AUDITING
THE FOOD & BEVERAGE
OPERATION

An Operational Audit Approach
Volume II

Hans L. Steiniger,
Certified Public Accountant,
Certified Internal Auditor

PublishAmerica
Baltimore

First printing

PublishAmerica has allowed this work to remain exactly as the author intended, verbatim, without editorial input.

ISBN: 1-60474-338-7 (softcover)
ISBN: 978-1-4489-2372-4 (hardcover)
PUBLISHED BY PUBLISHAMERICA, LLLP
www.publishamerica.com
Baltimore

Printed in the United States of America

TABLE OF CONTENTS

CHAPTER 13:
AUDITING MENU COSTING
Learning Objectives 13
Overview 13
In Practice 14
Purpose of Menu Costing 14
Cost Specification Sheets 16
Menu Mix 26
Standard Cost Calculation 30
Investigating Significant Variances 40
Updating Menu Mix Costs 42
Buffet Costing 44
Using Electronic Spreadsheets 48
Summary 49
Discussion Questions and Case Studies 49

CHAPTER 14:
AUDITING KITCHEN OPERATIONS
Learning Objectives 51
Overview 51
In Practice 52
Segregation of Duties 53
Order Entry Systems 54
Manual Dup Control Systems 55
Portion Control 61
Checker Function 62
Key Entrée Items 62
Non-Alcoholic Beverages 67
Spoilage and Waste 69
Linen Room Controls 70
China, Glass, Silverware 75

Kitchen Security 76
Summary 77
Discussion Questions and Case Studies 79

CHAPTER 15:
AUDITING PAYROLL

Learning Objectives 81
Overview 81
In Practice 83
Segregation of Duties 84
Sign In/Sign Out Sheet, Time Clocks, Time Keeping Systems 85
Signing and Approving Time Cards 90
Manual Adjustments 90
Adjustment Reports 92
Payroll Input 96
Tips Reporting & Minimum Wage 100
Tip Allocation 106
Payroll Reports 107
Documenting Payroll Testing 112
Signing for Payroll Checks 116
Manual Payroll Checks 119
Casual Employees 123
Overtime Paid at Straight Time 124
Productivity 126
Payout 128
Summary 131
Discussion Questions and Case Studies 134

CHAPTER 16:
AUDITING HUMAN RESOURCES

Learning Objectives 137
Overview 137

In Practice 139
Segregation of Duties 140
Human Resources Files 141
Security 142
Employee Maintenance Forms 143
Pay Rates 147
Drug Testing 148
I9 Documentation 150
Termination Checklist 155
Child Labor Laws 160
Alcohol Service Training 161
Documenting Human Resources Testing 163
Nepotism 167
Federal and State Poster Requirements 169
OSHA Reporting 170
Employee Discipline for Cash Overages/Shortages 172
Other Discipline 175
Summary 178
Discussion Questions and Case Studies 179

CHAPTER 17:
AUDITING INFORMATION TECHNOLOGY,
RISK MANAGEMENT, OTHER

Learning Objectives 183
Overview 183
In Practice 184
Segregation of Duties 185
Computer Back Up 185
Passwords 187
POS System Access 187
Hardware Security 188
Anti-Virus Software 189

Grill Hoods & Fire Suppression System Maintenance 190
CO2 and Propane Storage 191
Lease Compliance 192
Municipal Requirements 193
Record Retention 194
Licenses 196
Health Inspections 197
Photo Identification for Official Visitors 197
Summary 198
Discussion Questions and Case Studies 199

CHAPTER 18:
WRITING THE AUDIT REPORT
Learning Objectives 202
Overview 202
In Practice 203
Auditor's Workpaper Review 204
The Exit Conference 205
Scope 208
Executive Summary 209
Background 210
Findings and Recommendations 211
Required Response 214
Report Cover 216
Distribution 216
Table of Contents 218
Signature Page 218
Meetings with Subsidiary Management 219
Report Writing Tips 220
Summary 229
Discussion Questions 230

APPENDIX 1
Discussion Points Worksheet 233

APPENDIX 2
Jenny's Café—Denver
Internal Audit Report 263

APPENDIX 3
Sample Audit Program 303

APPENDIX 4
Sample Internal Control Questionnaire 391

VOLUME II

AUDITING THE FOOD AND BEVERAGE OPERATION
AN OPERATIONAL AUDIT APPROACH

AUDITING THE FOOD AND BEVERAGE OPERATION
AN OPERATIONAL AUDIT APPROACH

CHAPTER 13
AUDITING MENU COSTING

Learning Objectives

After reading this chapter, you should be able to:

1. Determine what each item on the menu costs to produce and how that cost is used in determining a selling price,
2. Review the items making up the Cost Specification Sheets and determine whether they are reasonable,
3. Know how the sales mix is used to calculate a standard cost to be compared to actual cost,
4. Check the standard cost calculation to ensure it is reasonable,
5. Determine whether the method used to calculate the buffet cost was reasonable.

Overview

This chapter discusses how menus are costed and how the cost of each menu item is used in determining a selling price for that item.

We will look at how Cost Specification Sheets are set up for each menu item and the different factors that go into costing each item.

We will discuss how the sales mix is used to calculate standard cost and how standard cost is compared to actual food cost to calculate a food cost variance.

Food cost variances greater than 2-3 percentage points need to be investigated. We will discuss different factors to consider in performing the investigation.

Buffet costing is quite different from menu costing because there are no standard servings that can be costed since the customers help themselves to whatever food they desire. Thus, buffet cost has unique features that need to be explored.

The auditor needs to be familiar with how menus are costed so she can review the work performed and determine whether it is reasonable.

Finally, we will discuss how electronic spreadsheets are used to simplify the number crunching to make it easier to update the spreadsheets when prices change.

In Practice

Aimee Stone walks over to Chef Stephan's office and asks him for copies of the menus and the Menu Costing book. Chef Stefan hands Aimee a set of menus and a three-ring binder stuffed with paper. "Can you save your files on my zip drive so I can see how the calculations work?" she asks the chef.

Chef Stephan takes Aimee's zip drive, puts it into his computer and saves a series of Excel spreadsheets. When Aimee returns to her desk, she saves each Excel spreadsheet onto her laptop in her Menu Costing directory.

Aimee looks at the menus and selects a few items for testing. She proceeds to look up the items she selected in the three ring binder and in her laptop. She reviews the calculations and puts together a list of invoices she will need to verify the cost prices used in the calculations.

Upon receiving the requested invoices from Heather, she ties the unit costs used in the menu testing to the appropriate invoices. She looks at the banquet menus and tests one of the banquet menus. Then she obtains the Menu Mix print out and tests a few days to see that the correct sales figures were used. Finally, she ties the standard cost from the Menu Mix to actual cost on the Standard to Actual Cost Comparison.

"32.3% Standard Cost versus 40.6% Actual Cost for June," she mutters. "I don't see Joey's signature. I wonder if he even looks at it!

"The costing is done correctly. Even the invoice costs are current with the exception of the produce costs that fluctuate weekly. The data are good but no one seems to look at the information available! There is a huge cost variance and no explanation! There is no evidence that any investigations are done at all! You can't manage a business successfully if you don't use the information provided to you!"

Purpose of Menu Costing

A menu is made up of a number of items, depending on the type of menu. In a full service restaurant there is a breakfast menu, a lunch menu, and a dinner menu. Each menu is divided into different sections, i.e. appetizers, soups, salads, main course, desserts, and beverages. There may also be separate banquet menus used when banquets are booked. Generally, the banquet menus have one price that includes different items that are priced separately on the regular menus, i.e. appetizer, soup or salad, main course, dessert, coffee or tea.

Each menu item is broken down by its ingredients and the cost of each ingredient used is calculated. Each cost for a menu item is added together to determine the total cost of that item. The menu cost is divided by the menu sales price to calculate the Standard Food Cost percentage for that menu item. This process is repeated for every item on the menu and every menu used in the restaurant.

The General Manager and Chef meet to determine the standard cost they need to achieve the planned food cost for the restaurant. Once all menus are costed, the General Manager and Chef begin to price the menu with the objective of achieving the desired food cost. They evaluate each menu item and assign a price that they believe the customer will be willing to pay.

Some menu items, i.e. lobster, are high cost items by nature. If the restaurant charges a price that brings lobster in line with the desired cost, no one will buy it because it will be too expensive. On the other hand, there are some items, i.e. pasta, that are low cost by nature. The restaurant can charge a price that will achieve a cost well below the desired cost and customers will still be willing to buy it. Thus, some menu items are set at prices that achieve above the desired cost and others are set at prices that achieve below the desired cost. If the menu is set up correctly, the high cost and low cost items will offset each other and the sales mix will achieve the desired cost.

Breakfast menus generally are low cost in nature while dinner menus tend to be higher in cost. Eggs, omelets, pancakes, waffles, bagels, etc. are all items that have low product costs. Steaks, fish, poultry, etc. tend to be higher cost items. Thus, the ratio of breakfast sales to dinner sales also plays a role in determining a restaurant's food cost.

Once all menu items are costed, the costs are entered into a menu mix software program. The program takes actual items sold during a specific period and calculates a standard cost for that period. When the standard cost is compared to actual cost, the variance should be within 2-3 percentage points. If the variance is higher that 2-3 percentage points, there are problems in the kitchen that need to be investigated and resolved. We will discuss these items further as we go through the chapter.

Cost Specification Sheets

The Cost Specification Sheets are Excel spreadsheets that list each item in a menu and are used to determine what each menu item costs to produce. To limit the number of spreadsheets that are created, a separate spreadsheet is used for each menu and a separate tab in the spreadsheet is used for each menu item.

The first thing the chef does is to list the items on the spreadsheet that make up the base. The base consists of those ingredients that are used in several items on the menu that make up a category of items. For example, breakfast items generally have toast, butter, and jam included in eggs any style and all omelets. The menu may have a ham and cheese omelet, western omelet, Spanish omelet, etc. but they all include toast, butter, and jam. Thus, the base used in costing each of these breakfast items will be toast, butter, and jam. When counting the number of slices of bread in a loaf, the two end pieces are discarded and thus should not be included in the number of slices making up a loaf.

When the chef lists the ingredients making up the ham and cheese omelet, the last ingredient is the base. Figure 13.1 shows how the base is costed and then costs the ham and cheese omelet. The columns are as follows:

Ingredient—Description of the individual items making up the menu item or base.

Unit—How the ingredient is measured, i.e. pound, dozen, box, case, etc.

Number per Unit—Number of smaller units in the Unit, i.e. 16 ounces = 1 lb., 12 pieces = 1 dozen, 200 pieces = 1 box (in this example).

Portion Size—Number per Unit used in a portion, i.e. 3 eggs in an omelet, 2 ounces of cheese in an omelet, 1 ounce of ham in an omelet, etc.

Unit Cost—Cost of one Unit, i.e. cost of a pound of butter, a dozen eggs, a box of jelly pieces, etc.

Extended Cost—Portion Size divided by Number per Unit, multiplied by Unit Cost.

Jenny's Café, Inc.
Denver Restaurant
Menu Costing - Base
31-Mar-06

Ingredient	Unit	Number per Unit	Portion Size	Unit Cost	Extended Cost
Bread	Loaf	16	2	$1.79	$ 0.22
Butter - pcs.	Box	200	2	$15.98	$ 0.16
Jelly - pcs.	Box	200	2	$8.55	$ 0.09
Orange Slice	Each	8	1	$0.55	$ 0.07
					$ 0.54

Jenny's Café, Inc.
Denver Restaurant
Menu Costing - Ham & Cheese Omelet
31-Mar-06

Ingredient	Unit	Number per Unit	Portion Size	Unit Cost	Extended Cost
Eggs	Dozen	12	3	$1.59	$ 0.40
Ham	Pound	16	1	$4.89	$ 0.31
Cheddar Cheese	Pound	16	2	$4.19	$ 0.52
Base					$ 0.54
					$ 1.77

Total Food Cost $ 1.77
Selling Price $ 8.50
Food Cost Percentage   20.8%

Figure 13.1

17

The cost of the base is added to the cost of the omelet ingredients to obtain the total cost of the omelet. The three lines at the bottom of the omelet costing are as follows:

Total Food Cost—Extended Cost Total,

Selling Price—Price for which the menu item sells,

Food Cost Percentage—Total Food Cost divided by Selling Price.

The date in the heading is the date that the menu costs were last updated. Thus, the chef can tell at a glance when product costs need to be reviewed and updated.

When determining a cost for an item where part is not usable, the chef needs to be sure that he includes the non-usable portion in the cost. For example, bell peppers have a core that is thrown away. Thus, in costing a Denver Omelet, the chef weighs the bell pepper, cuts out the core and discards it. He then cuts the rest of the bell pepper into small pieces and weighs them. He needs to adjust his cost per pound to take into consideration that the finished product weighs much less than the raw product.

For example, Chef Stephan uses bell peppers that cost $2.59 per pound, and an average bell pepper weighs half a pound. After removing the core, the pepper weighs 5 ounces. In his Denver Omelet, Chef Stephan uses half an ounce of chopped bell peppers. On his Cost Specification Sheet, Chef Stephan would indicate the following:

Bell Peppers—trimmed 0.5 oz. @ $4.14 per pound = $.13

To calculate the adjusted cost per pound, Chef Stephan divided the weight of the bell pepper after removing the core (5 ounces) by the raw weight of the bell pepper (8 ounces) = .625. Thus, the finished weight is 62.5% of the raw weight. The $2.59 cost per pound of the raw bell pepper is divided by .625 to arrive at $4.14, the cost of the trimmed bell pepper. A half ounce of bell peppers costing $4.14 (divided by 32 half ounce portions in a pound) is $.13.

Bases for dinners are normally more extensive than breakfast bases. They often include a chef's salad, rolls and butter, potato, vegetable, and a garnish. A garnish is something added to the entrée for presentation purposes to make the entrée look nicer. It could be an orange slice, an apple slice on a piece of Romaine lettuce, etc. and is included in the base. For example, if we have Filet Mignon on the menu, the costing of the base and the entrée would be as noted in Figure 13.2.

In costing the chef's salad in the base, one of the ingredients is salad dressing. The restaurant normally gives the guest several choices, such as Ranch Dressing, Italian Dressing, Thousand Islands Dressing, Honey Mustard Dressing, etc. Each one has a different cost. For purposes of determining the cost of the salad dressing, the chef would use an average cost of the different salad dressings.

Jenny's Café, Inc.
Denver Restaurant
Menu Costing - Dinner Base
31-Mar-06

Ingredient	Unit	Number per Unit	Portion Size	Unit Cost	Extended Cost
Lettuce	Head	1	0.25	$1.59	$ 0.40
Tomato	Pound	16	1	$2.29	$ 0.14
Onion	Pound	16	0.5	$1.79	$ 0.06
Salad Dressing	Gallon	128	2	$10.95	$ 0.17
Rolls	Dozen	12	2.5	$2.98	$ 0.62
Butter - pcs.	Box	200	2.5	$15.98	$ 0.20
Baked Potato	Case	80	1	$35.00	$ 0.44
Sour Cream	5- Gal Tub	640	1	$10.99	$ 0.02
Broccoli	Pound	16	4	$1.69	$ 0.42
Butter	Pound	16	1	$3.49	$ 0.22
Garnish					$ 0.10
					$ 2.78

Jenny's Café, Inc.
Denver Restaurant
Menu Costing - Filet Mignon
31-Mar-06

Ingredient	Unit	Number per Unit	Portion Size	Unit Cost	Extended Cost
Filet Mignon	Pound	16	10	$12.89	$ 8.06
Steak Sauce	12 oz.	12	.1	$2.49	$ 0.21
Base					$ 2.78
					$ 11.04

Total Food Cost $ 11.04
Selling Price $ 35.95
Food Cost Percentage   30.7%

Figure 13.2

19

The cost of the rolls in an entrée depends on the number of rolls a customer consumes. The waitress may be instructed to set 2 rolls on the table per customer. However, the customer may ask for additional rolls. Once the rolls are set out on the table, the unused ones need to be thrown in the trash. They cannot be later given to another table. For menu costing, we will assume that most people eat the two rolls given them and a few tables will ask for additional rolls. Thus, we will use 2.5 rolls and 2.5 butter pieces in our base.

During observations, the auditor should be aware of the number of rolls given to small tables. For example, a person sitting alone should not be given a half-dozen rolls because most of them will end up in the trash. The basket of rolls for one person should contain two rolls. She can always ask for more.

Jenny's Café uses a 10 ounce filet for the dinner entrée. There are only two ingredients to this entrée, the filet and the steak sauce. Some people will use more than one ounce while others will not use any at all. So for costing purposes, we will use an average of one ounce. The rest of the cost of the entrée is the base.

Some meat items are purchased in bulk and sliced by the chef into portions after the meat is cooked. An example is prime rib. The chef purchases a 16 pound piece of meat on average, cooks it and cuts it up into 15 pieces. The outer slices are thus well done and the inner slices are rare. The slices in between range from medium rare to medium well.

When costing prime rib, we need to use the raw weight because that is how the chef is buying it and how he is paying for it. Prime rib has a lot of fat and the chef will trim much of it and throw it away. In addition, as meat is cooked, the weight of the meat decreases because the fat drips off the meat. Thus, we cannot weigh cooked meat after it has been trimmed and multiply by the raw meat cost. If we do this, we will calculate a much lower food cost than the chef is actually incurring. Figure 13.3 shows how prime rib is costed.

Appetizers, soups, salads, desserts, and beverages are generally unique items and do not have bases. However, since they make up part of the menu mix, they must also be costed. Figure 13.4 shows an example where an appetizer and a soup are costed. The appetizer is generally straightforward. Each ingredient is costed and the costs summed to calculate the total food cost.

Soups tend to be a little different. If the restaurant is merely heating up soup from a can, the costing is easy. Figure how much soup comes from a can and determine the number of servings. However, most chefs make their own soup and costing becomes a little tricky.

The chef costs the ingredients that go into the soup pot and determines how much soup will be in the finished product. In our example, the chef is making French Onion Soup. He puts soup base, onions, and spices in the soup. He estimates that he uses approximately $.25 in various spices. The finished product will be 5 gallons of soup which he costs at $7.82.

In costing one serving of French Onion Soup, the chef assumes the unit is 5 gallons (640 ounces) and a bowl will hold 10 ounces. The bread going in the soup has 22 slices and he will use one slice. A slice of mozzarella cheese weighs 2 ounces. The total cost is $.95. French Onion Soup will sell for $7.95. Food Cost Percentage for the French Onion Soup is thus 12.0%.

Jenny's Café, Inc.
Denver Restaurant
Menu Costing - Prime Rib with Horseradish Sauce
31-Mar-06

Ingredient	Unit	Number per Unit	Portion Size	Unit Cost	Extended Cost
Prime Rib	16 lbs.	15	1	$111.84	$ 7.46
Horseradish	Gallon	128	1	$15.49	$ 0.12
Mayonnaise	Gallon	128	1	$8.59	$ 0.07
Base					$ 2.78
					$ 10.42

Total Food Cost	$ 10.42
Selling Price	$ 31.95
Food Cost Percentage	32.6%

Figure 13.3

Figure 13.5 shows the costing of a salad, dessert, and a beverage. For the salad, we costed a Caesar Salad. It consists of a quarter head of Romaine lettuce, one ounce of grated cheese, two ounces of Caesar dressing, and two ounces of croutons. The ingredients are broken down into .25 head Romaine lettuce, 1/16 pound of grated cheese, 2/128 of a gallon of Caesar Dressing, and 2/60 box of croutons. The Food Cost is the total of the ingredients ($1.43) divided by the selling price ($7.95) equals 16.3%. This Food Cost Percentage is considerable lower than our planned Food Cost of 32.0%, but it helps to offset the high Food Cost we are running on the Shrimp Cocktail (40.6%).

21

Jenny's Café, Inc.
Denver Restaurant
Menu Costing - Dinner - Appetizer - Shrimp Cocktail
31-Mar-06

Ingredient	Unit	Number per Unit	Portion Size	Unit Cost	Extended Cost
Jumbo Shrimp	Pound	15	4	$18.99	$ 5.06
Cocktail Sauce	Gallon	128	1	$15.29	$ 0.12
Lettuce	Head	1	0.05	$1.59	$ 0.08
					$ 5.26

Total Food Cost	$ 5.26
Selling Price	$ 12.95
Food Cost Percentage	40.6%

Jenny's Café, Inc.
Denver Restaurant
Menu Costing - Dinner - French Onion Soup - Bowl
31-Mar-06

Ingredient	Unit	Number per Unit	Portion Size	Unit Cost	Extended Cost
Soup Base	Quart	32	8	$15.95	$ 3.99
Onions	Pound	16	32	$1.79	$ 3.58
Seasoning					$ 0.25
Makes 5- Gallons Soup					$ 7.82
Soup	5 Gallons	640	10	$7.82	$ 0.12
Bread	Loaf	22	1	$3.19	$ 0.15
Mozzarella Cheese	Pound	16	2	$5.49	$ 0.69
					$ 0.95

Total Food Cost	$ 0.95
Selling Price	$ 7.95
Food Cost Percentage	12.0%

Figure 13.4

22

Jenny's Café, Inc.
Denver Restaurant
Menu Costing - Dinner - Salads - Caesar Salad
31-Mar-06

Ingredient	Unit	Number per Unit	Portion Size	Unit Cost	Extended Cost
Romaine Lettuce	Head	1	0.25	$2.89	$ 0.72
Grated Cheese	Pound	16	1	$4.79	$ 0.30
Caesar Dressing	Gallon	128	2	$12.79	$ 0.20
Croutons - oz.	Box	60	2	$6.19	$ 0.21
					$ 1.43

Total Food Cost $ 1.43
Selling Price $ 8.95
Food Cost Percentage   16.0%

Jenny's Café, Inc.
Denver Restaurant
Menu Costing - Dinner - Desserts - Pie ala Mode
31-Mar-06

Ingredient	Unit	Number per Unit	Portion Size	Unit Cost	Extended Cost
Apple Pie	Pie	8	1	$5.89	$ 0.74
Vanilla Ice Cream	3 Gallon	384	5	$17.99	$ 0.23
Whipped Cream - oz.	Can	40	1	$11.99	$ 0.30
					$ 1.27

Total Food Cost $ 1.27
Selling Price $ 7.95
Food Cost Percentage   16.0%

Jenny's Café, Inc.
Denver Restaurant
Menu Costing - Dinner - Beverages - Coffee
31-Mar-06

Ingredient	Unit	Number per Unit	Portion Size	Unit Cost	Extended Cost
Coffee Packet	Case	100	0.33	$35.99	$ 0.12
Creamer	Box	100	3	$6.79	$ 0.20
Sugar	Case	2000	3	$24.99	$ 0.04
					$ 0.36

Total Food Cost $ 0.36
Selling Price $ 1.95
Food Cost Percentage   18.5%

Figure 13.5

For a dessert item, we costed Pie ala Mode. While some restaurants make their own desserts, most buy them from a baker. If a chef decides to make his own desserts, he would list all the ingredients and cost them (as shown in Figure 13.4 for the French Onion Soup). Then he would divide the total cost of the batch by the number of servings to obtain the cost per serving. He would take the cost of one serving and add the additional items such as ice cream and whipped cream to obtain the total cost per serving.

In our example in Figure 13.5, we assumed the chef buys the pie. He obtains 8 slices from a pie. Thus, the cost of a slice is 1/8 the cost of the pie. To the cost of the pie, the chef adds 5 ounces of ice cream. Since ice cream is generally purchased in 3 gallon tubs, he uses 5/384 of a tub. Assuming that whipped cream comes in a 40 ounce can, he uses 1/40 of a can. The total cost of $1.27 is divided by the selling price of $7.95 to calculate the Food Cost of 16.0%.

When serving beverages, such as coffee and soda, the restaurant often gives free refills. Thus, when costing the beverage, we cannot cost only one serving because that will give an incorrect cost when the customer gets a refill. Therefore, the chef needs to make an assumption about how much of the beverage the average customer will consume. In the case of coffee, if the coffee sits on the warmer for more than 20 minutes, it will be discarded. Thus, a normal rate of spoilage must be considered.

In Figure 13.5, a pot of coffee serves ten 6 ounce cups. The chef assumes that between refills and normal spoilage, 1/3 of a pot will be used for an average customer. Cream and sugar are also ingredients in a cup of coffee. Some customers use two or three of each while others do not take any cream or sugar in coffee. Thus, the chef assumes the average customer will drink 3 cups of coffee and will take 1 cream and 1 sugar in each cup. The total ingredients thus cost $.36. When dividing the total cost by the selling price of $1.95, the Food Cost is 18.5%.

When auditing the cost specification sheets, it is not practical to watch a cook prepare the raw ingredients and weigh them to determine if the portions specified in the Cost Specification Sheets are accurate. Instead, the auditor selects some items from the menu and looks up the cost specification sheets. She reviews them to determine whether the assumptions that went into the Cost Specification Sheets appear to be reasonable.

For example, if the Shrimp Cocktail Cost Specification Sheet shows 3 shrimp, but when the auditor ordered shrimp cocktail for dinner, she received 4 shrimp, she may question the accuracy of the Cost Specification Sheet.

Then when the auditor observes shrimp cocktail prepared in the kitchen, she sees every one has 4 shrimp. Either the standard is wrong or the cooks are preparing it wrong. Either way, there is a significant impact on the Food Cost. She should discuss the discrepancy with the chef and write up the issue as a Discussion Point.

The auditor should test the mathematical accuracy of the Cost Specification Sheets for the items tested. She may ask the chef to save the Cost Specification Sheets on her zip drive so she can look at the Excel calculations. The idea is to check whether the formulas make sense, not whether Excel can multiply and divide properly.

While the chef cannot be expected to update the costs on the Cost Specification sheets every week, they should be updated quarterly. He would probably delegate this duty to one of the cooks or other kitchen help. The auditor should tie the costs of the items selected for testing to invoices. While food prices are constantly changing, a large company probably has pricing agreements with major suppliers for staples that hold prices for 6 months or a year. Thus, these items should not change.

Produce is usually purchased from a local supplier and these prices change constantly. Thus, the auditor should expect to see differences in produce prices. However, if tomatoes are listed on the March 31 Cost Specification Sheets at $1.19 per pound and the last five invoices the auditor looks at shows the following prices: $2.29, $2.69, $2.39, $2.79, $2.59, the auditor should question whether $1.19 is a good price. Even if the chef got a special price for one week of $1.19 per pound, he should be using a more realistic number if that would not be the long term price. Thus, the auditor should ask the chef about questionable prices. If there are solid reasons why the chef used the prices, then the auditor may conclude the Cost Specification Sheets are reasonable accurate. However, if the chef cannot support some of the unusual prices with reasonable explanations, the auditor would have a Discussion Point.

Dairy products, bread, meat, and fish are often purchased from local suppliers. Thus, the auditor should also check the reasonableness of the prices used for these suppliers on the Cost Specification Sheets against recent invoices. Again, if the prices are reasonable the auditor may accept them; otherwise, she should check with the chef for an explanation and consider whether she has a Discussion Point.

If the Company has a pricing agreement with a national meat or fish supplier, the invoice cost should be the same as the cost used on the Cost

Specification Sheets, unless there was a recent price increase issued to the Company. There is always the possibility that the national supplier increased prices in violation of the pricing agreement. Thus, the auditor should be alert to that possibility and notify the corporate purchasing department if that is the case.

Menu Mix

As we have seen, each item on the menu has a different food cost percentage based on the cost of the ingredients of each menu item and the selling price that the Chef and General Manager think they can get for the item. Thus, the Food Cost that the Chef should get during the inventory period, the Standard Cost, varies depending on the types of menu items sold.

Figure 13.6 shows a simplified menu for Jenny's Café for the month ending June 30, 2006 with the Food Cost for each menu item and the number of items sold for the month. The number of items sold can be obtained from the cash register (if it is the type that provides sales totals for the number of items sold) or the order entry system (from the sales report), i.e. Micros. The columns provide the following information:

Menu Item—Description of the item on the menu,

Selling Price—Sales price of the Menu Item,

Unit Cost—Standard Cost of producing the Menu Item, per the Cost Specification Sheets,

Food Cost Percentage—Unit Cost divided by Selling Price equals the Standard Food Cost Percentage,

Number Sold—Number of items sold per the cash register reading or the order entry system,

Extended Cost—Number Sold multiplied by Unit Cost,

Sales—Number Sold multiplied by Selling Price.

The line items on the bottom of the schedule are derived as follows:

Total Food Cost—Sum of the Extended Cost column,

Total Food Sales—Sum of the Sales column,

Food Cost Percentage—Total Food Cost divided by Total Food Sales.

Jenny's Café, Inc.
Denver Restaurant
Menu Mix
Month Ending June 30, 2006

Menu Item	Selling Price	Unit Cost	Food Cost %	Number Sold	Extended Cost	Sales
Ham & Cheese Omelet	$8.50	$1.77	20.8%	3,500	$ 6,195.00	$ 29,750.00
Pancakes	$7.50	$1.51	20.1%	1,900	$ 2,869.00	$ 14,250.00
Bagel & Cream Cheese	$3.95	$0.87	22.0%	2,100	$ 1,827.00	$ 8,295.00
Shrimp Cocktail	$12.95	$5.26	40.6%	6,900	$ 36,294.00	$ 89,355.00
French Onion Soup	$7.95	$0.95	11.9%	550	$ 522.50	$ 4,372.50
Caesar Salad	$8.95	$1.43	16.0%	1,200	$ 1,716.00	$ 10,740.00
Filet Mignon	$35.95	$11.04	30.7%	3,600	$ 39,744.00	$ 129,420.00
Prime Rib	$31.95	$10.42	32.6%	5,900	$ 61,478.00	$ 188,505.00
New York Strip Steak	$32.95	$9.98	30.3%	3,200	$ 31,936.00	$ 105,440.00
Barbecued Chicken	$15.95	$3.98	25.0%	1,800	$ 7,164.00	$ 28,710.00
Baked Salmon	$25.95	$7.59	29.2%	2,300	$ 17,457.00	$ 59,685.00
Pie ala Mode	$6.95	$1.27	18.3%	2,200	$ 2,794.00	$ 15,290.00
Orange Juice	$2.50	$0.43	17.2%	4,500	$ 1,935.00	$ 11,250.00
Coffee	$1.95	$0.36	18.5%	4,900	$ 1,764.00	$ 9,555.00
Soda	$1.95	$0.39	20.0%	9,800	$ 3,822.00	$ 19,110.00
					$ 217,517.50	$ 723,727.50

Total Food Cost	$ 217,517.50
Total Food Sales	$ 723,727.50
Food Cost Percentage	30.1%

Figure 13.6

The Food Cost Percentage in Figure 13.6 is 30.1%. Thus, based on the sales mix of the various items sold, the Standard Food Cost is 30.1%, the Food Cost that the Chef is expected to achieve. If the Actual Food Cost is 30.5%, the auditor would conclude that the Actual Food Cost is fairly close to standard.

Actual Food Cost often does not hit Standard Food Cost because of many factors that occur in the normal course of operations, such as the following:

• The cooks are human and may not provide the exact portions specified in the Cost Specification Sheets,

• There may be a normal amount of spoilage because food was prepped that could not be used, such as more melons were cut up for breakfast than

were needed and were no longer fresh the next day,
- Prices of goods purchased from local suppliers fluctuated from those used in the Cost Specification Sheets,
- Preportioned meats and fish were a little more or a little less than standard, but the operation is charged by the pound.

Generally, if Actual Cost falls within 2-3 percentage points of Standard Cost, the Chef is satisfied. Thus, if the company standard is + or - two percentage points, based on the Standard Cost of 30.1% in Figure 13.6, acceptable Actual Food Cost would range from 28.1% to 32.1%. Actual Food Cost outside this range should be investigated.

Figure 13.7 shows the same simplified menu for Jenny's Café for the month of May, but with a different sales mix. During May, Jenny's Café sold more low cost items than in June. Thus, the Standard Food Cost for the exact same menu was 27.7%. If Actual Food Cost for May was 29.9%, and the company standard was plus or minus two percentage points, the Chef would realize that he has a problem, even though May's Actual Food Cost is better than June's Actual Food Cost. But Standard Food Cost, the Food Cost the Chef expects to achieve, is much lower due to the sales mix, the higher proportion of low cost items. May's Actual Food Cost is outside the 2 percentage points outer limit.

The Chef's investigation may turn up one of the following reasons why Actual Food Cost is so much higher than standard:
- The cooks are over-portioning, such that they are serving portions that are much larger than the standard portions specified in the Cost Specification sheets. Retraining may be in order.
- There is an unusual increase in the prices of key menu items, such as meats or fish. If the increase is permanent, the Chef, in conjunction with the General Manager, may need to consider raising prices or reducing the portion sizes to attain the desired food cost.
- There may have been an error in the Food Cost calculation, i.e. some invoices for the current month were not included in the Food Cost calculation.
- There may have been an error in Actual Sales, such as one or more days' sales were not included in the Food Cost calculation.
- A cooler may have gone down overnight, resulting in an unusual amount of spoilage.

Jenny's Café, Inc.
Denver Restaurant
Menu Mix
Month Ending May 31, 2006

Menu Item	Selling Price	Unit Cost	Food Cost %	Number Sold	Extended Cost	Sales
Ham & Cheese Omelet	$8.50	$1.77	20.8%	4,500	$ 7,965.00	$ 38,250.00
Pancakes	$7.50	$1.51	20.1%	3,900	$ 5,889.00	$ 29,250.00
Bagel & Cream Cheese	$3.95	$0.87	22.0%	3,100	$ 2,697.00	$ 12,245.00
Shrimp Cocktail	$12.95	$5.26	40.6%	3,900	$ 20,514.00	$ 50,505.00
French Onion Soup	$7.95	$0.95	11.9%	2,500	$ 2,375.00	$ 19,875.00
Caesar Salad	$8.95	$1.43	16.0%	3,900	$ 5,577.00	$ 34,905.00
Filet Mignon	$35.95	$11.04	30.7%	3,600	$ 39,744.00	$ 129,420.00
Prime Rib	$31.95	$10.42	32.6%	4,900	$ 51,058.00	$ 156,555.00
New York Strip Steak	$32.95	$9.98	30.3%	2,200	$ 21,956.00	$ 72,490.00
Barbecued Chicken	$15.95	$3.98	25.0%	3,800	$ 15,124.00	$ 60,610.00
Baked Salmon	$25.95	$7.59	29.2%	1,900	$ 14,421.00	$ 49,305.00
Pie ala Mode	$6.95	$1.27	18.3%	3,200	$ 4,064.00	$ 22,240.00
Orange Juice	$2.50	$0.43	17.2%	5,500	$ 2,365.00	$ 13,750.00
Coffee	$1.95	$0.36	18.5%	5,900	$ 2,124.00	$ 11,505.00
Soda	$1.95	$0.39	20.0%	9,800	$ 3,822.00	$ 19,110.00
					$ 199,695.00	$ 720,015.00

Total Food Cost	$ 199,695.00
Total Food Sales	$ 720,015.00
Food Cost Percentage	27.7%

Figure 13.7

Order Entry Systems often have sales reports that accumulate number of items sold for the inventory period. The Sales Mix is often separate software where a clerk takes the sales data from the last day of the month and keys the number of each menu item sold into the Sales Mix software. If a cash register is used that provides the number of items sold each day, a clerk would key the daily sales figures into an Excel spreadsheet and total the columns to get the sales for the inventory period, i.e. month. The clerk would take the totals for the inventory period and key them into the sales mix.

Restaurants often have daily specials to add something to the menu that a regular patron may not have seen in the restaurant before or to use up extra product the restaurant has on hand. Whenever the Executive Chef adds a special to the menu, he should cost the special on a Cost Specification Sheet and add the item to the Menu Mix. Otherwise the Menu Mix will not be accurate.

In testing the Menu Mix, the auditor should tie the number of month to date items sold from the Order Entry System's last day of sales into the number of items sold in the sales mix. In the situation where cash register sales are keyed into an Excel spreadsheet, the auditor should take a few days cash register reading tapes and tie them into the spreadsheet. Then, she should take the spreadsheet sales and tie them into the Menu Mix. The auditor should also tie some of the selling prices into the actual menus and tie some of the costs into the Cost Specification Sheets.

Standard Cost Calculation

As we discussed in the previous section, the Standard Cost calculation calculates Standard Food Cost based on the sales mix. However, there are often adjustments that need to be made to the Standard Cost Calculation to arrive at the true standard cost.

Restaurants often provide free meals to its employees so they do not have to leave the premises to have lunch or dinner. The chef makes up a meal from leftovers and serves it in an employee cafeteria or lunchroom. If there are insufficient leftovers, the chef usually uses low cost ingredients to prepare the employee meal.

While there is no cost to the employee for the employee meal, there is a cost to the restaurant. While some companies take a credit to their Food Cost for the cost of the employee meal and charge an Employee Benefit account, many restaurants absorb the cost of the employee meal in their Food Cost. In this case, the Standard Food Cost calculated by the Menu Mix is adversely affected. The restaurant needs to take an adjustment in the Menu Mix software for the cost of the employee meals.

The Chef does not normally calculate a separate Food Cost for each employee meal given to the employees. He calculates an average per person cost and multiplies the cost of the employee meal by the number of employees who had lunch or dinner. The Chef should have a sign in sheet in the employee cafeteria or lunchroom so he knows how many employees consumed the employee meal. Each employee consuming a meal must sign the sign in sheet.

Figure 13.8 is an example of an Employee Meal Sign In Sheet for lunch. The first column is the row number. The row number allows the Controller to tell at a glance how many employees signed the sheet. Since there are 25 rows on a sheet, she takes the number of completed sheets and multiplies by 25. On the last sheet she can see how many signed by the last row number completed.

As an example, suppose the Chef has determined that the average Food

Cost for an employee meal is $2.25 per person. On May 25, there was one full Employee Meal Sign In Sheet completed and 1 partial with 17 lines completed. The Controller adds 25 + 17 = 42. She multiplies 42 meals by $2.25 to calculate the cost of the employee meals on May 25 at $94.50. She does the same thing for the other 30 days in May and calculates the employee meal credit for the month to be $3,345.75. In calculating Standard Food Cost, the Menu Mix software adds $3,345.75 to the Menu Mix Food Cost.

Jenny's Café, Inc.
Denver Restaurant
Employee Meal Sign In Sheet
Date: May 25, 2006

#	Print Name	Sign Name
1	George Smith	George Smith
2	Randy Jackson	Randy Jackson
3	Amanda Johnson	Amanda Johnson
4	Corey Briere	Corey Briere
5	Cynthia Carlyle	Cynthia Carlyle
6	Jessica Tremaine	Jessica Tremaine
7	Justin Jones	Justin Jones
8	Lloyd Nelson	Lloyd Nelson
9	Jimmie Smith	Jimmie Smith
10	Roseanne Reames	Roseanne Reames
11	Suzy Simpson	Suzy Simpson
12	Rhonda Bridges	Rhonda Bridges
13	Amy Adams	Amy Adams
14	Audrey Losman	Audrey Losman
15	Joseph Braun	Joseph Braun
16	Elizabeth Ostrowski	Elizabeth Ostrowski
17	Melissa Molson	Melissa Molson
18	Jasmine Miller	Jasmine Miller
19	Lorale Lisbon	Lorale Lisbon
20	Petula Petrowski	Petula Petrowski
21	Steven Adamczyk	Steven Adamczyk
22	Noel Nowaczyk	Noel Nowaczyk
23	John Johnson	John Johnson
24	Charlotte St. Claire	Charlotte St. Claire
25	Nicole Nesbitt	Nicole Nesbitt

Figure 13.8

31

To document the Employee Meal Credit calculation, the Controller should have a worksheet that shows the number of Employee Meals consumed each day and the cost value of those employee meals. Figure 13.9 shows the Controller's spreadsheet calculating the value of the employee meals for the month of May.

When auditing the Employee Meal Credit, the auditor should perform the following:

- Obtain the Controller's Employee Meal Credit Calculation spreadsheet and select a few days to test the calculation,
- Count the number of meals on the test days and tie the number of meals into the spreadsheet,
- Verify with the Chef the amount of credit per meal that should be given, i.e. $2.25 per meal is the amount the Chef determined is the average cost of the employee meal,
- Tie the total Employee Meal Credit for the month to the Menu Mix Standard Cost calculation.

To generate additional revenue, restaurants often run advertisements in the local newspapers with coupons. The coupon may offer $10 off a main entrée or a free entrée with the purchase of an equivalent or higher priced entrée. While the food cost on these revenues will be higher than normal, the restaurant hopes to impress the customer enough with the quality of its food and superior service that the customer will come back when the restaurant is not offering discounted meals. Some restaurants record the sale at full retail and charge Marketing Expense with the cost of the coupon. In this case, the value of the coupon has no impact on sales. Other restaurants subtract the value of the coupon from the selling price and record the discounted price as sales. In this case sales are adversely impacted.

Jenny's Café, Inc.
Denver Restaurant
Employee Meal Credit Calculation
May 31, 2006

Date	Day	Number Empl Meals	Value Per Empl Meal	Extended Value Empl Meals
1-May	Monday	44	$2.25	$ 99.00
2-May	Tuesday	50	$2.25	$ 112.50
3-May	Wednesday	54	$2.25	$ 121.50
4-May	Thursday	41	$2.25	$ 92.25
5-May	Friday	45	$2.25	$ 101.25
6-May	Saturday	46	$2.25	$ 103.50
7-May	Sunday	47	$2.25	$ 105.75
8-May	Monday	46	$2.25	$ 103.50
9-May	Tuesday	51	$2.25	$ 114.75
10-May	Wednesday	58	$2.25	$ 130.50
11-May	Thursday	45	$2.25	$ 101.25
12-May	Friday	47	$2.25	$ 105.75
13-May	Saturday	48	$2.25	$ 108.00
14-May	Sunday	46	$2.25	$ 103.50
15-May	Monday	45	$2.25	$ 101.25
16-May	Tuesday	49	$2.25	$ 110.25
17-May	Wednesday	53	$2.25	$ 119.25
18-May	Thursday	44	$2.25	$ 99.00
19-May	Friday	45	$2.25	$ 101.25
20-May	Saturday	47	$2.25	$ 105.75
21-May	Sunday	46	$2.25	$ 103.50
22-May	Monday	48	$2.25	$ 108.00
23-May	Tuesday	52	$2.25	$ 117.00
24-May	Wednesday	59	$2.25	$ 132.75
25-May	Thursday	43	$2.25	$ 96.75
26-May	Friday	45	$2.25	$ 101.25
27-May	Saturday	47	$2.25	$ 105.75
28-May	Sunday	48	$2.25	$ 108.00
29-May	Monday	47	$2.25	$ 105.75
30-May	Tuesday	52	$2.25	$ 117.00
31-May	Wednesday	49	$2.25	$ 110.25
				$ 3,345.75

Figure 13.9

While the Food Cost for the discounted items is the same as if they were not discounted, the revenue generated will be lower than what the Menu Mix software is calculating. Therefore, the Controller adds up the value of the coupons and takes a credit against Menu Mix sales so the Menu Mix sales will reflect actual sales. Thus, when Standard Food Cost calculated by the Menu Mix is compared to Actual Food Cost, the sales used in each calculation are comparable.

When accepting a coupon for a free entrée, the dining room cashier should write the Retail Value of the entree on the back of the coupon. The dining room cashier will need this figure to balance her cash register at the end of the shift. Also, the Controller will need to know the value of the coupon so she will know how much of an adjustment she needs to make to Menu Mix sales.

To calculate the credit to sales, the Controller adds the number of coupons of specific dollar values and lists them on the Coupon Credits Report. Figure 13.10 is an example of the Coupon Credits Report completed for the month of May. The Controller counts the number of $5 breakfast coupons each day and enters them in her Excel spreadsheet. The spreadsheet multiplies the number of $5 coupons by $5. When the Controller enters the number of $10 coupons for each day, the spreadsheet multiplies the number of $10 coupons by $10. For the Buy One Entrée, Get One Entrée Free coupon, the Controller adds the value of the coupons (noted on the back of the coupon) and enters the number of coupons in the spreadsheet and the total value of those coupons. The spreadsheet adds the values across and totals the daily values. The value of all coupons for the month of May is $17,380.05. The coupons should be collected by denomination, rubber banded, and put into a separate envelope for each day.

Jenny's Café, Inc.
Denver Restaurant
Coupon Credits Report
May 2006

| | $5 Breakfast | | $10 Dinner | | Buy 1, Get 1 Free | | Total |
Date	No.	Value	No.	Value	No.	Value	Value
1-May	5	$ 25.00	8	$ 80.00	7	$ 230.65	$ 335.65
2-May	6	$ 30.00	11	$ 110.00	9	$ 287.55	$ 427.55
3-May	4	$ 20.00	13	$ 130.00	11	$ 362.45	$ 512.45
4-May	8	$ 40.00	16	$ 160.00	13	$ 467.35	$ 667.35
5-May	3	$ 15.00	14	$ 140.00	15	$ 449.25	$ 604.25
6-May	7	$ 35.00	9	$ 90.00	17	$ 424.15	$ 549.15
7-May	2	$ 10.00	7	$ 70.00	18	$ 611.10	$ 691.10
8-May	5	$ 25.00	12	$ 120.00	15	$ 434.25	$ 579.25
9-May	7	$ 35.00	13	$ 130.00	17	$ 475.15	$ 640.15
10-May	13	$ 65.00	11	$ 110.00	14	$ 405.30	$ 580.30
11-May	4	$ 20.00	7	$ 70.00	9	$ 314.55	$ 404.55
12-May	7	$ 35.00	9	$ 90.00	14	$ 419.30	$ 544.30
13-May	1	$ 5.00	4	$ 40.00	8	$ 279.60	$ 324.60
14-May	8	$ 40.00	11	$ 110.00	15	$ 509.25	$ 659.25
15-May	15	$ 75.00	17	$ 170.00	23	$ 619.85	$ 864.85
16-May	3	$ 15.00	6	$ 60.00	7	$ 209.65	$ 284.65
17-May	16	$ 80.00	21	$ 210.00	24	$ 742.80	$ 1,032.80
18-May	8	$ 40.00	15	$ 150.00	16	$ 511.20	$ 701.20
19-May	6	$ 30.00	9	$ 90.00	9	$ 296.55	$ 416.55
20-May	3	$ 15.00	7	$ 70.00	13	$ 467.35	$ 552.35
21-May	5	$ 25.00	12	$ 120.00	17	$ 509.15	$ 654.15
22-May	14	$ 70.00	19	$ 190.00	24	$ 622.80	$ 882.80
23-May	13	$ 65.00	22	$ 220.00	28	$ 838.60	$ 1,123.60
24-May	15	$ 75.00	23	$ 230.00	31	$ 959.45	$ 1,264.45
25-May	9	$ 45.00	11	$ 110.00	17	$ 560.15	$ 715.15
26-May	5	$ 25.00	6	$ 60.00	5	$ 179.75	$ 264.75
27-May	3	$ 15.00	2	$ 20.00	7	$ 244.65	$ 279.65
28-May	4	$ 20.00	5	$ 50.00	4	$ 119.80	$ 189.80
29-May	7	$ 35.00	8	$ 80.00	6	$ 195.25	$ 310.25
30-May	5	$ 25.00	4	$ 40.00	3	$ 107.85	$ 172.85
31-May	2	$ 10.00	3	$ 30.00	3	$ 110.30	$ 150.30
			Total Value of Coupons Used				$ 17,380.05

Figure 13.10

To test the Coupon Credit Report, the auditor should perform the following:

- Select a few days and obtain the actual coupons supporting the numbers entered on the Coupon Credits Report for those days,
- Count the number of coupons in each denomination and agree the count to the count on the Coupon Credit Report,
- Check the accuracy of the multiplication,
- Add the values of the Buy One Entrée, Get One Free coupons and tie the total to the amount posted to the Coupon Credit Report.

During the course of normal business operations, location management may entertain people at the restaurant and provide complimentary food and beverage, including alcoholic beverages, to the group of people they entertain. For example, the General Manager may entertain someone from the corporate offices who is spending a couple of days at the operation to discuss various business matters. The Controller may entertain the auditor coming to the unit to perform the audit. The Marketing Manager may entertain someone from the local newspaper who is writing an article on the restaurant's food.

Many restaurants allow restaurant managers to eat in the dining room instead of in the employee cafeteria. This practice allows managers to sample different items on the menu and observe operations in the restaurant. Of course, managers are not precluded from eating in the employee cafeteria if they wish to have a quick lunch or dinner. They may also wish to eat in the employee cafeteria periodically to talk to the other employees on an informal basis. Managers who consume their meals in the dining room must sign the guest check and the meal is counted as a comp.

When the waitress presents the check to the management person at the table, the management person signs the check and writes comp on it. On the back of the guest check, she should indicate who is being entertained and the business purpose. If it is a management meal, she should write "management meal" and the names of the people consuming a management meal on the back of the guest check. Where the restaurant uses an order entry system, i.e. Micros, the restaurant cashier closes the check to the Comp key and puts the signed check in the cash drawer to be used as backup when balancing the cash register for the evening. If the restaurant has an ordinary cash register, the cashier puts the signed check into the cash register drawer to be used for balancing the cash register at the end of the evening.

When recording sales the following day, the Controller or designee adds up the comps (signed guest checks) and ties the total to the Comp Key on the order entry system's sales report. She makes sure that each comp has been signed by someone authorized to sign it. If there is a signature she does not recognize, the Controller follows up with the General Manager to ensure it is the signature of someone authorized to comp food and beverage.

The Controller or designee posts the comps to a Comp Report. She breaks down the complimentary guest checks by category, such as Food, Liquor, Beer, Wine, and Sales Tax, and totals the categories. The total amount should agree to the total of the comp guest checks. Figure 13.11 is an example of a Comp Report.

When calculating Standard Cost, the retail value of Food Sales must be deducted from Menu Mix sales because the Menu Mix is including the complimentary food in the sales calculation, but there are no actual sales recorded in the General Ledger system since the Controller backs out complimentary sales. Thus, in Jenny's Café, Heather would take a credit on the Menu Mix for $2,885.55 in May's Food Sales.

In auditing the Comp Report, the auditor should perform the following:
- Select a few days from the Comp Report and obtain the supporting guest checks,
- Tie the sales per the guest checks to the appropriate sales columns on the Comp Report,
- Check each guest check to ensure it was signed by a management person and that the business purpose or the notation "Management Meal" is written on the back. If she cannot read a signature, she should ask the Controller to identify the person who signed the check.

When calculating the Standard Cost, the adjustments to the Food Sales and Food Cost must be added to the Standard Cost calculation sheet to obtain the true Standard Food Cost. Figure 13.12 shows the same Menu Mix as in Figure 13.7 but has adjustments added to it. As a result of the adjustments, Standard Food Cost increased from 27.7% (Figure 13.7) to 29.0% (Figure 13.12).

If the variance between Standard Cost and Actual Cost is greater than two percentage points, the Executive Chef should investigate the reason for the large variance and should write an explanation on the comparison between Standard Cost and Actual Cost. In addition, the Executive Chef should sign the comparison sheet. The General Manager should also review and sign the comparison between Standard Cost and Actual Cost.

Jenny's Café, Inc.
Denver Restaurant
Comp Report
May 2006

Date	Day of Week	Total Comps		Food	Liquor	Beer	Wine	Sales Tax
1-May	Monday	$	97.94	$65.90	$11.00		$15.50	$5.54
2-May	Tuesday	$	166.10	$156.70				$9.40
3-May	Wednesday	$	32.81	$30.95				$1.86
4-May	Thursday	$	42.67	$40.25				$2.42
5-May	Friday	$	391.78	$275.60	$25.00	$24.00	$45.00	$22.18
6-May	Saturday	$	134.62	$127.00				$7.62
7-May	Sunday	$	122.22	$115.30				$6.92
8-May	Monday	$	528.20	$329.30	$45.50	$28.50	$95.00	$29.90
9-May	Tuesday	$	69.22	$65.30				$3.92
10-May	Wednesday	$	62.75	$59.20				$3.55
11-May	Thursday	$	31.69	$29.90				$1.79
12-May	Friday	$	132.92	$125.40				$7.52
13-May	Saturday	$	84.69	$79.90				$4.79
14-May	Sunday	$	283.02	$195.00	$18.00	$5.00	$49.00	$16.02
15-May	Monday	$	94.61	$89.25				$5.36
16-May	Tuesday	$	48.55	$45.80				$2.75
17-May	Wednesday	$	62.81	$59.25				$3.56
18-May	Thursday	$	-	$0.00				$0.00
19-May	Friday	$	73.14	$69.00				$4.14
20-May	Saturday	$	149.35	$115.00	$25.90			$8.45
21-May	Sunday	$	94.66	$89.30				$5.36
22-May	Monday	$	79.82	$75.30				$4.52
23-May	Tuesday	$	78.65	$74.20				$4.45
24-May	Wednesday	$	52.89	$49.90				$2.99
25-May	Thursday	$	37.05	$34.95				$2.10
26-May	Friday	$	-	$0.00				$0.00
27-May	Saturday	$	95.29	$89.90				$5.39
28-May	Sunday	$	411.97	$229.90	$10.50	$30.25	$118.00	$23.32
29-May	Monday	$	83.63	$78.90				$4.73
30-May	Tuesday	$	94.55	$89.20				$5.35
31-May	Wednesday	$	-	$0.00				$0.00
Totals		$ 3,637.60		$2,885.55	$135.90	$ 87.75	$322.50	$205.90

Figure 13.11

Jenny's Café, Inc.
Denver Restaurant
Menu Mix
Month Ending May 31, 2006

Menu Item	Selling Price	Unit Cost	Food Cost %	Number Sold	Extended Cost	Sales
Ham & Cheese Omelet	$8.50	$1.77	20.8%	4,500	$ 7,965.00	$ 38,250.00
Pancakes	$7.50	$1.51	20.1%	3,900	$ 5,889.00	$ 29,250.00
Bagel & Cream Cheese	$3.95	$0.87	22.0%	3,100	$ 2,697.00	$ 12,245.00
Shrimp Cocktail	$12.95	$5.26	40.6%	3,900	$ 20,514.00	$ 50,505.00
French Onion Soup	$7.95	$0.95	11.9%	2,500	$ 2,375.00	$ 19,875.00
Caesar Salad	$8.95	$1.43	16.0%	3,900	$ 5,577.00	$ 34,905.00
Filet Mignon	$35.95	$11.04	30.7%	3,600	$ 39,744.00	$ 129,420.00
Prime Rib	$31.95	$10.42	32.6%	4,900	$ 51,058.00	$ 156,555.00
New York Strip Steak	$32.95	$9.98	30.3%	2,200	$ 21,956.00	$ 72,490.00
Barbecued Chicken	$15.95	$3.98	25.0%	3,800	$ 15,124.00	$ 60,610.00
Baked Salmon	$25.95	$7.59	29.2%	1,900	$ 14,421.00	$ 49,305.00
Pie ala Mode	$6.95	$1.27	18.3%	3,200	$ 4,064.00	$ 22,240.00
Orange Juice	$2.50	$0.43	17.2%	5,500	$ 2,365.00	$ 13,750.00
Coffee	$1.95	$0.36	18.5%	5,900	$ 2,124.00	$ 11,505.00
Soda	$1.95	$0.39	20.0%	9,800	$ 3,822.00	$ 19,110.00
					$ 199,695.00	$ 720,015.00

Adjustments:
Employee Meals	$ 3,345.75	
Coupons		$ (17,380.05)
Comps		$ (2,885.55)
Cost & Sales after Adjustments	$ 203,040.75	$ 699,749.40

Total Food Cost	$ 203,040.75
Total Food Sales	$ 699,749.40
Standard Food Cost Percentage	29.0%
Actual Food Cost	$ 291,212.02
Actual Food Sales	$ 706,825.30
Actual Food Cost Percentage	41.2%
Variance	-12.2%

Main freezer went down resulting in $75, 230 in spoilage.

Stephan Richileau – Executive Chef

Joey Robertson – GM

Figure 13.12

Investigating Significant Variances

When the Controller has finished the Menu Mix report for the inventory period, she compares the Standard Cost calculated by the Menu Mix after adjustments to the Actual Cost calculated by the General Ledger system. If there is a difference between the two greater than 2-3 percentage points, depending on the Company standard, the Controller needs to investigate the reason for the significant difference.

The first thing the Controller should do is check the input to ensure that all data that should have been entered in the Menu Mix were in fact entered in the Menu Mix. She should look through the number of items sold on the Menu Mix for each menu item on each day of the inventory period to ensure they are reasonable. If one or more items appears to be too high or too low, the Controller should pull the source documents (detail cash register tapes or sales by item report) for each sales day, compare the number of items sold per the source document to what was entered on the Menu Mix, and correct any differences. For example, if the Controller sees that there were 10 Ham and Cheese omelets sold on Sunday when she would expect to see about 200 omelets sold, she would check the omelet sales for that day and make the correction to the Menu Mix.

Once the Controller has verified that the Menu Mix is correct, she needs to find out what happened that resulted in the large variance. She should check with the Executive Chef and ask him if something happened during the inventory period that would account for the large variance. For example, the Executive Chef may reply that a cooler broke one night early in the month and most of the food in the cooler spoiled. The Executive Chef should have taken an inventory of the spoiled food, determined the cost of each item, and given the extended and totaled inventory to the Controller as an explanation of the large variance. He may have the inventory in his office and was finishing up the extensions!

Another area the Controller should look at is the inventory. Was the physical inventory done properly? Does the value of the physical inventory look reasonable? If the physical inventory value is wrong, the Actual Cost percentage will be wrong. The Controller should look through the inventory and see if there are items whose counts appear to be too high or too low. These items should be recounted and the counts corrected if necessary. For example, the Controller scans through the inventory listing used to record the Food Inventory for the month and sees the following entry:

Prime Rib—Raw 41 lbs. @ 7.95 = $325.95

The Controller thinks to herself that prime rib is one of the restaurant's best sellers. Based on her experience, the Chef always has a few hundred pounds in storage. She does a recount with the inventory counters and finds out that while there were 41 pounds of prime rib in the cooler, the counters missed 636 pounds of prime rib in the walk in freezer, resulting in an understatement of inventory of $5,056.20.

If the extensions were done manually, the Controller should review the extensions to see if there is one or more that do not look reasonable. For example, the Controller sees the following entry:

Filets 335 lbs. @ $10.95 = $668.25

The Controller finds this entry while scanning the inventory extensions and sees it is an obvious error. She gets out her calculator and finds out that the extended cost is really $3,668.25 A few more errors like that and the inventory has a major impact on the Food Cost!

Was there an unusual amount of spoilage during the period? The Controller should check the Spoilage Sheets where kitchen personnel record product that spoiled and was thrown away. Was a new employee working in the kitchen who worked less efficiently than experienced help and threw away more than he should have? The Controller should talk to kitchen help and ask if they are aware of any unusual spoilage. Also, the Controller should observe the kitchen staff during production time to see if they are handling food in a manner that minimizes spoilage and waste.

Was there a large cost increase in seasonal products, i.e. produce, meat, seafood, etc.? The Controller should check with the person purchasing the product and compare invoice costs to the Cost Specification Sheets. If there was a large increase in seasonal items or a large permanent increase, the Cost Specification Sheets need to be updated and the new menu item costs entered into the Menu Mix.

Are cooks portioning correctly? The Controller should observe the kitchen during peak times to see if the portions served are reasonable. Is a cook portioning two ladles of vegetables and mashed potatoes when the standard is one? Is a cook portioning 8 ounces of roast beef when the standard is 4 ounces? Is a cook serving 2 filets on a plate when the standard is one? Is the cook serving 2 scoops of cheese sauce when the standard is one? The Controller should discuss any unusual observations with the Executive Chef to correct the over portioning problem.

The Controller should ask the Executive Chef about the possibility of theft. Did someone break into the kitchen or storage areas after the restaurant closed and stole product? Are the kitchen and storage areas properly secured at night? Are kitchen and storage areas properly manned during business hours to prevent employees from stealing cases of meat or other high cost items? After the Stores staff leaves, are all coolers, freezers, and dry goods areas locked so that only authorized personnel (Executive Chef, Manager on Duty) can gain access? If the storage areas are not properly secured, internal or external theft could be the reason for the excessive food cost.

The results of the investigation should be documented and filed with the Menu Mix Comparison of Standard Cost to Actual Cost. The Executive Chef and General Manager should sign the report documenting the results of the investigation. They should know what is going on at the restaurant. Their signatures indicate that if they did not participate in the investigation, they were at least informed of the situation and agree that the investigation was adequate.

When performing the audit, the auditor should review several comparisons of Standard Cost to Actual Cost. If there was a variance greater than the Company standard 2-3 percentage points, she should see whether there is documentation of an investigation of the large variance, signed by the Executive Chef and General Manager. The auditor should read the results of the investigation and decide whether there was an adequate effort made to determine why the cost was so high. If there is no documentation of an investigation of a variance greater than 2 percentage points signed by the Executive Chef and General Manager, the auditor has a Discussion Point.

Updating Menu Mix Costs

As with everything else in the economy, food prices generally go up over time. Purchasing departments try to keep food costs stable by negotiating prices with national suppliers for a set period of time, generally six months to one year. Eventually, the purchasing contracts expire and a new set of price increases go into effect.

The Controller needs to be aware of when the national contracts expire and needs to input the new costs into the Cost Specification Sheets. These updated menu costs from the Cost Specification Sheets need to be carried forward to the Menu Mix so the Standard Cost is calculated with the most updated product cost information.

As noted earlier, certain products purchased through local suppliers fluctuate frequently depending on market prices. If the Controller were to change the prices in the Cost Specification Sheets every week, she would have little time to do much else. Thus, the costs used in the Cost Specification Sheets should not be changed due to changes in prices from the local suppliers unless they have a significant impact on the Cost Specification Sheets.

For example, the price of tomatoes increases from $2.29 per pound to $2.79 per pound, a significant increase. But tomatoes are a minor part of most menu items and thus shouldn't have a significant impact on these items. However, if the price of filets went from $8.95 per pound to $10.95 per pound, this would affect the cost of filet mignon significantly. In this case, the Controller should change the cost of filets on the Cost Specification Sheet and in the Menu Mix.

As a general rule, the Controller should update the product costs in the Cost Specification Sheets once per quarter. She should look up the costs on recent invoices. After updating these costs, the Controller should transfer the new menu costs to the Menu Mix.

Some items on the menu are very popular and others never really seem to catch on with the customers. The Executive Chef should review the menu items at least annually to determine which items are the best sellers and which items do not sell well.

The Controller should be able to supply the Executive Chef with an Excel spreadsheet that shows the number of items sold each month and the total number of each menu item sold for the year. This information is easily obtained from the order entry system's sales report that provides daily and month to date number of each menu item sold. If the restaurant has a cash register that tracks items sold each day, the Controller needs to enter the number of items sold each day into an Excel spreadsheet and total these items each month. While this is a little more work, a clerk should be able to compile this information fairly easily if it is done each day.

Once he obtains the sales information for the year, the Executive Chef designs the menu for the upcoming year. For the new menu, the Executive Chef should drop the worst selling items from the menu and add new items that he thinks will sell better.

When performing the audit, the auditor should determine when the Cost Specification Sheets were last updated. There should be some type of notation in the Cost Specification Sheets indicating when the costs were last updated. For example, there could be a note in the beginning of the Cost Specification Sheet binder that reads as follows: "Updated unit costs on Cost Specification Sheets and menu costs in Menu Mix on May 15, 2006." If the

Cost Specification Sheets were not updated within the last three months, the auditor would have a Discussion Point.

To test the accuracy of unit costs in the Cost Specification Sheets, the auditor should select some items that play a significant part in the menu item costs. She should locate recent invoices and tie the Cost Specification Sheets' product costs into the invoice costs. Since costs often fluctuate without notice, a few differences should not cause alarm, especially if there is evidence that costs were updated within the past three months.

For example, if the auditor tested 10 significant items and noted that 8 of the 10 agreed to current invoice costs, the auditor can conclude that the Cost Specification Sheets are fairly current. However, if the auditor found that only 3 of 10 items agreed to current invoices, the auditor would conclude that the product costs in the Cost Specification Sheets are not current. In this case, the auditor would have a Discussion Point. If the results were somewhere in the middle, the auditor should select another 10 items to get a better idea whether product costs in the Cost Specification sheets are current.

Buffet Costing

One of the most popular features in a restaurant is the buffet. Some restaurants have a very extensive Sunday brunch buffet; others have a more limited daily breakfast buffet. Some restaurants have a Friday night seafood buffet; others have a Saturday night dinner buffet. Whatever the special feature, patrons seem to love buffets. They pay one price and eat all the food they like, but they can only take food home in their stomachs! No doggie bags allowed!

Since different people eat different items in the buffet and in different quantities, how do you calculate a standard cost that will be used in the Menu Mix? It is a problem! Generally, the Executive Chef costs the buffet on several different days and averages the cost of the buffets.

The first step in costing the buffet is for the Executive Chef to cost the different menu items going onto the buffet. The menu items should be prepared in standard dishes and the standard dishes should be costed. Figure 13.13 shows 4 dishes that appear on Jenny's Café's Seafood Buffet. Each item has been costed similar to the menu items costed earlier in the chapter with the exception that the total cost of each menu item on the buffet is the cost of preparing a tray, pan, or pot of the product. Thus, it costs $24.79 to produce a tray of shrimp cocktail, $47.45 to produce a tray of crab legs, $40.94 to produce a tray of haddock filets, and $3.95 to produce a tray of glazed carrots.

When costing the buffet, the Executive Chef should take an inventory of every item that will be going onto the buffet table, including whatever desserts and beverages are included in the selling price. As additional trays are added during the evening, the Executive Chef needs to add them to the inventory. When the buffet table is closed for the evening, the Executive Chef counts all usable food that is returned to the kitchen. If leftover food is to be thrown into the trash as spoilage, it should not be counted as returned.

Figure 13.14 is an example of a buffet costed on January 27, 2006. The columns used in the spreadsheet are as follows:

Menu Item—Description of the tray of product going on the buffet table,

Tray Cost—Cost of a tray of product, per the Cost Specification Sheets,

Beginning Count—Initial number of trays set on the buffet table,

Additions—Number of trays of the menu item added to the buffet table during the evening,

Total Available—Beginning Count plus Additions,

Ending Count—Number of trays left over at the end of the evening that will not be spoiled, counted by the nearest quarter tray,

Amount Used—Total Available minus Ending Count,

Cost of Usage—Amount Used multiplied by Tray Cost.

The information at the bottom of the schedule is the number of adults who purchased the buffet multiplied by the selling price to obtain the dollar amount of adult buffets sold, the number of children who purchased the children's portion multiplied by the selling price to obtain the dollar amount of children's buffets sold, and the total sales value of the buffets. This sales information is obtained from the order entry system or cash register.

The Food Cost percentage is the Total Food Cost divided by Total Food Sales. The schedule also lists the Food Cost percentage for the buffet from the 3 previous Friday night seafood buffets in January. By taking a simple average, i.e. the 4 food cost percentages divided by 4, the Executive Chef calculates the Standard Food Cost percentage for the Seafood Buffet to be 36.0%.

Jenny's Café, Inc.
Denver Restaurant
Menu Costing - Seafood Buffet - Shrimp Cocktail
31-Dec-05

Ingredient	Unit	Number per Unit	Portion Size	Unit Cost	Extended Cost
Shrimp 40-50/lb.	Pound	1	3	$6.99	$ 20.97
Cocktail Sauce	Gallon	1	0.25	$15.29	$ 3.82
					$ 24.79

Jenny's Café, Inc.
Denver Restaurant
Menu Costing - Seafood Buffet - Crab Legs
31-Dec-05

Ingredient	Unit	Number per Unit	Portion Size	Unit Cost	Extended Cost
Crab Legs	Pound	1	5	$8.99	$ 44.95
Butter Sauce	Pound	1	0.5	$4.99	$ 2.50
					$ 47.45

Jenny's Café, Inc.
Denver Restaurant
Menu Costing - Seafood Buffet - Fried Haddock Filets
31-Dec-05

Ingredient	Unit	Number per Unit	Portion Size	Unit Cost	Extended Cost
Haddock Filets	Pound	1	5	$7.99	$ 39.95
Flour Batter	Pound	1	1	$0.99	$ 0.99
					$ 40.94

Jenny's Café, Inc.
Denver Restaurant
Menu Costing - Seafood Buffet - Glazed Carrots
31-Dec-05

Ingredient	Unit	Number per Unit	Portion Size	Unit Cost	Extended Cost
Carrots	Pound	1	4	$0.89	$ 3.56
Glaze	Gallon	128	10	$4.99	$ 0.39
					$ 3.95

Figure 13.13

46

Jenny's Café, Inc.
Denver Restaurant
Seafood Buffet Costing
January 27, 2006

Menu Item	Tray Cost	Beginning Count	Additions	Total Available	Ending Count	Amount Used	Cost of Usage
Chef's Salad	$6.21	2.00	7.00	9.00	0.00	9.00	$ 55.89
Shrimp Cocktail	$24.79	2.00	8.00	10.00	1.25	8.75	$ 216.91
Smoked Salmon	$45.98	2.00	1.00	3.00	0.50	2.50	$ 114.95
Clams Casino	$35.67	2.00	7.00	9.00	0.75	8.25	$ 294.28
Raw Oysters	$36.89	2.00	3.00	5.00	0.00	5.00	$ 184.45
Salmon Filets	$39.78	2.00	9.00	11.00	1.25	9.75	$ 387.86
Crab Legs	$47.45	2.00	6.00	8.00	1.50	6.50	$ 308.43
Fried Haddock Filets	$40.94	2.00	7.00	9.00	1.00	8.00	$ 327.52
Fried White Fish	$24.95	2.00	6.00	8.00	1.75	6.25	$ 155.94
Fried Catfish	$25.43	2.00	9.00	11.00	0.25	10.75	$ 273.37
Flounder	$43.78	2.00	9.00	11.00	0.50	10.50	$ 459.69
Glazed Carrots	$3.95	2.00	5.00	7.00	0.00	7.00	$ 27.65
Green Beans	$5.86	2.00	4.00	6.00	0.00	6.00	$ 35.16
French Fries	$6.45	2.00	11.00	13.00	0.00	13.00	$ 83.85
Mashed Potatoes	$4.97	2.00	6.00	8.00	0.00	8.00	$ 39.76
German Potato Salad	$6.99	2.00	7.00	9.00	0.50	8.50	$ 59.42
Macaroni Salad	$5.19	2.00	3.00	5.00	0.25	4.75	$ 24.65
Carrot Cake	$9.97	2.00	9.00	11.00	1.25	9.75	$ 97.21
Mini Eclairs	$15.32	2.00	8.00	10.00	1.75	8.25	$ 126.39
Black Forest Cake	$12.39	2.00	9.00	11.00	1.00	10.00	$ 123.90
Brownies	$14.67	2.00	5.00	7.00	0.25	6.75	$ 99.02
Coffee - Pot	$1.25	0.00	55.00	55.00	0.00	55.00	$ 68.75
Soda - Gallon of Syrup	$7.95	5.00	0.00	5.00	3.75	1.25	$ 9.94
							$3,574.98

Total Cost of Buffet			$ 3,574.98

Buffet Sales:	No.	Price	Sales
Adults	239	39.95	$ 9,548.05
Children	38	15.95	$ 606.10
			$10,154.15

Food Cost Percentage - January 27, 2006	35.2%
Food Cost Percentage - January 20, 2006	32.9%
Food Cost Percentage - January 13, 2006	38.1%
Food Cost Percentage - January 6, 2006	37.8%
Four Week Average Food Cost Percentage	36.0%

Figure 13.14

47

In auditing the accuracy of the buffet's standard cost, the auditor reviews the Cost Specification Sheets used to cost the trays of product and the Seafood Buffet Costing spreadsheet. She should tie some of the costs into current invoices to ensure they are reasonably accurate.

The auditor should ask the chef how the buffet was costed and determine whether the method used was reasonable. If the chef has help in costing the buffet, the auditor should talk to the participants to determine whether the method used was reasonable. She should review the spreadsheets used to calculate the standard cost that is used in the Menu Mix.

Using Electronic Spreadsheets

As we noted earlier, the unit costs of the products used on the Cost Specification sheets should be updated quarterly. Since one menu may have 50 items or more on it, the product cost updating process seems to be a formidable task, particularly since most restaurants have several menus, i.e. breakfast, lunch, and dinner, menus, banquet menus, and possibly one or more buffets.

One way to make the task easier is to set up each menu item as a separate tab in an Excel spreadsheet and make the first tab an index tab of inventory items. The inventory items used to cost the recipes in the menu tabs should refer to the corresponding inventory items on the index tab. Thus, when the Controller changes an inventory item in the index tab, that change automatically changes the unit cost of that item on every menu tab included in the spreadsheet.

When setting up the menu costing on each menu tab, the Executive Chef or Controller must make sure that the same unit is consistently used on the index tab and every menu tab in the spreadsheet. For example, if horseradish is used in a recipe, the cost of horseradish on the index tab cannot be by the gallon and then by the quart on the prime rib recipe. Both the index tab and the recipe tab must use either gallon or quart. Both the index tab and recipe tab must specify the unit, i.e. gallon or quart, that is to be used in costing the item.

To make navigating through a large spreadsheet easier, the Executive Chef or Controller could add a Table of Contents tab before the index tab, listing each menu recipe tab. Hyperlinks could be set up so that clicking on the menu recipe tab in the Table of Contents takes the user to the actual Cost Specification Sheet. An additional hyperlink can be added to the bottom of each menu recipe tab to take the user back to the Table of Contents.

Summary

The purpose of Menu Costing is to determine what each item on the menu costs to produce. This cost is used in determining a selling price that will achieve a specified food cost percentage.

Cost Specification Sheets are listings of the ingredients making up the specific menu items and the costs of those items. The Executive Chef determines the cost of the base, items that are common to all menu items in a category, i.e. bread and butter, chef's salad, garnish, etc. The Executive Chef determines exact portion sizes by specifying number of ounces, ladle, etc. The auditor should review the reasonableness of the items making up the Cost Specification Sheets and check for mathematical accuracy.

The Menu Mix is a listing of the menu items and the costs of producing those menu items. The quantities of each item sold are entered into the menu mix to calculate the Standard Cost percentage based on the mix of menu items sold during a particular day since each one has a different Food Cost percentage.

Generally, Actual Food Cost variances greater than 2-3 percentage points from Standard Cost need to be investigated. The results of the investigation need to be documented and signed by the Executive Chef and General Manager. When the auditor sees Actual Food Costs outside the acceptable range, she should review the documented results of the investigation to determine whether the investigation was adequate.

Menu costs must be updated at least quarterly. The auditor should determine the last time the costs were updated.

Buffet costs vary depending on what patrons ate that day, high cost items versus low cost items. The Executive Chef should cost the buffet on several days and take an average as the Standard Cost percentage.

When using Excel spreadsheets in menu costing, the Executive Chef can ease the inventory updating process by setting up a separate tab for each Cost Specification Sheet, and drawing unit cost information from an index tab. A Table of Contents tab with hyperlinks to the Cost Specification Sheet tabs makes navigating through the many tabs of the spreadsheet much easier.

Discussion Questions and Case Studies

1. What is the purpose of Menu Costing?
2. What is a Cost Specification Sheet?
3. What is the purpose of the Menu Mix?
4. Chef Jermaine is costing his dinner menu. The first thing he does is cost

his base. What is a base? What types of items might be included in a base for a dinner menu?

5. Chef Jermaine is costing his breakfast menu. He is costing the 3 egg Denver Omelet. Using the following ingredients, determine the Food Cost percentage of the Denver omelet selling for $8.95.

Ingredient	Portion	Unit	Unit Cost
Eggs—Large	3	Dozen	$ 1.59
Bell Peppers—			
Trimmed	0.5 oz.	Pound	$4.59
Cheddar Cheese	1.5 oz.	Pound	$4.79
Base			$ .54

6. You are auditing Mama Maria's Mexican Cantina. The Actual Food Cost percentage for April was 38.3%. Looking at the Menu Mix, you notice that Standard Cost for April was 32.4%. There was no explanation of the variance documented in the Executive Chef's files or anywhere else. Do you have an audit issue? What is your recommendation to management?

7. You are auditing Bronco Bill's Beef Barbecue. You obtain the Cost Specification Sheets from the Executive Chef and notice that the dates on the Cost Specification Sheets are from one and a half years ago. Do you have an audit issue? What is your recommendation to management?

8. You are the Controller at Shirley's Seafood Emporium. Actual Food Cost for the month is 42.3% versus Standard Cost based on the Menu Mix of 35.4%. You start your investigation of the large variance. What procedures do you follow when investigating the large variance?

CHAPTER 14
AUDITING KITCHEN OPERATIONS

Learning Objectives

After reading this chapter, you should be able to:

1. Know how an order entry system works and how the order entry controls function,
2. Utilize portion controls in the kitchen to ensure stable food costs are achieved,
3. Determine whether the wait staff are charging for non-alcoholic beverages,
4. Minimize spoilage by documenting it on spoilage sheets and monitoring by the Executive Chef,
5. Ensuring kitchen security during the day and when the kitchen staff leaves for the night.

Overview

This chapter focuses on kitchen controls. It begins with a discussion of segregation of duties in the kitchen.

Order entry systems are useful in ensuring that everything that leaves the kitchen is recorded on a guest check. Manual dup controls need to be put into effect if an order entry system is not used. An effective checker function can also ensure that all items leaving the kitchen are recorded on a guest check.

To achieve Standard Food Cost, kitchen employees must utilize portion control. We will discuss how to implement portion control to achieve Standard Food Cost.

When regular theft of high cost items is suspected, performing daily inventories of high cost items susceptible to theft and accounting for usage is an effective method of detecting missing inventory.

Non-alcoholic beverages are considered to be low cost items. However, they can significantly impact operating results if the wait staff is not charging for them. We will discuss effective methods of ensuring all non-alcoholic beverages are recorded on guest checks.

Spoilage and waste can drive up Food Cost if they are not controlled. We will discuss how the Executive Chef can monitor spoilage and waste and how he can ensure his kitchen staff minimizes it.

Many restaurants lose money every year to linens that are stolen or end up in the trash. The linen company tracks the linens that it issues to each restaurant and charges the full retail value for any linens that are not returned. We will discuss effective methods of controlling linens so they are not stolen or discarded.

China, Glass, and Silverware are a large investment for any restaurant. Too often, employees are careless in how they handle china, glass, and silverware, resulting in excess breakage and silverware that ends up in the trash.

Kitchens must be properly secured. When the kitchen closes for the day, every cooler and freezer must be locked. When the kitchen staff leaves for the day, the kitchen should be locked.

In Practice

Aimee Stone walks into the kitchen of Jenny's Café in Denver to perform observations of its kitchen operations. She sees the cooks busy at work preparing the entrees for the patrons. One of the cooks takes the chit from the printer, reads it, and clips it on an overhead row of clips. He takes out a steak and drops it on the grill. Meanwhile, he pulls a steak off the grill, adds a baked potato to it, puts a ladle of vegetables on the plate, grabs a chit from the overhead rack, tears it halfway, and sets it next to the plate under the heat lamp. That's exactly the way it should work, Aimee thinks.

Aimee sees Stella walk into the kitchen who says to a young cook, "Hey Tony! I need a hamburger with French Fries."

"Sure Stella!" Tony replies, "Coming right up." Aimee can't believe her eyes. No chit printed on the printer, but Tony promptly walks over to the refrigerator, grabs a 1/3 pound hamburger patty and drops it on the grill. Twenty minutes later, the hamburger is sitting under the heat lamp waiting for Stella to pick it up. No sale was recorded in that transaction, Aimee thinks. I wonder how much of a tip Stella is getting for pulling off that trick, or is she just keeping the money for the burger?

Aimee walks over to the salad station. The young woman working at the salad station is busy filling orders coming off the Micros printer. After 10 minutes, the woman leaves for a few minutes. Meanwhile, Stella walks into the kitchen, goes behind the salad station, and opens a cooler. She grabs a premade shrimp cocktail, takes 2 additional giant shrimp from a pan, adds them to the shrimp cocktail, and walks out of the kitchen. Not only was that shrimp cocktail not recorded on the order entry system, but the portion is 50% larger than standard, Aimee thinks to herself.

Aimee goes to the dessert station, and once again observes a young man filling orders based on chits printing on the Micros printer. He sets the orders in front of him and puts the chit next to the order. He isn't tearing the chits halfway to ensure they can't be reused, Aimee thinks. Stella walks in and says, "Jimmie, I entered two apple pie ala modes but another customer at the table decided she would like one too. Give me a third pie ala mode and I'll enter it when I get back to the Micros station."

"Sure, Stella," Jimmie replies, and cuts a slice from a pie and puts a scoop of vanilla ice cream next to it. Wow! I bet that chit never comes out on the printer! Where is Chef Stephan? Aimee wonders.

Segregation of Duties

The Executive Chef is in charge of the kitchen. He schedules the kitchen employees and assigns them to the various jobs. His job is to ensure the kitchen staff is following company procedures while they are working in the kitchen.

Cooks are the only ones who work the broiler, deep fryer, grill, and stove. They remove product from the coolers to be grilled, cooked, and fried per the chits printing from the printer. No one else should be allowed behind the production line.

The salad station and dessert station should be set up separate from the production line. They should have their own staffs and should not share with the cooks. In other words, a cook should not work part of the time on the production line and also make salads at the salad station. The salad and dessert stations should have their own coolers. They should not share coolers with the cooks. The salad person and dessert person should by the only ones to go behind the station and get product from the salad and dessert coolers. Each station should have its own order entry printer and attendants should only fill orders based on what is printed on the chits.

Waiters and waitresses may not go behind the production line, salad station, or dessert station. They may only take product from the kitchen that has been recorded through the order entry system and set under the heat lamp or in front of the salad station or dessert station with the chit next to it, torn halfway to prevent reuse.

Large operations should have a separate linen room that is staffed by people who do not work in the kitchen. The linen room supervisor should report to the Dining Room Manager.

The auditor should observe kitchen operations to determine whether adequate segregation of duties is maintained. He should find a spot where he can observe what is going on but where he is not in the way of the kitchen workers working in the kitchen or the wait staff coming in to pick up orders.

Order Entry Systems

Order entry systems were designed to solve the problem of ensuring that product coming out of the kitchen was recorded on a guest check and ultimately paid for by the customer. The waiter or waitress walks over to the order entry station and enters the order into a computer terminal. For example, she enters 2 Shrimp Cocktails, Filet Mignon—Medium, Baked Potato, Sour Cream, Broccoli—No Butter; Filet Mignon—Rare, French Fries, Broccoli. A printer at the Salad Station prints "2 Shrimp Cocktail" and a printer at the Production Line prints "Filet Mignon—Medium, Baked Potato, Sour Cream, Broccoli—No Butter; Filet Mignon—Rare, French Fries, Broccoli."

The pantry worker at the salad station tears the chit off the printer, prepares two shrimp cocktails, tears the chit halfway to prevent reuse, and sets the chit next to the 2 shrimp cocktails. When the waitress comes to pick up the order, she reads her name on the chit to ensure the order is hers, picks up the order, and takes it to the dining room. She throws the chit in the trash.

The cook at the Production Line tears the chit off the printer, reads it, and puts two filets on the grill. He clips the chit on an overhead clip. When the steaks are ready, he puts each steak on a plate, pulls the chit from the clip, and reads it again. He puts a baked potato next to the one steak, puts a one ounce soufflé cup of sour cream next to it, and adds the broccoli and garnish. For the rare steak, he adds French Fries and lets a dab of butter melt over the broccoli. He tears the chit halfway to prevent reuse, and sets it next to the order under the warmer. The waitress reads her name on the chit to ensure the order is hers, picks up the order, takes it to the dining room, and drops the chit in the trash.

Later she enters the dessert order in the order entry system. "Pie ala Mode" and "Carrot Cake" print on the printer at the dessert station. The pantry person working at the dessert station tears the chit off the printer, reads it, fills the order, tears the chit halfway, and sets it down next to the pie ala mode and carrot cake. The waitress returns to the kitchen, reads her name on the chit to ensure it is her order, takes the order to the dining room, and discards the chit.

When taking orders for alcoholic beverages, the waitress enters the order into the order entry system and a chit prints at the bar. The bartender fills the order, tears the chit halfway, and sets it next to the order at the waitress station in the corner of the bar.

The purpose of tearing the chit halfway is to prevent the chit from being reused. A kitchen worker seeing a partially torn chit lying at the station knows this order has already been filled and did not fall from an overhead clip. An alternative to this procedure is to put spindles at each station. The kitchen worker puts the chit next to the completed order. The wait staff person reads the chit and drives it through the spindle. The hole in the spindle tells the kitchen worker that the order has been filled.

Obviously for this system to be effective, everyone must know how it works. During employee training sessions, the trainer should emphasize that no product may leave the kitchen without appearing on a chit. Kitchen workers may only fill orders based on what they read on a chit. No chit, no product. It's that simple. Trainers should also emphasize that failure to follow this policy will result in disciplinary action, up to and including termination.

The auditor should be familiar with the Company's policy on handling chits: torn in half or put through a spindle. As part of his audit procedures, he should observe kitchen operations to ensure the Company's policies are being followed. However, the auditor should find a spot in the kitchen where he can observe what is going on but is not in the way of people doing their jobs.

To document his observations, the auditor should do a write up on his observations of kitchen operations and insert the write up in the audit workpaper binder. Any exceptions from company policy should be documented and cross referenced to the Discussion Points worksheet.

Manual Dup Control Systems

Restaurants that do not have an order entry system should use a manual dup control system. Guest checks should be a two-part form that consists of a hard paper second copy with a non-carbon tissue copy on top. Dup pads should also be used.

The waiter or waitress writes the table number, waiter number, and number of patrons at the table in the appropriate places on the guest check. He writes the order on the hard guest check. The waiter also writes the drink order and appetizers on two separate copies of the dup pad, and writes the last four numbers of the guest check number on the dups along with his waiter number and table number. The waiter walks to the cashier station located in the kitchen.

The dining room cashier inserts the hard copy of the guest check into the cash register print slot. The cashier enters the guest check number in the cash register and proceeds to record the order. The machine prints the prices of each item recorded on the guest check.

The next time the cashier records orders for this guest check, she enters the guest check number in the cash register which brings the previous balance into memory and adds the new orders onto the previous balance to obtain the new balance.

When finished at the cashier station, the waiter walks over to the bar. The waiter tears off the dups from the pad, and gives one to the bartender and the second to the pantry person working at the salad station. He tears the tissue copy off the hard guest check and hands it to the cook on the production line.

The bartender reads the drink order and begins to fill it. When ready, the bartender sets the drink order down at the wait staff station and puts the dup next to it. The waiter picks up the drink order and drives the dup through a spindle located at the wait staff station.

The panty person working at the salad station reads the dup and prepares the order. He puts the dup next to the order waiting to be picked up. The Waiter picks up the order and drives the dup through the spindle located in the pick up area.

When the cook receives the tissue copy from the waiter, he reads it and clips it on one of the clips hanging overhead. He proceeds to prepare the order. When the order is ready, the cook sets it under the heat lamp and places the dup next to it. The waiter picks up the order and drives the dup (tissue copy) through a spindle near the heat lamps.

After dinner is over, the waiter returns to the patron's table and takes the dessert order. The waiter writes the dessert order on the hard copy of the main guest check and again on the dup pad. He writes the last four numbers of the main guest check number on the dup and takes the dup to the dessert station.

The waiter hands the dup to the pantry person who reads it and proceeds to fill the order. He also goes to the cashier so the order is recorded on the cash register and added to the patron's account. When completed, the pantry person sets the order down at the pick up station with the dup next to it. The waiter picks up the order and drives the dup through the spindle located at the dessert pick up station.

After dinner drinks and drinks ordered during the meal are handled the same way as the initial drink order. The waiter writes the orders on the main guest check and again on the dup with the last four digits of the main guest check number. The dups are taken to the bar to place the order. He goes to the cashier to have the order recorded on the cash register and added to the patron's account.

At the end of the day, someone is assigned to pick up the dups from each area and put them in separate bags labeled Bar, Salad Station, Dessert Station, and Production Line. He takes the bags with the dups to the Dining Room Manager's office or General Manager's office.

The following day, the Dining Room Manager or General Manager hands the bags containing the dups and the hard guest checks to a clerk. The clerk matches the tissue copy of the guest check to the hard copy and looks for the cash register validation to ensure the transactions were recorded for the correct amounts. He also locates the dups from the bar, salad station, and dessert station bags containing the last four numbers of the guest check. The clerk compares the orders written on the dups to the main guest check and checks to see that each item written on the dup is also written on the main guest check and validated by the cash register. If there is no cash register validation, the sale was not recorded. The clerk staples all dups to the main guest check.

After matching all dups with main guest checks, the clerk takes the exceptions to the Dining Room Manager or General Manager. The Dining Room Manager writes up a Record of Employee Conference for each waiter or waitress who had items written on dups that were not recorded on the main guest check. If there were items written on the main guest check that were not validated on the cash register, the Dining Room Manager writes up a Record of Employee Conference for the cashier because the cashier did not record all items listed on the guest check onto the cash register. The Dining Room Manager follows the normal progressive discipline procedures with the applicable employees, As you can imagine, comparing dups to guest checks is a lot of work and takes up the better part of the day for the clerk doing the comparison. Many restaurants do not perform this check daily but only do it periodically. If this is the case, the comparison should be done at least once a week, and it should be done on a different day each week selected randomly. If the same day is audited every week, the employees will soon learn this and make sure all procedures are followed to the letter on that day, but not on the other six days of the week.

The auditor should be cognizant of employees following proper procedures during his observations of kitchen operations. He should observe the dining room cashier to ensure the cashier is performing his duties properly. The auditor should document his observations of dup controls and the cashiering function in his kitchen observations memo.

Jenny's Café, Inc.
Denver Restaurant
Review of Dup Matching to Guest Checks - July 15, 2006
July 31, 2006

Guest Cks Audited	Guest Check Amount	Wait No.	----- Comparison of Dups to Guest Check -----		
			All Bar Orders on Guest Check?	All Salad Station Orders on G.C.?	All Dessert Station Orders on G.C.?
135068	$89.25	23	Yes	Yes	Yes
135075	$115.55	23	Yes	Yes	Yes
135081	$27.98	7	Yes	Yes	Yes
135089	$56.96	7	Yes	Yes	Yes
135097	$69.05	7	Yes	Yes	Yes
135108	$175.53	33	NO	NO	Yes
135116	$139.82	33	NO	Yes	NO
135124	$59.75	3	Yes	Yes	Yes
135132	$97.84	3	Yes	Yes	Yes
135139	$78.56	3	Yes	Yes	Yes
135148	$89.85	39	Yes	Yes	Yes
135154	$67.23	39	Yes	Yes	Yes
135161	$185.25	17	Yes	Yes	Yes
135169	$112.79	17	Yes	Yes	Yes
135176	$135.71	17	Yes	Yes	Yes
135183	$82.39	29	Yes	Yes	Yes
135189	$84.63	29	Yes	Yes	Yes
135191	$155.61	29	Yes	Yes	Yes
135198	$170.45	29	Yes	Yes	Yes
135207	$69.45	33	Yes	Yes	Yes

Figure 14.1

L1
A8
8/2/06

All Production Orders on G.C.?	Recorded on Cash Reg?	Record/Employee Conference?	Comments
Yes	Yes	N/A	
Yes	Yes	N/A	
Yes	Yes	N/A	
Yes	Yes	N/A	
Yes	Yes	N/A	
Yes	Yes	NO	Gin & Tonic on dup; not on GC 2 Shrimp Cocktails on dup; not on GC No Employee Conference Waitress: Stella Patenski **See Discussion Point #25**
Yes	Yes	NO	2 Beers on dup; not on Guest Check Pie ala Mode on dup; not on GC No Employee Conference Waitress: Stella Patenski **See Discussion Point #25**
Yes	Yes	N/A	
Yes	Yes	N/A	
Yes	Yes	N/A	
Yes	Yes	N/A	
Yes	Yes	N/A	
Yes	Yes	N/A	
Yes	NO	NO	1 Filet Mignon was not recorded. Cashier was April James No Employee Conference **See Discussion Point #26**
Yes	Yes	N/A	
Yes	Yes	N/A	
Yes	Yes	N/A	
Yes	Yes	N/A	
Yes	Yes	N/A	
Yes	Yes	N/A	

The auditor should select a day where the dups have been matched to the main guest check. He should select 20-50 guest checks with substantial sales activity, list them on a schedule, tie the orders from the dups to the main guest checks, and determine whether all orders were properly recorded and validated on the main guest checks. When selecting a day to test, it should be far enough away so that management has had a chance to take disciplinary action where appropriate. The auditor should check the personnel files of violators to determine whether disciplinary action was taken. Instances where a waiter or waitress did not follow Company policies but were not disciplined should be documented in the audit workpapers and cross referenced to the Discussion Points worksheet.

Figure 14.1 (above) is an example of a workpaper that documents the testing Aimee did in comparing dups to guest checks. The auditor answers "Yes" or "No" to each question and highlights all "Nos" in bold. "Nos" are explained in the Comments section. The spreadsheet columns are as follows:

Guest Checks Audited—Guest Check Numbers of the guest checks audited.

Guest Check Amount—Total Amount of the guest checks audited.

Waitress Number—Waitress Number on guest check used to identify the waitress who served the table.

All Bar Orders on Guest Check?—When matching dups to guest checks, were all bar orders on the dup recorded on the guest check?

All Salad Station Orders on Guest Check?—When matching dups to guest checks, were all salad station orders on the dup recorded on the guest check?

All Dessert Station Orders on Guest Check?—When matching dups to guest checks, were all dessert station orders on the dup recorded on the guest check?

All Production Orders on Guest Check?—When matching dups to guest checks, were all orders from the Production Line on the tissue copy of the guest check or dup recorded on the main guest check?

Recorded on Cash Register?—Was every entry on the main guest check validated on the cash register?

Record Employee Conference?—If there was an exception in the dup comparison to the main guest check, was there a Record of Employee Conference in the employee's personnel file?

Comments—Details of any "No" answer.

The auditor should cross reference any exceptions to the Discussion Points worksheet.

Portion Control

I can't emphasize enough that portion control is the key to controlling Food Cost. When the recipe calls for three ounces of meat on a sandwich, the sandwich maker has to put on three ounces of meat, not four or five. When the recipe calls for one ladle of carrots, the cook has to serve one ladle of carrots, not one and a half. When the recipe calls for a twelve ounce New York Strip steak, the meat cutter has to cut a twelve ounce steak, not a sixteen ounce steak. When the recipe calls for 15 slices from a 16 pound raw rib, the cook has to cut the rib into 15 slices, not 10.

Over-portioning is a major enemy of Standard Cost. Kitchen help think they are doing a good dead by making the portions a little bigger, but in fact they are sabotaging management's effort to make Plan. Bonuses depend on making Plan so if kitchen staff over-portion, management has a more difficult time making Plan and achieving its bonuses.

If some cooks are over-portioning and others are doing their jobs, patrons feel cheated. One time the patron gets a giant portion and another time he gets what appears to be a sub-standard portion, when in fact, the smaller portion is the correct portion. The patron is dissatisfied and may not come back a third time.

It is the Executive Chef's responsibility to ensure proper portions are consistently served by his kitchen staff. He should periodically observe the portions the kitchen staff is serving to ensure they are the proper size.

When making sandwiches or cutting steaks, kitchens often use portion control scales to ensure the portion is correct. A portion control scale weighs in ounces, rather than pounds. Often this scale weighs from one to twenty-four ounces. It is particularly effective for weighing cold cuts for sandwiches, but can also be used for weighing steaks, fish, etc.

For example, the sandwich maker puts some ham on the scale. If the standard is three ounces, and the scale weighs it at two and a half, he adds a little more ham until he has three ounces. If the scale weighs the ham at four ounces, the sandwich maker takes off some ham from the scale until he has three ounces.

For portioning mashed potatoes, vegetables, etc. the cook should use a standard ladle to measure a serving. When preparing a salad, the pantry person should be familiar with the standard recipe. She should fill the bowl with a normal amount of lettuce, the standard amount of tomato, onion, croutons, etc. Salad dressing should be served in a standard one ounce or two ounce (depending on the recipe) soufflé cup. The dessert person should cut the pie into the standard number of slices and add the standard amount of whipped cream and/or ice cream.

When performing observations of the kitchen staff, the auditor should observe the serving sizes the kitchen staff dish out. He should bring any serving sizes that seem out of the ordinary or inconsistent to the attention of the Executive Chef. The auditor should document any unusual serving sizes in his write up on kitchen observations. If the auditor notices severe violations of standard portion sizes, he should document his observations and cross reference them to the Discussion Points worksheet.

Checker Function

Restaurants that don't have order entry systems often utilize an expediter at the production line to get the orders out as quickly as possible. In this case, the expediter should also be performing a checking function to ensure that the entrees are listed on the guest check and were recorded on the cash register. Printing cash registers print the price of the item right on the guest check so the expediter can readily see whether the entrée was recorded.

Restaurants with order entry systems sometimes utilize a checker to ensure all items removed from the kitchen were recorded. The checker is located near the door to the dining room. As each waiter or waitress walks by the checker, the waiter or waitress hands the checker the chit. The checker compares each item on the tray to the chit, and drives the chit through a spindle.

Where restaurants use a checking system, the auditor should become familiar with how the checking system should work. During his kitchen observations, the auditor should observe the checking function to ensure it works as planned. Any exceptions should be reviewed with the Executive Chef and noted in the write up on kitchen operations. The auditor should include exceptions on his Discussion Points worksheet.

Key Entrée Items

Restaurants that consistently have high Food Costs have significant problems. Kitchen staff is over-portioning, there is excessive spoilage, or there is theft. It can be a combination of any two or all three.

When the auditor notes that a restaurant has high Food Cost, he can perform audit work that can help determine whether unusual amounts of high cost items are used. The auditor can perform daily counts of high cost items susceptible to theft, i.e. steaks, expensive cuts of meat, seafood, fish, etc., and compares the actual usage of these items to standard usage.

The auditor selects a dozen or more high cost items and counts them in the morning. He adds any receipts of product from the suppliers and subtracts the opening count from the next morning. The difference is the amount of product used. It is converted to number of portions served and compared to actual sales per the order entry system sales report or cash register reading. This process should be repeated for a week to see if there is a pattern.

When he retrieves the sales records from the previous day, the auditor multiplies the number of items sold by the standard portion for the entrée. He compares the calculated usage to actual usage to determine the variance from standard. Significant variances highlight problems that need to be investigated. One note of caution: the auditor must make sure that he includes the product usage from all menu items that use the inventory item he is tracking. For example, if 4 pieces of shrimp are used for the shrimp cocktail and for a shrimp salad, the auditor would need to add the number of shrimp salads to the number of shrimp cocktails for the number of orders.

Figure 14.2 is the first page of a schedule the auditor put together to track Jenny's Café's daily inventory of key items. Normally the auditor would select about a dozen or more items to track, but this schedule tracks four items so the reader can easily follow the first five days of activity.

The columns consist of the following information:

Item—A description of the inventory item being tracked,

Unit—The inventory unit the auditor is counting, i.e. pound, each, etc.,

Unit Cost—The invoice cost per one unit,

Number per Unit—Number of parts per unit, i.e. 15 shrimp per pound, 1 pound per pound, 1 piece per each,

Portion Size—Number of parts per portion, i.e. 4 shrimp per portion, 1.07 raw, untrimmed pounds per serving of prime rib, 1 tuna steak, 1 strip steak,

Beginning Count—Number of units counted at the beginning of the day; must be the same as previous day's ending count,

Received—Number of units received in the current day's supplier delivery,

Total Available—Beginning Count plus Received,

Ending Count—Number of units counted after close of business,

Actual Usage—Total Available minus Ending Count,

Number Orders Sold—Number of orders sold per the order entry system sales report or cash register z reading,

Standard Usage—Number Orders Sold multiplied by Portion Size divided by Number per Unit,

Variance—Standard Usage minus Actual Usage (overage is a positive number while shortage is a negative number),

Cost Value of Variance—Variance multiplied by Unit Cost.

Jenny's Café, Inc.
Denver Restaurant

Reconciliation of Key Item Usage to Sales
July 27 - August 2, 2006

Item	Unit	Unit Cost	No. per Unit	Portion Size	Beginning Count	Received	Total Available
July 27, 2006							
Shrimp Cocktail	Pound	$18.99	15	4	115		115
Prime Rib	Pound	$6.99	1	1.07	210		210
Tuna Steak	Each	$7.99	1	1	218		218
New York Strip	Each	$9.25	1	1	277		277
July 28, 2006							
Shrimp Cocktail	Pound	$18.99	15	4	102	120	222
Prime Rib	Pound	$6.99	1	1.07	95	367	462
Tuna Steak	Each	$7.99	1	1	115	240	355
New York Strip	Each	$9.25	1	1	157	360	517
July 29, 2006							
Shrimp Cocktail	Pound	$18.99	15	4	171		171
Prime Rib	Pound	$6.99	1	1.07	325		325
Tuna Steak	Each	$7.99	1	1	239		239
New York Strip	Each	$9.25	1	1	389		389
July 30, 2006							
Shrimp Cocktail	Pound	$18.99	15	4	109		109
Prime Rib	Pound	$6.99	1	1.07	127		127
Tuna Steak	Each	$7.99	1	1	91		91
New York Strip	Each	$9.25	1	1	179		179
July 31, 2006							
Shrimp Cocktail	Pound	$18.99	15	4	91	60	151
Prime Rib	Pound	$6.99	1	1.07	57	247	304
Tuna Steak	Each	$7.99	1	1	34	180	214
New York Strip	Each	$9.25	1	1	83	240	323

Figure 14.2

L2

莇

08/02/06

Ending Count	Actual Usage	No. Orders Sold	Standard Usage	Variance	Cost Value of Variance
102	13	49	13.07	0.07	$ 1.27
95	115	108	115.56	0.56	$ 3.91
115	103	102	102.00	(1.00)	$ (7.99)
157	120	119	119.00	(1.00)	$ (9.25)
171	51	129	34.40	(16.60)	$ (315.23)
325	137	112	119.84	(17.16)	$ (119.95)
239	116	80	80.00	(36.00)	$ (287.64)
389	128	87	87.00	(41.00)	$ (379.25)
109	62	164	43.73	(18.27)	$ (346.88)
127	198	139	148.73	(49.27)	$ (344.40)
91	148	108	108.00	(40.00)	$ (319.60)
179	210	162	162.00	(48.00)	$ (444.00)
91	18	68	18.13	0.13	$ 2.53
57	70	65	69.55	(0.45)	$ (3.15)
34	57	57	57.00	-	$ -
83	96	96	96.00	-	$ -
135	16	60	16.00	-	$ -
212	92	86	92.02	0.02	$ 0.14
34	180	179	179.00	(1.00)	$ (7.99)
83	240	237	237.00	(3.00)	$ (27.75)

By reviewing his schedule, the auditor can readily determine that on Friday, July 28 and Saturday, July 29, there is a serious shrinkage problem. The problem is not due to bad inventory counts because a bad count resulting in a large shortage one day would result in a large offsetting overage when the inventory is counted correctly the next day.

The auditor would bring the results of his audit work to the attention of the General Manager because it appears that inventory was stolen on Friday and Saturday. The cost of Friday's shrinkage was $1,102 and the cost of Saturday's shrinkage was $1,455. Shrinkage like that pays for a lot of additional security!

The auditor certainly has a Discussion Point in this situation, but there needs to be immediate corrective action. He should discuss possible remedies with the General Manager and Executive Chef.

The General Manager and Executive Chef should first look at current security. Are all freezers and coolers locked at night? Is Stores locked when its staff leaves for the day, including the receiving door and other means of entry? Is the kitchen locked when the kitchen staff leaves for the night? The problem may be lax security that is easily remedied or it may be that an unauthorized person has a key to the storage areas, i.e. a former employee. Perhaps changing the locks will remedy the problem.

The Controller should continue daily inventories of key items to monitor their usage and determine whether the shrinkage problem has been resolved by corrective action. If the above solutions do not remedy the shrinkage problem, it could be the result of theft by a current employee. In that case, management should consider installing cameras that point at all areas where the key items are stored, such as the walk in coolers and freezers. Anyone stealing product during the day or night would be caught on the camera and taped. Of course, someone would need to be monitoring the television cameras to catch the person stealing. Management might want to consider having the cameras installed and monitored by an outside professional security company.

Inventory of key entrée items is a time consuming process and is not a normal audit procedure. It is a response to unusually high Food Cost that the operation cannot explain with normal investigative procedures and theft is suspected. We are not considering the possibility of someone stealing a few pounds of meat but the theft of large quantities of product. Since this process would add to the cost of the audit, it is something that the Director of Internal Audit would clear with senior management in advance of performing these procedures.

Non-Alcoholic Beverages

An area that is often overlooked in the kitchen for proper controls is non-alcoholic beverages, i.e. coffee, tea, soda, and juices. Management often perceives non-alcoholic beverages as low cost, low revenue producers. Employees sometimes perceive non-alcoholic beverages as a way to give the customer something extra for nothing, thereby increasing the chances of getting a good tip. However, if employees are serving non-alcoholic beverages to customers without charging for them, the operation is losing out on a lot of revenue, and though the cost may be low, they are not free. Giving away any product increases Food Cost.

While most food items require a dup to be printed at the production line, salad station, or dessert station, coffee pots, soda dispensers, and juice dispensers are usually left in the wait staff area of the kitchen so time can be saved by allowing the wait staff to obtain their own non-alcoholic beverages. Requiring wait staff to obtain non-alcoholic beverages from the bar may tie up the bartenders and delay the service of higher priced alcoholic beverages.

This problem can be solved one of two ways. Utilizing a checker at the kitchen exit who takes the dup, reads it, and compares what is on the dup to what is on the waiter's or waitress's tray as they exit the kitchen, including non-alcoholic beverages ensures all non-alcoholic beverages are entered in the order entry system and thus added to the patron's check. The wait staff cannot just hand the checker the dup and continue out the exit. They must stop and wait until the checker does his job.

The other solution is to put the coffee pots, soda machine, and juice machines behind the salad station or dessert station, and program the order entry printer to print non-alcoholic beverage orders at this station. In this scenario, the wait staff pick up their non-alcoholic beverage orders from the pantry person who reads the order on the dup before filling it.

Refills become a problem. Most restaurants offer free refills of Coffee and soda. How do you ensure coffee and soda sales are properly recorded on a guest check but still offer free refills? The restaurant could require the waiter to bring the dirty glass or coffee cup back to the beverage station to obtain a new one. The coffee could be brewing at the waitress station in the dining room, but the cups could be obtained from the beverage station upon presentation of a dup. Either procedure would ensure that the original order was obtained from a dup but refills can be given for free.

If utilizing a checker, the checker would observe the waiter or waitress going into the kitchen with the dirty glasses and refilling them from the soda dispenser or coffee pot. Thus, the checker would know that there is no dup for the refill.

If there were coffee pots in the waitress station, the checker could see the coffee cups coming from the kitchen and check to be sure the coffee was recorded on a dup, but refills could be obtained from the coffee pots at the waitress station located in the dining room.

Non-alcoholic beverage sales is a difficult area to audit with the traditional set up because the order does not print on a dup printer and there is no second person involved in the transaction. When the auditor observes a waiter or waitress filling soda or juice glasses or coffee cups, he cannot determine whether the order was recorded in the order entry system because there is no dup printing the order.

Eating dinner at the restaurant, particularly if the auditor can arrange to have dinner prior to announcing he is at the operation conducting an audit, is the most effective method of determining whether wait staff are charging for non-alcoholic beverages. The auditor can eat dinner in the restaurant and order soda during the meal and/or coffee at the end of the meal. When presented with the check, the auditor should see whether all items ordered, including non-alcoholic beverages, appear on the check.

Even eating dinner at the restaurant has limited value because if only a few waiters or waitresses are serving non-alcoholic beverages without charging for them, the chances are that you will get a waiter that does charge his patrons for them. If the auditor is not charged for non-alcoholic beverages he ordered, he should report the incident to management during the introductory meeting so management can take action. Of course he should also document the incident and cross reference the documentation to a Discussion Point.

During the course of his audit and during his observations of the kitchen and dining room operations, the auditor should keep his eyes and ears open for anything unusual that indicates one or more waiters or waitresses are not charging for non-alcoholic beverages. The auditor will probably eat lunch in the dining room during the course of the audit. This is another good opportunity to keep an eye on the wait staff to see whether they are charging for everything they serve.

Employees who are caught serving non-alcoholic beverages without charging for them should be immediately disciplined. If not terminated, they should be subject to the progressive discipline process. Management should make it clear to its employees that it will not tolerate giving away the company's profits!

Spoilage and Waste

Spoilage and waste are areas that can lead to increased Food Cost if they are not controlled. Kitchen personnel who do not cut up food properly produce excessive waste that drives up Food Cost. New kitchen staff with little experience or who were not properly trained in previous jobs may need training in techniques for cutting fruits, vegetables, and meats in a manner than minimizes waste.

It is the Executive Chef's responsibility to ensure his staff is cutting up fruits, vegetables, and meats in a manner than minimizes waste. He needs to supervise his staff properly, observe their techniques, and train them where necessary. Minimizing Food Cost is the Executive Chef's responsibility.

One area that can lead to waste is accepting sub-standard produce or not rotating produce properly. If vegetables are blighted or starting to spoil, more fruits or vegetables will be thrown in the trash. It is the Executive Chef's responsibility to inspect any produce, meats, or fish that are delivered to the kitchen and reject product that does not meet the Company's specifications.

Sometimes spoilage is unavoidable. There may have been a large banquet that was cancelled at the last minute and the Executive Chef is not able to utilize all product elsewhere before it spoils. The Executive Chef should attempt to utilize this product in other ways to minimize spoilage, such as in a special for the dining room, in soups, or in employee meals. But if a lot of food was prepared for the banquet, it may be impossible to use all of it.

When there is spoilage, the Executive Chef should appoint a staff person to count the spoilage and document it on spoilage sheets before discarding it. The staff person should look up the cost values from the latest inventory and extend these values to calculate the value of the spoilage. The Executive Chef should review the spoilage sheet and sign it. A copy should be forwarded to the Controller so he will have a copy to support the high Food Cost that will result.

Sometimes a cooler or freezer goes down resulting in spoilage to much of its contents. In this situation where there is substantial spoilage, the Executive Chef should count the inventory that is spoiled and list it on a spoilage sheet. He should obtain the inventory costs from the most recent inventory and calculate the cost of each item spoiled and total the spoilage sheet. The Executive Chef should sign the spoilage sheet and give it to the General Manager for his review and signature. A copy of the signed spoilage sheet should be forwarded to the Controller to support the high Food Cost that will appear on the profit and loss statement for the month.

Figure 14.3 is an example of a Spoilage Sheet. The columns are as follows:

Description—Description of the inventory item that is discarded,

Unit—Unit of the item discarded. i.e. Pound, Gallon, #10 Can, etc.,

Unit Cost—Cost of one unit of product,
Quantity—Number of items that spoiled,
Extended Cost—Unit Cost multiplied by Quantity,
Reason—Reason the product is spoiled.

The two lines on the bottom of the Spoilage Sheets are the signatures of the person completing the Spoilage Sheet and the person approving it.

While the example documents an unusual situation, there are often smaller amounts of spoilage from product that was available but not completely used up. For example, the chef may have purchased fish for use over the next couple of days, but there were few orders for the fish, and a few remaining fish spoil in the walk in cooler. Even though the quantity of spoilage is relatively small, it must be documented on a Spoilage Sheet with the reason for the spoilage documented, signed by the person completing the Spoilage Sheet and the person approving it.

As part of his audit procedures, the auditor should review the spoilage sheet for the inventory period he is testing to determine whether proper procedures were followed, including proper signatures, in accounting for spoilage. Any exceptions should be documented and cross referenced to the Discussion Points worksheet.

Linen Room Controls

A lot of money is invested in linens, such as table cloths, cloth napkins, towels, aprons, chef's gowns, etc. Either the restaurant buys the linens or it rents them from a linen service. Either way, the restaurant is responsible for ensuring that all linens are returned after use. Linen services charge restaurants for linens that are lost or stolen.

Management of the linen room generally falls under the responsibility of the Dining Room Manager. While the linen room often has a supervisor, ultimately, the cost of linens is charged to the dining room.

The dining room has a certain number of tables that require table cloths and place settings. Of course, when the tables are turned over, a new table cloth is placed on the table with a new set of cloth napkins. A par should be established that consists of a certain number of table cloths that are issued to the dining room. It may include a certain number of extra table cloths and napkins.

The linen room should have its own staff under the supervision of the Linen Room Supervisor. It is the job of the Linen Room Supervisor to get the dirty linens washed, either with the restaurant's own washing machines or by a linen service. The Linen Room Supervisor is responsible for ensuring that records are kept of all linens issued and returned.

Jenny's Café, Inc.
Denver Restaurant
Spoilage Sheet
Date: *June 17, 2006*

Description	Unit	Unit Cost	Quantity	Extended Cost	Reason
Milk	Gallon	$3.99	15	$59.85	Dairy Cooler Compressor Broken
Sour Cream	Gallon	$4.74	12	$56.88	"
Whipped Cream	40 oz	$6.79	21	$142.59	"
Milk	Half Pint	$0.43	37	$15.91	"
Eggs	Case	$18.74	5.25	$98.39	"
Swiss Cheese	lb.	$4.87	29	$141.23	"
American Cheese	lb.	$4.49	45	$202.05	"
Gouda Cheese	lb.	$5.98	38	$227.24	"
Cannembert Cheese	lb.	$5.79	41	$237.39	"
Munster Cheese	lb.	$5.21	36	$187.56	"
Cheddar Cheese – Sharp	lb.	$4.98	55	$273.90	"
Cheddar Cheese – Mild	lb.	$4.98	37	$184.26	"
Cottage Cheese	5 Gallon	$24.78	4.75	$117.71	"
			TOTAL	$1,944.95	

Completed By: *Stephan Richileau*   Approved By: *Joey Robertson*

Figure 14.3

71

There should be a Linen Room Sign Out Sheet where the Head Waitress or Head Waiter signs for linens received and used in the dining room. It should indicate the type and number of linens received and returned. Once the par stock is issued for the day, additional linens are only issued upon returned of soiled linens. Since this is a one for one exchange, the transaction need not be documented on the sign out sheet, but the Linen Room Attendant must count the linens received and count out the linens issued with the Head Waitress or Head Waiter. The Head Waitress or Head Waiter takes the linens into the dining room, sets them down, and supervises the other waiters and waitresses in setting up the tables. The Head Waitress or Head Waiter is responsible for returning the same number of linens that was issued.

Aprons and chef's gowns received from the linen room must also be signed out on the sign out sheet. Each kitchen person obtaining an apron or chef's gown must sign the Linen Room Sign Out sheet. When towels are needed, a kitchen staff person goes to the linen room to sign for them.

As linens are returned at the end of the day, the Linen Room Attendant counts back the number of each type received and enters the ending count on the Linen Sign Out Sheet and initials the entry. Differences should be investigated. No linens may be discarded by employees during the normal course of business. Everything must be returned to the linen room at the end of the day no matter how soiled. Unused items should also be returned and stored in the linen room so that returns can be matched to issues.

Figure 14.4 is an example of a Linen Room Sign Out Sheet. The columns are as follows:

Date Received—Date linen item was received from the Linen Room,

Description—Description of the linen item received from the Linen Room,

Quantity—Quantity of linen items received from the Linen Room,

Received By—Print Name—Name of person receiving linen item from the Linen Room printed by the person receiving the item,

Signature—Signature of person receiving linen item from the Linen Room,

Date Returned—Date linen item was returned to the Linen Room,

Quantity Returned—Quantity of linen items returned to the Linen Room,

Linen Room Rep.—Initials of Linen Room Representative who received the linen item.

Jenny's Café, Inc.
Denver Restaurant
Linen Room Sign Out Sheet

Date Received	Description of Item	Quantity	Received By Print Name	Signature	Date Returned	Quantity Returned	Linen Room Rep
6/1/06	Chef's Coat	1	Stephan Richileau	Stephan Richileau	6/1/06	1	L.J.
6/1/06	Chef's Coat	1	Danielle Danielson	Danielle Danielson	6/1/06 .	1	L.J.
6/1/06	Apron	1	Tony Jones	Tony Jones	6/1/06	1	L.J.
6/1/06	Towels	25	Tony Jones	Tony Jones	6/1/06	25	L.J.
6/1/06	Apron	1	Rebecca Howard	Rebecca Howard	6/1/06	1	L.J.
6/1/06	Apron	1	Jessica Samson	Jessica Samson	6/1/06	1	L.J.
6/1/06	Apron	1	Jimmie Jones	Jimmie Jones	6/1/06	1	L.J.
6/1/06	Towels	5	Jimmie Jones	Jimmie Jones	6/1/06	5	L.J.
6/1/06	Apron	1	Donna Wozniak	Donna Wozniak	6/1/06	1	L.J.
6/1/06	Towels	5	Donna Wozniak	Donna Wozniak	6/1/06	5	L.J.
6/1/06	Table Cloths	98	Tuesday Thompson	Tuesday Thompson	6/1/06	98	L.J.
6/1/06	Cloth Napkins	392	Tuesday Thompson	Tuesday Thompson	6/1/06	392	L.J.
6/2/06	Chef's Coat	1	Danielle Danielson	Danielle Danielson	6/2/06	1	L.J.
6/2/06	Chef's Coat	1	Stephan Richileau	Stephan Richileau	6/2/06	1	L.J.
6/2/06	Apron	1	Rebecca Howard	Rebecca Howard	6/2/06	1	L.J.
6/2/06	Towels	25	Rebecca Howard	Rebecca Howard	6/2/06	25	L.J.
6/2/06	Apron	1	Jessica Samson	Jessica Samson	6/2/06	1	L.J.
6/2/06	Apron	1	Tony Jones	Tony Jones	6/2/06	1	L.J.
		562				562	

Figure 14.4

It is the Linen Room attendant's responsibility to ensure that each person picking up linens completes the entry on the Linen Room Sign Out Sheet properly. He should issue the linen requested only after verifying that the entry was properly made.

When using a linen service, the Linen Room Supervisor should count out all linens returned with the linen service representative each time the linen room service picks up dirty linens. The linen service rep should give the Linen Room Supervisor a receipt that shows how many linen items were returned by type, i.e. number of table cloths returned, cloth napkins, towels, chef coats, aprons, etc. The Linen Room Supervisor should count the linens received and compare the quantities to the invoice or packing slip. He should report any differences to the linen service immediately and follow up to ensure he receives appropriate credit on an invoice or credit memo.

As part of the planning process, the auditor should review the Linen account on the Profit and Loss statement and compare it to Plan. If there is a large variance to Plan, the auditor should ask the Executive Chef or Dining Room Manager the reason for the large variance. He should look through large invoices from the linen company to determine if the restaurant is being charged for lost linens, an indication that there is a linen control problem at the operation.

The auditor should observe the Linen Room to determine whether proper procedures are followed. He should look through several days of Linen Room Sign Out Sheets to determine that the entries were made properly. If possible, the auditor should observe a linen delivery and determine whether the Linen Room Supervisor is following proper procedures in counting out returned linens with the linen service representative and counting linens received. Any exceptions to normal procedures or problems noted should be documented in the workpapers and cross referenced to the Discussion Points worksheet.

China, Glass, Silverware

Another area where the Company has a large investment is China, Glassware, and Silverware. While some breakage is expected, management should be on guard for excessive breakage and waste.

Employees should exercise the same amount of care in handling the Company's China, Glassware, and Silverware as if it were their own. Bussers should be careful in removing dirty dishes, making sure they do not stack them so high that they will inevitably fall on the floor. Plastic bins should be used in collecting the dirty dishes to minimize plates, glasses, and cups from falling on the floor.

The Dining Room Manager and General Manager should periodically observe the bussers clear the tables to ensure they are clearing the tables in a manner than minimizes breakage. Retraining may be needed in some situations where breakage is excessive.

While bussers wouldn't dream of throwing their own silverware into the trash, some appear to think nothing of dumping knives and forks into the garbage as if they were plastic utensils. Glasses, cups, and plates sometimes end up in the trash, too. The Executive Chef, Dining Room Manager, and General Manager should routinely look into the trash bins that the bussers use to ensure there are no silverware, glasses, cups, and plates in there. If silverware is disappearing, management should make it a habit to periodically empty the trash on the floor and look through it to see if there is anything in the trash that shouldn't be there.

As part of the planning process, the auditor should review the China, Glass, and Silverware account and compare it to Plan. Are replacements significantly higher than Plan? Are China, Glassware, and Silverware replacements high in comparison to similar operations? It is possible that this operation historically has a high replacement cost due to poor handling practices and the high replacement cost is accepted and built into the Plan.

If China, Glassware, and Silverware replacements are high, compared to Plan or to similar operations, the auditor should bring this up to management during the introductory meeting or soon afterwards. While the Plan often spreads the cost evenly over the year or may lump the cost into a couple of months, the large replacement expenditures tend to be once or twice a year. Thus, the auditor's comparison may be a year's actual replacement against only a few months shown on the Plan, or the replacement costs may be hitting the profit and loss statement in one month and the Plan will show it in a subsequent month.

When discussing the large China, Glassware, and Silverware replacements with the General Manager and Dining Room Manager, the auditor should make sure their explanations are reasonable. If the explanation is reasonable, the auditor should note it in his audit workpapers. If not, the auditor should note the reasons given in the workpapers with an explanation why the reasons given are not reasonable and cross reference the workpaper to a Discussion Point.

While observing kitchen and dining room operations, the auditor should be alert to the sound of breaking dishes. He should observe the bussers clear tables and determine whether the methods used minimize breakage. Also, the auditor should be alert to what the bussers are dumping in the trash bins. Is silverware being dumped in the trash bins? Do plates and glasses end up in the trash bins?

Kitchen Security

There should be supervision of kitchen and dining room employees at all times. If the Executive Chef leaves the premises or is absent, the Sous Chef is in charge. One of them must always be in the kitchen supervising the kitchen staff.

In the dining room, the Dining Room Manager is in charge. When he is absent, someone else should be designated to be in charge. If there is no Assistant Dining Room Manager or Dining Room Supervisor, the General Manager may need to assume the responsibility of supervising the dining room staff during the Dining Room Manager's absence.

Employees should not be allowed to bring personal possessions into the dining room or kitchen. If possible, there should be locker rooms for changing into uniforms. Employees should be assigned lockers where they keep their clothing when changing into uniforms, hats, coats, purses, and other personal possessions. Company property, such as wrapped meats or fish, silverware, plates, etc., sometimes end up in large purses when management is careless about allowing purses into areas where these items are stored.

When the kitchen staff leaves for the day, all coolers and freezers must be locked. Only the Executive Chef, Sous Chef, and General Manager should have keys to the kitchen coolers and freezers. The room where the china, glassware, and silverware are kept must also be locked and keys limited to the Dining Room Manager, Executive Chef, and General Manager. The Linen Room must be locked when the Linen Room closes for the day. Only the Linen Room Supervisor, Dining Room Manager, and General Manager should have keys. The kitchen should also be locked when it closes. Only the Executive Chef, Sous Chef, and General Manager should have keys.

The restaurant should be locked and the alarm set when the last management person leaves for the day. Someone from management must remain in the restaurant until the last dish has been washed and put away. A dishwasher or waitress should not be given the responsibility of locking up for the night. That is management's responsibility. Being the closing manager should be rotated so that one person is not stuck with that duty every night.

The auditor should review the restaurant's policy of what employees do with their personal belongings and be alert to employees who violate these policies. He should discuss closing procedures with the General Manager and be alert to procedures that do not protect the company's assets. The auditor should document his observations and security discussions with management in the audit workpapers. Any procedures that do not promote strong security of the company's assets should be cross referenced to a Discussion Point.

Summary

The Executive Chef oversees kitchen operations. The salad station and dessert station should not share staff with the production line, but should have their own staffs. In large operations, the linen room should have a separate staff that does not participate in other kitchen operations. Waiters and waitresses should not be allowed behind the various stations. The auditor should observe kitchen operations to determine whether adequate segregation of duties is maintained.

Waiters and waitresses enter orders into the order entry terminal. A chit prints on the printer in the appropriate station, i.e. salad station, production line, and dessert station. The cook or pantry person fills orders based on what is printed on the chit. Chits are torn partway by the cook or pantry person to prevent reuse and set next to the order until picked up. The auditor should observe kitchen operations to determine that proper procedures are followed.

In manual dup systems, the waiters and waitresses write the orders on a two-part guest check. The top copy is torn off and given to the production line cook. Orders from the salad station and dessert station are written on a dup copy and presented to the pantry person to place the order. The following day, a clerk matches dups to guest checks to ensure all items were charged to patrons. The auditor should obtain the dups and match them against guest checks to ensure all items removed from the kitchen were put on a guest check.

To achieve standard cost, servers must serve the standard portion. Portion scales are often used for measuring the proper portion of meats for sandwiches. Standard ladles are used to ensure vegetables, mashed potatoes, etc. are the proper portion size. The auditor should observe portions served in the kitchen to ensure they agree to the menu specifications.

If an expediter is used to ensure product moves efficiently from the kitchen, he should perform a checking function. The checker should compare items on the waiters trays to the chits or guest checks to ensure everything taken out of the kitchen was recorded in the POS system.

When theft of key items is suspected, the auditor can select a dozen key entrée items to inventory daily and tie into usage per the POS system. The auditor should discuss differences with the Executive Chef and the General Manager.

Most restaurants do not have chit printers at the beverage station. Waiters and waitresses often obtain non-alcoholic beverages directly from the dispensers and coffee pots. Significant revenues can be lost if the wait staff is not charging customers for all beverages. The auditor should eat dinner in the restaurant and determine whether the wait staff is charging for beverages. He should keep his eyes and ears open to anything unusual in regards to charging for beverages served.

Spoilage must be documented on Spoilage Sheets, and approved by the Executive Chef. Unusual spoilage, such as resulting from a cooler going down, should be signed by the General Manager. Spoilage sheets provide some documentation for supporting the difference between theoretical and actual cost. The auditor should review Spoilage Sheets and determine whether proper procedures were followed.

There should be a par established for linens issued from the linen room. The person obtaining linens should sign a log for the items obtained. Soiled linens should be returned at the end of the day, counted and agreed to what was issued. When using a linen service, the linen room supervisor should count the linens returned with the linen service representative and should obtain a receipt for the items returned. The auditor should review linen room operations to determine whether proper procedures are followed.

When the kitchen closes for the day, all coolers, freezers, and storage areas should be locked. When the kitchen staff leaves, the kitchen should be locked.

Discussion Questions and Case Studies

1. You are the auditor auditing Mary's Marvels, a full service restaurant. What segregation of duties in the kitchen are you looking for?

2. Describe how the dup procedure works. Why are dups used in the kitchen?

3. If the restaurant does not have an order entry system, describe how a manual dup system would work?

4. You are performing observations in the kitchen at Mary's Marvels. You observe a cook at the production line filling orders from the waitresses based on verbal orders. You look over at the chit printer a see a string of chits hanging from it. Every once in a while, the cook tears off the chits and throws them in the garbage. What audit issues do you have? What are your recommendations to management?

5. You are performing observations at Kyle's Korner Kafe. The pantry person at the salad station is preparing a large order based on a chit she has taken from the printer. You see another chit print. A few minutes later, a waitress walks up to the cooler, grabs four shrimp cocktail, and says the following, "Janie, I know you are busy. I'm taking the four shrimp cocktail I ordered. It's on that chit I printed on your printer." Janie replies, "Sure thing, Heather!" and continues working. Do you have an audit issue? What is your recommendation to management?

6. You are observing the production line at Rob's River Roost making luncheon sandwiches. The amount of meat that is placed on the sandwiches varies substantially from one sandwich to the next. You also notice that the amount of coleslaw served with the sandwiches also varies substantially from one order to the next. Do you have an audit issue? What is your recommendation to management?

7. You are auditing Mama Maria's Mexican Cantina. While observing Linen Room operations, you see that every item that is issued is logged in a log and signed by the person receiving the linen. After the restaurant closes, you observe the waiters and waitress clearing the tables, taking the dirty linen to the Linen Room, and handing it to the Linen Room Supervisor. What audit issues do you have? What are your recommendations to management?

8. You review the menu mix at Joey's Jumbo Steakhouse and notice that Actual Food Cost is 42.5% versus standard cost of 33.6%. In discussing the high Food Cost with the General Manager, he thinks some employees might be stealing some steaks at night. What audit procedure can you perform to document whether steaks are disappearing?

9. You have documented that substantially more steaks are used each day at Joey's Jumbo Steakhouse than can be accounted for with steak sales. What recommendations would you make to stop the theft of steaks?

CHAPTER 15
AUDITING PAYROLL

Learning Objectives

After reading this chapter, you should be able to:

1. Check time cards for employee signatures, proper approvals, and approval of manual adjustments,
2. Audit tip reporting from sub-minimum wage employees to determine whether the wages received plus tips puts the employee over the minimum wage threshold, and know what the field location must do to bring the employee up to minimum wage,
3. Reconcile payroll input to the Payroll Register to ensure all payroll input into the payroll system was actually paid to the employees,
4. Know what types of controls should be in place to properly control the issuance of manual checks and ensure the wages paid are reported in the payroll system,
5. Know the rules about paying hourly employees for overtime and auditing the payroll to ensure the field location is in compliance with these rules,
6. Perform a payout to ensure there are no ghosts (fictitious employees) on the payroll.

Overview

The restaurant business is very labor intensive. Labor is used to place orders, receive product, store product, and issue product. More labor is used in preparing the raw materials for consumption. Additional labor is used to serve the customers and clean the tables. More labor is used to clean the kitchen and dining room after the restaurant closes. Finally, labor is used in reporting sales, payroll, inventory, and other necessary paperwork. As you can see, labor is one of the highest cost areas of the restaurant operation. Thus, controlling labor is one of the keys to profitability.

Most companies pay their hourly staff weekly, although some companies pay them biweekly (every two weeks). Salaried employees, including salaried field employees, are often paid semi-monthly (twice a month) on a separate payroll run. Where salaried employees are paid on the weekly field location payroll, they would of course be paid weekly.

There must be proper segregation of duties in the payroll area. We will examine the different roles that various people play in the payroll function and we will see where duties must be segregated to ensure proper internal control.

Some locations use sign in sheets to document time worked. Others use time clocks where each employee punches in and out, and the time cards are used to calculate hours worked. With modern computers, time keeping systems have been developed where the employee swipes her ID card when clocking in and again when clocking out. The computer tracks the time worked of each employee, calculates the hours worked, and the gross wages earned by each employee. We will examine the controls that should be in place for each system and how the auditor will audit them.

Time cards must be signed by the employee, acknowledging that the time recorded is correct. Each time card must be approved by the department manager. Manual adjustments made by the department manager must be initialed to document approval. We will examine how the auditor tests time cards to ensure that Company procedures are followed.

The Payroll Clerk calculates time worked from sign in sheets and some time clock systems. She inputs these hours worked into the payroll system and prints reports that provide the number of hours worked, adjustments made from prior weeks, and gross wages to be paid. We will examine how the auditor reviews these reports to ensure that wages paid for the test week are correct.

Federal minimum wage for tipped employees is $2.13 per hour, provided the employee reports sufficient tips to bring her up to the Federal or State minimum wage, whichever is higher. We will examine tip reporting to ensure it meets governmental reporting requirements. In addition, we will look at testing hourly wages plus reported tips to ensure that the employee reached minimum wage, and we will see what needs to be done if the minimum wage plateau is not achieved.

Each week, the Payroll Clerk should reconcile the hours and wages per the input report to the Payroll Register and explain any differences. We will discuss how the auditor reviews this reconciliation to ensure it was done correctly.

The Controller or General Manager should review the Payroll Register, Employee Maintenance Report, and High Dollar report, sign them and date them. We will review these reports and discuss the purpose of each one.

Manual checks should only be issued in the case of an emergency or in states where final payment is due on the date an employee is terminated. We will discuss proper internal controls over manual payroll checks and how the auditor audits them.

Productivity is the measurement of sales per employee. This calculation is used to determine how productively the field location is operating in comparison to the company standard. We will discuss how the auditor tests productivity reports to ensure the field location is calculating it properly.

The payout is an effective audit tool for ensuring that every paycheck issued to the field location is going to an actual employee. The auditor intercepts the payroll going to the unit and personally hands out every paycheck to each applicable employee. We will discuss the procedures the auditor follows in performing an effective payout.

In Practice

Aimee Stone walks over to the desk of Bob McCarthy, the Payroll Clerk.

"Here are the time cards and payroll reports for the month of June, as you requested," Bob says.

"Thanks," says Aimee.

Aimee takes the binder of documents with her to her desk. She pulls out the time cards of the waiters and waitresses, makes her selection, and enters the number of hours and the $2.13 minimum wage that they are paid on the Excel spreadsheet. Then she enters the charge tips and value of the employee meals from the Payroll Register on the spreadsheet. Aimee looks for cash tips but doesn't see any entries in the Payroll Register. She looks at the results of the calculations on the spreadsheet and walks over to the Controller's office.

"Heather, I don't see any entries in the Payroll Register for cash tips," Aimee says.

"The employees keep telling me they don't receive any cash tips," Heather replies.

"That's impossible," Aimee says. "A substantial portion of the restaurant's sales are in cash. They must be receiving cash tips!"

"I agree," Heather say, "But try telling them that! I keep hearing that they don't receive any cash tips."

"Are they signing a tip declaration with zero tips?" Aimee asks.

"No, since they always declared zero, I stopped giving them the tip declaration to sign," Heather replies.

"The Federal government requires every tipped employee to sign a tip declaration, even if they declare zero tips," Aimee says. *"What's worse is that you have some employees who are not making minimum wage when I add the wages paid plus charge tips paid through the payroll system and the value of the employee meals. If an employee's earnings, wages plus tips and employee meals, do not equal minimum wage, the Company has to make up the difference."*

"We are not about to reward an employee for not reporting cash tips we know she is receiving by paying her more money!" Heather exclaims.

"What I suggest is that Joey sits down with each waiter and waitress who does not make minimum wage and explain that if he or she is such a bad waiter or waitress that they cannot earn at least enough in tips to bring them up to minimum wage, that they cannot work in this restaurant. I think you will suddenly find that they take in lots of cash tips!"

Segregation of Duties

With so many dollars paid out in payroll, it is imperative that there be strong segregation of duties in the payroll function. The person inputting payroll checks may not handle the paychecks at any time. Payroll checks from the Corporate Offices should be delivered directly to the Controller or the General Manager. After completing the payroll review, the checks should be given to someone besides the Payroll Clerk for distribution.

At the end of the payroll period, the department managers should calculate the number of hours worked from the time cards or sign in sheet. This function should not be the job of the Payroll Clerk. The department manager is in a better position to determine whether the number of hours each employee in her department worked is reasonable.

The person performing master file maintenance or inputting hours worked should not perform the Human Resources function. These two functions must be separated to ensure that every employee added to the Payroll system is a legitimate employee.

The Payroll Clerk should not cut manual payroll checks. This function should be performed by someone at the Corporate Offices. If manual payroll checks must be cut at the field location, someone besides the Payroll Clerk should cut the checks based solely on the information documented on a Manual Check form, completed by the Payroll Clerk and approved (signed) by the General Manager or Controller.

The auditor should review the duties of the different participants to determine whether duties are properly segregated. She should note any exceptions in the audit program or in the workpapers and cross reference the exceptions to the Discussion Points Worksheet.

Sign In/Sign Out Sheet, Time Clocks, Time Keeping Systems

Hourly employees must document time worked by signing in and out on a Sign In Sheet, clocking in and out on a time clock, or swiping in and out on a computerized time keeping system. We will look at each system and describe how it works.

Employers who use Sign In/Sign Out sheets have employees sign in and out when checking in at their departments. For example, the bar employees sign in and out at the bar, the kitchen employees sign in and out in the kitchen, etc. The Employee prints her name and signs next to the name. Then the employee writes the time in the appropriate column. When taking lunch, the employee writes the time out and after lunch the time in. At quitting time, the employee writes the time out.

Each day, the department manager or supervisor calculates the time worked from the time the employee signed in to the time the employee signed out, minus the time documented for lunch. She enters the time worked in the appropriate column and initials next to it. At the end of the week, the department manager or supervisor sends the sign in sheets to the Payroll Clerk who keys the hours worked into the Payroll system.

Figure 15.1 is an example of a Payroll Sign In/Sign Out sheet. Each day, the department manager or supervisor writes the Department Name and Date at the top of the form. The information contained in the columns is as follows:

Print Name—Employee arriving for work prints her name,

Signature—Employee signs her name,

Time In—Employee writes the time she reported for work,

Time Out—Employee writes the time she started her lunch break,

Time In—Employee writes time she came back from lunch break,

Time Out—Employee writes the time she finished work and left the premises,

Total Hours—Supervisor calculates the number of hours worked, rounded to the nearest quarter hour and writes the total in the column,

Supervisor's Initials—Supervisor initials the entry.

When calculating time worked, the supervisor rounds the time worked to the nearest quarter hour. She must include time worked from the time the employee signed in, even if the employee was not scheduled to begin work until later. Federal labor laws require employers to pay their employees from the time they arrive at the premises. The employer should tell the employees that they may not arrive for work more than 7 minutes before starting time. Employees who continuously violate this policy should be subjected to discipline (See Chapter 16).

In our example, one employee, Robert Robinson, arrived for work one half hour early and signed in. The supervisor did not begin paying him until the time he was scheduled to begin work at 4:00 p.m. This practice is in violation of Federal Labor Laws and was noted as a Discussion Point. Similarly, another employee, Summer Simmons, did not sign out for lunch, but was not paid for this time. If Summer did forget to enter the time out for lunch, the supervisor should require her to write the time she left for lunch on the Sign In Sheet. If Summer did not take a lunch, she must be paid for 8.5 hours. Violations of the company's policy to take a half hour lunch when scheduled without a good excuse, i.e. Dining Room Manager agreed she was too busy to take a lunch break, should be subject to discipline.

When reviewing Sign In/Sign Out sheets, the auditor should be aware of employees who sign in for several employees. She should examine the Sign In/Sign Out sheets for identical handwriting on several consecutive employees, indicating that one employee signed for several employees. This practice is against Company policy. If the auditor sees this, she should make a copy of the Sign In/Sign Out sheet, circle the incident, insert it in the workpapers, and cross reference the comments to the Discussion Points Worksheet.

Some employers use time clocks to record the time the employee worked. The time clock is located near the employee entrance. Each employee grabs her time card from a rack, clocks in, and returns the time card to the rack. The advantage of the time clock is that a machine records when the employee inserts her card into the clock. With the Sign In Sheet, the employer is relying on the honesty of the employee to write down the time she reported for work. It is easy to write 5 or 10 minutes earlier than when the employee actually arrived or 5 to 10 minutes later than when the employee left. With the clock, the employee cannot cheat because the clock prints the time the card was inserted.

Jenny's Café, Inc.
Denver Restaurant
Payroll Sign In Sign Out Sheet
Department: *Dining Room*
Date: *July 14, 2006*

M2
AB
8/3/2006

Print Name	Signature	Time In	Time Out	Time In	Time Out	Total Hours	Supervisor's Initials	
Robert Robinson	*Robert Robinson*	3:29	8:30	9:01	12:32	8	*AB*	α
April James	*April James*	3:55	8:00	8:30	12:30	8	*AB*	
Tuesday Thompson	*Tuesday Thompson*	3:55	7:30	8:00	12:31	8	*AB*	
Stella Palenski	*Stella Palenski*	3:56	7:00	7:30	12:31	8	*AB*	
Willie Wei	*Willie Wei*	3:56	7:30	8:00	12:31	8	*AB*	
Jeremy Choi	*Jeremy Choi*	3:57	7:00	7:30	12:32	8	*AB*	
Summer Simmons	*Summer Simmons*	3:58			12:33	8	*AB*	μ
Tammie Topaz	*Tammie Topaz*	3:58	8:01	8:29	12:34	8	*AB*	
Ellen Estophan	*Ellen Estophan*	3:59	6:30	7:00	12:30	8	*AB*	
Henry Hernandez	*Henry Hernandez*	4:00	7:00	7:30	12:30	8	*AB*	
April Choi	*April Choi*	4:00	7:30	8:00	12:30	8	*AB*	
Jennifer Choi	*Jennifer Choi*	4:00	7:30	8:00	12:30	8	*AB*	
Miradije Muhammed	*Miradije Muhammed*	4:01	8:00	8:30	12:30	8	*AB*	
Hasim Abdullah	*Hasim Abdullah*	4:01	8:00	8:30	12:30	8	*AB*	
Bilal Muhibuddin	*Bilal Muhibuddin*	4:02	7:30	8:00	12:35	8	*AB*	
George Barker	*George Barker*	4:05	7:30	8:00	12:36	8	*AB*	
Emily O'Brien	*Emily O'Brien*	4:15	8:30	9:00	12:35	7.75	*AB*	
Jennifer Nydahl	*Jennifer Nydahl*	4:17	8:30	9:00	12:30	7.75	*AB*	
Gary Chester	*Gary Chester*	4:32	8:00	8:30	12:30	7.5	*AB*	

α - *Employee signed in at 3:30, out at 12:30, and clocked in and out for a half hour lunch. Paid for 8 hours when time clocked in and out equals 8.5 hours. Discussed with Linda Barton, Dining Room Manager. Linda said that starting time is 4:00 p.m. and this employee was paid from 4:00 p.m. Labor laws require the employer to pay the employee from the time he signs in. Thus, the employee should not be allowed to come to work any earlier than 7 minutes before the 4:00 p.m. starting time. Jenny's Caf. owes employee 1/2 hour back pay. See Discussion Point # 42*

μ - *Employee did not sign out for lunch but was not paid for the lunch period that was not documented. Discussed with Linda Barton, Dining Room Manager. She said that all employees are required to take a half hour lunch, but sometimes they forget to sign in and out for lunch. If the employee did take a lunch, the Dining Room Manager should ask the employee to sign in and out. If no lunch was taken, employer must pay from time signed in to time signed out. See Discussion Point #43*

Figure 15.1

Figure 15.2 is an example of a completed time card. The first two lines of the time card are for the Employee Name and the Week Ending Date. The Time In and Time Out are printed by the time clock as follows: Day of the Week, Date, Time. The time clock calculates the difference between time in and time out and keeps a running total in the final column.

The auditor should spend some time observing employees punch in and out. She should watch for employees taking time cards from their friends and punching them. Even if the friends are with the employee, punching a time card for someone else is strictly forbidden. If the auditor sees someone punching more than one time card, she should note the observation in the audit program or in the workpapers, and cross reference the notation to the Discussion Points Worksheet. The auditor should also notify the General Manager immediately so she can take corrective action.

A Time Keeping system is a computerized system with a scanner. Each employee swipes her time card in front of the scanner. The computer reads the employee number and matches the employee number against an internal table to obtain the employee name. The time in is thus recorded for the employee. When the employee breaks for lunch, she swipes her ID card again and the computer records the time out. After lunch, the employee swipes her ID card to clock back in and one final time when she leaves for the day.

One of the advantages of the Time Keeping system is that employees keep their ID cards with them. Therefore it is not so easy to clock in for a friend because the employee needs her friend's ID card to do so. Nevertheless, if an employee is not planning to work, she could give a friend her ID card so the friend can swipe in and out on that card. Thus, the auditor should observe the employees swiping in at check in time. If the auditor sees someone swiping two or more cards, she should note the observation in the workpapers and cross reference the deficiency to the Discussion Points Worksheet. The auditor should also inform the General Manager of the incident immediately so the General Manager can take corrective action.

Jenny's Café, Inc.
Time Card

Name: Tammie Topaz
Week Ending: July 15, 2006

IN	MO 071006	3:58 PM	
OUT	MO 071006	7:31 PM	3:33
IN	MO 071006	7:59 PM	
OUT	TU 071106	12:32 AM	8:06
IN	TU 071106	3:59 PM	
OUT	TU 071106	8:02 PM	12:09
IN	TU 071106	8:30 PM	
OUT	WE 071206	12:31 AM	16:10
IN	WE 071206	4:01 PM	
OUT	WE 071206	7:30 PM	19:39
IN	WE 071206	8:02 PM	
OUT	TR 071306	12:29 AM	24:06
IN	TR 071306	3:58 PM	
OUT	TR 071306	8:01 PM	28:09
IN	TR 071306	8:29 PM	
OUT	FR 071406	12:34 AM	32:14
IN	FR 071406	3:57 PM	
OUT	FR 071406	8:01 PM	36:18
IN	FR 071406	8:31 PM	
OUT	SA 071506	12:33 PM	40:20

40.25 *Hrs.*

LB

Tammie Topaz

Figure 15.2

Signing and Approving Time Cards

At the end of the week, the department manager or supervisor reviews the time cards to ensure all time was correctly entered. At the bottom of the time card, the supervisor rounds the time worked to the nearest quarter hour and initials the time card, approving the time worked. The employee signs the bottom of the time card, acknowledging that the calculated time is correct. Figure 15.2 (above) is a properly signed and approved time card.

The auditor should select 20-30 time cards to determine whether the department manager or supervisor initialed the time card. In addition, the auditor should check to see that the employee signed the time card. The names of the employees whose time cards were selected should be listed on a workpaper with an indication of whether the proper signatures and initials were on the time card. We will discuss documentation of these audit procedures later in this chapter.

Manual Adjustments

If an employee forgets to punch in or out, the department manager or supervisor must write the time in or out on the time card and initial the entry. The time clock will not calculate all time worked because there is information missing. At a certain time (as programmed) in the early morning, the time clock resets itself and starts calculating time worked again. When reviewing the time card at the end of the week the department manager or supervisor manually adds the time calculated by the clock for the two periods where there was good information to the manually calculated time.

Figure 15.3 is a good example of what the department manager or supervisor should do to report time worked where an employee failed to punch out at the end of the shift. After discussing the situation with Tammy Topaz, Linda learning that Tammy forgot to clock out when she left at 12:30. Thus, Linda wrote 12:30 AM on the time card and initialed the entry. At the end of the week, Linda took the 12 hours and 9 minutes for the first day and a half, added the 24 hours and 12 minutes for the last 3 days, and added the 4 hours for the second half of Tammy's shift on Tuesday to calculate 40 hours and 21 minutes worked for the week. Linda rounded the time worked to 40 ¼ hours. Tammy's signature on the time card acknowledges that all time recorded on the time card, including adjustments, is correct.

The auditor should look through the sample time cards to see if any manual adjustments on these cards were handled properly. If there were no adjustments on the time cards selected, the auditor should look through the remaining time cards until she finds 5 time cards with manual entries. She should add these employees to the workpaper and report on whether the manual adjustments were properly handled. Any exceptions should be noted in the workpapers and cross referenced to the Discussion Points Worksheet.

		Jenny's Café, Inc.			
		Time Card			
	Name:	Tamie Topaz			
	Week Ending:	July 15, 2006			
IN	MO 071006	3:58 PM			
OUT	MO 071006	7:31 PM	3:33		
IN	MO 071006	7:59 PM			
OUT	TU 071106	12:32 AM	8:06		
IN	TU 071106	3:59 PM			
OUT	TU 071106	8:02 PM	12:09		
IN	TU 071106	8:30 PM			
OUT		12:30 AM LB	4		
IN	WE 071206	4:01 PM			
OUT	WE 071206	7:30 PM	3:29		
IN	WE 071206	8:02 PM			
OUT	TR 071306	12:29 AM	7:56		
IN	TR 071306	3:58 PM			
OUT	TR 071306	8:01 PM	11:59		
IN	TR 071306	8:29 PM			
OUT	FR 071406	12:34 AM	16:04	12:09	
IN	FR 071406	3:57 PM		4:00	
OUT	FR 071406	8:01 PM	20:08	24:12	
IN	FR 071406	8:31 PM		40:21	
OUT	SA 071506	12:33 PM	24:12	40.25 Hrs.	
				LB	
		Tammie Topaz			

Figure 15.3

91

Adjustment Reports

The Time Keeping system calculates the time worked based on the scans and keeps a running total of the hours worked for the week. The Payroll Clerk prints a daily report that the department manager reviews, makes adjustments, and signs the report. The Payroll Clerk enters all adjustments into the Time Keeping system.

Figure 15.4 is an example of the Daily Time Worked Report for July 14, 2006, sorted in alphabetical order for the Dining Room. It contains the following information in each column:

Employee Name—Name of each employee who swiped in and out,

Employee Number—Number that identifies the employee in the Time Keeping system,

Time In—Time the employee swiped in,

Time Out—Time the employee swiped out for lunch,

Time In—Time the employee swiped in after lunch,

Time Out—Time the employee swiped out at the end of the shift,

Total Hours Worked—Total hours worked in decimal format.

While hours worked by day is in the normal 60 minutes to an hour format, the Total Hours column is in decimal format. For example 15 minutes is printed in the total column as .25 hours. Linda Barton, the Dining Room Manager wrote the time in and out for lunch and corrected the hours worked for Summer Simmons after talking to her and learning that Summer had taken a half hour for lunch, but forgot to swipe in and out. She documented her conversation at the bottom of the report. Once satisfied that the Daily Time Worked Report is correct, the department manager signs and dates it.

The auditor should review one week's Daily Time Worked Reports to determine whether adjustments were handled properly. Any exceptions should be noted in the workpapers and cross referenced to the Discussion Points Worksheet.

At the end of the week, the Payroll Clerk prints the Weekly Time Summaries and distributes them to the applicable department managers or supervisors. The department managers or supervisors review the Weekly Time Summaries to ensure all changes were made correctly. If there are any differences, the department manager or supervisor would note these for the Payroll Clerk to correct. Once satisfied that the Weekly Time Summary is correct, the department manager or supervisor signs the Weekly Time Summary and returns it to the Payroll Clerk.

Jenny's Café, Inc.
Denver Restaurant
Daily Time Worked Report
Dining Room
July 14, 2006

Employee Name	Empl #	Time In	Time Out	Time In	Time Out	Total Hours	
Abdullah, Hasim	15986	4:01 PM	8:00 PM	8:30 PM	12:30 AM	7.98	
Barker, George	17843	4:05 PM	7:30 PM	8:00 PM	12:36 AM	8.02	
Choi, April	13894	4:00 PM	7:30 PM	8:00 PM	12:30 AM	8.00	
Choi, Jennifer	13895	4:00 PM	7:30 PM	8:00 PM	12:30 AM	8.00	
Choi, Jeremy	13896	3:57 PM	7:00 PM	7:30 PM	12:32 AM	8.08	
Estophan, Ellen	12257	3:59 PM	6:30 PM	7:00 PM	12:30 AM	8.02	
Hernandez, Henry	16392	4:00 PM	7:00 PM	7:30 PM	12:30 AM	8.00	
James, April	10352	3:55 PM	8:00 PM	8:30 PM	12:30 AM	8.08	
Muhammed, Miradije	18110	4:01 PM	8:00 PM	8:30 PM	12:30 AM	7.98	
Muhibuddin, Bilal	17328	4:02 PM	7:30 PM	8:00 PM	12:35 AM	8.05	
O'Brien, Emily	16820	4:15 PM	8:30 PM	9:00 PM	12:35 AM	8.33	
Palenski, Stella	10287	3:56 PM	7:00 PM	7:30 AM	12:31 AM	8.08	
Robinson, Robert	14792	3:29 PM	8:30 PM	9:01 PM	12:32 AM	8.03	
Simmons, Summer	17946	3:58 PM	12:33 AM	7:30 PM	8:00 PM	8.58	8:08 *LB*
Thompson, Tuesday	10783	3:55 PM	7:30 PM	8:00 PM	12:31 AM	8.10	
Topaz, Tammie	11957	3:58 PM	8:01 PM	8:29 PM	12:34 AM	8.13	
Wei, Willie	14820	3:56 PM	7:30 PM	8:00 PM	12:31 AM	8.08	
Total Hours						137.54	137 *Hrs.*

*Talked to Summer Simmons — She did take lunch from 7:30 to 8:00 but
forgot to clock out and back in. — LB*

Linda Barton
7/14/06

Figure 15.4

Figure 15.5 is an example of the Dining Room's Weekly Time Summary at Jenny's Café—Denver for the Week Ending July 15, 2006. The columns present the following information:

Employee Name—Name of each employee who worked during the week,

Employee Number—Number that identifies the employee in the Time Keeping system,

The next 7 columns are the number of hours worked on each day of the week,

Total—Sum of the 7 columns containing the hours worked on each day of the week.

Linda Barton, the Dining Room Manager, signed and dated the bottom of the report, documenting her review and approval of the hours worked by each person in her department.

The auditor should review the Weekly Time Summary for the week tested, tie corrections from the Daily Time Worked Reports to the Weekly Time Summary, and determine whether the department managers and supervisors have signed the Weekly Time Summaries for their departments, thus authorizing those hours to be paid.

Jenny's Café, Inc.
Denver Restaurant
Weekly Time Summary
Dining Room
Week Ending July 15, 2006

Employee Name	Empl #	7/9/06	7/10/06	7/11/06	7/12/06	7/13/06	7/14/06	7/15/06	Total
Abdullah, Hasim	15986	8.04			7.52	8.02	7.98	8.02	39.58
Barker, George	17843			8.04	8.05	7.98	8.02	8.04	40.13
Choi, April	13894	7.98			8.02	8.04	8.00	7.98	40.02
Choi, Jennifer	13895	7.98			8.02	8.04	8.00	7.98	40.02
Choi, Jeremy	13896			8.00	8.05	8.02	8.08	7.96	40.11
Estophan, Ellen	12257		8.02	8.02		7.58	8.02	8.04	39.68
Hernandez, Henry	16392			7.96	8.05	8.02	8.00	7.98	40.01
James, April	10352			7.98	8.05	8.04	8.08	8.02	40.17
Muhammed, Miradije	18110		8.04	8.02	7.98		7.98	8.00	40.02
Muhibuddin, Bilal	17328	8.02	8.04			8.02	8.05	7.96	40.09
O'Brien, Emily	16820		7.98	7.50		8.02	8.03	7.95	39.48
Palenski, Stella	10287			8.00	8.02	8.02	8.08	7.96	40.08
Robinson, Robert	14792	8.05			8.02	7.96	8.03	8.03	40.09
Simmons, Summer	17946		8.02	7.98		8.02	8.08	7.98	40.08
Thompson, Tuesday	10783	7.98			8.04	8.05	8.10	7.56	39.73
Topaz, Tammie	11957		8.10	8.07	7.93	8.10	8.13		40.33
Wei, Willie	14820			8.02	7.98	7.96	8.08	8.02	40.06
Total Hours		48.05	48.20	87.59	103.73	127.89	136.74	127.48	679.68

Linda Barton
7/17/06

Figure 15.5

Payroll Input

On Monday morning, the signed time records (Payroll Sign In/Sign Out sheets, time cards, or Weekly Time Summaries) from each department should be on the Payroll Clerk's desk. The Payroll Clerk enters her password to access the Payroll System, and keys the hours worked from the time records into the Payroll System. It is the job of the department managers or supervisors, not the Payroll Clerk, to calculate the hours worked by each employee in their departments for the week and to enter the totals on the time records. The Payroll Clerk also keys miscellaneous adjustments into the Payroll System based on properly approved source documents.

Prior to keying hours and other wage information, the Payroll Clerk performs file maintenance. She adds new employees and deletes terminated employees from the Payroll Master file. She keys various changes to employees' files, such as address changes, wage rate changes, 401K contribution changes, garnishments, etc. Each addition, deletion, or change transaction must be supported by a properly authorized (signed) Employee Maintenance Form.

Some payroll systems have a routine where the Payroll System calculates employee meals based on a formula. For example, the formula may add $2.25 (determined to be the average cost of an employee meal by management) for days when the employee works at least 5 hours per day. In New York, Texas, California, and Oregon, the value of employee meals is added to gross wages for purposes of calculating the employer's State unemployment taxes.

Once the Payroll System calculates State unemployment taxes for the applicable states, employee meals are subtracted from gross wages prior to calculating the employee's withholding taxes. In the remaining states, employee meals are not subject to State unemployment taxes and no calculation is made. However, the cost of employee meals can be added to wages of tipped employees to see if they achieved minimum wage when adding declared tips to the hourly wage.

The Payroll Clerk keys charge tips and cash tips into the payroll system. Since tips are taxable to the employees, they are reluctant to declare cash tips received. The Dining Room Manager prepares a spreadsheet each payroll period that lists the total charge tips (tips that a customer adds to the credit card slip) received that should be paid through the payroll system. Once completed, the Dining Room Manager should sign the spreadsheet, certifying its accuracy. The Payroll Clerk keys cash tips from the Cash Tips Declaration slips signed by the reporting employees. Cash tips are added to

Gross Wages in the Payroll system for calculating tax withholdings and are subtracted from Gross Wages before Net Pay is calculated.

The Payroll Clerk may key various deductions into the payroll system, such as uniform charges, parking fees, etc. Each deduction entered should be supported by properly approved source documents, such as a list of uniform charges listed by employee and signed by the Linen Room Supervisor. It must also be supported by a form signed by the employee where the employee authorizes the employer to make the deduction.

When the Payroll Clerk has finished keying all payroll information into the Payroll system, she prints the Wage and Hour Report. This report lists everything that was keyed by employee. The Payroll Clerk ties all hours and other information into the Wage and Hour Report to ensure it was keyed correctly. If a Time Keeping system is used, the Payroll Clerk ties the total hours per the Weekly Time Summary to the total hours on the Wage and Hour Report. If time cards or Sign In/Sign Out sheets are used, the Payroll Clerk takes an adding machine tape of all hours worked and compares the total hours on the adding machine tape to the total hours on the Wage and Hour Report.

Once satisfied that all data were keyed correctly, the Payroll Clerk gives the Wage and Hour Report and all supporting documentation to the Controller for review. The Controller compares the total hours per the adding machine tape or the Weekly Time Summary to the total hours on the Wage and Hour Report. She compares the Total Adjustments to the approved source documents, the Total Charge Tips to the Dining Room Manager's Charge Tips Listing, and the Cash Tips to the Dining Room Manager's Listing of Cash Tips, supported by the employee signed tip declarations. The Controller checks off each total and ties it in to the supporting documentation. Once satisfied that everything on the Wage and Hour Report is in order, the Controller signs and dates the report. The Payroll Clerk now transmits the payroll to Corporate to be processed or to the outside payroll service bureau for processing.

Figure 15.6 is an example of a Wage and Hour Report for the Dining Room employees for the Week Ending July 15, 2006. The columns provide the following information:

Employee Name—Name of each employee who worked during the week,

Employee Number—Number that identifies the employee in the Time Keeping system,

Position—Name of position that the employee worked,

Hourly Rate—Rate of pay per hour that the employee will receive,

Total Hours—Total hours the employee worked during the week, per the Sign In/Sign Out sheets, Time Cards, or Weekly Time Summary from the Payroll Timekeeping System,

Regular Wages—Hourly Rate multiplied by Total Hours up to 40 hours, calculated by the Payroll System,

Overtime Wages—Total Hours minus 40 hours, multiplied by 1.5 (some states have laws that require more than time and a half for overtime under certain circumstances),

Adjustments—Adjustments to wages from prior weeks, due to hours missed or overpayments,

Charge Tips—Charge tips due to employees that will be paid through the Payroll System,

Cash Tips—Cash tips received and declared by the employees.

Where the restaurant is part of a chain of restaurants that transmits its payroll to Corporate, the Corporate Office runs the payroll when received from the field location. It runs processes that pull the pay rates from the payroll system and calculates gross wages, adds benefit data (health insurance, dental insurance, 401K contributions, etc.) and calculates payroll tax withholdings and other deductions. The Corporate Payroll Clerk checks for tax and benefit errors and corrects them. When the payroll is error free, the Corporate Payroll Clerk sends an email to the field location's Payroll Clerk and advises her that she can run the Payroll Register and other payroll reports.

The field location's Payroll Clerk runs payroll reports and reviews them for errors. Any errors are noted on an email and sent to the Corporate Payroll Clerk for correction. Once satisfied that the payroll is correct, the field location's Payroll Clerk emails or telephones the Corporate Payroll Clerk indicating the payroll is correct. When all field locations have reported that their payrolls are correct, the Corporate Payroll Department runs the payroll checks and sends them to the field locations via an overnight delivery service.

Some states have laws where the employee is entitled to more than time and a half for some overtime hours. For example, in California an employee is entitled to time and a half after working 8 hours in a day and double time after working 12 hours in a day. Thus, the auditor should familiarize herself with the State's overtime requirements before going to the field location. The Corporate Human Resources Department often has information on each State's overtime requirements. If not, the auditor can telephone the State's Department of Labor to learn about its overtime requirements.

Jenny's Café, Inc.
Denver Restaurant
Wage and Hour Report
Week Ending July 15, 2006

Dining Room

Employee Name	Empl #	Position	Hourly Rate	Total Hours	Regular Wages	O/T Wages	Adjust	Charge Tips	Cash Tips
Abdullah, Hasim	15986	Busser	$5.15	39.58	$203.84	$0.00			
Barker, George	17843	Busser	$5.15	40.13	$206.00	$1.00			
Choi, April	13894	Wait	$2.13	40.02	$85.20	$0.06		$100.50	$0.00
Choi, Jennifer	13895	Wait	$2.13	40.02	$85.20	$0.06		$98.65	$0.00
Choi, Jeremy	13896	Wait	$2.13	40.11	$85.20	$0.35		$115.25	$0.00
Estophan, Ellen	12257	Wait	$2.13	39.68	$84.52	$0.00		$96.75	$5.00
Hernandez, Hen	16392	Wait	$2.13	40.01	$85.20	$0.03		$105.20	$0.00
James, April	10352	Cashier	$10.00	40.17	$400.00	$2.55			
Muhammed, Mir	18110	Busser	$5.15	40.02	$206.00	$0.15	$10.30 √		
Muhibuddin, Bilal	17328	Busser	$5.15	40.09	$206.00	$0.70			
O'Brien, Emily	16820	Busser	$5.15	39.48	$203.32	$0.00	-$5.15 √		
Palenski, Stella	10287	Wait	$2.13	40.08	$85.20	$0.26		$150.25	$0.00
Robinson, Rober	14792	Wait	$2.13	40.09	$85.20	$0.29		$100.75	$0.00
Simmons, Sum	17946	Wait	$2.13	40.08	$85.20	$0.26		$95.25	$0.00
Thompson, Tues	10783	Head Wa	$4.50	39.73	$178.79	$0.00		$115.25	$0.00
Topaz, Tammie	11957	Wait	$2.13	40.33	$85.20	$1.05		$125.70	$0.00
Wei, Willie	14820	Wait	$2.13	40.06	$85.20	$0.19		$90.25	$0.00
Totals				679.68 √	$2,455.26	$6.96	$5.15	$1,193.80 √	$5.00

Heather Smith
7/17/06

Figure 15.6

The auditor should audit the Wage and Hour Report by tying the totals to the source documents. She should agree the adding machine tape of hours worked to the Wage and Hour Report, Adjustments to the approved source documents, Charge Tips to the Dining Room Manager's list of Charge Tips to be Paid, and Cash Tips to the Dining Room Manager's list of Cash Tips Declared. The auditor should test these listings by tying individual time cards, entries on the Sign In/Sign Out sheets, time cards, or Weekly Time Summaries to the individual entries on the Wage and Hour Report. She should tie Adjustments to Wages to the approved source documents. She should test the Charge Tips by tying the Charge Tips Total on the Wage and Hour Report to the sum of each day's charge tips reported on the Daily Sales Journals (See Chapter 11). The auditor should test the Cash Tips reported by comparing signed individual employee Cash Tip Declaration forms to the entries on the Dining Room Manager's Cash Tips Declared spreadsheet.

All audit steps performed should be documented in the workpapers. Any exceptions should be noted in the workpapers and cross referenced to the Discussion Points Worksheet.

Tips Reporting & Minimum Wage

The Federal Minimum Wage for employees is $5.15 per hour. (Effective July 24, 2007, the Federal minimum wage increased to $5.85 per hour. Additional increases are scheduled to take effect as follows: July 24, 2008—$6.55 per hour, July 24, 2009—$7.25 per hour.) However, many States have minimum wage laws that are much higher than the Federal minimum wage. For example, effective January 1, 2007, the minimum wage in New York State is $7.15 per hour. Restaurants that operate in states that have a higher state minimum wage must pay its employees the higher State minimum wage.

The Federal government allows employers to pay $2.13 per hour (can be higher under State labor laws) to tipped employees where these employees earn at least the difference between the minimum wage and $2.13 per hour in tips. This is called the tip credit. Of course, for the tip credit to count, the employee must declare tips. Charge tips are recorded in the Payroll System and added to the employees' Gross Pay for tax purposes since the employer has a record of them. However, cash tips received by the employee but not declared cannot be used in the minimum wage calculation.

Where the employer pays its tipped employees (waiters, waitress, bartenders, etc.) below minimum wage, the Payroll Clerk should prepare a spreadsheet to ensure each employee has met the minimum wage calculation. The cost of employee meals can be added to wages for purposes of calculating the minimum wage. If the spreadsheet shows that an employee did not make minimum wage, the Payroll Clerk must enter an adjustment to Gross Wages to bring the employee up to minimum wage.

Figure 15.7 is an example of a spreadsheet that calculates whether each tipped employee received minimum wage. The Minimum Wage Testing schedule (Figure 15.7) assumes a minimum wage of $5.15. It would be updated for the current minimum wage, i.e. $5.85, effective July 24, 2007, $6.55, effective July 24, 2008, or $7.25, effective July 24, 2009. According to the spreadsheet, April Choi's Gross Wages for the week ending July 15, 2006 are $9.14 under minimum wage. The Payroll Clerk would enter $9.14 in the Payroll system as an Adjustment to wages. The columns in Figure 15.7 are as follows:

Employee Name—Name of the tipped employee,

Hourly Rate—Amount the employee receives per hour,

Total Hours—Number of hours the employee worked per the Wage and Hour Report,

Regular Wages—Hourly Rate multiplied by Total Hours, up to 40 hours,

Overtime Wages—Hours over 40 hours multiplied by the Hourly Rate times 1.5,

Charge Tips—Amount of Charge Tips per the Wage and Hour Report,

Cash Tips—Cash tips declared by the employee per the Wage and Hour Report.

Cost of Employee Meals—Number of days the employee worked (5 hours or more) multiplied by the average cost per meal ($2.25 in Figure 15.7),

Total Wages—Regular Wages plus Overtime Wages plus Charge Tips plus Cash Tips plus Cost of Employee Meals.

The next section of the spreadsheet is the calculation of minimum wage. Its columns contain the following information:

Regular Minimum Wages—Total Hours up to 40 multiplied by the minimum Hourly Wage ($5.15 in Figure 15.7),

Overtime Minimum Wages—Total Hours (if over 40) minus 40 multiplied by Hourly Wage times 1.5,

Total Minimum Wages—Regular Wages plus Overtime Wages.

The last column is the amount of minimum wage shortfall, if any. If the result is a negative number, the employer must pay the shortfall to the employee.

Amount Over (Under) Minimum—Total Wages minus Total Minimum Wages.

Jenny's Café, Inc.
Denver Restaurant
Minimum Wage Testing
Week Ending July 15, 2006

Emloyee Name	Hourly Rate	Total Hours	Regular Wages	Overtime Wages	Charge Tips	Cash Tips	Cost of Employee Meals
Choi, April	$2.13	40.02	$ 85.20	$0.06	$ 100.50	$0.00	$ 11.25
Choi, Jennifer	$2.13	40.02	$ 85.20	$0.06	$ 98.65	$0.00	$ 11.25
Choi, Jeremy	$2.13	40.11	$ 85.20	$0.35	$ 115.25	$0.00	$ 11.25
Estophan, E.	$2.13	39.68	$ 84.52	$0.00	$ 96.75	$5.00	$ 11.25
Hernandez, H.	$2.13	40.01	$ 85.20	$0.03	$ 105.20	$0.00	$ 11.25
Palenski, S.	$2.13	40.08	$ 85.20	$0.26	$ 150.25	$0.00	$ 11.25
Robinson, R.	$2.13	40.09	$ 85.20	$0.29	$ 100.75	$0.00	$ 11.25
Simmons, S.	$2.13	40.08	$ 85.20	$0.26	$ 95.25	$0.00	$ 11.25
Thompson, T.	$4.50	39.73	$ 178.79	$0.00	$ 115.25	$0.00	$ 11.25
Topaz, T.	$2.13	40.33	$ 85.20	$1.05	$ 125.70	$0.00	$ 11.25
Wei, Willie	$2.13	40.06	$ 85.20	$0.19	$ 90.25	$0.00	$ 11.25
Totals		440.21	$1,030.10	$2.56	$1,193.80	$5.00	$ 123.75

Figure 15.7

The auditor should test minimum wages for tipped employees by preparing a spreadsheet similar to the one the Payroll Clerk Prepares. She can use IF statements to calculate Regular Minimum Wages and Overtime Minimum Wages so the spreadsheet does it automatically. The auditor clicks on the Function (fx) button on the first line of the Regular Minimum Wages column, selects IF and clicks on OK to start the formula. There are three statements to the IF formula, the Logical Test, the Value if True, and the Value if False.

For Regular Minimum Wages, the Logical Test is "If Total Hours are greater than 40." If the value is true, then 40 is multiplied by $5.15 (the hourly minimum wage). If the value is false (less than 40 hours), Regular Wages is multiplied by $5.15. After keying the three statements of the formula, the user clicks on OK. For example, in Figure 15.7, the information for April Choi appears on Line 9 of the Excel spreadsheet and Total Hours is in Column C. When clicking on the fx button in Excel, the function arguments the user would enter would be as follows: (current minimum wage is substituted for 5.15 in the formulas)

Logical Test: C9>40
Value if True: 40*5.15
Value if False: C9*5.15

In the Overtime Minimum Wages column, the auditor also uses the IF

| Total Wages | Minimum Wage ($5.15) Calculation | | | Amount Over (Under) Minimum |
	Regular Wages	Overtime Wages	Total Wages	
$ 197.01	$ 206.00	$ 0.15	$ 206.15	$ (9.14)
$ 195.16	$ 206.00	$ 0.15	$ 206.15	$ (10.99)
$ 212.05	$ 206.00	$ 0.85	$ 206.85	$ 5.20
$ 197.52	$ 204.35	$ -	$ 204.35	$ (6.83)
$ 201.68	$ 206.00	$ 0.08	$ 206.08	$ (4.40)
$ 246.96	$ 206.00	$ 0.62	$ 206.62	$ 40.34
$ 197.49	$ 206.00	$ 0.70	$ 206.70	$ (9.21)
$ 191.96	$ 206.00	$ 0.62	$ 206.62	$ (14.66)
$ 305.29	$ 204.61	$ -	$ 204.61	$ 100.68
$ 223.20	$ 206.00	$ 2.55	$ 208.55	$ 14.66
$ 186.89	$ 206.00	$ 0.46	$ 206.46	$ (19.57)
$2,355.21	$ 2,262.96	$ 6.18	$ 2,269.14	

statement. The Logical Test is "If Total Hours are greater than 40." If the value is true, then Total Hours minus 40 is multiplied by $7.725 ($5.15 multiplied by 1.5). If the value is false (Total Hours are less than 40), 0 is entered in the column. Thus, continuing with our example, the function arguments for April Choi would be as follows:

Logical Test: C9>40
Value if True: ((C9-40)*(5.15*1.5))
Value if False: 0

The auditor prints the spreadsheet and inserts it into her workpaper binder. If the spreadsheet shows that some employees earned below minimum wage, the auditor looks in the adjustment column of the Payroll Register to see if the Payroll Clerk paid the minimum wage shortfall to the employees. If not, the auditor notes the deficiency on the spreadsheet and cross references the notation to the Discussion Points Worksheet.

In Figure 15.8, Aimee tested the wages of the dining room tipped employees to determine whether they achieved minimum wage, as she noted in her Basis of Selection. Her conclusion was that 8 of 11 tipped employees did not achieve minimum wage and Denver Restaurant did not give the affected employees a wage adjustment that would bring them up to minimum. She cross referenced her conclusion to Discussion Point Number 44.

Jenny's Café, Inc.
Denver Restaurant
Minimum Wage Testing
Week Ending July 15, 2006

Employee Name	Hourly Rate	Total Hours	Regular Wages	Overtime Wages	Charge Tips	Cash Tips	Cost of Employee Meals
Choi, April	$2.13	40.02	$ 85.20	$0.06	$ 100.50	$0.00	$ 11.25
Choi, Jennifer	$2.13	40.02	$ 85.20	$0.06	$ 98.65	$0.00	$ 11.25
Choi, Jeremy	$2.13	40.11	$ 85.20	$0.35	$ 115.25	$0.00	$ 11.25
Estophan, E.	$2.13	39.68	$ 84.52	$0.00	$ 96.75	$5.00	$ 11.25
Hernandez, H.	$2.13	40.01	$ 85.20	$0.03	$ 105.20	$0.00	$ 11.25
Palenski, S.	$2.13	40.08	$ 85.20	$0.26	$ 150.25	$0.00	$ 11.25
Robinson, R.	$2.13	40.09	$ 85.20	$0.29	$ 100.75	$0.00	$ 11.25
Simmons, S.	$2.13	40.08	$ 85.20	$0.26	$ 95.25	$0.00	$ 11.25
Thompson, T.	$4.50	39.73	$ 178.79	$0.00	$ 115.25	$0.00	$ 11.25
Topaz, T.	$2.13	40.33	$ 85.20	$1.05	$ 125.70	$0.00	$ 11.25
Wei, Willie	$2.13	40.06	$ 85.20	$0.19	$ 90.25	$0.00	$ 11.25
Totals		440.21	$1,030.10	$2.56	$1,193.80	$5.00	$123.75

Basis of Selection: Selected all tipped employees working in the Dining Room for the week ending July 15, 2006.

Conclusion: 8 of 11 tipped employees tested did not declare enough in tips minimum wage of $5.15 per hour, but Denver Restaurant to achieve did not pay these employees wage adjustments that would bring them up to minimum wage.See Discussion Point #44

Figure 15.8

Where the union contract requires the employer to pay Charge Tips to the employees in cash the day they were earned, the Payroll Clerk must still input the Charge Tips into the Payroll System for Internal Revenue Service (IRS)

M3

AS

8/3/06

Total Wages	Minimum Wage ($5.15) Calculation					Amount Over (Under) Minimum
	Regular Wages		Overtime Wages		Total Wages	
$ 197.01	$	206.00	$	0.15	$ 206.15	$ (9.14)
$ 195.16	$	206.00	$	0.15	$ 206.15	$ (10.99)
$ 212.05	$	206.00	$	0.85	$ 206.85	$ 5.20
$ 197.52	$	204.35	$	-	$ 204.35	$ (6.83)
$ 201.68	$	206.00	$	0.08	$ 206.08	$ (4.40)
$ 246.96	$	206.00	$	0.62	$ 206.62	$ 40.34
$ 197.49	$	206.00	$	0.70	$ 206.70	$ (9.21)
$ 191.96	$	206.00	$	0.62	$ 206.62	$ (14.66)
$ 305.29	$	204.61	$	-	$ 204.61	$ 100.68
$ 223.20	$	206.00	$	2.55	$ 208.55	$ 14.66
$ 186.89	$	206.00	$	0.46	$ 206.46	$ (19.57)
$2,355.21	$	2,262.96	$	6.18	$ 2,269.14	

reporting purposes. In this case, the Payroll System will add Charge Tips to Gross Wages to calculate tax withholdings and then subtract Charge Tips from Gross Wages when calculating Net Pay (same treatment as Cash Tips).

Every pay period, each tipped employee must declare cash tips on a form that the employer provides and must sign the form. The employer must require the employees to declare cash tips even if the employee declares zero tips.

There are two exceptions to the Fair Labor Standards Act (FLSA) rules relating to the minimum wage. Restaurants with less than $500,000 in annual revenue qualify for the *Low Revenue Exception*. Where the revenues of a restaurant's entire operation (food, bar, banquet room, valet parking, etc.) are less than $500,000, the restaurant may pay its employees below the Federal minimum wage.

The second exception to the FLSA rules allows employers to pay a *Training Wage* of $4.25 per hour for newly hired employees under the age of 20 for the first 90 days of employment. There is no specific training required during this period. Restaurant employers should consult state laws in the state where the restaurant is located to determine whether these federal exceptions are permitted under the state labor laws.

Tip Allocation

Each week, the Payroll Clerk obtains the sales generated by the Dining Room, Bar, Banquet Room, etc. and enters them into the Payroll System. At year end, the Payroll System allocates sales in the area (Dining Room, Bar, Banquet Room, etc.) to each tipped employee based on the number of hours worked. The Payroll System takes Total Tips reported for each employee and divides by Allocated Sales. It compares employee reported tips to Allocated Sales multiplied by 8%. If the declared tips are below 8% of Allocated Sales, the Payroll System allocates the difference to the employee as additional wages on the W-2 statement that is filed with the IRS. The employee will thus be required to pay personal income taxes on the allocated tip amount.

For example, Ellen is a waitress who had $50,000 in Dining Room Sales allocated to her based on hours worked. Ellen was paid $2,500 in charge tips during the year and declared $500 in cash tips. The Payroll System multiplied $50,000 by 8% to obtain $4,000. Since Ellen only had taxes withheld on $3,000, the Payroll System will allocate and additional $1,000 to Ellen on her Form W-2 at year end as additional wages. Ellen will need to include the entire $4,000 on her Federal and State income tax returns as wages.

The auditor should test the accuracy of sales entered in the Payroll system by comparing the sales for one week to the Daily Sales Journals (See Chapter 11) for that week. She should document her work on a workpaper and insert it in the workpaper binder. Any significant difference should be noted in the workpapers and cross referenced to the Discussion Points Worksheet.

Payroll Reports

Normally the payroll is due into Corporate or the payroll processing bureau by the end of the day on Tuesday. It takes a day to process the payroll checks and send them to the field locations via an overnight delivery service. The field location can expect to receive the payroll checks on Thursday morning for distribution to the employees on Friday.

When the package containing the payroll checks arrives at the field location, it should be received by the Controller or General Manager, not the Payroll Clerk. The Payroll Clerk may not have access to the payroll checks. This control is necessary because if the Payroll Clerk added a name to the Payroll Master File for an employee who does not exist and keyed hours for the fictitious employee, she would be able to remove and cash the payroll check if she had access to the package containing these checks.

The Controller should run the Payroll Reports which typically include a Payroll Register, Employee Maintenance Report, and some type of High Dollar Report. She should compare the Wage and Hour Report to the Payroll Register to see that the Total Hours by Department, Regular Wages, Overtime Wages, Adjustments, Charge Tips, and Cash Tips agree. Any differences should be researched by the Payroll Clerk and reconciled. The Controller should check off the Department Totals on the Payroll Register as she ties them to the Wage and Hour Report. Once she is satisfied that the numbers are correct, the Controller signs and dates the Payroll Register.

Figure 15.9 is a Payroll Register. The columns contain the following information:

Employee Name—Name of the employee receiving a payroll check,

Position—Name of the position that the employee worked,

Employee Number—Number that identifies the employee to the Payroll system,

Hourly Rate—Rate of pay that the employee will receive,

Total Hours—Number of hours that the employee worked,

Regular Wages—Total Hours up to 40 multiplied by Hourly Rate,

Overtime Wages—Total Hours over 40 multiplied by one and a half times the hourly rate, or some other rate as required by the State labor laws,

Adjustments—Adjustments to wages from prior weeks, due to hours missed or overpayments,

Charge Tips—Charge tips due to employees that will be paid through the Payroll System,

Cash Tips—Cash tips received and declared by the employees,

Total Gross Wages—Regular Wages plus Overtime Wages plus Adjustments plus Charge Tips plus Cash Tips,

Federal Withholding—Federal income taxes withheld for the employee and paid to the IRS,

F.I.C.A.—Social Security taxes withheld for the employee (6.2%) and paid to the IRS,

Medicare Withholding—Medicare taxes withheld for the employee (1.45%) and paid to the IRS,

State Withholding—State income taxes withheld for the employees and paid to the State taxing authority,

Disability—Amount withheld from the employee's gross wages, per the state's labor statutes, and applied to the cost of Disability Insurance,

Cash Tips—Cash Tips declared by the employee which will be subtracted from Gross Pay since it is not due to the employee,

Miscellaneous Deduction—Miscellaneous deduction, i.e. Garnishments, Uniforms, Parking Fees, etc. that the employee has authorized in writing (through completion of a form) to be deducted from her payroll check,

Deduction Code—Alphabetical code that identifies the type of deduction (G = Garnishment, U = Uniform in Figure 15.9),

Net Pay—Total Gross Wages minus Federal Withholding minus F.I.C.A. minus Medicare Withholding minus State Withholding minus Disability minus Cash Tips minus Miscellaneous Deduction,

Check Number—Check Number of the payroll check used to pay the employee.

The Controller runs an Employee Maintenance Report that lists every new employee added to the Payroll database, every terminated employee removed from the active list of employees, and any changes to the employees' master files, i.e. address change, pay rate change, miscellaneous deduction changes etc. Every entry on the Employee Maintenance Report must be supported by a completed Employee Maintenance Form that is signed by the employee and the department head. The Controller should compare the entries on the Employee Maintenance Report to the supporting Employee Maintenance Form. Once satisfied that everything is in order, the Controller signs and dates the Employee Maintenance Report.

The third important report that the Controller reviews is the High Dollar Report. The purpose of this report is to flag gross wages over a certain dollar amount so the reviewer can check the source documents to ensure that this amount is not in error. For example, if Denver Restaurant sets the dollar limit at $400, April James would appear on the High Dollar Report at $402.55. Heather Smith would check the hours entered to ensure they are correct and then check off April James on this report. Once satisfied that all employees paid more than $400 were paid correctly, Heather would sign and date the High Dollar Report.

Once the Controller has completed her audit of the payroll, she sends the Payroll Registers to the Department heads for their review. The Department heads should review the hours and gross pay paid to each employee to ensure they are correct. When satisfied that the Payroll Register is correct, the Department head signs and dates the Payroll Register and returns it to the Controller. Signed Payroll Registers are due back in the Controller's office by 5:00 p.m. on Thursday. At this point, the payroll checks are ready for Friday distribution.

Any errors noted when reviewing payroll checks or by an employee who received her payroll check should be noted on a Payroll Adjustment form. The department head completes the form with the details of the error and signs it. The Payroll Adjustment forms are turned in to the Payroll Clerk for inclusion in the following period's payroll as adjustments.

Payroll reports are highly confidential since they contain pay rate information on all employees. Thus, the Payroll Clerk and Controller should take care not to leave payroll reports lying around for other employees to see. When working with payroll reports and leaving her desk, the Payroll Clerk or Controller should cover up the reports or put them in a drawer so people walking by the desk can't look through them. At night, all payroll reports should be stored in a locked file cabinet.

The auditor should select 4-5 sets of payroll reports and check them for proper signatures. She would look at the Payroll Register and see whether there is evidence that the hours and dollars were tied back to the Wage and Hour Report. Evidence of tying hours and dollars would be check marks on the Payroll Register or a note describing what the Controller did. The auditor would also look for proper signatures and dates. In addition, the auditor would check the Employee Maintenance Report and High Dollar Report for the Controller's or General Manager's signature and date, documenting her review and approval.

As part of reviewing the Internal Control Questionnaire with the Payroll Clerk and Controller, the auditor should ask where the payroll reports are stored at night. Any exceptions to Company policies or sound internal control practices that are noted while reviewing the payroll reports should be noted in the workpapers and cross referenced to the Discussion Points Worksheet.

Jenny's Café, Inc.
Denver Restaurant
Payroll Register
Week Ending July 15, 2006

Dining Room

Employee Name	Position	Empl No.	Hourly Rate	Total Hours	Regular Wages	O/T Wages	Adjust	Charge Tips
Abdullah, Hasim	Busser	15986	$5.15	39.58	$203.84	$0.00		
Barker, George	Busser	17843	$5.15	40.13	$206.00	$1.00		
Choi, April	Wait	13894	$2.13	40.02	$85.20	$0.06		$100.50
Choi, Jennifer	Wait	13895	$2.13	40.02	$85.20	$0.06		$98.65
Choi, Jeremy	Wait	13896	$2.13	40.11	$85.20	$0.35		$115.25
Estophan, Ellen	Wait	12257	$2.13	39.68	$84.52	$0.00		$96.75
Hernandez, Henry	Wait	16392	$2.13	40.01	$85.20	$0.03		$105.20
James, April	Cashier	10352	$10.00	40.17	$400.00	$2.55		
Muhammed, Miradije	Busser	18110	$5.15	40.02	$206.00	$0.15	$10.30	
Muhibuddin, Bilal	Busser	17328	$5.15	40.09	$206.00	$0.70		
O'Brien, Emily	Busser	16820	$5.15	39.48	$203.32	$0.00	-$5.15	
Palenski, Stella	Wait	10287	$2.13	40.08	$85.20	$0.26		$150.25
Robinson, Robert	Wait	14792	$2.13	40.09	$85.20	$0.29		$100.75
Simmons, Summer	Wait	17946	$2.13	40.08	$85.20	$0.26		$95.25
Thompson, Tuesday	Hd Wait	10783	$4.50	39.73	$178.79	$0.00		$115.25
Topaz, Tammie	Wait	11957	$2.13	40.33	$85.20	$1.05		$125.70
Wei, Willie	Wait	14820	$2.13	40.06	$85.20	$0.19		$90.25
Totals				679.68 √	$2,455.3 √	$6.96 √	$5.15 √	$1,193.80 √

Heather Smith
7/19/06

Figure 15.9

110

Cash Tips	Total Gross Wages	Federal Withhold	F.I.C.A.	Medcre W/H	State W/H	Disblity	Cash Tips	Misc. Deduc	Ded Cde	Net Pay	Check Number
	$203.84	$30.58	$12.64	$2.96	$7.13	$0.60	$0.00	$0.00		$149.93	245290
	$207.00	$31.05	$12.83	$3.00	$7.25	$0.60	$0.00	$25.00	G	$127.27	245291
$0.00	$185.76	$27.86	$11.52	$2.69	$6.50	$0.60	$0.00	$0.00		$136.59	245292
$0.00	$183.91	$27.59	$11.40	$2.67	$6.44	$0.60	$0.00	$0.00		$135.22	245293
$0.00	$200.80	$30.12	$12.45	$2.91	$7.03	$0.60	$0.00	$0.00		$147.69	245294
$5.00	$186.27	$27.94	$11.55	$2.70	$6.52	$0.60	$5.00	$10.00	U	$121.96	245295
$0.00	$190.43	$28.56	$11.81	$2.76	$6.67	$0.60	$0.00	$0.00		$140.03	245296
	$402.55	$80.51	$24.96	$5.84	$14.09	$0.60	$0.00	$0.00		$276.56	245297
	$216.45	$32.47	$13.42	$3.14	$7.58	$0.60	$0.00	$0.00		$159.25	245298
	$206.70	$31.00	$12.82	$3.00	$7.23	$0.60	$0.00	$10.00	U	$142.04	245299
	$198.17	$29.73	$12.29	$2.87	$6.94	$0.60	$0.00	$0.00		$145.75	245300
$0.00	$235.71	$42.43	$14.61	$3.42	$8.25	$0.60	$0.00	$0.00		$166.40	245301
$0.00	$186.24	$27.94	$11.55	$2.70	$6.52	$0.60	$0.00	$0.00		$136.94	245302
$0.00	$180.71	$27.11	$11.20	$2.62	$6.32	$0.60	$0.00	$0.00		$132.85	245303
$0.00	$294.04	$52.93	$18.23	$4.26	$10.29	$0.60	$0.00	$0.00		$207.72	245304
$0.00	$211.95	$31.79	$13.14	$3.07	$7.42	$0.60	$0.00	$0.00		$155.93	245305
$0.00	$175.64	$26.35	$10.89	$2.55	$6.15	$0.60	$0.00	$0.00		$129.11	245306
$5.00 √	$3,666.17	$585.95	$227.30	$53.16	$128.32	$10.20	$5.00	$45.00		$2,611.25	

Documenting Payroll Testing

Throughout this chapter, we have discussed various audit tests that the auditor should perform in the Payroll section. Many of these tests can be documented on one Payroll Testing worksheet. As part of the planning process, the auditor should obtain the current Payroll Master File from the Corporate Payroll Department. From the Payroll Master file, the auditor should select 15-30 employees that she will test for Payroll and Human Resources. In auditing a restaurant that uses a payroll service bureau to process its payroll, the auditor will make her selection of employees to be tested when she arrives at the restaurant and obtains the location's Payroll Master File. We will discuss the selection process in more detail when we discuss Human Resources in Chapter 16.

As the auditor selects the employees whose records she will test, the auditor lists them on an Excel spreadsheet. She indicates the Cost or Profit Center where the employee works, the employee's position, the Hourly Rate, and the Birthday. The Birthday is important because minors have restricted hours that they are allowed to work (See Child Labor Laws in Chapter 16). The minors working in the unit should be separated into a separate section at the bottom of the worksheet, labeled "Minors" so the auditor will pay extra attention to ensure minors are not working more than the maximum number of hours that they are allowed to work.

During the planning phase, the auditor enters abbreviations on the right side of the spreadsheet as column headings for the audit steps she will perform. These audit steps will be the ones outlined in the audit program.

As part of the List of Documents that the auditor requests from the Controller prior to arrival at the unit or upon arrival is the test month for payroll testing. The auditor requests all Time cards, Sign In/Sign Out sheets, or Time Keeping Reports for the test month. She also requests all tip reporting documentation and documentation for all adjustments, miscellaneous earnings, and special payroll deductions. Once the auditor has received these documents, she selects one week that she will test.

As the auditor performs the audit steps outlined in the audit program and abbreviated as column headings on the Excel spreadsheet, she enters a "Yes," "No," or "N/A" for each employee tested in the appropriate column. If the employee's record meets the test criterion, she enters "Yes." If the employee's record does not meet the test criterion, she enters "No." The "No" is in bold type to make it stand out on the workpaper. If the criterion does not ʼply to the employee, the auditor enters "N/A."

Figure 15.10 is Aimee's worksheet for her payroll testing. Minimum wage testing is not included here because it was already documented on Worksheet **M3** (Figure 15.8). The columns in Figure 15.10 contain the following information:

Employee Name—Name of the employee selected for testing,

Center—Name of the Profit Center (Center contains revenues and associated costs) or Cost Center (Center that contains only costs and minimal or no revenue i.e. Warehouse or Maintenance),

Position—Type of job to which the wage rate applies,

Hourly Rate—Hourly rate of pay that the employee earns,

Birthday—Date the employee was born,

The next set of columns is abbreviations for the audit steps the employee performs, as outlined in the audit program. The ones Aimee performed in Figure 15.10 are as follows:

Hourly Rate Agrees to Approved Employee Maintenance Form?—Does the Hourly Rate on the Payroll Register agree to the current Employee Maintenance form signed by the General Manager?

Hourly Rate Agrees to the Union Contract?—Does the Hourly Rate on the Payroll Register agree to the current rate in effect per the union contract?

Time Card Initialed by the Supervisor?—Was the Time Card initialed by the department supervisor?

Hours per Time Card Agree to Payroll Register?—Do the total hours on the Time Card agree to the hours on the Payroll Register?

Charge Tips per Dining Room Manager's Spreadsheet Agree to Payroll Register?—Do the Charge Tips listed on the Dining Room Manager's Charge Tips Spreadsheet agree to the charge tips on the Payroll Register?

Employee Signed Payroll Check Log Acknowledging Hours Worked?—Did the employee sign a Payroll Check Log, thereby acknowledging the accuracy of the hours worked (See Signing for Payroll Checks below)?

Jenny's Café, Inc.
Denver Restaurant
Payroll Testing
Week Ending July 15, 2006

Employee Name	Center	Position	Hourly Rate	Birthday	Hrly Rate Agrees to Apprvd Empl Maint Form?	Hrly Rate Agrees to Union Contract	Time Card Initialed by Supervisor?
Lopez, Laura	Bar	Bartend	$7.50	11/23/80	Yes	Yes	NO
Robinson, Bobbie	Bar	Bartend	$7.50	06/01/81	Yes	Yes	NO
Smith, Jane	Cash Rm	Attend	$11.00	04/28/75	NO	N/A	Yes
Abdullah, Hasim	Dining	Busser	$5.15	04/17/88	Yes	Yes	Yes
Barker, George	Dining	Busser	$5.15	03/04/88	Yes	Yes	Yes
Choi, April	Dining	Wait	$2.13	02/11/79	Yes	Yes	Yes
Choi, Jennifer	Dining	Wait	$2.13	10/28/77	Yes	Yes	Yes
Choi, Jeremy	Dining Rm	Waiter	$2.13	08/09/75	Yes	Yes	Yes
James April	Dining Rm	Cashier	$10.00	12/25/66	NO	Yes	Yes
Muhammed, Muhibiddin, Bilal	Dining	Busser	$5.15	09/05/87	Yes	Yes	Yes
	Dining	Busser	$5.15	07/14/87	Yes	Yes	Yes
Tamme Topaz	Dining	Wait	$2.13	06/15/76	Yes	Yes	Yes
Wei, Willie	Dining	Wait	$2.13	09/04/74	Yes	Yes	Yes
Howard, Rebeca	Kitchen	Cook	$15.25	03/12/68	NO	Yes	NO
Jone, Jimmie	Kitchen	Dessert	$8.50	01/01/79	Yes	Yes	NO
Jons, Tony	Kitchen	Cook	$15.25	04/24/75	Yes	Yes	NO
Woniak, Donna	Kitchen	Salad	$8.50	02/13/86	Yes	Yes	NO
Josphson, Linda	Linen Rm	Spvsr	$12.50	08/07/55	NO	N/A	Yes
Arrivo, Raul	Maint	Cleaner	$9.25	09/20/51	Yes	Yes	Yes
Byon, Joe	Whse	Receiv	$9.50	11/07/71	Yes	Yes	Yes
O'rien, Kelly	Whse	Receiv	$9.50	11/11/69	Yes	Yes	Yes
Mnors							
Vatsworth, Willie	Valet Pk	Attend	$5.15	05/20/90	Yes	Yes	Yes
Ortez, Jimmy	Valet Pk	Attend	$5.50	07/17/89	Yes	Yes	NO
uarez, Suzie	Valet Pk	Attend	$5.50	06/30/90	Yes	Yes	NO
Complied					20	22	16
Exceptions					4	0	8
No. Tested					24	22	24
Exception Percentage					16.7%	0.0%	33.3%

Basis of Selection: Selected same employees selected in Human Resources Test -
See N1 for details.

nlusion: Payroll testing revealed exceptions as follows:
. 4 of 24 Employee Maintenance Forms tested, the rate on the Payroll Register did not agree to the Employee Maintenance Form,
. 8 of 24 Time Cards tested were not initialed by the supervisor,
. 5 of 7 manual entries on the Time Cards were not initialed by the supervisor, **See Discussion Point #41**

Figure 15.10

Hours per Time Card Agree to P/R Regstr?	Chrg Tips / DR Mgr's SS Agree to P/R Regstr?	Empl Sign P/R Ck Log Acknow Hrs Wkd?	Time Card Manual Entries Initialed?	If Minor, Hrs Hours Worked Legal?	Comments
Yes	Yes	Yes	N/A	N/A	
Yes	Yes	Yes	NO	N/A	Man Entry- time out 7/13 not initialed
Yes	N/A	Yes	N/A	N/A	Hrly rate-last apprvd M.F.-$10.50
Yes	N/A	Yes	N/A	N/A	
Yes	N/A	Yes	N/A	N/A	
Yes	Yes	Yes	N/A	N/A	
Yes	Yes	Yes	N/A	N/A	
Yes	Yes	Yes	NO	N/A	Manual entries for time out on 7/11 & 7/14 not initialed
Yes	N/A	Yes	N/A	N/A	Hrly rate on last apprvd M.F.-$9.65
Yes	N/A	Yes	N/A	N/A	
Yes	N/A	Yes	N/A	N/A	
Yes	Yes	Yes	Yes	N/A	
Yes	Yes	Yes	Yes	N/A	
Yes	N/A	Yes	N/A	N/A	Hrly Rate-last apprvd M.F.-$14.75
Yes	N/A	Yes	NO	N/A	Man entry-time out-7/13 not initialed
Yes	N/A	Yes	N/A	N/A	
Yes	N/A	Yes	N/A	N/A	
Yes	N/A	Yes	N/A	N/A	Hrly rate-last apprvd M.F.-$12.10
Yes	N/A	Yes	N/A	N/A	
Yes	N/A	Yes	N/A	N/A	
Yes	N/A	Yes	N/A	N/A	
Yes	N/A	Yes	N/A	Yes	
Yes	N/A	Yes	NO	Yes	Man entry-time out 7/14 not initialed
Yes	N/A	Yes	NO	Yes	Man entry-time out 7/14 not initialed
24	7	24	2	3	
0	0	0	5	0	
24	7	24	7	3	
0.0%	0.0%	0.0%	71.4%	0.0%	

Time Card Manual Entries Initialed?—Were manual entries on the Time Card initialed by the department supervisor?

If Minor, Hours Worked Legal?—If the employee is a minor, were the hours worked legal? (See Chapter 16 for a discussion of Child Labor Laws?

Comments—This column is used to provide further details on a "NO" answer to one of the criterion in the previous columns.

The next section on the worksheet is a summary of the testing. The auditor enters the number of employee records that met the criterion, the number of exceptions, the total number tested (does not include N/A's), and the exception percentage. The auditor can count these items manually or can use the COUNT IF function to have the Excel spreadsheet automatically count these items (See Chapter 8, Setting Up the Workpaper to Test Invoices).

On the bottom of the worksheet, Aimee indicated her Basis of Selection. Since these are the same employees that she is using for the Human Resources test, she referred to the Human Resources Testing worksheet for details on how she made her selection. In the Conclusion, Aimee summarized the exceptions that she noted and cross referenced the workpaper to the Discussion Points Worksheet.

Signing for Payroll Checks

Each employee should sign an acknowledgement that the hours she is paid are correct. One way to do this is to have the employee sign the Time Card where the total hours worked are noted at the bottom. Many companies have the Pay Master (not the Payroll Clerk) paper clip the Time Card to the payroll check. When the employee picks up the payroll check, the employee signs the Time Card. After all payroll checks have been picked up, the Pay Master (person who distributes the payroll checks) returns the signed Time Cards to the Payroll Clerk who files them with the Payroll.

When picking up her payroll check, the employee should sign the Payroll Check Log. The Payroll Check Log can be sorted by department and set up so there is a page break after each department. In this way, the Pay Master can divide up the payroll checks by department and hand the payroll checks and Payroll Check Log to each department supervisor. When the department supervisor distributes the payroll checks to her direct reports, she asks the employee to sign the Payroll Check Log acknowledging receipt of the check. When all checks have been distributed on pay day, the supervisor returns the Payroll Check Log to the Payroll Clerk for filing with the week's payroll records and reports. Undistributed checks are returned to the Pay Master who locks them in a file cabinet until claimed by the employee. In this way, if an employee later says that she did not receive her payroll check, the Payroll Clerk looks up the employee's name in the Payroll Check Log and shows the employee where she signed for her payroll check.

Many companies have the Payroll Check Log printed along with the payroll reports. The Payroll System can be programmed to print the number of hours each employee worked, and an acknowledgement that the number of hours worked is correct can be printed at the top of each page. If this system is implemented, the employee does not need to sign the Time Card.

Employees should be required to pick up their payroll checks in person. If an employee does not pick up a payroll check and the Pay Master mails it to the employee's home, i.e. in the case where the employee quits without picking up her final payroll check, the Pay Master should note on the Payroll Check Log that the payroll check was mailed and the date it was mailed.

Figure 15.11 is an example of one page of the Payroll Check Log for the Dining Room. The week ending date is noted in the heading. Each page of the Payroll Check Log has the following certification, "Your signature certifies that you received your payroll check and you agree that the hours for which you were paid (noted to the right of your name) are correct." The information contained in the columns is as follows:

Employee Name—Name of the employee receiving a payroll check,

Hours Worked—Number of hours that the employee worked during the week noted in the heading,

Received Check—Signature of the employee, acknowledging receipt of the payroll check and that the number of hours worked are correct.

Jenny's Café, Inc.
Denver Restaurant
Payroll Check Log
Week Ending July 15, 2006

**Your signature certifies that you received your payroll check and you agree that the hours
for which you were paid (noted to the right of your name) are correct.**

Dining Room

Employee Name	Hours Worked	Received Check
Abdullah, Hasim	39.58	*Hasim Abdullah*
Barker, George	40.13	*George Barker*
Choi, April	40.02	*April Choi*
Choi, Jennifer	40.02	*Jennifer Choi*
Choi, Jeremy	40.11	*Jeremy Choi*
Estophan, Ellen	39.68	*Ellen Estophan*
Hernandez, Henry	40.01	*Henry Hernandez*
James, April	40.17	*April James*
Muhammed, Miradije	40.02	*Miradije Muhammed*
Muhibuddin, Bilal	40.09	*Bilal Muhibuddin*
O'Brien, Emily	39.48	*Emily O'Brien*
Palenski, Stella	40.08	*Stella Palenski*
Robinson, Robert	40.09	*Robert Robinson*
Simmons, Summer	40.08	*Mailed on 7/31/06*
Thompson, Tuesday	39.73	*Tuesday Thompson*
Topaz, Tammie	40.33	*Tammie Topaz*
Wei, Willie	40.06	*Willie Wei*

Figure 15.11

The auditor should use the same sample of employees that she used to test the time cards or other time recording device to test whether the employees signed for their payroll checks. The results of the testing should be noted on that worksheet (Figure 15.10). Any discrepancies should be cross referenced to the Discussion Points Worksheet.

Department supervisors should return any payroll checks that were not picked up by the employees to the Pay Master who should store them in a locked file cabinet. If the employee later comes to pick up the payroll check, the Pay Master should obtain the Payroll Check Log from the Payroll Clerk and ask the employee to sign the Payroll Check Log. Unclaimed payroll checks may not be returned to the Payroll Clerk because they could be the result of the Payroll Clerk adding a fictitious employee to the payroll.

The auditor should look through the Payroll Check Log of the test week to see if there are any entries for payroll checks that were not signed. She should ask the Pay Master for the actual payroll checks to ensure that the Pay Master still has them. If there are checks missing, the auditor should ask the Pay Master for an explanation. The auditor can make a copy of any pages of the Payroll Check Log that have entries without signatures. She can index these pages and put them in her workpaper binder. The auditor would use a tick mark to document her examination of payroll checks for entries on the Payroll Check Log without signatures. She should also note any explanations or exceptions on these pages and cross reference the exceptions to the Discussion Points Worksheet.

Manual Payroll Checks

Manual payroll checks should be avoided, whenever possible. If an employee was underpaid a few hours in the current payroll, those hours should normally be added to the following period's payroll, unless delaying the payment of those hours will cause hardship to the employee.

There are situations where manual checks are unavoidable. Some states, i.e. California, require an employer to provide a terminating employee with her final payroll check on the last day of work. It doesn't matter whether the employee is terminating voluntarily or involuntarily. Where an employee was missed when the payroll was keyed into the payroll system, a manual payroll check is required.

The Company should have detailed procedures in place for requesting a manual payroll check. There should be a Manual Payroll Check Request form for the Payroll Clerk to complete. This form should include all information necessary for the Corporate Payroll Department to process the employee's payroll check. Where a restaurant is stand alone, the Manual Payroll Check Request should be the source document for cutting the manual check at the restaurant.

Figure 15.12 is an example of a properly completed Manual Payroll Check Request form. The information on this form is as follows:

Date—Date the Manual Check Request is completed,

Subsidiary—Name of the subsidiary where the employee works,

Location—Name of the location where the employee works,

Date Check Needed—Date the manual check is needed,

Employee Name—Name of the employee for whom the manual check is requested,

Position—Name of the position that the employee is paid to work,

Hourly Rate—Hourly rate that the employee receives for working that position,

Overtime Rate—Rate of pay the employee receives for working overtime (time over 40 hours or however overtime is defined in the State Labor Laws),

Monthly Rate (if salaried)—If the employee is a salaried employee, Annual Salary divided by 12,

Number of Regular Hours—Number of hours to be paid at the regular hourly rate, generally hours up to 40,

Number of Overtime Hours—Number of hours to be paid at the Overtime Rate,

Total Gross Pay—Number of Regular Hours multiplied by Regular Rate plus Number of Overtime multiplied by Overtime Rate,

Reason why manual check is needed—Explanation why the field location needs a manual check for this employee,

Requested by—Signature of the person who requested the manual payroll check,

Date—Date the person requesting the manual payroll check signed the request,

Approved by—Signature of the person who approved the manual payroll check request,

Date—Date the person approving the manual payroll check request approved the request.

Great American Restaurant Company

Manual Check Request Form

Date: *June 15, 2006*

Subsidiary: *Jenny's Café*

Location: *Denver*

Date Check Needed: *June 16, 2006*

Employee Name: *Bobbie Robinson*

Position: *Bartender*

Hourly Rate: *$8.25*

Overtime Rate: *$12.38*

Monthly Rate (if salaried):

Number of Regular Hours: *40*

Number of Overtime Hours: *1.53*

Total Gross Pay: *$348.94*

Reason why manual check is needed:

Time card stuck to the back of the previous employee's time card.
Thus, did not see Bobbie's time card and did not key it.

Requested By:	Approved by:
Bob McCarthy	*Heather Smith*
Date: 6/15/06	Date: 6/15/06

Figure 15.12

When the Payroll Clerk has completed the Manual Payroll Check Request, she brings it to the Controller or General Manager with the documentation of the hours worked for her approval. The Controller or General Manager reviews the information on the Manual Payroll Check Request, compares the hours to the Time Card or other time record, and signs the request. The Payroll Clerk faxes the Manual Payroll Check Request to Corporate by the deadline, i.e. 2:00 p.m. The Controller should receive the manual check via overnight delivery the following morning. The manual check data will be included in the next regular payroll's set of reports, flagged on the Payroll reports as a manual check.

Field locations should not be allowed to cut manual payroll checks even if they have checking accounts for beverage purchases and other special situations (See Chapter 8). Since there are deductions from gross wages for various purposes (taxes, garnishments, miscellaneous, etc.), it is better to control all payroll from Corporate. Once the check has been issued to the employee, it is difficult to recover deductions that the field location did not subtract from gross wages.

Corporate Payroll should be able to turn around a Manual Payroll Check Request in 24 hours if it receives the request by its cutoff time. Upon receipt of the check, the Controller should review the Gross Wages to ensure they are correct and check the deductions for reasonableness. The Controller should manually print the employee's name on the most recent Payroll Check Log, write the number of hours paid next to it, draw a line, and ask the employee to sign for the check.

Alternatively, the Controller can create a separate Manual Check Acknowledgment on her P.C. with the number of hours noted on the acknowledgement and the statement that says the employee received the check and agrees that the number of hours paid are correct. After the employee signs the acknowledgment, the Controller inserts it in the applicable payroll file.

The auditor should select a few manual payroll checks that were cut in the last few months and determine if the proper procedures were followed. Was the Manual Payroll Check Request form properly completed, signed, and approved? Did the employee sign an acknowledgment that she received the payroll check and the number of hours paid were correct?

The auditor should document her work on a workpaper, listing the names of the employees whose manual checks she tested. She should use tick marks to document the audit procedures performed. Any deviations from company procedures should be documented on the workpaper and cross referenced to the Discussion Points Worksheet.

Casual Employees

There are times when employees are needed only for a special event or a limited period of time. There may be an unusually large banquet requiring extra employees or a series of unusually large special events that require extra employees. The General Manager may decide to request employees from a temporary help agency. This is probably the best place to obtain extra help because the personnel are employees of the temporary help agency. As such, the agency pays the employees, handles all deductions, and pays all employer taxes and benefits.

At the end of the week or on the last day temporary help is needed, the temporary help agency employees present the department manager with a time sheet that shows the time started and ended each day, the total hours worked each day and for the week. The department manager signs each person's time sheet and keeps a copy. When the field location receives the invoice from the temporary help agency, the applicable department head approves the invoice, staples the time sheet to the back of the invoice, and sends it to the Accounts Payable Clerk for Accounts Payable processing (See Chapter 8).

As an alternative to using a temporary help agency, the General Manager may decide to hire additional employees for the limited time period. The advantage is that the General Manager does not pay the temporary agency's profit on the service it provides, and the employees wouldn't be eligible for benefits since they are only working for a limited period of time. The disadvantage is finding personnel who are willing to work for a short period of time. Assuming the General Manager is able to find these people, he must hire them as employees of the company even though she considers them to be casual labor. She must put them through the normal hiring procedures (See Chapter 16), and add them to the payroll.

Some General Managers, in an effort to cut costs, find people who are willing to work for a limited period without being added to the payroll if they are paid in cash. The General Manager does not pay employer taxes for the casual labor and the individuals do not pay income taxes. It works well for both sides, but it is illegal. If discovered during a Labor Department audit, the employer will be fined.

The auditor should be on the look out for personnel who worked at the field location but were paid through petty cash or through an on site checking account. She should question any payments made to individuals without adequate receipts or explanations. If the auditor finds these types of transactions, she should document them in her workpapers and cross reference her comments to the Discussion Points Worksheet.

Overtime Paid at Straight Time

For hourly employees, overtime hours worked, i.e. time over 40 hours in a week, must be paid at time and a half. The Federal Labor Laws do not specify when these hours may be worked or how many hours can be worked in a day at the normal hourly rate. The employee can work 16 hours in a day or Saturday and Sunday and still be paid at the normal rate as long as total hours in a week do not exceed 40. Some states have more stringent requirements. Where the State labor laws are more stringent than the Federal laws, the state labor laws supersede the Federal laws. For example, California labor laws require the employer to pay time and a half (hourly rate multiplied by 1.5) for hours worked in a day over 8, up to 12 hours. Hours worked over 12 hours in a day must be paid at double time (hourly rate multiplied by 2). Hourly employees are often referred to as Non-Exempt employees, i.e. non-exempt from overtime pay.

Salaried employees do not need to be paid overtime for hours over 40 in a week. They are often referred to as Exempt employees, i.e. exempt from overtime pay. However, the employer cannot put all his employees on salary and not pay them for overtime worked. To be an Exempt employee, the employee must manage other employees or must be a professional, i.e. Accountant, Lawyer, Human Resource Professional, Marketing Specialist, etc,

To qualify under the *manager exemption*, the employee must meet a duties test and a salary test. The employee's duties must include managing the business or a portion of it and regularly directing the work of two or more employees. In addition, the employee must either (a) be paid at least $250 per week in salary (not an hourly wage), or (b) have the authority to hire, terminate, or promote and be paid at least $155 per week in salary. If either of these conditions applies, the employee may be treated as a manager and thus exempt from overtime. The minimum salary amounts specified are taken from the Federal Fair Labor Standards Act. State laws may require a higher minimum salary.

Whether an employee's duties are sufficient to pass the manager's test is not only a matter of the number of hours spent performing managerial duties compared to other tasks. A court will also review the significance of the employee's managerial duties compared to other responsibilities, how frequently the employee uses discretion in carrying out her tasks, and her independence from supervision. The court evaluated these factors in Dole v. Papa Gino's of America, Inc.

A chain restaurant claimed its lowest-level manager, whose job title was Associate Manager, was an executive position and therefore exempt from overtime pay. The job, an entry-level position, included work that regular crew members do (preparing pizzas, salads, and other food, running the cash register, waiting on customers and cleaning), tasks described by the company as "learning by doing," and studying company manuals to prepare for management tests. Associate managers perform little or no supervision of other employees, are not in charge of a restaurant, and do not supervise shifts. Not surprisingly, the court held that the position of Associate Manager was not an executive position.

Dole v. Papa Gino's of America, Inc., 712 F.Supp.1038 (Mass. 1989)

Some employers make verbal agreements with employees who want to work extra hours. The employee works as many hours as she wishes, i.e. 50, 60, 70 hours, and the employer pays all hours at straight time (normal hourly rate). The employee may have even suggested the arrangement. Everyone benefits. The employee receives extra pay; the employer keeps her payroll costs down. But it is illegal, in violation of Federal and State Labor Laws, and subjects the employer to large fines.

The employee may have been eager to receive the extra pay at the standard hourly rate and may work under this agreement for years. One day, there is a disagreement between the employee and the employer and the employee becomes disgruntled. She goes over to the State Labor Department and tells them that she has been paid hours over 40 at straight time. The State Labor Department sends an investigator to the restaurant, finds the complaint to be true, demands that the employer pay back pay for all the years that the employee worked overtime hours at straight time, and fines the restaurant.

When auditing payroll, the auditor should be aware of the possibility of certain employees working time over 40 hours at straight time, particularly if the location is not audited very often due to its small size. If she finds this situation, the auditor should document the situation in her workpapers and cross reference the comment to the Discussion Points Worksheet.

Productivity

To track the efficiency of Labor, many Companies require the field locations to prepare a Productivity Analysis each day. Sales are summarized by area (Dining Room, Bar, Valet Parking) and compared to the number of employees working in that area. Sales are divided by the number of employees to calculate Sales Per Employee. This statistic is compared to a Company standard to determine whether the restaurant is properly staffed for the amount of sales generated. Low Sales per Employee equates to high labor cost. Thus, if Sales per Employee is low, the restaurant should be reducing the number of employees working to bring productivity closer to standard.

Of course, there is a minimum number of employees required to operate the restaurant. Once this level is reached, the General Manager cannot provide the required service with fewer employees. If a restaurant is consistently at this level of staffing and cannot meet Company productivity standards, senior management may consider permanently closing the restaurant because it is losing money.

Figure 15.13 is an example of a Productivity Report that was completed for July 14, 2006 for Denver Restaurant. It is divided into four sections: Dining Room, Bar, Valet Parking, and Total Restaurant. Each section has the sales generated by that area and the number of employees working in that area, broken down by position. For example, the bar generated $10,000 in sales (does not include sales tax) and there were 7 employees working in the bar over two shifts: 3 bartenders, 2 cocktail waitresses, 1 cleaner, and 1 bar manager. The $10,000 in sales was divided by the 7 employees to calculate $1,429 in Sales per Employee. When compared to the Company standard of $1,400 per employee, it is $29 favorable to the Company standard.

When looking at the Dining Room, Denver Restaurant is $112 unfavorable to standard. This statistic indicates that Dining Room staffing is too high and should be reduced to bring the staffing level in line with standard. Likewise, in Valet Parking, Revenues per Employee of $226 is $74 below the standard of $300. Thus, staffing should be reduced, or revenues increased by tightening the Valet Parking controls (See Valet Parking in Chapter 11) so all revenues collected are turned in to the Cash Room. When reviewing the overall productivity, Sales per Employee of $423 is well below the Company standard of $525. Since the variance from standard is so large, reducing staffing in operations may not be sufficient to bring overall productivity in line with the Company standard. Overhead also appears to be overstaffed. The General Manager should look at these areas to see if some staffing can be reduced to bring Sales per Employee for the entire restaurant in line with the Company standard of $525.

Jenny's Café, Inc.
Denver Restaurant
Productivity Analysis
July 14, 2006

Dining Room Sales		Bar Sales:		Valet Parking:		Total Restaurant:	
Food	$20,810	Liquor	$ 4,120	Valet Parking	$ 903	Food	$20,810
Liquor	$ 826	Wine	$ 858			Liquor	$ 4,946
Wine	$ 4,023	Beer	$ 5,022			Wine	$ 4,881
Beer	$ 701	Total	$10,000	Total V. Parking	$ 903	Beer	$ 5,723
Total	$26,360					Valet Parking	$ 903
						Total	$37,263

Dining Room Staffing:		Bar Staffing:		Attendants	3		
Wait Staff	20	Bartenders	3	Supervisor	1		
Head Wait	2	Cocktail Wait	2		4	Total Staffing:	
Bussers	10	Cleaner	1			Dining Room	36
Cashiers	2	Manager	1			Kitchen	18
Manager	2	Total Bar	7			Bar	7
Total D.R.	36					Valet Parking	4
						Total Oper.	65

Kitchen Staffing:							
Cooks	6					Warehouse	
Salad	2					Manager	1
Dessert	2					Clerk	1
Dishwasher	4					Receivers	4
Cleaner	2					Total Whse	6
Exec Chef	1						
Sous Chef	1					Linen Room:	
Total Kitchen	18					Attendants	2
						Supervisor	1
Total	54					Total L.Rm.	3

		Cash Room:	
		Attendants	2
		Manager	1
		Total C.Rm	3
		Maintenance	2
		Office:	
		Accounting	4
		Human Res.	3
		Marketing	1
		General Mgr	1
		Total Office	9
		Total Staffing	88

Sales per Empl	$ 488	Sales per Empl	$ 1,429	Rev. per Empl	$ 226	Sales per Empl	$ 423
Company Std	$ 600	Company Std	$ 1,400	Company Std	$ 300	Company Std	$ 525
Over (Under)	$ (112)	Over (Under)	$ 29	Over (Under)	$ (74)	Over (Under)	$ (102)

Heather Smith
7/15/2006

Figure 15.13

The Sales Reporting Clerk completes the Productivity Analysis each day on an Excel spreadsheet. After the Controller reviews, signs, and dates the report, the Sales Reporting Clerk keys it into the statistical system. Corporate produces statistical reports that summarize productivity for the month and issues them to Senior Executives. The Regional Vice President of Operations uses these reports to determine whether payroll is in line with Company standards at each operation.

The auditor should test a few days of Productivity Analysis by tying the sales to the Daily Sales Journal and the number of employees working that day to the payroll records. She should make a copy of the Productivity Analysis for the days tested and use tick marks to document the audit work performed. Any errors in sales or number of employees reported on the Productivity Analysis should be documented in the workpapers and cross referenced to the Discussion Points Worksheet.

If the field location consistently fails to meet Company productivity standards, the auditor should document this concern in the workpapers and cross reference the comment to the Discussion Points Worksheet. This is one of those areas where the auditor can help make the field location more profitable by pointing out that reducing staffing would bring the restaurant in line with Company standards and reduce excessive payroll costs.

Payout

A Payout is an audit procedure where the auditor intercepts the payroll checks going to the field location and personally distributes them. This tends to be a very time consuming process and is generally not done in a typical audit. The payout is normally performed when management suspects that there are ghosts on the payroll, i.e. fictitious employee names have been added to the payroll with fictitious hours and someone is cashing these checks.

When a Payout is performed, the auditor makes arrangements to obtain the payroll checks from the Payroll Department on Wednesday afternoon. The auditor travels to the city where the field location is located on Wednesday night or Thursday morning with the payroll checks. After introducing herself to the General Manager, the auditor advises the General Manager and Controller that she has the payroll checks and will be personally distributing them to the employees on Friday. The Controller can run payroll reports as usual and perform her normal review to ensure all payroll checks are correct. On Thursday, the General Manager should advise the employees that they will need to bring photo ID on Friday to pick up their payroll checks.

The auditor should not let the payroll checks out of her sight. If the Company prints Payroll Check Logs for the employees to sign, the auditor uses them to document the checks that were distributed. Where Payroll Check Logs are not printed, the auditor must design her own Payout Log and list every employee for whom she has a payroll check.

On Friday afternoon, the auditor sets up a payroll check pick up station where she has the payroll checks and the Payout Log. Each employee presents photo ID to pick up her payroll check. The auditor should look at the photo carefully to ensure it is a photo of the person picking up the payroll check. She looks at the name on the photo ID and finds the payroll check. The employee signs the Payout Log and the auditor gives her the payroll check. Each employee must personally pick up her payroll check. She cannot send a friend of a relative with her photo ID.

Figure 15.14 is an example of one page of a Payout Log. It contains the following information:

Employee Name—Name of the employee signing for a payroll check,

Check Number—Check number of the payroll check,

Received Check—Signature of the employee receiving the check,

Comments—Comments the auditor has concerning how checks were distributed.

At the end of the audit, the auditor takes any remaining payroll checks back to Corporate. She obtains a copy of the initial Employee Maintenance form that was completed when the employee was hired and any address changes. Once back at Corporate, the auditor sends a letter to the employee, with a stamped return addressed envelope, at the last address via certified mail. The letter should advise the employee that the payroll check is at Corporate. It should request the employee to send a photocopy of photo ID and sign on the line at the bottom of the letter, and return it in the envelope.

Jenny's Café, Inc.
Denver Restaurant
Payout Log
Week Ending July 15, 2006

M4
AS
8/15/06

Dining Room

Employee Name	Check No.	Received Check	Comments
Abdullah, Hasim	245290	*Hasim Abdullah*	
Barker, George	245291	*George Barker*	
Choi, April	245292	*April Choi*	
Choi, Jennifer	245293	*Jennifer Choi*	
Choi, Jeremy	245294	*Jeremy Choi*	
Estophan, Ellen	245295	*Ellen Estophan*	
Hernandez, Henry	245296	*Henry Hernandez*	
James, April	245297	*April James*	
Muhammed, Miradije	245298	*Miradije Muhammed*	
Muhibuddin, Bilal	245299	*Bilal Muhibuddin*	
O'Brien, Emily	245300	*Emily O'Brien*	
Palenski, Stella	245301	*Stella Palenski*	
Robinson, Robert	245302	*Robert Robinson*	
Simmons, Summer	245303		*Mailed letter on 8/7/06. Received reply on 8/15/06. Examined copy of driver's license. Signature on letter matched Employee Maintenance form completed upon hiring. Mailed check on 8/15/06 AS*
Thompson, Tuesday	245304	*Tuesday Thompson*	
Topaz, Tammie	245305	*Tammie Topaz*	
Wei, Willie	245306	*Willie Wei*	

Basis of Selection: Selected every payroll check for the payout.

Conclusion: All employees who received payroll checks appear to be legitimate employees.

Figure 15.14

Figure 15.15 is an example of a letter that Aimee sent to an employee who did not pick up her payroll check while she was at the Denver Restaurant. In the letter, Aimee asks the employee to sign on the line at the bottom of the letter and to return the letter with a photocopy of her photo ID. Upon receipt of the letter from the employee, the auditor matches the signature at the bottom of the letter to the initial Employee Maintenance form completed when the employee was hired. If the signatures match, she mails the payroll check to the employee. Often the certified letter is returned and marked "undeliverable."

When the Payout has been completed, the auditor reports the results of the payout in the audit report or in a separate memo to senior management.

Summary

The person inputting payroll should not handle the payroll checks. Department managers should calculate the number of hours worked from the Time Cards or Sign In/Sign Out sheets. The person inputting hours and performing master file maintenance should not be performing Human Resources functions. The Payroll Clerk should not cut manual checks. The auditor should review the duties of the different parties to determine whether duties have been properly segregated.

When using Sign In/Sign Out sheets for documenting hours worked, each employee should print her name, sign her name, and write the time in and time out. The Department Manager calculates the time worked for each employee. If time clocks are used, employees must clock in and out. Where time keeping systems are used, the employees swipe their ID cards when clocking in and again when clocking out. The auditor should watch out for employees signing in, clocking in, or swiping ID cards for other employees.

Jenny's Café, Inc.
One Great American Drive
Buffalo, New York 14214

Ms. Summer Simmons
375 Chestnut Street
Denver, Colorado 80216

August 7, 2006

Dear Ms. Simmons:

Jenny's Café's Internal Audit Department has conducted payroll audit tests at its Denver location whereby it distributed payroll checks for the Week Ending July 15, 2006 to all employees upon presentation of photo ID.

Since you were not working at Jenny's Café during the two week period that we were at the Denver location (July 24–August 4), and did not come to the restaurant to pick up your payroll check, we have it in our Buffalo New York Corporate Office.

Please sign on the line below and return this letter and a photocopy of your photo ID in the enclosed stamped envelope. Upon receipt of the signed letter and photocopy of your photo ID, we will send your payroll check to the above address.

Sincerely,
Jenny's Café, Inc.
Aimee Stone
Senior Auditor

Please sign on the line below:

_____
Summer Simmons

Figure 15.15

Department managers must calculate hours worked from the time cards and initial the time cards. Employees must sign an acknowledgment that the time paid through the payroll check is correct. The auditor should take a sample of employees worked during the test period to determine whether proper signatures and initials appear on the time cards.

All manual adjustments to time cards must be initialed by the Department Manager. The auditor should determine whether manual adjustments on time cards were properly approved.

Time keeping systems print a daily report of time in and out and the total hours worked, printed by department. Department managers should review the department report daily, make any adjustments to the report, and initial the adjustments. Upon receipt of the signed reports, the Payroll Clerk enters the adjustments into the time keeping system. The auditor should review the adjustment reports and determine whether proper initials and signatures appear on these reports.

The Payroll Clerk keys the data from Employee Maintenance forms, i.e. additions, deletions, and changes to the employee master files. She inputs the calculated hours worked for each employee off the Sign In/Sign Out sheets, time cards, or time keeping reports. The Payroll Clerk also keys wage adjustments, employee meals, charge tips, cash tips, and deductions from appropriate source documents. The auditor compares the Wage and Hour Report totals to supporting documentation, looks for evidence that the Controller checked the accuracy of the Wage and Hour Report, i.e. checking off the appropriate numbers, and looks for her signature and date.

The Federal minimum wage for tipped employees is $2.13 per hour, provided the employee reports sufficient tips to bring her up to the Federal minimum wage of $5.15 ($5.85—effective July 24, 2007, $6.55—effective July 24, 2008, $7.25—effective July 24, 2009), or the State minimum wage, whichever is higher. The Payroll Clerk needs to check all sub-minimum wage employees to ensure that wages plus tips plus the cost of employee meals exceed the applicable minimum wage. The auditor should take a sample of sub-minimum wage waiters and waitresses and determine whether the employer paid the difference to the employees as additional wages.

Payroll reports typically include a Payroll Register, Employee Maintenance Report, and some type of High Dollar Report. The auditor should review the reports for a month and determine whether the General Manager or Controller signed and dated the reports.

The restaurant should have a Payroll Check Log where each employee signs for her payroll check when she receives it. The auditor should select a sample of employees from the Payroll Register and determine whether the employees signed for their payroll checks.

Manual payroll checks should only be issued in the case where any employee will not otherwise receive a payroll check, an employee will suffer hardship if an error is not corrected in the current week, or the employee is terminated in a State that requires employers to give terminating employees their payroll checks on the last day of work. Manual payroll checks should only be cut from the Corporate office.

All personnel working at the field location must be on the payroll or must be employees of a temporary agency. The auditor should be on the lookout for personnel working at the location who were paid through petty cash or the onsite checking account.

Productivity is the measurement of sales per employee, compared to a company standard. It is used to determine whether an operation is properly staffed for the amount of sales generated. Where a productivity analysis is performed, the auditor should test several events by tying the sales per the Productivity Analysis to the Daily Sales Journal and the number of employees who worked per the Productivity Analysis to the payroll records.

Discussion Questions and Case Studies

1. Why should the Department Manager initial manual entries made on the time cards? What does the Department Manager's initials next to the total hours on the time card indicate?
2. Why should the employee sign the time card or some other acknowledgement that the hours paid are correct?
3. What is the minimum wage for tipped employees? What happens if the hourly wages plus declared tips plus the cost of employee meals do not equal the minimum wage? What happens when the State minimum wage is higher than the Federal minimum wage?
4. What type of information appears on the Payroll Register? What type of information appears on the Employee Maintenance Report? What type of information appears on the High Dollar Report? What is the purpose of the High Dollar Report?
5. In what situations should manual payroll checks be issued? Describe manual payroll check procedures that represent strong internal control.
6. You are auditing payroll at the Lone Hombre Bar and Grill. In reviewing the time cards, you notice that every once in a while, there is a manual time

in or time out written on a time card, but you don't see any initials next to the entry. There is no indication of the time card being approved and no employee signature on the time card. When you ask Lidia Chen, the Controller, for the Payroll Check Log where the employees sign for their payroll checks, Lidia asks, "What's a Payroll Check Log? Gina, my Payroll Clerk separates the payroll checks by department and gives them to the department managers for distribution. The department managers hand the employees their payroll checks. Any left over checks come back to Gina, who holds them until the employee comes to pick up her check." Do you have any audit issues? What are your recommendations to management?

7. You are auditing payroll at Grandma's Kitchen. The location has a time keeping system where the employees swipe their ID cards when they clock in, when they clock out for lunch, when they clock back in after lunch, and when they clock out to go home. You ask Franklin Joseph, the Controller, for the time keeping reports that are printed off the system. He hands you the Wage and Hour Reports. When you ask again for the Daily Time Worked Report and the Weekly Time Summary, Franklin replies, "Oh, those reports! Once we key the information from them, we throw them out. The information is all in the Wage and Hour Reports anyway. I don't want to clutter my files with a lot of duplicate paperwork." Do you have any audit issues? What are your recommendations to management?

8. You are auditing Connie's Mexican Cantina. While counting the operating fund, you see completed petty cash vouchers for the following cash payments:

> May 5, 2006 Carlos Garcia $100,
> May 5, 2006 Juan Hernandez $100,
> May 5, 2006 Raul Reyna $100,
> May 5, 2006 Fernando Paloma $100,
> May 5, 2006 Jorge Jimenez $100,
> May 5, 2006 Jose Alvarado $100,
> May 5, 2006 Lorenzo Lopez $100,
> May 5, 2006 Vidal Padilla $100.

You ask Consuela Martinez, the General Manager, why these payments were made. Consuela answers, "Cinco deMayo is such a huge day for us that we cannot handle the volume with our normal staff. I get a few friends to help out for that one day and pay them $100 in cash. It is not worthwhile to put them on the payroll for the one day and take them off again. I pay them out of petty cash and code the reimbursement as Temporary Labor. My friends are happy because they don't have to report the $100 as income, I am happy because I have the help I need, and Corporate is happy because I cut costs by not having to pay payroll taxes. It's a win/win for all sides!" Do you have any audit issues? What are your recommendations to management?

9. You are auditing Bronco Buck's Texas Barbeque. While looking through the Payroll Register for week ending August 19, 2006, you see the following entries:

Name	Pay Rate	Reg Hrs	O/T Hrs	Gross Pay
Adams, Joe	$7.75	70	0	$ 542.50
Cheng, Charlie	$7.50	65	0	$ 487.50
Ledesma, Larry	$7.65	75	0	$ 573.75
Taylor, Willie	$7.40	60	0	$ 444.00

You ask Mike Davidson, the General Manager, why he isn't paying these employees time and a half for the hours worked over 40 in a week. Mike replies, "About six months ago, Joe, Charlie, Larry, and Willie came into my office and said, 'We can't make any money just working 40 hours a week. We know that Corporate will scream if you pay us for overtime so we've got a proposition. You let us work all the hours we want and just pay us straight time. That way, we'll make extra money and you can keep your payroll costs in line.' I could see they were four really motivated guys and I said 'sure, why not?' I like helping out a group of eager beavers like them!" Do you have any audit issues? Explain your answer.

10. You are auditing Francois's French Delights. Corporate management asked you to perform a payout because they suspected there might be some fictitious employees on the payroll. While at the restaurant, you asked employees to present photo identification and sign your Payout Log to receive their payroll checks. You are now back at Corporate Headquarters with 5 payroll checks that no one claimed while you were at the restaurant. When you asked Cathy Carlisle, the Controller, about these employees, she said all five had just left on vacation and will be back in a month. What do you do now?

CHAPTER 16
AUDITING HUMAN RESOURCES

Learning Objectives
After reading this chapter, you should be able to:
1. Know what type of information is required when hiring an employee and the documentation that should be in each Human Resources folder,
2. Review I9 documentation and know whether all Department of Immigration and Naturalization Service requirements have been met,
3. Obtain information on the State's Child Labor Laws and know how to audit the field location for compliance to these laws.
4. Examine the Federal and State posters that are posted at the field location and know whether the postings comply with all Federal and State Department of Labor laws,
5. Determine whether employee discipline is consistently applied in cases of employee violations of Company policies.

Overview
Restaurants are part of the service industry. As such, Human Resources play a major role in the success of the restaurant. The Company depends on people to buy the food, receive and store the food, prepare the food, and serve it to customers. To be successful, management must hire competent people, train these people, compensate them fairly, and manage them adequately. As there are books on the market that discuss how to manage Human Resources, we cannot condense Human Resources management into one chapter. As such, our focus will be on Human Resources from an internal control perspective and compliance to company policies and governmental regulations.

Each employee should have a Human Resources folder that contains information about the employee, including his history of employment with the company. We will discuss what should be in each employee's Human Resources folder and how the auditor determines whether the folders of the employees selected are complete.

137

When an employee is hired, an Employee Maintenance form is completed with the new hire information. We will look at the type of information that most employers request, including information required by Federal agencies, and the types of approvals needed.

To foster a drug free environment, many employers require prospective employees to be drug tested. We will examine how this process works, the type of documentation needed, and the auditor's role in ensuring the field location is in compliance with Company policy.

The Immigration and Naturalization Service (INS) requires employers to hire only those people who are eligible to work in the United States. Severe penalties can he levied on employers who hire people who are not eligible to work in this country, or do not obtain proper documentation from prospective employees. We will examine the INS requirements, the best way to ensure compliance, and how the auditor audits I9 documentation to ensure the field location is in compliance.

As part of performing their jobs, employees are often assigned company property for use while working for the Company, i.e. company ID card, uniform, keys, laptop computer, cell phone, palm pilot, black berry, etc. The employee is entitled to vacation pay, possibly severance pay, and the option to continue certain benefits at the employee's expense. We will look at how the employer ensures that all company property is returned and all employer obligations are met.

Child Labor Laws are unique to each state but generally restrict the number of hours that a child can work and the hours when a child is allowed to work. Severe penalties can be levied for violations of the State's Child Labor Laws. We will examine Child Labor Laws and how the auditor selects minor employees and tests them to ensure the field location is in compliance.

Courts have held restaurants that serve alcoholic beverages liable for a customer involved in an automobile accident while intoxicated. Insurance premiums for establishments that serve alcohol have sky rocketed as a result. Thus, it is imperative for a large company to have an Alcohol Service Training program in place that emphasizes responsible drinking, teaches employees to recognize when a patron becomes intoxicated, and trains them to handle the situation. We will look at how the auditor ensures that the field location has an effective Alcohol Service Training program that ensures all alcohol service employees are properly trained.

Federal and State Labor Departments require the employer to display required posters in a place frequented by its employees. OSHA has reporting requirements for certain workplace injuries. We will examine these requirements and discuss how the auditor ensures that the field location is in compliance with these requirements.

Companies penalize their employees for cash variances (overages and shortages) and violations of Company policies. We will discuss how progressive discipline is administered and how the auditor determines whether it is administered consistently.

In Practice

Aimee Stone walks over to the office of Emily Nguyen, the Manager of Human Resources.

"Here are the employee files you requested," Emily says.

"What about the I9 files?" Aimee asks.

"The I9's and supporting documentation are in the employee folders," Emily replies.

"There should be a separate I9 binder that contains all I9's with attached copies of the ID's that support them. If the INS comes to audit I9's, you don't want to hand them any more documentation than they require. You don't want them looking through other documentation you maintain on each employee. They may find something they weren't originally looking for."

Aimee walks over to her desk. She begins her audit of I9's by looking through each employee folder and reviewing the I9 and copies of the supporting documentation. After completing her I9 audit and review of the employee files, she sets up a meeting with Emily Nguyen for later that day. At the meeting, Aimee gives Emily a copy of the workpaper that shows the exceptions she found during her audit. Aimee talks about the I9 exceptions.

"Emily, I tested 24 I9's and found that half of them do not meet the INS requirements and would be flagged if the INS were to conduct such an audit. Each violation is subject to a $10,000 fine. Let's go over them."

"I didn't realize the I9's were such a big deal," Emily says, although I thought we were doing them correctly."

"Roberta Robinson's I9 does not have the attest section completed where she declares she is a US citizen, registered alien, or an alien eligible to work.

"Hasim Abdullah is in the United States on a student visa. It says right on his Social Security card that supports the I9, 'Not eligible for work.' We need to terminate his employment immediately.

"George Barker's I9 has a copy of his driver's license and social security card attached but they were not listed in the Employer Review and Verification section of the I9.

"April, Jennifer, and Jeremy Choi were hired on the same day, but the

Employer Certification was not completed for any of them.

"In the attest section, Miradije Muhammed checked that he is a registered alien but his Alien registration number was not entered on the form."

"Also, in the attest section, Bilal Muhibuddin checked that he is an alien authorized to work but did not note the work permit expiration date.

"James Jones and Donna Wozniak are over-documented. The List A, List B, and List C columns were all completed on the I9. The INS requires that only a List A item be noted on the I9 or a List B and a List C item. As far as the INS is concerned, over-documentation can be seen as discriminatory and is as bad as under-documentation.

"William Wei was hired on January 23 but the employer certification on the I9 was dated February 5. The employer must certify the I9 within 3 days of hire."

"Tammie Topaz's social security number was copied incorrectly on the I9. The copy of her social security card shows her social security number to be 128-42-7926. On the I9, it is noted as 128-24-7926."

"Many of these I9's were verified by Doreen Sanders, my assistant," Emily said. *I thought she knew what she was doing."*

"When an employee is hired and the paperwork is completed, a second person should be reviewing the paperwork to ensure it was completed properly before it is filed," Aimee said. *"That should be you, Emily."*

Segregation of Duties

Payroll and Human Resources should be separated. The Payroll Clerk should report to the Controller and the Human Resources person should report to the General Manager. The person hiring new employees should not be paying them. If possible, the Human Resources Department should perform file maintenance to the employee master file in the Human Resources system. This system should automatically update the payroll master file so that the Payroll Clerk cannot perform maintenance to the employee master file.

If there is no separate Human Resources system that links to the Payroll system, the Human Resources Department should complete the paperwork to hire the employee, obtain all required signatures and bring the paperwork to the Payroll Clerk to be keyed.

The Human Resources Manager should be the approver on the Employee Maintenance Form (EMF), not the Human Resources Clerk. If there is no Human Resources Manager, the General Manager should be the second approver on the Employee Maintenance Form that hires the employee. The Employee Maintenance Report should be printed by the Controller or General Manager who should compare all entries on the report to the signed EMF's.

The auditor should review the duties of the various participants to determine whether the duties are properly segregated. Any segregation of duties concerns should be documented in the Internal Control Questionnaire and cross referenced to the Discussion Points worksheet.

Human Resources Files

There should be a separate Human Resources folder for each employee. Each Human Resources folder should contain the completed employment application and resume. Generally, resumes are only required for salaried positions. There should be room on the employment application for the applicant to list prior jobs he has held and a contact at each former employer. Human Resources should contact each former employer to determine whether the employee had a satisfactory relationship.

Whenever someone from the Human Resources Department contacts an outside source regarding an inquiry about an applicant or a reference, he should complete an Applicant Inquiry form where the questions asked and the answers received are documented. It should also document the name of the applicant, the position for which he is applying, the date of the telephone call, the Human Resources person making the telephone call, and his signature.

The completed Employee Maintenance Form (EMF) with required signatures to hire the employee should be in the employee folder along with properly approved EMF forms for status changes, such as change of address, new pay rate, promotion, termination, etc. (See Employee Maintenance Forms below).

Where the Company requires employees to be drug tested, the completed Drug Test Consent and Release form with applicable signatures is put in the employee's Human Resources file. Drug testing is discussed in greater detail in the Drug Testing section (below).

The Federal government requires every employee to have a current W-4 form on file with the employer. On this form, the employee claims the number of tax exemptions the employee is entitled to receive. The number of tax exemptions claimed determines how much in federal and state taxes will be withheld from the employee's payroll check. On the back of the W-4 are instructions that help the employee determine how many exemptions he may claim. The larger the number of exemptions claimed the less in taxes is withheld. However, if the employee claims a lot of tax exemptions, it does not mean he will pay less in taxes.

When the employee files his tax return at year end, he calculates taxes due based on his income and legal exemptions, not on what he claimed on his W-4.

If not enough taxes were withheld from his payroll checks, he will need to pay the amount of taxes due plus any penalties and interest, if applicable. Thus, it is to the employee's benefit to make sure the number of exemptions claimed is correct.

Some employers have various certifications that the employee signs that are kept in the Human Resources folder. If the Company has an Employee Handbook, there is often a tear out page at the end of the book that the employee signs and turns in to the Human Resources Department. The certification states that the employee has read the Employee Handbook and agrees to abide by all the rules and regulations stipulated in the Employee Handbook. Alcohol serving employees may sign a certification stating that they have been trained in Alcohol Awareness and understood the training. Cash Handlers may sign a certification stating that they agree to various rules regarding the handling of cash.

Some employees are disciplined for various infractions. The details of the infractions and disciplinary action are documented on a Record of Employee Counseling that is signed by the supervisor and the employee being disciplined. Completed Records of Employee Counseling are kept in the Human Resources folder. We will discuss more about the Record of Employee Counseling in the sections on Employee Discipline later in this chapter.

The auditor should select a sample of employees and determine whether the employees have folders and whether each folder has the required documentation signed by the applicable personnel. In the Documenting Payroll Testing section of this chapter, we will discuss how the documentation is accomplished.

Security

Employee files contain confidential information, such as pay rates, social security numbers, home telephone numbers, etc. that should not be available to anyone who enters the field location's office. As such, all employee files must be locked in a file cabinet whenever the Human Resources personnel leave the area. They should not be left lying on a desk while the Human Resources person takes a break or goes to lunch. If Human Resources is located in a separate office, the Human Resources person can lock the office door when leaving the room. Otherwise, the files must be put in a desk drawer or file cabinet and locked whenever the Human Resources person leaves.

At night, the employee files must be locked in a locked file cabinet. Preferably, the locked file cabinet is kept in a separate room that can be locked. If this is not possible, the field location office should be locked when the last office person leaves for the day.

Through observations and direct questioning of the Human Resources personnel, the auditor should determine whether security over the Human Resources files is adequate. Using the Internal Control Questionnaire (ICQ), the auditor can ask the Human Resources Manager how the files are secured. He should document the Human Resources Manager's comments on the ICQ.

As the auditor performs his work, he should verify the Human Resources Manager's answers by observing the way the Human Resources people handle the employee files. Do they lock the Human Resources room when they leave? Do they return all employee files to the file cabinet and lock it at night? The auditor should document any exceptions on the ICQ and cross reference them to the Discussion Points Worksheet.

Employee Maintenance Forms

The Employee Maintenance Form (EMF) is the form that is used to update the Employee Master Files in the Payroll System. It can be used for adding a new employee, deleting a terminated employee, or changing information for a particular employee, such as address changes, pay rate, marital status, etc.

For a New Hire, the Human Resources Clerk completes the EMF from the information obtained on the Employment Application, and other information that the employee supplies on the first day of work. When a New Hire reports for work on his first day, he is ushered to the Human Resources Department to complete all paperwork. The Human Resources Clerk will have already completed whatever information was available on the Employment Application, but there is other required information that the employee must supply.

When the EMF is completed, the employee signs the form. The Human Resources Clerk brings the form over to the employee's department manager for his signature. Once the hiring manager has signed the EMF, the Human Resources Clerk brings the form to the Manager of Human Resources or the General Manager for the second signature. Each EMF must have the employee's signature and the signatures of two managers, one of whom should be the hiring manager. This requirement ensures that at least two people are aware of the New Hire added to the Payroll.

Figure 16.1 is an example of a properly completed EMF. It provides the following information.

Company Code—Code that identifies the field location in the Human Resources and Payroll systems,
Subsidiary—Name of the subsidiary to which the field location belongs,
Effective Date—Date the information on the EMF becomes effective,

143

Employee Number—Number that identifies the employee in the Human Resources and Payroll systems,

Social Security Number—Employee's Social Security Number,

Home Department Number—Number that identifies the employee's home department in the Human Resources, Payroll, and General Ledger systems,

Home Department Name—Name of the Profit Center or Cost Center.

Add, Change, Delete—Type of action this form will be used to accomplish—Write "A" to Add a new employee, "C" to Change the status or some information for an existing employee, or "D" to Delete an employee from the Human Resources and Payroll systems,

Employee Name, Last, First, Middle—Employee's last name, first name, and middle name,

Address—Street address where the employee resides,

City, State, Zip—City, State, Zip Code of the street address where the employee resides,

Home Phone—Telephone number of the employee's home,

Cell Phone—Telephone number of the employee's cell phone,

Other Phone—Other telephone number where the employee can be reached,

New Hire, Terminate, Other Action—Write "N" if this employee is a New Hire, write "T" if the employee is to be terminated, or Write "O" for any changes to the employee's master file,

Position—Name of the position the employee has at the field location, i.e. Waitress, Bartender, Cook, etc.

Job Code—Number that identifies the position in the Human Resources and Payroll systems,

Pay Rate—Amount of pay the employee receives per hour, if hourly, or annually, if salaried,

Hourly—Enter "H" if the employee is paid hourly—otherwise leave blank,

Salaried—Enter "S" if the employee is a salaried employee—otherwise leave blank,

Full Time—Enter "F" if the employee meets the Company's definition or Full Time Employee, i.e. 35 or more hours worked per week—otherwise leave blank,

Part Time—Enter "P" if the employee does not meet the Company's definition of a Full Time Employee, i.e. works less 35 hours per week—otherwise leave blank,

Birthday—Date the employee was born,

I9 Expiration Date—Date the temporary Alien Registration expires, if applicable,

Emergency Contact Name—Name of person that the employee would like the Company to contact in case of an emergency,

Address—Residence of the emergency contact,

City, State, Zip—Residence city, state, and zip code of the emergency contact,

Relationship—Relationship of the emergency contact to the employee,

Telephone Number—Telephone number where the emergency contact can be reached,

Ethnic Group—For Equal Employment Opportunity Commission statistical purposes, mark the box that the employee believes describes his ethnic background,

I9 Status—From the I9 the employee completed, mark the box that the employee marked on the I9—for temporary aliens, enter the I9 expiration date and the Alien Registration Number,

Notes—Write any notes regarding the employee, such as in a termination, the reason for termination,

Military Status—Military Status, i.e. Veteran,

Tipped Status—Tipped or Non-Tipped,

Federal, State Marital Status—For Tax Purposes, Single, Married, Head of Household, Married Filing Separately, per the W-4,

Withholding Allowances—Number of allowances claimed on the W-4,

Additional Withholding—Additional dollar amount to be withheld from wages for tax purposes,

Worked State—State where the employee works,

Employee Signature and Date—Signature of the employee and the date signed,

First Manager's Signature and Date—Signature of the first manager (to whom the employee reports) and date signed,

Second Manager's Signature and Date—Signature of the second manager (Human Resources Manager or General Manager) and date signed.

Utilizing the sample of employees selected for Human Resources testing, the auditor should review the EMF for these employees to determine whether they were properly completed, and signed and dated by the employee and two managers. Any exceptions should be noted on the worksheet and cross referenced to the Discussion Points worksheet.

GARC
Great American Restaurant Company
Employee Maintenance Form (EMF)

Co. Code: JCDEN	Subsidiary:	Jenny's Café, Inc.		Effective Date:	3/6/06
Employee No.	13894	Social Security Number:		459-82-3679	
Home Dept. No.	3301010	Home Department Name:		JC Denver Dining Room	

Add (A) Change (C) Delete (D) A	Employee Name Last, First, Middle	Choi, April Mae	Home Phone:	303-789-3309
	Address:	37 Acorn Drive	Cell Phone:	303-597-1854
	City, State, Zip	Denver, Colorado 80207	Other Phone:	

New Hire (N) Terminate (T) Other Action (O) N	Position:	Waitress	Pay Rate:	$2.13
	Job Code: 1706		Hourly (H)	H
Emergency Contact: Name	Mary Choi		Salaried (S)	
Address:	37 Acorn Drive		Full Time (F)	F
City, State, Zip	Denver, Colorado 80207		Part Time (P)	
Relationship:	Mother		Birthday:	2/11/79
Telephone No.	303-789-3309		I9 Expiration Date:	3/15/10

Ethnic Group:	I9 Status		Military Status:	N/A
☐ White	☐ US Citizen/Naturalized		Tipped Status:	Tipped
☐ Hispanic/Latino	☐ Alien Permanent		Federal/State	
☐ American Indian/Alaska Native	☒ Alien Temporary		Marital Status	Single
☐ Native Hawaiian/Other Pac Island	Expiration Date:	3/15/10	W/H Allow.	1
☐ Black/African American	Alien Admission #:	R5860639	Additional W/H	N/A
☒ Asian			Worked State	Colorado

Notes:

Employee Signature:	*April M. Choi*	Date:	3/6/06
First Manager's Signature:	*Linda Barton*	Date:	3/6/06
Second Manager's Signature:	*Joey Robertson*	Date:	3/6/06
Completed By: *Doreen Sanders*	Keyed By: *Bob McCarthy*	Date:	3/7/06

Figure 16.1

Pay Rates

When the Human Resources Manager makes an offer of employment, he will quote the Pay Rate that has previously been determined for that position. If there is a union representing the employee, the Rate of Pay is specified in the union contract. Every employee working that position is paid the same rate. Where there is no union contract, there may be some flexibility in wage offers that vary on the amount of experience the applicant had with other employers. Whatever the policy is, the Human Resources Manager makes an offer with a pay rate that the General Manager has approved.

Where the employee has agreed to the employment offer, the Human Resources Department prepares the Employee Maintenance Form (EMF) for the New Hire with the Pay Rate that the new employee will receive. Once the EMF has been completed, the employee is asked to sign it, verifying the Pay Rate that will be used in paying the employee. The hiring manager and a second manager (can be the Human Resources Manager) should also sign the EMF, verifying their agreement with the Pay Rate.

When an employee's Pay Rate is changed, the Human Resources Department completes an EMF for every employee affected by the rate change. The Human Resources Clerk only completes the information required to enter the new rate in the Human Resources and/or Payroll System, i.e. Company Code, Subsidiary, Effective Date, Employee Number, Home Department Number and Name, Change Code (C), Employee Name, Position, and Pay Rate. The EMF is signed by the employee, and two managers.

Where a blanket increase affects all employees, such as with a rate increase stipulated in the union contract, the rate change can be documented with a memo written by the General Manager that lists the old rate and new rate for each union position and the effective date of the new rates. The General Manager signs the memo, and the Human Resources Clerk inserts a copy into the employee file of each affected employee. The Human Resources Clerk should put together a list of employees affected by the blanket increase that lists each employee's Name, Employee ID, Position, Old Rate, and New Rate. Using the list, the Payroll Clerk makes the maintenance changes to the applicable Payroll Master Files.

Utilizing the sample of employees the auditor has selected for Human Resources testing, the auditor should tie the wage rates on the EMF's to the union contract rates to ensure they are correct. He should also check to see that each employee folder has an EMF with the current Pay Rate that was signed by the employee and two managers. Alternatively, the employee file can contain a memo signed by the General Manager listing the old and new rates for blanket pay increases, based on the union contract. Any exceptions should be documented in the workpapers and cross referenced to the Discussion Points worksheet.

Drug Testing

Many employers drug test applicants to provide a drug free environment for its employees and customers. Drug free employees tend to be more reliable and do not pose safety threats to themselves and fellow employees. While there is a cost to utilizing a drub test lab for testing applicants, the cost is much less than dealing with lost workdays and possible safety situations.

When the hiring manager has decided to make an offer to an applicant, he asks the applicant to take a drug test. Since there is a cost involved in obtaining the drug test, the applicant should not be asked to take a drug test unless the field location is planning to make an employment offer. The drug test is the last step in determining whether the applicant will make a suitable employee.

Where the Company has a policy of drug testing new applicants, the employer should have a standard Drug Test Consent and Release form that the employee signs. If the employee is a minor, the parent must sign the bottom of the form agreeing to have his son or daughter drug tested. In the form, the employee agrees to be drug tested and recognizes that the results of the drug test will be one of the factors used in evaluating the applicant's suitability for employment. In reality, if the employee tests positive for drugs, the field location may not hire him.

When the Human Resources Clerk receives the signed Drug Test Consent and Release form, she makes an appointment at the lab for the applicant to be drug tested. She files the Drug Test Consent and Release form with the applicant's paperwork. The applicant arrives at the drug test lab on the appointed day at the appointed time. He provides a urine sample in a bottle that the lab supplies. The lab analyzes the sample and reports directly to the employer several days later.

The Human Resources Manager should maintain a Drug Test Log that is used to track each applicant who is sent to the drug test lab for drug testing. The Drug Test log can be a manual form or it can be an Excel spreadsheet that is maintained on the computer. If Excel is used, the Human Resources Manager should maintain a separate file for each year. To ensure the Drug Test Log is not lost if the hard drive goes down, the Human Resources Manager should maintain a back up copy of the file. Also, the Drug Test Log should be printed once a month (once a week if a lot of employees are hired) so that if all file copies are destroyed, the Drug Test Log can be recreated. The current paper copy of the Drug Test Log should be stored in a locked file cabinet with the employee files. When a new Drug Test Log is printed, the prior Drug Test Log should be shredded.

Figure 16.2 is an example of a Drug Test Log. The information contained in the columns is as follows:

Drug Test Appointment Date—Date the applicant has an appointment at the lab to be drug tested,

Last Name—Last name of the applicant,

First, Middle Initial—First name and middle initial of the applicant,

Social Security Number—Social Security number of the applicant,

Telephone Number—Telephone number of the applicant,

Department—Field location department where the applicant is applying,

Results Date—Date the results are received from the lab (applicant cannot be hired before the negative results are received),

Results—"N" = Negative, "P" = Positive—Can also use "1" = Negative and "2" = Positive.

The field location may not hire an employee until the drug test results are received from the lab and a negative result is obtained. If the applicant tests positive, the applicant may not be hired or retested at a later date.

If a Company owns restaurants in Canada, the Canadian applicants may not be drug tested because Canadian labor laws forbid employers from drug testing applicants as a requirement for hiring them.

Utilizing the sample the auditor selected for Human Resources testing, the auditor should tie each employee to the Drug Test Log that shows where the employee was drug tested and that a negative result was obtained. If the Drug Test Log is maintained in an Excel spreadsheet, the auditor asks the Human Resources Manager to email the Drug Test Logs for the years needed. When the file is opened, the auditor puts the curser at the top of the Last Name column. The auditor clicks on "Edit, Find" in the Excel menu. He types the last name of the employee he wishes to find and clicks on the "Find Next" button. Excel will bring the curser to the first match in the file. If this is not the right name, the auditor clicks on the "Find Next" button again and Excel will bring the curser to the next match in the file. The auditor should look up the hire date and make sure he is looking for the employee in the correct year.

If the auditor finds an employee who tested positive or an employee who was not drug tested, he should note the exception on the workpaper. He should cross reference his comment to the Discussion Points Worksheet.

Jenny's Café, Inc.
Denver Restaurant
Drug Test Log
2006

Drug Test Appt Date	Last Name	First, Mid. Init.	SS Number	Telephone No.	Department	Results Date	Results
1/3/06	Wozniak	Donna K.	389-45-2874	303-359-2794	Kitchen	1/6/06	N
1/5/06	Chung	Emily	235-42-7952	303-357-3296	Cash Room	1/9/06	N
1/9/06	Samuels	David R.	487-28-1956	303-342-8031	Kitchen	1/12/06	P
1/11/06	Davidson	Helen C.	380-45-6732	303-349-8612	Dining Room	1/16/06	P
1/17/06	Wei	William R.	259-83-1297	303-343-6671	Dining Room	1/23/06	N
1/25/06	Hernandez	Amanda L.	521-79-2943	303-379-3119	Office	1/30/06	N
1/31/06	Abdullah	Hasim	386-13-2813	303-363-1063	Dining Room	2/3/06	N
2/7/06	O'Brien	Kelly J.	289-28-3108	303-247-3901	Warehouse	2/10/06	N
2/13/06	Topaz	Tammie L.	387-31-3749	303-349-3193	Dining Room	2/16/06	N
2/22/06	Johnson	Jason G.	532-63-7301	303-249-4281	Dining Room	2/27/06	P
2/27/06	Choi	Jeremy J.	279-54-6931	303-341-5925	Dining Room	3/3/06	N
2/27/06	Choi	April M.	459-82-3679	303-789-3309	Dining Room	3/3/06	N
2/27/06	Choi	Jennifer J.	457-83-6459	303-789-3871	Dining Room	3/3/06	N
3/13/06	Howard	Rebecca	398-23-4156	303-341-1327	Kitchen	3/16/06	N
3/21/06	McCarthy	Robert D.	201-76-3812	303-249-1123	Office	3/24/06	N
3/29/06	Suarez	Susan S.	312-67-2701	303-247-3790	Parking	4/3/06	N
3/29/06	Valenzuela	Ricardo	289-15-3294	303-452-8601	Parking	4/3/06	P
4/6/06	Muhammed	Miradije	439-36-2174	303-316-2799	Dining Room	4/11/06	N
4/10/06	Watsworth	William S.	143-88-3285	303-345-8121	Parking	4/13/06	N
4/18/06	Alexander	Angela A.	254-81-9494	303-347-2683	Office	4/21/06	N
4/25/06	O'Brien	Emily M.	129-66-3179	303-241-3388	Dining Room	4/28/06	N
5/1/06	Sanchez	Angelina P.	458-21-5734	303-348-3557	Bar	5/5/06	P
5/7/06	Kambrowski	Paula A.	376-28-7482	303-446-3751	Bar	5/11/06	N
5/16/06	Chester	Gary J.	497-25-3188	303-246-3441	Dining Room	5/22/06	N
5/23/06	Barker	George T.	257-34-2886	303-247-3293	Dining Room	5/26/06	N
5/26/06	Hernandez	Henry J.	438-18-2755	303-447-3118	Dining Room	5/31/06	N
6/13/06	Braun	Jennifer A.	379-54-2289	303-362-4434	Dining Room	6/19/06	P
6/20/06	Williams	Roger C.	169-53-2874	303-345-5588	Bar	6/23/06	P
6/27/06	Muhibuddin	Bilal	312-73-8731	303-239-3002	Dining Room	7/3/06	N
7/6/06	Robinson	Robert N.	275-75-3630	303-249-0031	Dining Room	7/11/06	N
7/19/06	Estophan	Ellen R.	136-44-3287	303-455-7381	Dining Room	7/24/06	N

Figure 16.2

I9 Documentation

In an effort to abolish the employment of illegal aliens, Congress passed a law that requires all employees hired after November 6, 1986 to complete an I9 form. This form is used to prove the new employee's identity and his eligibility to work. Figure 16.3 is an example of the front of the Form I9.

All employees must complete Section 1 of the I9 form. This section requires the employee to write his Name (Last, First, Middle Initial, Address,

Maiden Name (if applicable), Date of Birth, and Social Security Number. The employee must also attest under penalty of perjury that one of the following applies:

* The employee is a citizen or national of the United States,
* The employee is a lawful permanent resident (must list the Alien Registration Number),
* The employee is an alien authorized to work until (date must be entered and the Alien Number or Admission Number must be entered).

The employee signs and dates the form. It is the employer's responsibility to check the documents the employee presents and verify them against the information the employee completes in Section 1. The Human Resources Manager should check to make sure the date is the correct date.

If the new hire does not speak sufficient English to complete the I9 by himself, a translator can be used to explain the I9 form to the new hire and write down the required information in Section 1. In this case, the translator must complete the Preparer and/or Translator Certification at the bottom of Section 1. The translator acknowledges that he assisted in the completion of the form and to the best of his knowledge, the information is correct. The Translator signs the certification and prints his name, address, and the date.

The Employer completes Section 2 of the I9 form. This section should normally be completed by the Human Resources Manager, but could be completed by the Human Resources Clerk if she has been trained by the Human Resources Manager in proper I9 completion. The employee at his option must present either a List A item or a List B and a List C item. The List A items prove identity and eligibility to work. The List B items prove identity and the List C items prove eligibility to work. The back of the Form I9 lists the various documents that are acceptable as List A, List B, and List C items.

The List A items (prove identity and work eligibility) taken from the back of an I9 form are as follows:

* U.S. Passport (expired or unexpired),
* Certificate of U.S. Citizenship (*Form N-560 or N-561*),
* Certificate of Naturalization (*Form N-550 or N-570*),
* Unexpired Foreign Passport, with *I-551 stamp* or attached *Form I-94* indicating unexpired employment authorization,
* Permanent Resident Card or Alien Registration Receipt Card with photograph (*Form I-151 or I-551*),
* Unexpired Temporary Resident Card (*Form I-688*),
* Unexpired Employment Authorization Card (*Form 688A*),

- Unexpired Reentry Permit (*Form I-327)*
- Unexpired Refugee Travel Document (*Form 1-571),*
- Unexpired Employment Authorization Document issued by DHS that contains a photograph (*Form I-688B),*

The following are List B items (prove identity) that can be used together with a List C item (prove work eligibility):

- Driver's license or ID card issued by a state or outlying possession of the United States provided it contains a photograph or information such as name, date of birth, gender, height, eye color, and address,
- ID card issued by federal, state, or local government agencies or entities, provided it contains a photograph or information such as name, date of birth, gender, height, eye color, and address,
- School ID card with a photograph,
- Voter's registration card,
- U.S. military card or draft record,
- Military dependent's ID card,
- U.S. Coast Guard Merchant Mariner card,
- Native American tribal document,
- Driver's license issued by a Canadian government authority,

For persons under 18 years of age who are unable to present a document listed above:

- School Record or report card,
- Clinic, doctor, or hospital record,
- Day-care or nursery school record.

The following are List C items (prove work eligibility) that can be used with a List B item (prove identity):

- U.S. social security card issued by the Social Security Administration (*other than a card stating it is not valid for employment*),
- Certificate of Birth Abroad issued by the Department of State (*Form FS-545 or Form DS-1350*),
- Original or certified copy of a birth certificate issued by a state, county, or municipal authority or outlying possession of the United States bearing an official seal,
- Native American tribal document,
- U.S. Citizen ID Card (*Form I-197*),
- ID Card for use of resident citizen of the United States (*Form I-179*),
- Unexpired employment authorization document issued by DHS (other than those listed under List A).

Department of Homeland Security	OMB No. 1615-0047; Expires 03/31/07
U.S. Citizenship and Immigration Services	**Employment Eligibility Verification**

Please read instructions carefully before completing this form. The instructions must be available during completion of this form. ANTI-DISCRIMINATION NOTICE: It is illegal to discriminate against work eligible individuals. Employers CANNOT specify which document(s) they will accept from an employee. The refusal to hire an individual because of a future expiration date may also constitute illegal discrimination.

Section 1. Employee Information and Verification. To be completed and signed by employee at the time employment begins.

Print Name: Last	First	Middle Initial	Maiden Name

Address (Street Name and Number)		Apt. #	Date of Birth (month/day/year)

City	State	Zip Code	Social Security #

I am aware that federal law provides for imprisonment and/or fines for false statements or use of false documents in connection with the completion of this form.

I attest, under penalty of perjury, that I am (check one of the following):
- [ ] A citizen or national of the United States
- [ ] A Lawful Permanent Resident (Alien #) A _____
- [ ] An alien authorized to work until _____
  (Alien # or Admission #)

Employee's Signature	Date (month/day/year)

Preparer and/or Translator Certification. (To be completed and signed if Section 1 is prepared by a person other than the employee.) I attest, under penalty of perjury, that I have assisted in the completion of this form and that to the best of my knowledge the information is true and correct.

Preparer's/Translator's Signature	Print Name

Address (Street Name and Number, City, State, Zip Code)	Date (month/day/year)

Section 2. Employer Review and Verification. To be completed and signed by employer. Examine one document from List A OR examine one document from List B and one from List C, as listed on the reverse of this form, and record the title, number and expiration date, if any, of the document(s).

List A	OR	List B	AND	List C
Document title:				
Issuing authority:				
Document #:				
Expiration Date (if any):				
Document #:				
Expiration Date (if any):				

CERTIFICATION - I attest, under penalty of perjury, that I have examined the document(s) presented by the above-named employee, that the above-listed document(s) appear to be genuine and to relate to the employee named, that the employee began employment on (month/day/year) _____ and that to the best of my knowledge the employee is eligible to work in the United States. (State employment agencies may omit the date the employee began employment.)

Signature of Employer or Authorized Representative	Print Name	Title

Business or Organization Name	Address (Street Name and Number, City, State, Zip Code)	Date (month/day/year)

Section 3. Updating and Reverification. To be completed and signed by employer.

A. New Name (if applicable)	B. Date of Rehire (month/day/year) (if applicable)

C. If employee's previous grant of work authorization has expired, provide the information below for the document that establishes current employment eligibility.

Document Title:	Document #:	Expiration Date (if any):

I attest, under penalty of perjury, that to the best of my knowledge, this employee is eligible to work in the United States, and if the employee presented document(s), the document(s) I have examined appear to be genuine and to relate to the individual.

Signature of Employer or Authorized Representative	Date (month/day/year)

NOTE: This is the 1991 edition of the Form I-9 that has been rebranded with a current printing date to reflect the recent transition from the INS to DHS and its components.

Form I-9 (Rev. 05/31/05)Y Page 2

Figure 16.3

153

The person verifying the employment eligibility of the new hire must accept whatever valid documentation the new hire presents. He cannot specify specific documentation. However, it must be one List A item or a List B and a List C item. It cannot be two List B items or two List C items. If the employee presents a List A, List B, and List C item, the person verifying work eligibility cannot list all three items because that would be over-documentation. The Immigration and Naturalization Service (INS) has determined that over-documentation is discriminatory. The employer may not refuse to hire an applicant because his work eligibility documents will expire in the future if they are currently valid.

While the person reviewing the documentation does not need to make copies of the documentation, it makes sense to copy it and attach the copies of the documentation to the I9. The person is required to record the document title, issuing authority, document number, expiration date if any, and the date the employment begins. Attaching a copy of the documentation to support the I9 does not relieve the Human Resources person from listing it on the I9. Failure to list the documentation on the I9 is an INS violation.

The person reviewing the documents must sign and date the certification. He must also print his Name, Title, Business Name, and Business Address. The date must be within three days of the hire date, i.e. within three days of the date that the employee signed and dated Section 1.

When reverifying (rehiring) or updating the I9 (original work permit expired), the Human Resources person must complete Section 3 of the I9. The I9 must be reverified on or before the expiration date noted in Section 1. Section 3 requires the Human Resources person to print the employee's Name, Date of Rehire, and Document Title, Number, and Expiration Date. The Human Resources person must sign and date the reverification. He cannot specify what documents the employee must present for reverification as long as they are valid documents that are either a List A item or a List B and a List C item.

Human Resources may photocopy Form I9 as long as both sides are copied. The employee must be provided with a set of instructions for completing this form. The completed I9 must be kept for 3 years from the date of hire or one year after the employee terminates, whichever is later.

I9's should not be kept in employee files but should be retained in a separate I9 binder. If the INS does an I9 audit, you do not want them looking through other paperwork contained in the employee files. The I9 binder should have alphabetical dividers and the I9's should be filed in alphabetical order. When an employee terminates, his I9 should be removed from the active I9 binder and filed in a separate terminated I9 binder.

Human Resources should be very careful in reviewing the I9 that the employee has completed and the Human Resources Department has verified. Each incident of an improperly completed I9 uncovered during an INS audit carries a potential $10,000 fine. If one person does the documentation, a second person should verify the I9 to ensure it was completed properly.

Utilizing the sample of employees selected for Human Resources testing, the auditor should determine whether INS regulations regarding I9 completion have been followed. Any differences should be documented on the workpaper and cross referenced to the Discussion Points Worksheet.

Termination Checklist

When an employee terminates voluntarily or involuntarily, there are a lot of items that need to be resolved. The employee is entitled to certain benefits, such as vacation pay and possibly termination pay, if it is an involuntary termination. Under Federal law, the employee is entitled to a continuation of health insurance at the employee's expense (COBRA). He is also entitled to leave his 401K holdings in the Company's 401K Plan or transfer the plan assets into an IRA or another 401K Plan. The employee may be in possession of company assets, such as a uniform, POS access card, laptop computer, company ID card, etc.

With a termination, there are administrative matters that the Human Resources Department needs to resolve. The employee must be terminated in the payroll system, particularly in the case of a salaried employee because the payroll system will continue printing payroll checks until the employee is terminated. In the case of management, office or cash room employees, the passwords to Company software, i.e. the Payroll system and Human Resources system, must be changed and the combinations to all safes must be changed.

Human Resources should take the I9 out of the Active I9 binder and put it in the Terminated I9 binder. The employee file should be removed from the Active drawer of the file cabinet and put into the Terminated file cabinet drawer. To prevent the employee from tampering with the computer system, all computer access for the terminated employee, i.e. email, POS systems, etc. must be deleted.

In some states, such as California, the employee must be presented with his final payroll check on the date of termination. In this situation, the Human

Resources Manager must complete the paperwork to request a manual payroll check from the Corporate Payroll Department prior to actual termination (See Chapter 15). The Corporate Payroll Department should be able to process a manual check within 24 hours if the request is made by Corporate's deadline (e.g. 2:00 p.m.).

As you can see, when an employee terminates, there is a lot of behind the scenes activity that must be completed prior to the termination. A Termination Checklist is a necessity to ensure that all steps leading to termination and after termination are completed. The Human Resources Manager completes the Termination Checklist as the steps noted on it are completed. When all steps have been completed, the Department Manager, Human Resources Manager, and the General Manager sign the Termination Checklist and the checklist is placed in the employee's folder.

When terminating an employee, an Employee Maintenance Form (EMF) must be completed and the reason for the termination must be explained in the Notes section of the form. If the termination is due to unsatisfactory performance or violation of work rules, there should be a brief description of the violation or a reference to an Employee Evaluation or Record of Employee Counseling. The employee is asked to sign the terminating EMF. If he refuses to sign, the Human Resources Manager notes "Refused to Sign" on the Employee Signature line. Two managers must sign the EMF, usually the Human Resources Manager and the General Manager.

Figure 16.4 is a properly completed Termination Check List. The information on the Check List is as follows:

Employee Name—Name of the employee who is terminating employment with the Company,

Employee Department ID—Department Identification Number where the employee worked,

Employee Title—Title or Position of the terminating employee,

Last Day Worked—Last day the terminating employee worked,

Date of Termination Interview—Date that the Department Manager interviewed the employee (involuntary termination) or Date the Human Resources Department conducted the exit interview (voluntary termination),

Date of Hire—Date the employee was originally hired,

Reports To—Name of the Department Manager or supervisor to whom the employee reports,

Termination Conducted By: Name of person who conducted the termination, normally the Department Manager in the case of an involuntary termination or the Human Resources Manager in the case of a voluntary termination,

If Voluntary, Date Letter of Resignation Received—If the employee terminated voluntarily, the date the Letter of Resignation was received,

If Involuntary, Date Termination Issued—If the termination was involuntary, the date the employee was terminated,

Reason for Termination—Reason the employee was terminated, such as Resignation, Job Elimination, Performance, etc,

Number of Vacation Days—Number of unused vacation days for which the employee is entitled to receive payment,

Days Paid in Lieu of Notice—Number of days the employee will be paid in lieu of giving notice of the termination,

Date of Final Check—Date the final check is given to the employee or mailed,

COBRA Benefits—Date that the employee's right to continue Health Insurance at employee's expense is explained,

401K Plan—Date that 401K Plan options are explained to the employee,

Outstanding Expense Reports—Date outstanding expense reports were received from the employee to be processed for reimbursements,

Company ID Card—Date the employee's Company identification card was received,

Laptop—Date the laptop issued to the employee was received,

Cell Phone/Pager—Date the cell phone or pager issued to the employee was received,

Palm Pilot/Black Berry—Date the palm pilot or black berry issued to the employee was received,

Books/Software—Date any company owned books or software issued to the employee was received,

Uniform—Date the uniform(s) issued to the employee was received,

POS Access Card—Date the POS Access Card was received,

Miscellaneous Keys—Date any keys issued to the employee were received, i.e. office keys, desk keys, file cabinet keys, etc.

Other—Date any other Company property issued to the employee was received, or employee property was returned, listed on the blank lines (e.g. If a minor, "working papers returned"),

Passwords Changed on Software—For management and office employees who have access to Company software, i.e. Payroll system, Human Resources system, etc, date that the password was changed,

Safe Combinations Changed—For management and cash room personnel who have access to the safe, date that the combinations were changed to all safes,

EMF Submitted—Remove from Payroll—Date the Employee Maintenance Form was submitted to the Payroll Clerk to remove the terminated employee from the Payroll,

Transfer I9 to Termination Binder—Date the terminating employee's I9 is removed from the Active I9 Binder to the Inactive I9 Binder,

Removal From All Automated Systems—Date the terminating employee is removed from all computerized systems, including email, POS systems, etc,

Transfer Employee File to Terminations—Date the employee's file is transferred from the Active Employees file drawer to the Terminated Employees file drawer,

Department Manager Signature and **Date**—Signature of the Department Manager and the date of the signature,

Human Resources Manager Signature and **Date**—Signature of the Human Resources Manager and the date of the signature,

General Manager Signature and **Date**—Signature of the General Manager and the date of the signature.

The auditor should select about 5 terminated employee files and determine whether the Termination Checklist was properly completed and whether the reason for termination was explained on the terminating EMF. Any exceptions should be documented on the workpaper and cross referenced to the Discussion Points Worksheet.

Jennie's Café, Inc.
Termination Checklist

Employee Name:	Stella Palenski	Date of Termination Interview:	8/7/06
Employee Dept ID	3301010	Date of Hire:	3/13/95
Employee Title	Waitress	Reports To:	L. Barton
Last Day Worked	8/4/06	Termination Conducted by:	L. Barton

If Voluntary, Date Letter of Resignation Rec'd: _____

If Involuntary, Date Termination Issued: 8/7/06

Reason for Termination: (Resign. Job Elim. Perform.) Performance

EMF Form:		Benefits:	
No. of Vacation Days:	20	COBRA	8/7/06
Days paid in lieu of notice:	10	401 K Plan	8/7/06
Date of Final Check	8/11/06		
		Management & Office Employees:	
Outstanding Expense Reports	N/A	Passwords Changed on Software	N/A
		Safe Combinations Changed	N/A
Company Issued Properly:			
Company ID Card	8/7/06	EMF Submitted-Remove from Payroll	8/7/06
Laptop	N/A	Transfer I9 to Termination Binder	8/7/06
Cell Phone/Pager	N/A	Removal from all Automated Systems	8/7/06
Palm Pilot/Black Berry	N/A	Transfer Employee File to Terminations	8/7/06
Books/Software	N/A	*Linda Barton*	
Uniform	8/7/06		8/7/06
POS Access Card	8/7/06	Department Manager Signature	Date
Miscellaneous Keys	N/A	*Emily Nguyen*	
Other (list):			8/7/06
_____	N/A	Human Resources Mgr. Signature	Date
_____	N/A	*Joey Robertson*	
			8/7/06
		General Manager's Signature	Date

Figure 16.4

Child Labor Laws

The U.S. government's Fair Labor Standards Act allows 14 and 15 year old minors to work in non-hazardous jobs (may not operate power slicers and grinders), but for a limited number of hours and during certain time periods. Minors who are 14 and 15 years old may only work according to the following rules:

When School is in session, minors under 16 years old may work
• During non-school hours, 3 hours in a school day,
• 18 hours in a school week,
• 8 hours on a non-school day.

When School is not in session, minors under 16 years old may work
• 8 hours per day,
• 40 hours per week.

Minors under 16 years old may only work from 7:00 a.m. to 7:00 p.m., except from June 1 through Labor Day, when they may work until 9:00 p.m.

The Fair Labor Standards Act does not restrict minors who are 16 years old or older, but State Labor Laws often limit the number of hours 16 and 17 year olds may work. Before leaving for the field location, the auditor should obtain a summary of the State's Child Labor laws from the Corporate Human Resources Department. If the Human Resources Department does not have this information, the auditor should contact the State Department of Labor or go on its website to obtain Child Labor Law information. Where there is a difference between the Federal Child Labor laws and the State's Child Labor laws, the stricter of the two laws applies.

Many states require the employee to obtain a work permit and give it to the employer before the minor can begin working. The employer must keep the work permit on file for inspection by a State Labor Department auditor when requested. When the minor employee terminates employment, the employer must return the work permit to the employee.

Many states require the employer to post the work schedule for all minors. In these states, the work schedule should be posted on the employee bulletin board, over the time clock, or some other place where the employees congregate, i.e. the employee break room.

It is the Human Resources Manager's responsibility to be familiar with the applicable child labor laws and train department managers and supervisors in observing these laws. The restaurant can be subject to severe penalties for violations of the Child Labor Laws.

The requirement for minor employees to stop work at the designated time is very easy to miss. The employee often wants to make as much money as possible and may continue working even when he is aware that he should be quitting. A different color time card for 14 and 15 year olds and a third color for 16 and 17 year olds will help alert the department manager or supervisor to the quitting time and maximum hours worked requirements.

Each week, the Human Resources Manager or General Manager should audit the minors' time cards and flag any working hours' violations. Managers and supervisors should be disciplined for repeated violations of minors working beyond the legal maximum number of hours permitted by law.

During the sample selection process, the auditor should select 5-10 minors and determine whether the minors worked only the maximum number of hours permitted and within the legal starting and quitting times. Where work permits are required, the auditor should examine the work permits of the minors selected. In locations where the State requires the work schedule to be posted, the auditor should determine whether the schedule for minors working during the current week has been posted as required. Any exceptions should be documented on the workpaper and the comments should be cross referenced to the Discussion Points Worksheet.

Alcohol Service Training

When a customer of the restaurant leaves the premises and is involved in an automobile accident where injuries have occurred due to the driver's negligence, courts have held the restaurant liable for damages to the injured party. Particularly where the restaurant is owned by a large corporation, prosecuting attorneys have asked for and received large judgments against the party perceived to have deep pockets, the large corporation. For this reason, it is imperative for a Company to have an effective Alcohol Awareness Training program in place.

The Alcohol Awareness Training program should be documented on paper by the restaurant's trainer, most likely the Human Resources Manager. Each year, the documented program should be updated, approved by the General Manager in writing, and submitted to the Corporate Human Resources Department for approval. Either the Vice President of Human Resources or the Director of Human Resources should approve the field location's Alcohol Awareness Program in writing. An email from the Vice President of Human Resources or Director of Human Resources to the General Manager or the restaurant's Human Resources Manager approving the program is sufficient as long as the email is printed and stapled to the written program.

Each alcohol serving employee must attend an Alcohol Awareness training session each year where the employee is trained on how to determine when a customer is intoxicated and how to politely tell the customer that he cannot buy any additional alcoholic beverages.

At the training session, the employee is trained to ask for photo identification from any young customer who appears to be under 30 years of age. In many states, employees serving alcohol to underage customers can be arrested and the restaurant can lose its liquor license. Some State Liquor Commissions aggressively pursue violations of sales to underage consumers by hiring underage employees to go to establishments selling alcoholic beverages and attempt to purchase one. When the bartender completes the sale, State Liquor Commission agents have been known to move in immediately and arrest the bartender who committed the violation. The arrest is shortly followed by the State Liquor Commission suspending the establishment's liquor license.

Upon conclusion of the training session, the employee must sign a certification that states the following:

> On [date] I attended an Alcohol Awareness training session at [location name]. During the training session, I was given the opportunity to ask questions, had my questions answered to my satisfaction, and I understood the training content.

Each signed (by the employee) Alcohol Awareness training certification must be filed in the applicable employee's Human Resources folder.

Companies should require attendance at an Alcohol Awareness training session every year to ensure the employee has not forgotten the lessons learned. Some states, i.e. Texas and California, require alcohol serving employees to attend an alcohol serving certification program prior to working as an alcohol server. Other states require state recertification every two years. Field locations in these states should require their alcohol servers to attend a Company Alcohol Awareness training session the year the state does not conduct one.

Utilizing the sample selected for Human Resources testing, the auditor should check the employee folders of alcohol serving employees to determine whether the folder contains an employee certification of attendance at an Alcohol Awareness Training session within the last year. If the auditor does not feel there is a sufficient number of alcohol serving employees in the original sample, he can select a few additional alcohol serving employees for this test. The auditor should note any exceptions on the workpaper and cross reference them to the Discussion Points Worksheet.

Documenting Human Resources Testing

In this chapter we have discussed various tests of the Human Resources files that the auditor should conduct and said that the auditor should document the results of his testing. Much of this documentation can be done on one spreadsheet. The names of the employees whose files will be tested can be listed in the first column while the audit steps per the audit program can be the column headings for subsequent columns. The audit steps are worded as questions that require a "Yes" or "No" answer. The Comments column is used to provide more detail for "No" answers.

Figure 16.5 is an example of the Human Resources Testing Worksheet that Aimee used for her audit of Jenny's Café—Denver. The columns provide the following information:

Employee Name—Name of the employee whose file is tested,

Position—Job title of the employee,

Birthday—Date the employee was born,

Hire Date—Date the employee was hired,

The next columns are the audit steps from the audit program that the auditor is testing. The audit steps used in this example are as follows:

EMF is Properly Completed?—Was all required information written on the Employee Maintenance Form?

EMF Signed by Employee?—Was the EMF signed by the employee?

EMF Signed by First Manager?—Was the EMF signed by the first manager, normally the manager the employee reports to?

EMF Signed by Second Manager?—Was the EMF signed by a second manager, i.e. Human Resources Manager or General Manager to ensure the department manager is not acting alone?

Passed Drug Test?—Did the employee listed on the Drug Test Log have a negative result?

Drug Test Procedures Proper?—Were all procedures relating to the drug test properly followed, i.e. completing and signing a Consent & Release form, parents signing the Consent & Release form for minor children, employee hired after negative results obtained from the lab, etc.

Jenny's Café, Inc.

Denver Restaurant

Human Resources Testing

Week Ending July 15, 2006

Employee Name	Birthday	Hire Date	EMF is Properly Completed?	EMF Signed by Employee?	EMF Signed by 1st Mgr?	EMF Signed by 2nd Mgr
Lopez, Laura	11/23/80	10/10/05	Yes	Yes	Yes	Yes
Robinson, Roberta	06/01/81	7/11/05	Yes	Yes	Yes	Yes
Smith, Jane	04/28/75	8/9/04	Yes	Yes	Yes	Yes
Abdullah, Hasim	04/17/88	2/3/06	Yes	Yes	Yes	Yes
Barker, George	03/04/88	5/26/06	Yes	NO	NO	NO
Choi, April	02/11/79	3/3/06	Yes	Yes	Yes	Yes
Choi, Jennifer	10/28/77	3/3/06	Yes	Yes	Yes	Yes
Choi, Jeremy	08/09/75	3/3/06	Yes	Yes	Yes	Yes
James, April	12/25/66	10/7/91	Yes	Yes	Yes	Yes
Muhammed, Miradije	09/05/87	4/11/06	Yes	NO	Yes	NO
Muhibuddin, Bilal	07/14/87	7/3/06	Yes	Yes	NO	NO
Tammie Topaz	06/15/76	2/16/06	Yes	Yes	Yes	Yes
Wei, Willie	09/04/74	1/23/06	Yes	Yes	Yes	Yes
Howard, Rebecca	03/12/68	3/16/06	Yes	Yes	Yes	Yes
Jones, James	01/01/79	4/18/05	Yes	NO	Yes	NO
Jones, Anthony	04/24/75	2/23/04	Yes	Yes	Yes	Yes
Wozniak, Donna	02/13/86	1/6/06	Yes	Yes	Yes	Yes
Josephson, Linda	08/07/55	3/23/92	Yes	Yes	Yes	Yes
Arroyo, Raul	09/20/51	10/21/96	Yes	Yes	Yes	Yes
Byron, Joseph	11/07/71	9/1/97	Yes	Yes	Yes	Yes
O'Brien, Kelly	11/11/69	2/10/06	Yes	Yes	Yes	Yes
Minors						
Watsworth,	05/20/90	4/13/06	Yes	Yes	NO	NO
Cortez, James	07/17/89	11/28/05	Yes	Yes	Yes	Yes
Suarez, Susan	06/30/90	4/3/06	Yes	NO	NO	NO
Complied			24	20	20	18
Exceptions			0	4	4	6
No. Tested			24	24	24	24
Exception Percentage			0.0%	16.7%	16.7%	25.0%

Basis of Selection: Selected employees on a judgment basis to include several foreigners

Conclusion:

Exceptions noted in the Human Resources testing are as follows:

• 4 of 24 EMF's were not signed by the employee, 4 of 24 were not signed by either manager, and an additional 2 were not signed by a second manager.

• 2 of 21 employees did not sign a Consent and Release form prior to being drug tested and 3 of 3 minors did not have their parents signature on the Consent & Release Form.

Figure 16.5

Passed Drug Test?	Drug Test Procedures Proper?	I9's Properly Completed?	If Alien, Alien No. Noted?	Alcohol Training Certificate?	Comments
Yes	Yes	Yes	Yes	NO	No Curr't Alcohol Aware Train Certificat'n Attest section not completed
Yes	Yes	NO	N/A	NO	No Curr't Alcohol Aware Train Certificat'n
Yes	Yes	Yes	N/A	N/A	
Yes	Yes	NO	Yes	N/A	SS Card says "Not eligible for work"
Yes	Yes	NO	N/A	N/A	Driver's License & SS Card attached but not listed on I9
Yes	Yes	NO	Yes	Yes	Employer Cert not Complete
Yes	Yes	NO	Yes	Yes	Employer Cert not Complete
Yes	Yes	NO	Yes	Yes	Employer Cert not Complete
Yes	Yes	Yes	N/A	N/A	
Yes	Yes	Yes	NO	N/A	In Attest Section, Checked Register Alien but Alien Registration No. not on Form
Yes	Yes	NO	Yes	N/A	In Attest Section, Checked Alien Authorized to work but did not note work permit expiration date
Yes	Yes	NO	N/A	Yes	SS # is 128-42-7926- on I9 128-24-7926
Yes	Yes	NO	Yes	Yes	Hired on 1/23/06, Employer Cert. on 2/5 - More than 3 days apart
Yes	NO	Yes	N/A	N/A	Consent & Release not Signed by Emplyee
Yes	Yes	NO	N/A	N/A	I9 has List A, B & C Items
Yes	Yes	Yes	N/A	N/A	
Yes	Yes	NO	N/A	N/A	I9 has List A, B & C Items
Yes	Yes	Yes	N/A	N/A	
Yes	Yes	Yes	Yes	N/A	
Yes	Yes	Yes	N/A	N/A	
Yes	NO	Yes	N/A	N/A	Consent & Release not Signed by Emplyee
Yes	NO	Yes	N/A	N/A	C & R not signed by Parent
Yes	NO	Yes	Yes	N/A	C & R not signed by Parent
Yes	NO	Yes	Yes	N/A	C & R not signed by Parent
24	19	13	10	5	
0	5	11	1	2	
24	24	24	11	7	
0.0%	20.8%	45.8%	9.1%	28.6%	

to test for work eligibility.

- 11 of 24 I9's were not properly completed - exceptions noted in the comments section.
- 1 of 11 Alien's did not have Alien Registration no. noted on the I9 in the Attest Section.
- 2 of 7 alcohol serving associates who were trained last year did not have a current Alcohol Training Awareness certification in their files. **See Discussion Point #46**

I9's Properly Completed?—Was the new hire's I9 properly completed by the employee and the Human Resources person, including maintaining the I9 in a separate I9 binder, proper ID's were listed with all required information (expiration dates) on the I9, and copies attached, etc.?

If Alien, Alien Number Noted?—If the employee is an alien eligible to work, was the Alien Registration Number documented in the certification section of the I9?

Alcohol Training Certificate?—If the employee is an alcohol serving employee, is there an Alcohol Training Certificate in the employee's file that documents that the employee attended an Alcohol Awareness training session within the last year?

In this example, there is no audit step regarding work permits for minors or the posting of minor work schedules because these are not requirements in the State of Colorado. In states where child labor laws require work permits and/or the posting of minor work schedules, these steps can be added to the workpaper.

In selecting employees for this test, random selection was not used because the auditor wants to select employees who may be aliens that need work permits. If a random selection was used, the auditor may not select any employees with work permits. Since significant penalties can be levied on employers who knowingly or unknowingly hire illegal aliens who are not eligible to work, it is imperative that the auditor determine whether proper Company procedures are followed in hiring new employees.

While some employees are selected on a random basis, the auditor looks through the Human Resources or Payroll master file to select employees who have a greater likelihood of being foreigners. Thus, the auditor selects some employees with Hispanic, Asian, African, Eastern European, and Middle Eastern names. While there may be Western European immigrants working at the location, the odds of testing foreign workers are better with the former types of names.

The Conclusion is used to summarize the findings of the testing. The COUNT IF function can be used to count the numbers of "Yes" and "No" answers (See Chapter 8). Exceptions should be cross referenced to the Discussion Points Worksheet. When summarizing the exceptions, it is best to indicate the number of exceptions and the number of items tested. This method gives management a better feel whether the exceptions are isolated or pervasive.

Nepotism

Nepotism is the term used to describe an employee related by blood or marriage to an employee to whom he is reporting directly or indirectly. The most obvious forms of nepotism include a wife reporting to her husband, husband reporting to his wife, son or daughter reporting to a father or mother, a brother or sister reporting to another brother or sister. It also includes a grandson or granddaughter reporting to a grandmother or grandfather, a niece or nephew reporting to an aunt or uncle, and in-laws reporting to each other. Significant others, i.e. two unrelated people living together, should be included in nepotism.

Nepotism can result in collusion between the two related people because the one relative is reviewing and approving the work done by the other. It is thus a breakdown in the system of checks and balances that make up good internal control. For example, the Bar Manager's wife works as a bartender and reports to the Bar Manager. The wife does not record all sales on the cash register that she makes at the bar and steals approximately $200 per night. Since she does not record these sales, the cash register always balances to the cash. A theft this large should drive up liquor, beer, and wine costs that would stand out on the profit and loss statement. However, the Bar Manager counts the inventory at the end of the month and adds enough in non-existent inventory to the counts to make the product cost come out close to Plan. Since the bartender and Bar Manager are in collusion, they are able to cover up a theft that would normally raise red flags and trigger an investigation. In this case, the General Manager and Controller think everything is running well at the bar because the Product Cost percentage is always close to Plan.

Of course, to keep the product cost in line, the inventory balances would continually go up until they are significantly higher than Last Year. This is one reason why the auditor compares this year's Balance Sheet to Last Year to determine whether there are any significant changes in asset and liability balances (See Chapter 3).

While collusion can exist between friends, it is less likely because the one friend cannot be sure that the other friend will go along when the subject of collusion is brought up. If the friend does not agree to the collusion, he may decide that a clean conscience is more important than their friendship and report the friend to the department manager or General Manager. Where there are relatives involved in collusion, one of the relatives may have a guilty conscience if he knows about theft or fraud of another relative but will probably have a guiltier conscience if he turns in the relative. Thus, even if he does not agree to go along with the fraud or theft, he probably won't turn in his relative.

Nepotism can also involve indirect reporting such that there is a relative two levels below the manager. For example, the General Manager's daughter is a bartender at a small restaurant where there is no Controller. The General Manager reviews the inventories and sends them to Corporate Accounting. The General Manager knows that his daughter is stealing $200 in bar sales every night but keeps her in his employ. To cover up his daughter's theft, he changes the inventory his Bar Manager submits to him every month by adding enough in fictitious beer, liquor, and wine inventory to cover up his daughter's thefts.

As we have illustrated, nepotism should be discouraged. However, there are times when nepotism is unavoidable, such as when a Company buys an existing restaurant chain that has poor internal control, including nepotism among its employees. The Company may not feel right about terminating a good performing employee because he is related to his supervisor. If there is a union, it would be impossible to terminate the unionized worker because it is unlikely that nepotism is listed in the union contract as a cause for dismissal.

If possible, one of the employees should be reassigned so that he does not report to his relative. For example, if the bartender is related to the Bar Manager, the General Manager could make the bartender a waiter, reporting to the Dining Room Manager. If the bartender is represented by a union, this may also be impossible where the bartender does not wish to be a waiter.

The Company should have a policy that discourages nepotism. Its policy should state that where one relative or significant other reports to a related person, the relationship should be reported to the subsidiary President and the Corporate Vice President of Human Resources. The General Manager should send an email to the subsidiary President and the Corporate Vice President of Human Resources, with a carbon copy to the Regional Vice President of Operations, disclosing the relationship and asking for permission for the reporting relationship to continue.

If permission is granted, the subsidiary President and Corporate Vice President of Human Resources should each send an email to the General Manager acknowledging the relationship and agreeing to let it continue. Upon receipt of the return emails, the General Manager should print them and put a copy in each employee's Human Resources folder. The purpose of this procedure is to make senior management aware of the relationship so it can be monitored.

When performing his audit of Human Resources, the auditor should ask the Human Resources Manager and other management personnel if anyone at the field location reports directly or indirectly to a relative or significant other. If there is such a relationship, the auditor should examine the personnel files to determine whether there are written approvals from the subsidiary President and Corporate Vice President of Human Resources.

While examining employee files, the auditor should be aware of possible nepotism. Where a supervisor has the same last name as a subordinate, the auditor should see if the home addresses of the two people are the same. If not, the auditor should ask the Human Resources Manager if the two people are related. Of course, where a wife does not take the husband's last name or where a sister marries and takes her husband's name, it is impossible to determine where nepotism exists by merely looking at last names. For this reason, it is important to ask the Human Resources and other management personnel whether there are any related people reporting to each other. If there is such a relationship, the Human Resources Manager will often tell the auditor if asked.

Where the auditor uncovers nepotism that has not been disclosed to management or approval has not been documented, the auditor should note the situation in the audit program with the names of the related individuals. The comments should be cross referenced to the Discussion Points Worksheet.

Federal and State Poster Requirements

Employers are required under Federal and State labor laws to post certain posters that inform workers about labor law. The employer is required to hang these posters in a conspicuous place that is frequented by all employees. Thus, hanging the posters in the back of the kitchen where most employees do not go does not qualify as a conspicuous location. The posters should be hung near the time clock, the employee break room, the employee cafeteria, the employee bulletin board, or some other place where all employees go.

The Federal Department of Labor requires the following posters to be posted:

- Uniformed Services Employment and Reemployment Rights Act (USERRA),
- Equal Employment Opportunity is the Law,
- Federal Minimum Wage,
- Employee Polygraph Protection Act,
- Family and Medical Leave Act,
- OSHA-Job Safety & Health Protection.

Rather than obtaining six individual posters, the field location can purchase the Federal 6 in 1 poster (all six posters on one poster board) from companies that specialize in printing these posters. Thus, posting the one poster covers the location's Federal poster requirements. Some states require the Federal posters to be in English and Spanish. If the Human Resources Manager telephones the Department of Labor, they will tell him how to obtain the Federal posters or where he can purchase the Federal 6 in 1 poster (in Spanish, too). Alternatively, the Human Resources Manager can find information on obtaining these posters from the internet.

Each state has its own labor laws that in many cases are stricter than the Federal requirements. The employer is required to post the applicable state's posters along with the Federal posters. For example, Colorado requires the following to be posted:

• Workers' Compensation Parts 1 & 2,
• Discrimination Notice,
• Pay Day Notice,
• Unemployment Insurance,
• Minimum Wage Poster.

The Human Resources Manager can obtain the state posters from the state's Department of Labor. Alternatively, there are companies that print an all inclusive poster that includes the Federal and State poster requirements. Thus, in Colorado, there would be an 11 in 1 poster that can be purchased. The advantage of this poster is that by hanging the one poster, the Human Resources Manager can be sure he is covered for all required posters. If individual posters are posted, one or more posters can fall off the wall unnoticed and the restaurant is no longer in compliance with the posting requirements.

Many companies have various posters that they have designed and require their field locations to post in the same place as the governmental posters. They may be posters having to deal with Sexual Harassment, Safety Issues, Whistle Blower Hotline, etc. Company employment opportunities should be posted for a two-week period.

Prior to traveling to the field location, the auditor should get a list of the state required posters from the Corporate Human Resources Department or the State Department of Labor. While at the field location, he should check the posters that are displayed against his list to ensure all required Federal, State, and Company posters (including job postings) have been posted. He should also determine whether the posting location is a place that is frequented by all employees. The auditor should note on the audit program any required posters that are missing, and cross reference the comments to the Discussion Points Worksheet.

OSHA Reporting

The Federal government's Occupational Safety and Health Administration (OSHA) has been charged with ensuring that workers work in a safe work environment. As such, OSHA has the power to act upon complaints by sending an inspector to the workplace to investigate the validity of those complaints and take appropriate action. As such, OSHA can fine the employer if it determines that the employer is subjecting its employees to an unsafe work environment.

OSHA requires employers to maintain an OSHA 300 Log during the year. This log is summarized at year end on the OSHA 300A Summary. The OSHA 300A Summary must be posted for a three-month period every year in February following the completed year. This posting must continue through the end of April. The Human Resources Manager should be responsible for maintaining the OSHA 300 Log and summarizing this activity to the OSHA 300A Summary at year end and posting the Summary with the other government posters.

The instructions that accompany the OSHA 300 Log state that a work related injury should only be reported on an OSHA 300 Log if the injury or illness results in one of the following:

- Fatality, hospitalization of 3 or more employees, or a catastrophe,
- Medical treatment beyond defined first aid,
- Loss of consciousness,
- Days away from work, restricted work activity or job transfer,
- Any significant injury or illness diagnosed by a physician or licensed health care professional,
- Cases involving cancer, chronic irreversible disease, a fractured or cracked bone, or a punctured eardrum,
- Any needle stick or cut from a sharp object that is contaminated with another person's blood or potentially infectious material,
- Positive skin test or diagnosis by a physician for tuberculosis infection after exposure to a known case of active tuberculosis.

The OSHA 300 Log is a log of work-related injuries and illnesses. Each line is a separate incident. It provides the injured employee's name, job title, date of injury, where the event occurred, description of injury, injury classification, number of days the worker was away from work, transferred to another job, or job restriction, and the type of illness.

The OSHA 300A Summary is a summary of work-related injuries and illnesses. It summarizes the information on the OSHA 300 log by number of cases, number of days away from work, number of days on job transfer or restriction, and number of injuries and illnesses by type (injuries, skin disorders, respiratory conditions, poisonings, hearing loss, and all other illnesses).

The Human Resources Manager can obtain the OSHA 300 Log and the OSHA 300A Summary from OSHA. Information on these forms can also be obtained from OSHA's website at www.osha.gov.

The auditor should ask the Human Resources Manager to see the OSHA 300 Log. If the Human Resources Manager cannot produce it, even if there were no reportable incidents, it means he is not maintaining it. The auditor should look over the OSHA 300 Log and determine whether the incidents reported are reportable incidents and were reported correctly on the log. If the fieldwork occurs during the months of February through April, the auditor should determine whether the OSHA 300A Summary was posted. He should note any exceptions on the audit program and cross reference them to the Discussion Points Worksheet.

Employee Discipline for Cash Overages/Shortages

With modern cash registers and POS systems, the system tells the cashier the total amount due, the cashier enters the amount tendered, and the system tells the cashier how much change to give to the customer. With all this technology, there really is no reason for cash overages or shortages. Yet, some cashiers always seem to have a cash variance. A cash overage is as bad as a cash shortage because a cash overage means that the cashier short changed one or more customers.

The restaurant is not concerned about minor variances in the cash register, i.e. under $5 or $10, but when certain cashiers always seem to have a significant variance, there is a problem with the cashier. Management needs to put the cashier on notice that variances will not be tolerated. This is done through the progressive discipline process.

The General Manager needs to establish a cash variance policy in writing and make all cash handlers aware of this policy. One way to make cash handlers aware of the policy is to have each one sign a written statement acknowledging his awareness and understanding of the policy. The original signed statement is filed in the employee's Human Resources folder and a copy is given to the employee for his records. Figure 16.6 is an example of Jenny's Café's certification that each cash handling employee signs acknowledging his awareness of the Cash Variance policy.

When a restaurant sets a Cash Variance policy, the General Manager determines the amount that will be considered to be a notable variance, i.e. $10. When a cashier has an overage or shortage that is greater than $10, the cashier will be subject to the progressive discipline policy. Progressive discipline starts with a verbal warning, followed by a written warning, final warning, suspension, and termination if the fifth notable variance occurs within one year of the first.

Jenny's Café, Inc.
Denver Restaurant
Cash Variance Policy

Jenny's Café requires that every cashier's cash in his/her cash register balances to sales recorded on the POS system for every shift. A cash overage or shortage greater than $10 for a shift is considered to be a Notable Variance and subjects the cashier to Jenny's Café's progressive discipline policy.

Jenny's Café's cash variance policy requires each notable variance that occurs within one year of the first notable variance to be handled in a progressive manner. Jenny's Café's progressive discipline policy for cash variances follows the following sequence.

- First Notable Variance—Verbal Warning,
- Second Notable Variance—Written Warning,
- Third Notable Variance—Final Warning,
- Fourth Notable Variance—One Week Suspension,
- Fifth Notable Variance—Termination.

A major cash variance, i.e. a cash variance over $100 will result in the immediate suspension of the employee, pending an investigation. If the investigation does not resolve the cash variance, the employee will be terminated.

I have read Jenny's Café—Denver Restaurant's cash variance policy. I understand the policy and agree to abide by it.

Name: April James
Signature: *April James*

Date: October 7, 1991

Figure 16.6

Each stage of the progressive discipline process is documented on a Record of Employee Counseling. A new Record of Employee Counseling form is completed for each type of warning. While the first notable variance is considered to be a verbal warning, the warning must still be documented on a Record of Employee Counseling.

When a notable variance occurs, the cashier's department manager should complete the Record of Employee Counseling (supplied by the Human Resources Department) by indicating the date of the incident and describing the situation. For example, Accounting determined that on July 15, 2006, sales were \$3,550 and the cashier turned in \$3,510, a \$40 shortage. The department manager indicates on the form where the employee is on the progressive discipline scale, i.e. this is the first or verbal warning. He should state on the form the consequences of additional notable variances, i.e. a second notable variance will result in a written warning, a third notable variance will result in a final warning, a fourth will result in a one week suspension, and a fifth will result in termination. Some companies do not have a final warning, and suspend the employee on the third notable variance and terminate the employee on the fourth notable variance.

The department manager should sign and date the Record of Employee Counseling. He meets with the employee to discuss the incident and listens to any comments the employee may have. There should be a place on the Record of Employee Counseling for the employee to note any comments he may have regarding the incident. At the end of the meeting, the department manager should ask the employee to sign and date the form. The department manager makes a copy for the employee and files the original in the employee's Human Resources folder.

If the employee goes through an entire year after the first warning without additional warnings, or goes through the second, third, and fourth step without reaching the fifth step in one year, the process starts over. For example, John Jones receives a verbal warning on February 21, 2006 for being \$35 short. He receives a written warning on June 15, 2006 for being \$25 over, and a final warning on September 27, 2006 for being \$55 short. On March 16, 2007, John is \$45 short. Since a year has passed from the time he received the original verbal warning, the verbal, written, and final warnings expired on February 20, 2006 and John receives a verbal warning for the shortage on March 16, 2007.

A major variance, i.e. a cash variance over \$100, generally results in the immediate suspension of the employee pending an investigation by the

Controller and the Human Resources Manager. If the Controller is not able to resolve the cash variance, the employee is terminated. The investigation and its results should be documented and signed and dated by the Controller and Human Resources Manager

The auditor should ask the General Manager to give him a copy of the location's cash variance policy. Where there is no written cash variance policy (a discussion point), the auditor should ask the General Manager to explain the field location's cash variance policy. As part of the audit process, the auditor should select at least one week in the prior month and list each notable difference that he sees during the test period. The auditor does not want to select the most recent week because he wants to be sure that management had a chance to complete the progressive discipline process.

The auditor should examine the applicable employees' Human Resources files and determine whether progressive discipline was documented on a Record of Employee Counseling form. If not, the auditor should note this on the workpaper and cross reference the notation to the Discussion Points Worksheet.

Other Discipline

Normally, if an employee is performing a task incorrectly or unsatisfactorily, the supervisor corrects the individual and the employee begins performing the task as desired. This is part of the training process and is considered to be normal. However, some employees persist in performing the task in an unsatisfactory manner, even after being corrected. In this situation, the supervisor contacts the Human Resources Manager and explains the situation. The Human Resources Manager will advise the supervisor to document the situation on a Record of Employee Counseling form, the first step in the progressive discipline process.

The purpose of the progressive discipline process is to make the employee aware that he is performing in an unsatisfactory manner or engaging in inappropriate behavior. The progressive discipline process gives the employee a chance to correct the problem and demonstrate that he can and will perform in a satisfactory manner.

The Record of Employee Counseling form should include the following information:

- Dates and brief summary of any previous counselings and/or discussions,
- Detailed description of the incident that needs to be addressed, including dates and examples,

- Detailed description of the standards that must be met (must be measurable, understandable, reasonable, and within the employee's influence),
- Time period during which improvement must be made, i.e. 30 days, 60 days, 90 days, etc.
- Section for the employee to note comments,
- Signatures and dates of the employee and supervisor.

Most companies have a four-step progressive discipline process, as follows: Verbal Warning, Written Warning, Final Warning and Termination. Progressive discipline for non-cash variance issues may differ somewhat from the cash variance process, i.e. the fourth step is termination rather than suspension. Reasons for subjecting employees to discipline include the following (not all inclusive):

- Unsatisfactory performance or failure to meet minimum performance standards,
- Carelessness, negligence, incomplete work,
- Endangering the safety of oneself, fellow employees, or others,
- Sanitation violations,
- Falsifying company records,
- Punching a co-worker's time card or swiping a co-worker's ID card,
- Failure to record sales for product served to a customer,
- Failure to work overtime when requested or working overtime without management's permission,
- Conducting excessive personal business on the job, i.e. mail, e-mail, telephone calls, etc.),
- Lack of professionalism in performing one's tasks,
- Infractions of dress code or grooming policy,
- Violations of the company's anti-harassment policy,
- Sexual Harassment,
- Refusal to work or accept job assignments,
- Misusing identification cards,
- Excessive absence,
- Leaving early without permission,
- Excessive tardiness,
- Excessive breaks.
- Not returning promptly from breaks.

When the employee demonstrates consistent improvement in the performance that resulted in the commencement of progressive discipline, the supervisor completes a Record of Employee Counseling form that officially removes the employee from counseling. The employee's supervisor signs the Record of Employee Counseling form and discusses the action with the employee who signs the Record of Employee Counseling form that removes him from counseling. If after removal from counseling, the employee reverts back to the unsatisfactory performance, the next step in the progressive discipline process can be taken.

The union contract often lists major offenses that result in immediate dismissal. When an employee commits a major offense, he is suspended pending an investigation. The Human Resources Manager should contact the Human Resources professional at Corporate who is assigned to the field location and the Corporate Labor Relations Department (if a union is involved) to make them aware of the situation.

The field location's Human Resources Manager should conduct an investigation of the situation. He should talk to witnesses, document their statements, and have the witnesses sign the statements. When he is finished with the investigation, he should document the results in a report, sign, and date the report. The Human Resources Manager puts the original report in the employee's Human Resources folder with the copies of the signed witness statements stapled to the report. He sends copies of the report to the Corporate Human Resources representative and the Corporate Director of Labor Relations. If the Human Resources Manager verifies the cause for dismissal during his investigation, the employee is terminated.

The following are examples of major offenses (not all inclusive) that can result in immediate suspension pending an investigation and dismissal if found to be true:

- Theft of cash or property,
- Intoxication on the premises,
- Consuming alcoholic beverages while working,
- Illegal drug possession on the premises,
- Possession of a fire arm on the premises,
- Dishonesty, i.e. undercharging or overcharging a customer,
- Willfully damaging Company property,
- Fighting, displaying abusive behavior that causes physical harm to other persons,
- Verbally abusing or physically assaulting another individual,
- Accepting or offering bribes.

While reviewing employee files during Human Resources testing, the auditor should be alert to files containing a Record of Employee Counseling or other documentation of disciplinary action taken. He should review the Record of Employee Counseling to see whether the situation was handled according to Company procedures. If the employee discipline was not properly documented or did not comply with Company procedures, the auditor should note the situation in the workpapers. He should cross reference the comment to the Discussion Points worksheet.

Summary

Human Resources personnel should not process Payroll. The Human Resources Manager should be the approver on the Employee Maintenance Form, not the Human Resources Clerk. The auditor should review the duties of the various participants in the Human Resources process to determine whether duties are properly segregated.

Each employee should have a separate Human Resources folder that contains the employment application and resume (if applicable), Employee Maintenance Forms (hiring form and status changes, i.e. raises, address changes, promotions, terminations, etc.), Drug Test Consent & Release Form, W-4, disciplinary action documentation, etc. The auditor should select a sample of employees and determine whether each employee has a Human Resources folder and whether each folder has the required documentation signed and dated by the applicable personnel.

All employee files must be locked in a file cabinet and stored in a locked room overnight. The auditor should determine whether all employee files are properly secured.

The employee must sign the Employee Maintenance Form (EMF) that documents the hire and other EMF's that document status changes. EMF's that document new hires and major changes, i.e. pay raises, promotions, terminations, must be signed by two managers; one must be the Department Manager or General Manager. The auditor should select a sample of employees and determine whether their EMF's were properly completed and contain all required signatures.

Many companies drug test applicants to ensure the workplace is a drug free environment. The applicant should sign a Drug Test Consent and Release form; if a minor, the parents must also sign. The auditor should select a sample of employees and determine whether all new hires have been properly drug tested.

All employees hired after November 6, 1986 must have a completed and properly signed I9 form in a separate I9 binder. The I9 is used to prove identity and work eligibility. The auditor should select a sample of employees and determine whether the I9 requirements have been met.

A Termination Checklist should be completed each time an associate terminates. The Termination Checklist is a reminder for the Human Resources Department to retrieve all company assets, change passwords and safe combinations (if applicable), and provide the employee with all payments due and explain COBRA eligibility. The auditor should select a sample of recently terminated employees and determine whether a Termination Checklist was properly completed, including all signatures.

While there are Federal Child Labor Laws, each state has its own requirements; the stricter of the two apply. They generally limit the number of hours the child can work and the hours during which the child is permitted to work. The auditor should select 5-10 minors and determine whether all applicable Child Labor Laws were followed.

Every establishment that serves alcohol should have an Alcohol Awareness training program in place. Each alcohol serving employee should attend an Alcohol Awareness training session annually, evidenced by a certification signed by the employee. The auditor should select a sample of alcohol serving associates and determine whether each one has a certification signed by the employee in the last year in his Human Resources folder.

The Federal and State governments require employers to post certain posters in a conspicuous location frequented by the employees. The auditor should have a list of the required posters for the State where he is conducting the audit and determine whether all required posters are posted.

The restaurant should have a written progressive discipline policy in place that progresses from a verbal warning to termination. Notable cash variances and other violations of work rules and company policy should subject the employee to progressive discipline. The auditor should determine whether notable variances were followed up with documented progressive discipline and other violations were properly handled.

Discussion Questions and Case Studies

1. Why should there be a separate Human Resources folder for each employee? What types of documents should there be in each folder?
2. What is the purpose of the I9? Is the completed I9 normally filed in the employee's Human Resources folder? Explain your answer.
3. What type of information is normally contained on the Employee

Maintenance Form that is used to hire a new employee? Whose signatures should be on the form?

4. What is the purpose of the Termination Checklist? What type of information should be found on the Termination Checklist?

5. You are auditing Route 55 Bar & Grill during early February 2006. The State requires minors to bring a work permit to the employer on the first day of work, and it requires the employer to post the work schedule for all minors. Minors under 16 may work 3 hours a day on days that school is in session and 8 hours a day on days that school is not in session, up to 18 hours per week. In addition, minors under 16 years of age may not work before 7:00 a.m. or after 7:00 p.m. In looking through the time cards, you notice there are two minors aged 15, three minors aged 16 and one minor aged 17. The minor work schedule is posted is for the week ending January 28, 2006. Each minor is scheduled to work from 4:00 p.m. to 7:00 p.m. Monday through Friday. In looking through the time cards for the week ending January 28, 2006, you notice that each minor generally punches out between 7:15 p.m. and 7:30 p.m. In adding up the hours worked for the week, each minor has worked just under 18 hours. Do you have any audit issues? What are your recommendations to management?

6. You are auditing Pier 27 Seafood Emporium in May 2006. In reviewing the I9's, you notice the following:

- On Juan Garcia's I9, the employee's signature in Section 1 is dated January 9, 2006 and the employer's certification in Section 2 is dated January 16, 2006,
- On Jennifer Chin's I9, in Section 1, she checked off "A Lawful Resident Alien" but did not fill in any details,
- On Justin Ostrowski's I9, copies of his driver's license and Social Security Card are stapled to the I9 but Section 2 is not completed,
- Simon Mabutu's I9 had Section 1 fully completed, except for the Maiden Name,
- On Ellen Smith's I9, Section 1 was dated February 15, 2006 but the Employer Certification in Section 2 says that Ellen began employment on February 27, 2006,
- On Larry Petrovich's I9, Section 2 was completed with a U.S. Passport, Driver's License, and Social Security card,
- On Erika Schultz's I9, the Address, Social Security Number, and Date of Birth were not completed,

- Rosalina Perez's I9 is supported with a driver's license and Social Security card that is marked "Not eligible for employment without additional work permit,"
- Wilson Chen's I9 was supported with a Driver's License that expired on June 13, 2012, and Social Security Card,
- On John Li's I9, Section 1 was checked "An Alien Authorized to work until December 28, 2005"—Section 3 was not completed,
- On Ivan Malikov's I9, Section 3 was completed with an Employment Authorization Card, Form 688A, but no Expiration Date was noted,
- On Kimberly Johnson's I9, Section 1 was dated March 20, 2006, Section 2 indicated that Kimberly began work on March 21, and the Section 2 certification was dated on March 22.

  Do you have any audit issues? What are your recommendations to management?

7. You are auditing the Star 88 Sports Bar and Café, a chain of 44 restaurants located in most major cities throughout the United States. Star 88 Sports Bar and Café has a Corporate policy that requires every alcohol serving employee to take annual Alcohol Awareness Training and certify that they attended the training, had a chance to ask questions, and understood the training. When you examine the employee folders of a sample of bartenders, waiters, and waitresses, you do not see any certifications in the folders. When you ask Lenore Lennon, the Human Resources Manager why there are no signed certifications in the employee folders, Lenore gives the following explanation, "We have annual training meetings for each existing employee and monthly training sessions for new employees. For each meeting, I set up an Alcohol Awareness Meeting Sign In Sheet with the date of the meeting noted at the top. Each employee attending the session prints his name and signs next to his printed name." You are able to tie each employee in your sample to the Alcohol Awareness Training Meeting Sign In Sheet. However, you notice that new alcohol serving employees often start working in their jobs before attending the Alcohol Awareness Training Meeting. Do you have any audit issues? What are your recommendations to management?

8. You are auditing the Great California Bear Bar & Grill, one of 50 restaurants owned by State Themed Restaurants, Inc. Corporate policy dictates that each restaurant posts all required federal and state posters plus the company's Sexual Harassment poster, Safety poster, and

Company Hotline poster. Each restaurant is also required to post new jobs for two weeks. You look at the employee bulletin board in the employee cafeteria and notice that the restaurant has the Federal 5 in 1 poster in English and Spanish and all required California state posters. When you ask Rachel Slade, the Human Resources Manager, why there are no job postings on the bulletin board, Rachel says, "The only job openings sent over from Corporate in the last month were jobs in New York, Boston, Dallas, and Washington. I know no one here is interested in relocating to any of those cities so it would be a waste of my time to post those job postings." Do you have any audit issues? What are your recommendations to management?

9. You are auditing The Daily Catch Restaurant. When you ask Robert Robbins, the General Manager, what the restaurant's policy is regarding Cash Variances, he says, "Any cash shortage over $10 is written up as a notable shortage. We utilize the Company's Record of Employee Counseling to document all shortages over $10." When you ask if overages over $10 are written up as notable variances, Robert replies, "A cash overage doesn't hurt us, it helps us. I'm not going to penalize an employee for helping us." When you ask Robert if the department manager discusses the Record of Employee Counseling with the employee, Robert replies, "Angela, our Controller tells the employee that he had a shortage over $10 and that he will be written up." Do you have any audit issues? What are your recommendations to management?

CHAPTER 17
AUDITING
INFORMATION TECHNOLOGY,
RISK MANAGEMENT, OTHER

Learning Objectives

After reading this chapter, you should be able to:

1. Know what types of computerized systems should be password protected, how often the password should be changed, and how to create a password that is not easily deciphered.
2. Determine whether computer hardware is properly secured to prevent unauthorized access,
3. Know how CO_2 tanks, propane tanks, and tanks under pressure should be secured to prevent injuries from tanks tipping over, and determine whether these tanks are properly secured,
4. Determine whether field location personnel ask for photo identification from official visitors before granting them access to company assets and records or allowing them into restricted areas.

Overview

Computers are a fact of life in the business world. POS systems are used to record sales and balance cash to those sales. PC's are used to crunch numbers that provide the users with information to run the business. Main frame computers are used to process information that is summarized into the General Ledger. We will discuss how to backup the information that computers process so it can be retrieved in the event the primary data storage device breaks down.

PC's and mainframe systems accessed by field personnel should require passwords to access them so their data are protected. We will look at how passwords should be created and how the auditor determines whether users have followed Company guidelines in creating their passwords.

POS system access should be limited to personnel who need to use it. Types of access should be based and limited to job responsibilities. We will examine who should have access and how the auditor determines whether POS system access promotes strong segregation of duties.

Computer equipment, such as PC's, main frame terminals, file servers, etc. should be properly secured to prevent unauthorized access. We will discuss how the auditor reviews hardware security throughout the premises and notes any problem areas for discussion with management.

Each PC should have anti-virus software that is regularly updated whether or not it is connected to the internet. We will look at how the auditor determines whether all PC's at the field location have current anti-virus software.

Grill hoods must be cleaned every 6 months. Fire suppression systems must also be inspected every 6 months. Fire extinguishers must be inspected annually. We will examine how the auditor determines whether the grill hoods were cleaned and fire suppression systems and fire extinguishers were inspected on schedule.

CO_2 and propane tanks contain gases under pressure. If a tank falls over and the top breaks off, the top will be propelled like a missile and could seriously injure someone. We will discuss how the auditor determines whether these tanks are properly secured to prevent them from tipping over.

There are miscellaneous compliance areas that the auditor needs to review, such as lease requirements, municipal requirements, record retention requirements, license requirements, Health Department requirements, etc. We will examine each of these areas and discuss what the auditor should examine to determine whether the field location is in compliance.

Location personnel should request photo identification from official visitors before showing them company records or allowing them into restricted areas. We will discuss how the auditor determines whether field location personnel examine photo identification from official visitors.

In Practice

Aimee Stone walks into Chef Stephan's office, adjacent to the Main Kitchen. Aimee says to the Chef, "I have pulled the latest invoices from Easy Does It Fire Prevention Company, the company that cleans the grill hoods and inspects the fire suppression systems and the fire extinguishers. These invoices are 18 months old. Company standards require the grill hoods to be cleaned every 6 months, the fire suppression system to be inspected every 6 months, and the fire extinguishers to be inspected annually."

"You're right, Aimee. I totally forgot about it," Chef Stephan replies.

"On the day Easy Does It comes in, you should set up the next appointment so you won't forget to call them later. Then you can mark the next visit on your calendar so you'll know when they are coming."

"I'll get on it right away," Chef Stephan replies.

"I've noticed that the CO2 tanks throughout the building are not secured to the wall with a chain. In the warehouse, the CO2 tanks are standing unsecured in a corner. If someone knocked over one of these tanks, someone could get injured. Even the empties should be chained up so the weight of the tank does not injure someone."

"I'll have to get with Joey on that so he can get Roger Sanchez to screw chains into the walls where we have CO2 tanks," Chef Stephan replies.

"That would be good," Aimee says.

Segregation of Duties

The Controller should periodically review the miscellaneous areas, such as computer technology, risk management, etc. to determine whether proper segregation of duties exists and these areas comply with sound principles of internal control. POS systems should be set up so that cashiers and waiters only have access to those areas they need to perform their functions. Void approval, file maintenance, and report printing should be reserved for management. For restaurant chains, the Corporate Help Desk should be available to help with computer issues.

During the audit, the auditor should review the miscellaneous areas to determine whether there is adequate segregation of duties. Any internal control weaknesses noted should be documented in the Internal Control Questionnaire and cross referenced to the Discussion Points Worksheet.

Computer Back Up

You come to work one day, turn on your computer, and try to open the file you worked on yesterday. You find out that the file is no longer there. Not only that, but every other file that was on your hard drive is gone. You telephone your service rep who comes over, examines your computer, and declares that your hard drive is defective and needs to be replaced.

"What about all the files I saved on the hard drive?" you ask the service rep.

"They're gone," the service rep replies. "You saved everything on back up, of course. Once I replace the hard drive, you transfer the files from the back up disks to your new hard drive and you're back in business."

But did you save everything on back up disks or a flash (zip) drive? It is amazing how many people do not bother backing up their files. If they lose the data on the hard drive, it is gone forever.

If companies do not back up their POS systems, Accounts Payable system, Payroll system, and General Ledger system on disk or tape, they risk losing all data that they need to operate. Not only should these systems be backed up every day, but once a week, these systems should be backed up on a tape or other portable storage device and taken to an offsite location for storage. In the event of a fire or other catastrophe, the tape can be removed from the offsite location, inserted into a computer, the current week's activity is entered, and reports can be processed.

Large companies have a file server at Corporate Headquarters that dials up the file server at each field location every night after the location has closed and data processing has stopped. The Corporate file server backs up the online systems, such as the General Ledger subsystems (Sales/Accounts Receivable, Accounts Payable, etc.) at Corporate Headquarters. However, the field locations are still responsible for backing up offline systems, such as the POS system, inventory control systems, etc, each day. If there is no Corporate backup, the restaurant must perform this function.

Important spreadsheets should be backed up onto a disk or zip (flash) drive any time changes are made. As a matter of practice, every PC user should be in the habit of backing up each file onto a disk or zip drive whenever they make a change to the file.

The auditor should ask the Controller how the location backs up the data on its systems, and whether data is stored offsite. When was the last time the data were backed up and a tape taken to the offsite location? She should verify the Controller's answers by questioning the office employees about their back up practices. Any system or important spreadsheet that is not backed up daily is an internal control deficiency. If a current day tape was not taken to the offsite storage location within the last week, it is an internal control deficiency. The auditor should note any deficiencies in the audit program or Internal Control Questionnaire and cross reference the notation to the Discussion Points Worksheet.

Passwords

All online systems, such as Accounts Payable, Payroll, Sales Reporting, etc. should be password protected so that only authorized individuals are able to process transactions. Likewise, each PC should be password protected to prevent unauthorized access to company files, word processing documents, and spreadsheet files. The Company's Information Technology network should prompt each user to change her password every 30 days.

Passwords should be unique words unrelated to the system the password is accessing. For example, jennyscafe, payroll, accountspayable, inventory, etc. are all bad choices for passwords because they would be too easy for an unauthorized person to guess. The user's name, husband's name, child's name, etc. are also poor choices because they are also easy to guess but are often used. If possible, the password should be a combination of letters, words, and special characters. For example, "&%snowy3#@" would be an excellent choice for a password.

Hackers can obtain software that goes through most of the common words in the English language. The software program tries every word in its dictionary in sequence until it finds a match. If there are no other numbers or symbols in the password, the software will eventually find a match and the hacker will have access to the data on your PC. Once in, the hacker not only has access to the data on the PC's hard drive, but also to whatever data in the network the user has been given security clearance to access.

The Company's data security should shut out any user who enters six incorrect passwords. Once shut out from the Company's network, data security should not allow the user to log in until the Information Technology Department resets the password. If a user fails six times to enter her correct password, she needs to call the Help Desk at Corporate. The Help Desk resets the password and gives the user a temporary password that the network requires the user to change after the first log in.

The auditor should select several PC and mainframe users and ask each user whether the password is unique and the features noted above are in place, i.e. a combination of words, numbers, and special characters. Any deficiencies should be noted on the Internal Control Questionnaire or Audit Program and cross referenced to the Discussion Points Worksheet.

POS System Access

Access to the Point of Sale (POS) system should be limited to those who need to use it, i.e. waiters, waitresses, bartenders, supervisors, etc. Each person with access is issued a swipe card and a unique access code. When the waitress swipes the card into the POS reader, the waitress keys her access code. The system recognizes that the access code goes with that specific swipe card and it will accept transactions entered by the waitress for which she has been granted POS security. For example, the POS system will allow the waitress to enter orders to the kitchen and bar, but it won't grant the waitress access to the screen that allows the user to obtain the sales report for the cashier station.

The Dining Room Manager has security clearance in the POS system to grant access levels to the employees who need access. She should grant POS system access to employees based on and limited to job responsibilities. Thus, bussers and kitchen staff are not granted any access to the POS system because they do not need it. Waiters and waitresses are granted the first level of access that allows them to enter orders. The cashier is granted a second level of access that allows her to look up guest checks and to enter cash tendered. Supervisors are granted the third level of access that allows them to void erroneous transactions entered by the waitress or cashier and to obtain sales reports from the POS system. The Dining Room Manager is granted a fourth level of access that allows her to grant POS security access to other employees.

The cashier should close the cash drawer after every transaction. She should not keep the drawer open for multiple transactions. Staff should keep their POS swipe cards in their pockets when not using them. They should not lay them down next to the order entry terminal or other places where they can lose them or unauthorized personnel can take them.

The auditor should ask different types of employees what types of transactions they can make in the POS system and determine whether that level of security is appropriate for the position. She should note any instances of inappropriate security access levels in the Internal Control Questionnaire or Audit Program and cross reference the comments to the Discussion Points Worksheet.

Hardware Security

Computer hardware, including PC's, peripheral equipment (printers, scanners, etc.) needs to be properly secured so it is not stolen or intentionally damaged. Individual offices that contain PC's should be locked at night when the occupier leaves. When the last person in the office leaves, the office should be locked. When the restaurant closes and the last employee leaves the premises, she should be sure that all doors leading into the restaurant are locked with a dead bolt. File servers should be located in a separate room that is kept locked 24 hours a day so unauthorized personnel cannot tamper with them.

Laptop computers are particularly vulnerable to theft since they are portable. If a laptop is sitting on someone's desk, it is easy for someone passing by to unplug the laptop from the adapter and walk out with it. When leaving for the day, the user should unplug the laptop and lock it in a locked file cabinet or locked overhead cabinet. The keys should not be kept somewhere that is easy to find, i.e. as a desk drawer unless the drawer is also locked. If the user has an office that will not be opened by cleaners, the laptop can stay on the desk provided the office is locked when the user leaves.

The auditor should review the computer security situation through observations during the period she is conducting the audit. Do managers with PC's lock their offices when they leave? Are laptops properly secured at night? Is the file server located in a room that is locked 24 hours a day? If the auditor is the first to arrive in the morning, is the office locked? When the auditor leaves late at night, does the Manager on Duty check all doors to make sure they are locked? Do the outer doors to the premises have deadbolt locks?

The auditor should note any computer security exceptions in the Internal Control Questionnaire or Audit Program. Any comments should be cross referenced to the Discussion Points Worksheet.

Anti-Virus Software

A virus is a computer program that someone builds into a file that was designed to systematically destroy every file on the PC's storage devices and the network. It is often picked up through email, but can be picked up from a contaminated disk or even from your Company's internal network. There is nothing worse that logging into your PC and finding that all files are corrupted because you picked up a virus. Once your PC has a virus, it spreads to any external storage devices that are inserted into the PC, i.e. disks and zip drives.

Every PC should have anti-virus software that detects viruses when they appear, attacks them, and destroys them before they damage your files. There are several good anti-virus programs that the Company can purchase and the IT Department can support, i.e. Norton Anti-Virus and McAfee. All field locations must purchase the anti-virus software that is designated as the Company standard. There are new viruses developed every day that are immune to current anti-virus software. The company that designed the anti-virus software is constantly updating it for new viruses that are discovered. As the updates are issued, they are immediately sent to all license holders via email.

Upon receipt of an update, IT will update all PC's within the company that are hooked up to the Company's internal network. If someone has anti-virus software made by another software company, she will not get the benefit of the Company update. Unless she constantly updates her anti-virus software through the internet, it quickly becomes out of date and useless. If the restaurant is stand alone, the Controller, General Manager, or designee should be alert to anti-virus updates received via email and update all PC's throughout the internal network.

Most companies have spam filters that filter out unsolicited emails the system does not recognize. The user goes to the spam quarantine on her PC and selects which emails caught in the filter should be sent to her regular email to be read and which should be deleted. Once caught in the spam filter, the user can designate the sender as a trusted sender and the sender's email will be accepted in the future. Users should be careful about opening attachments from unfamiliar sources. If there is a virus in the attachment, opening the attachment will release the virus.

The auditor should discuss anti-virus software with the Controller and General Manager to find out if the restaurant is using the Company standard software. Then the auditor should select several PC's and determine whether the PC has the current Company specified software. By looking at the symbols on the bottom right corner of the screen, the auditor should be able to recognize the symbol for the Company approved software. She should note any exceptions in the Internal Control Questionnaire or audit program and cross reference them to the Discussion Points Worksheet.

Grill Hoods & Fire Suppression System Maintenance

Normally there are grill hoods over the stoves with fans that suck up the steam and evaporating grease from the kitchen and blow it outside through ventilation ducts. As the stoves are constantly in use, grease and grime build up inside the grill hoods. If they are not periodically cleaned, a fire could start. The Executive Chef should make arrangements to have the grill hoods cleaned every 6 months.

All restaurants should have a fire suppression system. When a fire breaks out and the temperature hits a certain level, water sprays from the nozzles and douses the fire. The Dining Room Manager or General Manager should make arrangements with a service provider to test the fire suppression system every 6 months to ensure there is sufficient water pressure in the system and that it is working properly.

There should be fire extinguishers in the kitchen, dining room, bar, banquet room, warehouse, offices, etc. To ensure the fire extinguishers are ready for use in the event of a fire, the General Manager should make arrangements with a service provider to have them inspected once a year. The inspectors put a new tag on the fire extinguisher with the month and year punched on the tag.

The auditor should review recent invoices from the service providers to determine when the grill hoods were last cleaned and the fire suppression system was last tested. She should look for fire extinguishers throughout the facility and check the inspection tags to ensure they were inspected within the last year. Any exceptions to the maintenance and inspection schedules should be noted in the Internal Control Questionnaire and cross referenced to the workpapers.

CO2 and Propane Storage

CO2 tanks are hooked up to soda dispensers and draft beer systems. Most soda dispensers are post mix systems that mix one part syrup to five parts water to produce soda when mixed with CO2. The CO2 is also used as the propellant to drive the syrup to the dispenser tower where it is mixed with water. In draft beer systems, the CO2 is the propellant that drives the beer from the keg to the draft beer dispenser.

Propane is used for cooking. Generally, propane is used for cooking on a portable stove outdoors. However, it can be used for indoor cooking in some restaurants that do not have natural gas available.

Both CO2 and propane tanks have contents under high pressure. If a tank fell over and the top broke off, the top would be propelled like a missile and would seriously injure anyone that it would hit. To prevent an accident, all CO2 and propane tanks (in storage and in operation) must have chains going around the tank that are chained to a wall to prevent them from falling over. The chain must be tight around the tanks because a slack chain will not prevent the tank from falling over. Even CO2 and propane tanks that are hooked up to dispensers and stoves must have a chain going securely around the tank. Empty tanks should also be chained to prevent them from falling on someone's foot because they are still quite heavy. CO2 or propane tanks should definitely not be used as door props, whether they are full or empty.

As part of the audit, the auditor should go to each location where CO_2 and propane tanks are kept, including the warehouse, bar, kitchen, banquet room, etc. and determine whether all full and empty CO_2 and propane tanks are properly secured by chaining them to a wall or other means of preventing them from tipping over. Any exceptions should be noted on the audit program or on a separate workpaper and cross referenced to the Discussion Points worksheet.

Lease Compliance

Restaurants typically lease the buildings where they are located. Even where the building is company owned, the title to the building is often in the name of a separate subsidiary and a lease would have been executed between the two subsidiaries. When a new restaurant opens, the Corporate Law Department writes or at least reviews the lease prior to the Company President or one of the Vice Presidents signing the lease.

The lease is typically for a set number of years and may have one or more options to renew. The lease specifies the amount of rent that the Company will pay the landlord and the date it is due. It typically is a flat fee but could also include a percentage of sales. Leases that specify a flat fee as rent typically have a rent escalator that increases the rent each year of the lease based on the Consumer Price Index. For example, the lease could specify that the rent will increase by the Consumer Price Index plus 1%. Thus if the monthly rent is $5,000 and the Consumer Price Index in the first year of the lease was 4%, the monthly rent would increase by 5% or $250 in the second year of the lease.

Where the Company is operating a restaurant in a national or state park, the rent could be entirely a percentage of revenues. Sometimes the percentage of sales is subject to a rent guarantee. For example, if Jenny's Café were to operate a restaurant in a national park, it might negotiate a lease that pays 20% of revenues as rent, subject to an annual rent guarantee of $2 million. If 20% of revenues does not equal $2 million dollars or more during the calendar year, Jenny's Café would pay the difference as additional rent.

The lease may specify that the landlord is entitled to dine at the restaurant at a reduced price. For example, the lease may specify that the landlord can entertain guests at the restaurant and receive a 25% discount off the menu prices. If there is a percentage of sales component in the rent, the lease generally specifies that discounted sales are not subject to the rent percentage.

In the case where all or part of the rent is in the form of a percentage of sales, the Controller would prepare a rent statement each month that summarizes the sales for the month and multiplies it by the applicable percentage. Any fixed rents or rent guarantees are added to the percentage rent. The Controller encloses the rent check with the rent statement and mails it to the landlord.

The lease typically specifies who is responsible for cleaning, maintenance, and repairs to the facility. Generally, the tenant is responsible for cleaning and routine maintenance, but the landlord is responsible for major repairs to the building, i.e. a new roof, painting the interior and exterior of the building, new plumbing, etc.

The auditor should have read the lease as part of the planning phase of the audit and taken notes on the unique features of the audit. Referring to those notes, the auditor checks the field location's operations for compliance to the lease provisions. She designs tests or observations that measure whether the field location is in compliance with those provisions. The auditor should obtain the most recent rent payment and determine whether the correct amount of rent was paid. Any exceptions to the lease provisions should be noted in the audit program or on a separate workpaper and cross referenced to the Discussion Points Worksheet.

Municipal Requirements

The Controller and General Manager should be familiar with any unique municipal requirements in the area and should ensure that the restaurant is in compliance. For example, the municipality may have a requirement that paper, plastics, bottles, and cans are separated from normal garbage and recycled. In this case, the General Manager must be sure that cans and plastic containers are cleaned, put in a separate recycling bin, and arrangements made with the trash collection company to recycle this waste. Failure to follow the municipality's recycling ordinance would subject the restaurant to fines. Even more costly than the fine might be the bad publicity surrounding the incident when the media learns of the restaurant's failure to comply with the local ordinance. Customers may stop patronizing the restaurant if they believe the Company is not a good corporate citizen.

During the initial meetings with the local management, the auditor should ask if there are any unique municipal requirements. The auditor could also ask the Corporate Legal Department if it is aware of any unique municipal requirements in the municipality where the restaurant is located. She should ask local management how the employees become aware of these requirements. Management should make employees aware of their responsibilities during orientation and periodic training meetings.

During the audit, the auditor should observe whether the municipal requirements are being followed by all employees. For example, if during kitchen observations, the auditor sees that the cooks are throwing dirty jars, cans, and bottles into trash cans along with food waste, they are not complying with the municipality's recycling requirement. The auditor should note any exceptions in the audit program or in the workpapers and cross reference the comments to the Discussion Points Worksheet.

Record Retention

The accounting function inevitably produces a lot of reports and other records that must be retained as supporting documentation. The POS system produces sales reports by cashier and the overall food and beverage operation that are used to produce the sales journal. Sign In/Sign Out Sheets, Time Cards, and Time Keeping Reports are used to enter time worked into the payroll system to produce payroll checks and various payroll reports. Purchase orders, packing slips, and invoices are used to order product, receive it, and pay for it. Inventory reports are produced each time a physical inventory is taken. Each of these records must be stored in a place where they can be easily retrieved if needed for an audit.

Records should be clearly labeled and stored in file cabinets. Normally, the restaurant would have the current year's records and the prior year's records in a metal file cabinet so they are easily retrieved. Invoices should be stored in folders. Each folder has the name of the vendor whose invoices are kept inside. One drawer is used for the current year, and a second drawer for the prior year.

Sales reports and the sales journals should be kept in folders such that there is a separate folder for each sales day. Supporting documentation can be kept in separate accordion folders, marked by sales day, if they are too bulky to keep with the sales reports. The supporting documentation can be kept in a separate file drawer. If the Accounting Department runs out of file cabinet space, the Sales Reporting Clerk can move the oldest accordion folders containing supporting documentation and put them into record retention boxes or regular boxes and put them in storage. The boxes should be clearly labeled as to their contents, i.e. Sales Documentation: January 1–31, 2006. The boxes for the current year and prior year that are put in the record retention room should be put in a place that is easily accessible because these records will probably be used throughout the year for reference in answering questions that arise.

Payroll Sign In Sheets, Time Cards, or Time Keeping Reports should be stored in accordion folders with other payroll information, such as tips, payroll adjustment sheets, etc, by Pay Week. The Payroll Clerk should store payroll records for the current year and prior year in a locked file cabinet along with the payroll reports.

Invoices with attached purchase orders and packing slips (where applicable) should be filed in folders by vendor name. The Accounts Payable Clerk should store the current year's and prior year's invoices in separate drawers of a metal file cabinet.

Inventory reports are sent to the Controller once they are completed. The Controller should file all inventory reports for an inventory period in one folder, labeled with the period end date. The Controller should keep the inventory reports for the current year and the prior year in a file cabinet.

In January, office staff personnel take the files that are now two years old from the metal file cabinets and put them into paper retention boxes or regular cardboard boxes. They label the boxes with their contents and bring the boxes to a room that has been designated as the record retention room. The boxes should be stacked with the contents labeled on the boxes to the front so they are easily seen. Boxes should be organized in logical sequence so a particular file is easy to locate. Thus, if sales records are stored, the January box should be followed by the February box, and the March box, etc. Boxes should be stacked in rows with aisles so people can move among the boxes and easily retrieve the ones they are trying to find.

Since confidential records from prior years are stored in the record retention room, this room must always be locked. Only the General Manager, Controller, Dining Room Manager, and the Bar Manager should have keys to this room. In loaning the keys to other employees to retrieve needed records, the managers should make sure the keys are promptly returned.

People typically are reluctant to throw any records away in case they may be needed. As the years go by, the restaurant is scrambling for places to store records. Boxes are often thrown on top of old boxes and aisles are filled. Thus, while the box someone is trying to find is somewhere in the record retention room, it is nearly impossible to find because it is buried under a pile of other boxes.

By law, sales records, payroll records, bank statements, and invoices must be retained for 6 years for audit purposes. After 6 years have elapsed they can be discarded. Monthly inventory records should be retained for the current year and the prior year. In January, the inventory records from two years ago can be discarded. However, the year end inventory reports must be retained for 6 years.

When confidential documents, such as financial statements, payroll reports, sales reports, bank statements, cancelled checks etc., are to be discarded, they should be shredded. Anything with an account number, pay rate, or personal information should be shredded. Invoices, inventory reports, time cards, and other less sensitive records can be thrown in the dumpster. General Ledgers must be retained indefinitely because they are the official books of the Company. When destroying records, it is often worth the cost to have a commercial record destruction company shred the documents. With the type of shredders available to the typical office, it could take someone days and possibly weeks to shred everything.

January is a good time for the General Manager and Controller to go through the record retention room and mark those boxes older than six years for destruction. Those boxes to be shredded commercially should be separated in the room until ready to be picked up. The Controller should designate a clerk to make a list of the records to be destroyed and supervise their removal. The list should indicate the type of records and their dates, copied from the front of the boxes. When the commercial destruction company's truck arrives, the Controller should observe a porter carrying the boxes to the loading dock to be loaded onto the truck. She should check off each box on the list as it is placed on the loading dock.

The auditor should discuss the restaurant's record retention policies with the General Manager and Controller. During the audit, she should determine whether records appear to be well organized and readily retrievable. She should ask to see the record retention room and determine whether this room is properly organized so records can be readily retrieved. Also, the auditor should determine whether the record retention room contains records older than 6 years that could be destroyed. Any exceptions should be noted in the audit program or Internal Control Questionnaire and cross referenced to the Discussion Points Worksheet.

Licenses

A restaurant must have a general business license that should be hanging somewhere in the restaurant visible to the patrons. A restaurant that sells alcoholic beverages must have a liquor license that is also hung in a place that is visible to the public.

The auditor should examine the licenses at the restaurant. She should determine whether the general business license and liquor license (if applicable) are hanging in a conspicuous place, such as in the lobby or waiting area. She should also check that they are still valid and have not expired. The auditor should note any exceptions in the audit program or workpapers and cross reference them to the Discussion Points Worksheet.

Health Inspections

Periodically, the County Board of Health sends an inspector to the restaurant to perform a health inspection. The health inspector checks to see that the restaurant is operating in a sanitary manner and completes a standard health inspection report as she performs her inspection. If there are any health violations, the health inspector notes them on the report. When completed, the health inspector meets with the General Manager and advises her of any deficiencies that need to be corrected. Before leaving the premises, the health inspector gives the General Manager a copy of the heath inspection report. The General Manager must correct any deficiencies noted.

The auditor should ask the General Manager for a copy of the most recent health inspection report. She should check to see that any deficiencies noted have been corrected. Any uncorrected deficiencies should be noted in the audit program or workpapers and cross referenced to the Discussion Points Worksheet.

Photo Identification for Official Visitors

Throughout the year, the restaurant may be visited by various people on official business. The health inspector may arrive to perform a health inspection. The sales tax auditor may arrive to conduct a sales tax audit. OSHA may send an inspector to investigate an accident that occurred in the workplace. External auditors may arrive to count cash and perform other financial audit work. Corporate internal auditors may arrive to conduct an audit of operations.

While each of these people has legitimate reasons for obtaining access to company records, there have been cases of imposters posing as someone with legitimate business reasons for obtaining access to company records and/or company assets. The General Manager does not want someone counting his cash or snooping around the kitchen or warehouse who has no legitimate business purpose for doing so. Likewise, she does not want someone reviewing confidential records where there is no legitimate business reason for obtaining access to them.

Whenever someone identifies herself as representing a government or other agency, or someone from the Corporate Offices who the General Manger has not met, she should ask the person for Government or Company logo photo identification. A business card is easy to obtain and proves nothing except the name the person would like you to call her. All government agencies and corporate employees carry photo identification with them. Look at the photo and compare it to the person standing in front of you. Make sure they match.

When arriving at the unit, the auditor should introduce herself and explain the purpose for the visit. She should not produce a photo identification card until asked to do so. If the General Manager or other management person does not ask for photo identification prior to showing the auditor to the cash room or providing her with records requested, it is an internal control deficiency. The auditor should note the deficiency in the audit program and cross reference the notation to the Discussion Points Worksheet.

Summary

All computer systems must be backed up nightly. A tape with current data must be taken to an offsite storage location weekly. Important spreadsheets should be backed up onto a disk or zip (flash) drive. The auditor should ask the Controller about data backup and offsite data storage practices.

All PC's should have passwords that are needed to log in to protect the data stored on the PC. All online systems should have passwords to prevent unauthorized use. If possible, each password should be a combination of words, numbers, and/or symbols. After six unsuccessful attempts to enter a password, the system should shut down to prevent future attempts until the password is reset by Corporate IT. The auditor should select several PC users and ask whether the password is unique with a combination of words, numbers, and/or symbols.

POS access should be limited to personnel who need to use it and should require a swipe card with an access code. Types of access should be based and limited to job responsibilities. The cash drawer and POS swipe cards should be secured from theft. The auditor should ask location personnel about POS security and note any deficiencies uncovered from the discussions.

The office should be locked when the last office person leaves for the day.

The restaurant should be locked at night. File servers should be located in a room that is kept locked all day to prevent unauthorized access. Laptops should be locked in a cabinet or office at night to prevent theft. The auditor should review hardware security throughout the premises and note any problem areas for discussion with management.

Each computer should have anti-virus software whether or not it is connected to the internet since PC's can pick up viruses from contaminated disks. Anti-virus software must be updated regularly since new viruses are constantly introduced. The auditor should discuss anti-virus software and regular updates with the Controller or General Manager. The auditor should select several PC's and determine whether the PC's have current anti-virus software.

Grill hoods must be cleaned every 6 months, fire suppression systems must be inspected every 6 months, and fire extinguishers must be inspected once a year. The auditor should examine invoices to determine when the grill hoods were last cleaned and the fire suppression system was last inspected. She should examine the inspection tags on the fire extinguishers throughout the restaurant to determine when they were last inspected.

CO_2 and propane tanks have contents under high pressure that can cause serious injury if a tank fell over and the top broke off. The auditor should check that each tank (including empties) is chained to a wall to prevent it from tipping over.

The auditor should determine whether the field location is following record retention guidelines and legal retention requirements. Sales records, payroll records, bank statements, and invoices must be maintained for 6 years. A locked room should be designated as the record retention room where labeled boxes of documents are neatly organized to facilitate easy retrieval when records are needed.

Location personnel should request photo identification from any official visitors before showing them any company records or allowing them into restricted areas. The auditor should determine whether the Controller, General Manager, or other person who showed her around the premises asked to see Company ID.

Discussion Questions and Case Studies

1. How often should computer systems be backed up? How often should back up tapes be taken to offsite storage? What is the purpose of an offsite storage location?

2. Why are passwords needed to access computer systems and PC's? Why is it important to create passwords that are made up of more than words? Give an example of a good password.

3. Why is hardware security important? Describe how to make computer hardware secure.

4. How often should grill hoods be cleaned? Why? How often should fire suppression systems be tested? How often should fire extinguishers be tested? How does the auditor determine whether the grill hoods were cleaned and fire suppression systems and fire extinguishers were tested frequently enough?

5. You are auditing Randy's Bar and Grill. You ask Marguerita Martinez, the Controller whether there is anti-virus software on the PC's. "Of course," Marguerita replies, "every time we buy a new PC, we install anti-virus software along with Microsoft Office and some other standard software." You ask Marguerita how the anti-virus software is updated. "What do you mean updated?" she asks. "We install the anti-virus software and it detects viruses. What else is there to do?" Do you have any audit issues? What are your recommendations to management?

6. You are auditing Good Morning, a restaurant specializing in breakfasts. On Sundays, during the summer, Good Morning has an outdoor patio where cooks make omelets to order on a propane stove while the customer watches. You notice that the propane tanks are not secured to the stove. In looking around the restaurant, you notice that a full CO_2 tank is being used as a door stop to hold the kitchen door open. When you ask Reynaldo, the Executive Chef, about the CO_2 tank propping the door open, he says, "We need some air circulating in here. Otherwise it gets unbearably hot." You also notice that the CO_2 tanks attached to the soda dispensers throughout the restaurant are not secured to the wall. There are soda tanks standing next to the CO_2 tank attached to the soda dispenser. When you ask Rita Reynolds, the Dining Room Manager about the CO_2 tanks, she answers, "The tanks are attached to the soda dispensers with the hose. The other tanks are empty. When one runs out of CO_2, we get a porter to bring one from the warehouse. When you go to the warehouse, you see 25 CO_2 tanks standing on the floor in one corner in five rows of five tanks. Do you have any audit issues? What are your recommendations to management?

7. You are auditing Mermaid's Seaside Café. You have selected January 20-23, 2006 as the dates you wish to audit the Sales Journals. You have asked Virginia Watkins, the Controller, if she can get them for you. Virginia

replies, "I'd prefer if you could select a more recent date. Those dates are in the retention room and it'll take me all day to find them. Here, I'll show you why." You follow Virginia to the retention room. Virginia opens the door and walks in. You see boxes scattered everywhere. Looking around the room, you look at the dates on the boxes and see boxes labeled with sales documentation going back as far as 1990. Do you have any audit issues? What are your recommendations to management?

8. You are entering The Flaming Grill and Eatery to commence your audit. You introduce yourself to Roscoe Williams, the General Manager and explain the purpose of your visit. Roscoe shakes your hand and asks, "What can I show you first?" You tell him you would like to count the operating fund. "Sure," Roscoe replies. "Right this way." You count the operating fund and tie out the fund to the General Ledger balance. It balances within $.43. "What would you like to see next?" asks Roscoe. You ask Roscoe to give you a tour of the premises. Roscoe takes you to the kitchen and introduces you to the Executive Chef. He takes you to the warehouse and introduces you to the Warehouse Manager. He introduces you to the Dining Room Manager and Bar Manager. Finally, he introduces you to the Controller with instructions to give you whatever you need. You present your list of documents to the Controller and she gives it to one of her clerks to retrieve the documents. Before you realize it, you are sitting in a conference room with a cup of coffee, a danish pastry, and all the documents you requested. You begin your audit. Do you have any audit issues? What are your recommendations to management?

AUDITING THE FOOD AND BEVERAGE OPERATION
AN OPERATIONAL AUDIT APPROACH

CHAPTER 18
WRITING THE AUDIT REPORT

Learning Objectives

After reading this chapter, you should be able to:

1. Lead the Exit Conference, reviewing the findings with local management and obtaining agreement on the facts,
2. Know the various components making up the audit report and how to write each one,
3. Know how to write an effective report that does not burden the reader with a lot of detail he does not want to know,
4. Review the draft of the report with subsidiary management before it is issued.

Overview

The audit report is the culmination of the audit. It is where the auditor communicates the audit findings to management and makes recommendations to remediate the deficiencies noted. A good audit report can be a dynamic tool that compels management to initiate corrective action on the auditor's findings or it can be a boring recitation of a long list of deficiencies that puts the reader to sleep.

Appendix 2 is the audit report that Aimee wrote at the conclusion of her audit of Jenny's Café—Denver. As the reader reads this chapter, he can refer to Appendix 2 for an illustration of how the concepts discussed in the chapter are put into practice. Appendix 1 is the Discussion Points Worksheet that Aimee used to summarize her findings. Each finding in the audit report (Appendix 2) can be traced to a Discussion Point in Appendix 1.

The Exit Conference is where the auditor meets with the field location's management and reviews the findings and recommendations. We will learn how to conduct an effective Exit Conference and ensure all findings are discussed.

The audit report generally consists of several sections. We will discuss how to write the Scope Section, an effective Executive Summary, Background, Findings and Recommendations, and Required Response.

The audit report is distributed to the General Manager, Location Controller, subsidiary management, corporate management, the Audit Committee, and the external auditors. Distribution should be limited to executives who have a direct interest in the operations of the field location. We will discuss who at corporate should receive a copy of the audit report and why distribution should be limited.

When writing the report, the auditor should keep the report as brief as possible. This is not always easy, particularly when there are a lot of audit findings. We will discuss the type of information that should go into the audit report and what information is better left out. We will also discuss various tips to make the audit report more effective.

Once the audit report has been written, the auditor should review it with subsidiary executive management. We will discuss the purpose for reviewing the draft with subsidiary executives and when the auditor may need to change conclusions reached.

In Practice

Aimee Stone walks into the Denver Restaurant Conference Room at 1:00 p.m. on Friday for the Exit Conference. Seated around the conference table are Joey Roberson, General Manager, Heather Smith, Controller, Jason Smith, Bar Manager, Linda Barton, Dining Room Manager, Wally Dobranski, Warehouse Manager, and Stephan Richileau, Executive Chef. Aimee hands each person a copy of the Discussion Points Worksheet.

"Let me review the process with you before we go through the findings and recommendations," Aimee says.

"I have spent the last two weeks reviewing every aspect of your business. During that time, I documented any deficiencies that I found in the Discussion Points Worksheet. We will go over each deficiency in the order that I have noted it. If you have any questions, I will answer them as we go along. If you do not agree with a conclusion I reached, bring it up and we will discuss it. I can be persuaded to change my mind if I have missed something. Once I return to the Corporate Offices, I will write the audit report and discuss it with Jenny's Café management.

"You should receive the final report in 2-3 weeks. At that time, you will have 30 days to respond to the report. Your response should include an

Action Plan that addresses each item in the report and explains how you will correct the deficiency and the timetable for implementing corrective action."

Two hours later, the group has reviewed the last discussion point. Joey says, "I can see there are a lot of areas where we need to improve. Overall, how would you rate this location in comparison to other locations you have audited?"

"Generally, I find that most locations have areas where they need to improve. I think you have a lot of work to do to bring Denver to where it needs to be."

"Spoken like a politician!" Joey exclaims.
Aimee smiles.

Auditor's Workpaper Review

The night before the Exit Conference, the auditor should go through the audit program to ensure he has completed all audit steps that must be completed in the field. Then he goes through the To Do List and checks to see that all To Do's that need to be done in the field have been completed. This review can be done at the field location before the auditor leaves for the day or in the hotel room that night or early the next morning. This step is critical because the auditor does not want to return to the Corporate Office to discover that there was something he wanted to do in the field but now cannot do because he is back at Corporate.

The third thing the auditor should do the night before the Exit Conference is to go through the workpaper binder to make sure all exceptions have been cross referenced to the Discussion Points Worksheet. He looks at each workpaper, checks each exception noted and the workpaper's conclusion, and makes sure that each exception has been cross referenced to the Discussion Points worksheet. If there are Discussion Points that need to be written, the auditor should write them now so he does not forget to write them later.

The auditor does not want to be in the position where he goes through the workpapers back in the office, and finds one or two exceptions that should go in the report but he did not discuss them with the General Manager while he was at the field location. In this case, the auditor must telephone the General Manager and explain the additional exception that will be added to the report.

The best time to schedule the Exit Conference is right after lunch to allow the auditor time to wrap up loose ends in the morning. This may not always be possible, depending on airline scheduling. If the field location is on the west coast and the Corporate offices are on the east coast, the last flight out will be at 1:00 or 2:00 o'clock in the afternoon. In this case, the auditor must ensure that all To Do's have been completed before he leaves the field location the night before the Exit Conference.

Once he is sure that the field work is complete, the auditor makes copies of the Discussion Points Worksheet for each attendee at the Exit Conference. The auditor should ask the General Manager who will be attending so he will have sufficient copies for everyone. Some General Managers will only invite the Controller to attend the Exit Conference, while others invite the entire management staff. Since the General Manager is ultimately responsible for corrective action, it is up to him to decide who will attend the Exit Conference.

The Exit Conference

The Exit Conference is the last meeting the auditor has with field location management. Once the exit conference is over, the auditor may follow up on a few items that were brought up in the meeting. After that he packs his bags and heads for the airport.

Prior to reviewing the findings and recommendations, the auditor should explain how the report is written, with whom the auditor will review the report, and management's responsibility to write a response to the report within 30 days of the issuance date. The response should include an Action Plan that addresses each finding and recommendation, explains how each deficiency will be corrected, and provides a timetable for implementing corrective action.

The auditor should stress that he is not the final authority on whether a recommendation that requires an expenditure of funds should be implemented. The General Manager should not buy something based solely on the auditor's recommendation. It is only a recommendation and not a mandate. The General Manager and Controller should set up a meeting or conference call with the Regional Vice President of Operations to discuss each issue and determine how the issue should be resolved. Based on this meeting, the Regional Vice President of Operations may decide that there are certain issues that they will not resolve due to their cost. Or they may decide to include the cost of the recommended system in next year's capital expenditures budget. Whatever is decided should be documented in the field location's Audit Response.

Regardless of the number of discussion points the auditor has on his

Discussion Points Worksheet, he should keep the tone of the meeting positive. The auditor should avoid negative comments, such as "things look pretty bad" or "I've never seen a place where so many things are done wrong." Instead, say something like, "There is a lot of work to be done," "there is much room for improvement," or "there are many challenges." You want management to gear up for the challenge of improving its performance. You don't want management to despair that they can never make all the required changes.

Even if management asks you how their operation compares with others you have audited, avoid making comparisons. It doesn't do anyone any good to know that they were the worst location you have ever audited. Besides, there probably was a location that was just as bad. Or if the audit was good, there probably was a location you've audited that was just as good. Each location is unique and should be treated that way.

Never make a comment where you say that you think someone should be fired, even if asked. That is management's decision, based on the circumstances. Your comment should be that people who violate Company policy should be subject to progressive disciplinary action, including termination, if appropriate.

As the auditor reviews each finding and recommendation with location management, he should listen to whatever comments management has on the topic. While the auditor should not let management talk him into eliminating a legitimate deficiency that he noted, the auditor should keep an open mind in discussing the findings. Management is not always right, but the auditor is not always right either. Sometimes there may be circumstances where the method the location uses is the only practical way of handling the situation even if it is not entirely compliant with company policy.

For example, the Company has a contract to manage a historic restaurant in a national park. The Company has a policy that it requires three bids on all capital projects and that the work is to be awarded to the lowest bidder. The auditor noted in his workpapers and Discussion Points Worksheet that for restoration work done on the exterior of the building, there was no bidding process in awarding the work. In the Exit Conference, the auditor explains this deficiency to the attendees. The General Manager states that the reason there was no competitive bidding on the project was because the Park Director mandated that the Company use the only company that has experience in performing restorations to historic buildings. In this case, the auditor would note this explanation on the Disposition side of the Discussion

Points Worksheet and would not include the item in the report.

There may be some areas where the General Manager, Controller, or one of the other managers disagrees with a Discussion Point. The auditor should jot down notes on any points of disagreement and revisit the issue after the meeting to ensure the findings are correct. Wherever possible, the auditor should get agreement on the facts. The interpretation of the impact the facts have on the operation may differ, but management can provide its opinion of the impact on operations in its reply to the audit report.

Sometimes management agrees with the finding but feels it should be worded a little differently. If revised wording does not substantially alter the facts but makes management more comfortable with the report, the auditor should agree to the revision. While it is difficult to be comfortable with criticism, the auditor should try to make management as comfortable with the report as possible without allowing management to dictate what goes into the report and what stays out. Remember, the auditor is the final judge, not the General Manager.

There may be one or two items where additional information may be needed to resolve an audit issue. For example, when testing I9's, the auditor noted that there were two employees for whom the Human Resources Manager could not find the I9's. In the Exit Conference, the Human Resources Manager says that she knows the I9's were completed and she is sure that they are with a stack of forms that need to be filed. He has been busy preparing for an upcoming jobs fair and has not had time to look for them. The auditor gives the Human Resources Manager one week to fax the I9's to him. Four days later, the I9's appear on the fax machine. The auditor notes on the Disposition column of the Discussion Points worksheet that the properly completed I9's were received, and removes the comment from the audit report.

Where management requests copies of workpapers so it can correct the deficiencies noted, the auditor should provide copies of those workpapers. For example, the auditor noted various deficiencies in completing I9's. The Human Resources Manager asks for a copy of the workpaper so he can ensure the I9's are corrected. The auditor should make a copy of the workpaper where the I9 deficiencies are noted and give it to the Human Resources Manager.

Scope

The Scope Section is the opening section of the report and consists of a few short paragraphs where the auditor describes how the audit was conducted. In the first paragraph, the auditor identifies the name of the field location that he audited and the businesses within the location, i.e. Jenny's Café—Denver Restaurant Food and Beverage and Valet Parking operations. If there was a banquet hall, the auditor could say "Jenny's Café—Denver Restaurant Food and Beverage, Catering, and Valet Parking operations. He identifies the names of the General Manager and the Controller, if there is one. These are the people responsible for how the location operates. They are the ones who will take charge of implementing corrective action to remediate the deficiencies.

In the second paragraph, the auditor indicates how the audit was conducted and what was done. Generally, the auditor would say that the audit was conducted utilizing the standard audit programs designed for that specific type of operation, such as a Food and Beverage operation of that particular subsidiary. A parent company may have different subsidiaries involved in different types of food and beverage operations. Jenny's Café is a chain of restaurants. However, the parent company may have other subsidiaries that operate cafeterias in office buildings, bid on food and beverage operations in airports, stadiums or arenas, national parks, etc. Each type of operation has its own unique characteristics and has a set of audit programs designed specifically for that type of operation.

The second paragraph should also identify the type of work done at the field location. Generally, the auditor would test transactions, perform management inquiries, and observe the operation in progress. The paragraph should also state that the auditor considers the audit work performed to adequately evaluate the key areas of internal control. The auditor probably did not evaluate every internal control because that would require a lot more time than he wanted to spend in the field. But he should have identified the key internal controls and tested them to ensure they were working adequately to detect errors and potential fraud. There should be a system of checks and balances so that if one person makes an error, someone reviewing the work will catch the error and correct it.

The third paragraph should state that the key findings are summarized in the Executive Summary. It should also identify the management people with whom the auditor reviewed the findings and recommendations. Generally, it would be the General Manager, the Controller, and the subsidiary operations people at Corporate Headquarters, i.e. the subsidiary's Regional Vice President of Operations, the Vice President of Finance, and possibly the subsidiary President. Normally, the auditor would not review the report with the parent company's executives. They would receive a copy of the report for information purposes.

Appendix 1 is the Discussion Points Worksheet for Jenny's Café—Denver. Each reference to the Discussion Points Worksheet throughout the book is identified and explained in Appendix 1. It includes audit findings identified in the In Practice sections in the beginning of each chapter. Some of the Discussion Points refer to workpaper indexes that do not actually exist in this book, but they would have existed in Aimee's workpaper binder. I tried to make the format as realistic as possible.

Appendix 2 is the audit report written for Jenny's Café—Denver. It is a sample audit report that includes all findings that were discussed throughout the book, including issues that were brought up in the In Practice sections in the beginning of each chapter. This report is longer than most reports that are normally written because I tried to show the reader how each deficiency discussed in the book would be handled in an audit report.

I realize that some of the findings are inconsistent. For example, one finding may discuss deficiencies in the Sign In Sign Out sheet while the next one may discuss deficiencies in approving time cards. Generally an operation would have either Sign In Sign Out Sheets or time cards, not both. Please overlook the inconsistencies and concentrate on the format of the report.

Executive Summary

The Executive Summary is a brief summary of the key findings. It should not be an attempt to list all the details in a condensed version with the recommendation. Instead, it should be a brief description in 1 to 3 sentences of the key findings. The recommendation will be contained in the Findings and Recommendations section. The Executive Summary should just give enough information for senior management to decide whether it wants to learn more about the finding by reading the details in the Findings and Recommendations section.

I have seen Executive Summaries that are almost as long as the Findings and Recommendations section. Once senior management reads this "summary," it no longer needs to read the Findings and Recommendations. I have also seen Executive Summaries that try to summarize every finding in the report. The Executive Summary should only include the most important findings.

The Executive Summary should be written after the Findings and Recommendations section is complete. The auditor should initially write the findings and recommendations in chronological order, the same order as they appear in the Discussion Points worksheet. Then the auditor can arrange the topics in order of importance and decide which findings are important enough to go into the Executive Summary.

The topics in the Executive Summary should be arranged according to order of importance. The most important findings are listed first. If the auditor discovered misappropriation of cash, this finding should come first. Theft of merchandise, unrecorded sales, violations of governmental requirements, etc. should also be near the front of the summary.

The titles used in the Executive Summary should correspond to those used in the Findings and Recommendations. There may only be one finding in a section that is a key finding while there may be several other findings in the section that are not as important. Only the key finding is included in the Executive Summary.

Bullets are generally used to separate the key findings in the Executive Summary, instead of numbers. When location management replies to the audit report, it replies to the individual findings in the Findings and Recommendations section, not the Executive Summary. Thus, there is no reason for anyone to refer to specific bullet points in this section.

Background

Often the audit report contains a background section on the field location. This section can be useful in providing the reader, who may not be familiar with this specific location, with some information that can be used to put the findings and recommendations in perspective. The reader will probably want to know how long the field location has been operating and how long the General Manager and Controller have managed this location. If the location is a new operation, the reader would expect to see more deficiencies than if the location has been in operation for a long period of time. Locations with new General Managers or Controllers might be expected to have more deficiencies than locations with veteran management because the new management is still becoming familiar with Company policies and procedures.

The reader would be interested in the term of the lease. If the lease expires within the next year and the landlord has decided to sell the building to a developer who wants to build a golf course, senior management will probably decide not to invest in the liquor dispensing system the auditor is recommending.

The size of the location could have an impact on the amount of segregation of duties the reader can expect. If the operation is small, the risk of a large fraud would be smaller than a large operation because there is less available to steal. Thus, the auditor should include This Year's Revenues, Planned Revenues, and Last Year's Revenues through the audit date. In addition, he should include This Year's Net Income or Loss, Planned Net Income or Loss, and Last Year's Net Income or Loss. To give the reader a better idea of the size of the operation, the auditor should also include planned revenues for the entire year.

If there is anything unique about the operation or of special interest, the auditor should include that information in the Background section. For example, if the restaurant is located in a historic building, there may be limits to the types of renovation that can be done to the restaurant. Special building permits may be needed before any renovations can proceed.

Findings and Recommendations

The Findings and Recommendations section is the bulk of the report. This is where the auditor explains each finding and provides his recommendation to correct the deficiency noted, to increase revenues, or to reduce cost. Sufficient detail should be provided so management can understand why the issue is a deficiency, an opportunity to increase revenues, or reduce expenses.

The auditor should not go into a lot of detail explaining how the tests were conducted. Generally, management is not interested in how the auditor selected his sample. Rambling on about information management does not care about may cause the reader to stop reading the report and dropping it into a file. If an executive wants to know how a sample was selected, he can always ask the auditor. Audit reports tend to be fairly long anyway. Don't make them longer by including information that does not help explain why a finding needs to be corrected. Remember, senior management has a lot to do. It does not want to spend an hour or more reading your report. Keep it as brief as possible.

Findings involving procedures that were not followed by a Corporate Department should not be addressed in the Internal Audit Report. This is a report on the field location, not the Corporate Department. The auditor should not ignore the issue. He should cross reference the issue to the Discussion Points Worksheet like any other audit issue. However, the disposition should be that he discussed the issue with the Department Director or Manager and wrote a separate memo to the Department Director or Manager addressing the issue.

The auditor should read the prior audit report to determine which findings are repeat items from the last audit report. These items should be highlighted so that senior management knows that they were not corrected from the previous audit. In Appendix 2, recommendation #5 in the Cash section (page 23 of the audit report) is a repeat issue from the prior report. "**REPEAT ISSUE**" is in uppercase letters and in bold type.

In writing the Findings and Recommendations, the auditor should use titles to describe topics. The names of the audit sections are often used as titles, such as Cash, Accounts Receivable, Inventory, Bar Operations, etc. These are fine. If there are more specific topics, the name of the specific topic may be used as well. For example, in Appendix 2, Valet Parking (page 8 of the audit report) was audited as part of the Sales Audit Program. The auditor could have named the topic "Sales," but chose a more specific topic "Valet Parking Revenues" as the title for this section.

After the auditor has written each finding with the corresponding recommendation, he should go through his report, topic by topic and arrange the findings within a topic in order of importance, most important finding first. Then the auditor rearranges the topics within the report in order of importance. When the report is completed, the topics in the Findings and Recommendations should be in the same order as in the Executive Summary.

In the Findings and Recommendations section, the auditor should number the recommendations. The numbering system should not number consecutively throughout the report but should start at Number 1 in each new section. The General Manager does not want to be reminded that he has 96 recommendations that need to be addressed, and would prefer that senior management not be reminded that there were 96 issues in the audit. As he is addressing the recommendations in his reply, the General Manager can just as easily refer to Payroll Recommendation #5 as he can refer to Audit Recommendation #31.

When describing exceptions, the auditor should indicate the number of items tested. This gives management an idea of the significance of the problem. Where the auditor states that 5 time cards were not signed by the supervisor, approving the time worked, management does not get a perspective of the significance of the situation. While any exception means that Company policy is not consistently followed, do 5 exceptions represent a major problem or a minor one? If the auditor states that 5 of 50 time cards tested were not signed by the supervisor, it is not as big a problem as if 5 of 10 time cards tested were not signed by the supervisor.

When quantifying cost inefficiencies, the auditor should quantify at cost, not at retail. For example, in the In Practice session of Chapter 10, the auditor might have quantified the amount of beer that was lost through sloppy bear pouring techniques by inventorying the beer each day for a week and comparing the beer usage to draft beer sales recorded in the Point of Sales system. She might have determined that over the course of a week, 4 kegs of beer were wasted, costing $75.85 each or $303 per week. In the audit report, the auditor could say that the bar had $16k in excess beer cost ($303 x 52 = $15,756) per year through sloppy beer dispensing techniques.

I have known some auditors who would try to make the waste sound more impressive by stating that the bar lost $58k in sales (124 glasses [1,984 oz. per keg] of 16 oz beers in a glass at $2.25 per glass multiplied by 208 kegs) per year through sloppy beer pouring techniques. The bar did not lose $58,000 in sales because sales would be the same whether all beer went into the glass or only 25% of the beer went into the glass and 75% was wasted. Sales were not lost, but Beer Cost rose substantially. Trying to inflate the effect of inefficiencies only causes the auditor to lose credibility with management.

Extrapolating the effect of a test period over a year (taking the result of a sample and projecting it across the entire population) is a legitimate method of conveying to management the impact of the cost inefficiency or theft if the situation is allowed to continue. In Appendix 2, the section on Valet Parking (pages 8-10 of the audit report) describes cash misappropriation. Through comparing tickets used to cash turned in, Aimee determined that on July 15, Valet Parking was short $384. To drive the point home that significant revenues were lost, Aimee extrapolated her finding over the entire year, and reported that the estimated misappropriation for a year would be $110,000. This statement would certainly catch management's attention and it is a fair statement based on the evidence available.

One thing the auditor should always keep in mind is the cost-benefit relationship of corrective action. This means that if the cost of correcting a deficiency exceeds the potential loss, it is not worthwhile to implement corrective action. For example, liquor dispensing and metering systems are used to control the amount of liquor that the bartender dispenses into the drink glass. If a liquor metering system is used, the Bar Manager can determine how much liquor should have been used for the amount of liquor sales recorded. Where liquor usage exceeds recorded sales, the Bar Manager can take disciplinary action against the bartender. However, if the restaurant has a bar where liquor sales are low, the cost of installing the liquor dispensing system will be far greater than the benefits to be derived from controlling liquor sales. In this situation, the auditor would not recommend that the restaurant purchase a liquor dispensing system for the bar.

Where the Company has a policy that the field location is not following, the auditor should include the item in the report even where there is no positive cost-benefit relationship. For example, the Company may have a policy that field locations must use national suppliers whenever possible. During his review, the auditor finds 10 items that are covered by a national supplier agreement that the field location can purchase cheaper from a local supplier. The auditor should include this exception from Company policy in his report even though the field location, from its perspective, is getting a better deal. Unknown to the field location, the national supplier agreement includes a rebate to Corporate that escalates with the volume of business done with the supplier. With the rebate, the Company overall is paying less for the products when purchasing them from the national supplier.

Required Response

When the General Manager and Controller receive the audit report, they need to know what they are expected to do with it. The Required Response section is where the auditor states how the General Manager and Controller should respond to the report. It states that the General Manager and Controller should put together an Action Plan that addresses each issue brought up in the report and sets a timetable for implementing corrective action. The Required Response should also set a deadline when the response is due to Internal Audit. Normally, this is 30 days from the issuance date of the report.

After receiving the audit report, the General Manager should meet with his management team to discuss the audit report and decide how best to implement the recommendations. In some cases, they may come up with a better way of resolving the issue. After this meeting, the General Manager should set up a meeting or a conference call with the Regional Vice President of Operations to discuss the audit report. Some of the recommendations may involve capital expenditures that need the Regional Vice President of Operations' and other executives' approvals. He may decide that the capital expenditure is not warranted or that the capital purchase should be included in next year's capital budget.

Once the management team has addressed the issues and the planned corrective action has been approved by the Regional Vice President of Operations, the General Manager should assign responsibility for implementing corrective action to the applicable department managers. It is the General Manager's responsibility to follow up with the department managers to ensure that corrective action has been implemented.

The General Manager should draft the audit response or assign someone to do so. The response should list each audit topic and each recommendation within the topic. It should indicate the corrective action to be taken to remediate the deficiency. If no corrective action will be taken, the response should explain management's reasons for not implementing corrective action.

When the draft is completed, the General Manager should give each person on the management team a copy of the draft. He should set up a meeting where the response is discussed. After input is received from the management team, the General Manager should finalize the response and send it to Internal Audit, with copies to senior management at Corporate.

The auditor's job is not finished after issuing the report. He should put the due date of the response on his calendar. If he does not receive the response by the due date, the auditor should telephone the General Manager or email him to ask when he can expect the reply. The auditor should continue following up with the General Manager each week until he receives the reply. When the report is 30 days past due, the auditor should discuss the tardiness of the reply with the Regional Vice President of Operations.

Once the reply is received, the auditor needs to review it to ensure the field location's response addresses each item satisfactorily. There may have been some misunderstanding on one or more issues resulting in a reply that the auditor did not expect. The auditor should send a memo or email to the General Manager with a copy to the Regional Vice President of Operations stating which responses did not adequately address the issues noted. He may need to clarify some of these items in his memo or email.

Where there are one or more items that require an additional reply, the auditor should continue to follow up with the General Manager to ensure each item receives a satisfactory reply. A satisfactory reply may be that after discussions with senior subsidiary management, the decision has been made not to implement the auditor's recommendation. However, the reply should state why management has decided not to implement the auditor's recommendation.

There should be a separate file drawer in Internal Audit that contains the audit reports that have been issued. Each report should be in a separate folder, labeled with the field location name and issuance date. The auditor should put the audit reply and any further correspondence regarding the audit report in this audit report file.

Report Cover

In this day of email, it is easy to distribute the report electronically. However, there is something to be said for mailing the report to the recipients. This allows the Internal Audit Department to put a distinctive cover on the report that immediately identifies the report on the recipient's desk among the various memos and other papers lying on the desk as an Internal Audit Report.

The report cover probably should not be red or orange. It should not convey the idea that the report is hot. A neutral color should be used, i.e. blue, green, or yellow, but the color should be unique so it is not confused with some other department's report. The cover should be printed on colored paper, with the rest of the report printed on white paper. If the report is stapled in the corner, a colored cover should be sufficient. Where the report is bound with a binding machine, the last page (blank) should also be colored paper.

The report cover should have the parent company's logo at the top of the report. It should include the subsidiary name, the name of the location audited, the names of the General Manager and Controller, the date of the last audit, the dates of the field work, the issue date, and the distribution list.

Distribution

The report should be issued 2-3 weeks after conclusion of the field work, if possible. If issuance of the report is delayed much longer than that, it begins to lose its value. After the exit conference, local management is generally eager to begin remedial action and anticipates the receipt of the audit report. As the weeks go by, the enthusiasm for implementing corrective action begins to ebb. If it takes 2 months or longer before the field location receives the report, the audit has long been forgotten.

Internal Audit may make the case that the field location has a copy of the Discussion Points Worksheet that they can use to begin remedial action. This certainly is true and location management probably will make some changes immediately. However, there is nothing like an official report to drive the local management team into action.

The auditor should perform any follow up work as quickly as possible and begin writing the report. He should try to complete the draft of the report in a week, two weeks at the most. This gives the Director a week to review the draft, make his changes and get them back to the auditor to input the changes and issue the report.

Distribution of the report should be limited to as small a list as possible. The auditor does not want his audit report to be used as ammunition in the political battles between subsidiaries. There is no reason why the management of a sister company should receive a copy of the audit report. Likewise, unless there is an issue that directly affects a corporate department head, there is no reason why corporate department heads should receive copies.

The General Manager and Controller should each receive a copy of the report. Once he receives his copy, the General Manager can make additional copies and distribute them to his management team, as he deems appropriate.

The Internal Audit Department should also distribute the report to the subsidiary President, Vice President of Finance, and the Regional Vice President of Operations who has responsibility for the field location that was audited. There is no reason to send copies to the Vice Presidents of Operations for other regions within the subsidiary. There is no point in airing dirty linen among those people without a direct relationship to the field location. Nothing good can come out of it and the auditor does not want to supply fuel for fires igniting regional rivalries.

Senior corporate executives will want copies of the Internal Audit report. A copy should be issued to the Corporate President and the Vice Presidents. As noted earlier, department directors should not receive copies unless there are major issues noted in the report that affect their departments. In this case, the department director can receive a copy of this report. However, the department director should not be added to the standard distribution list for future reports. Internal Audit does not want the audit to become the source of gossip at the water cooler or lunch room.

Since the Internal Audit Department reports to the Audit Committee, the members of the Audit Committee should each receive a copy of the audit report. Most likely, the Director of Internal Audit will address the audit committee quarterly with a report that summarizes the most important issues in each audit report issued during the quarter.

The external auditors should also receive a copy of the audit report. Since they perform the year end audit and report on the Company's system of internal controls, receipt of audit reports provide them with evidence that the Company has an effective Internal Audit Department, a key ingredient in the Company's system of internal controls.

Table of Contents

If the report is short, a Table of Contents may not be necessary, but most reports should have one. The Table of Contents should be the page after the cover page. The reader should be able to look at the Table of Contents to find a topic he wants to review and locate the page number where he can start reading.

The Table of Contents should list the sections of the report, i.e. Scope, Required Response, Executive Summary, Background, and Findings and Recommendations, with the appropriate page numbers. The Findings and Recommendations section should be further broken down into the audit report topics with the appropriate page numbers.

In most cases, the Table of Contents should be double spaced so it fills the entire page. The auditor does not want to start the Scope on this page, but by single spacing it, half the page is empty.

Signature Page

The signature page is beneath the Required Response section. It does not have a title and is thus not officially a separate section in the report. However, it is where the auditors and the Internal Audit Director sign the report.

Prior to the signatures, there is often a paragraph where the auditor thanks the General Manager and his staff for the cooperation received during the audit. Obviously, if the auditor feels that there was little cooperation during the audit or the location staff actually impeded the auditor's efforts to conduct the audit, this paragraph would be left out of the report.

If several auditors performed the field work, each auditor signs the report. Where an auditor helped the auditor in charge to prepare for the audit or assisted in some follow up work without actually going to the field, he should not sign the report. Field personnel will wonder who this person is that they have never met. There should be a line on the signature page for each auditor signing the report with the auditor's name and title printed beneath the signature line.

Once the report is ready for distribution, the Internal Audit Administrative Assistant should make the required number of copies and staple or bind them. The report copies should go to each auditor for his signature. While it takes longer to sign each copy than signing the original and copying it with the signatures, it makes the recipient feel like he has received a personalized copy of the report.

The last person signing the report should be the Director of Internal Audit. The caption "Approved" should be above his name. Once the Director has signed the reports, the Administrative Assistant puts the report copies in Inter-Departmental envelopes and takes them to the mail room.

Meetings with Subsidiary Management

When the auditor has completed the draft of the report, he should review it with subsidiary management. Generally, the auditor would review the report draft with the Regional Vice President of Operations and the Vice President of Finance. If the Regional Vice President of Operations is located in a different city, the auditor should email the report to him. If email is not feasible, the auditor should fax the draft to him or send it via an overnight delivery service. Where the report is lengthy, it might be easier to use the overnight delivery service. The auditor would telephone the Regional Vice President of Operations to discuss the report.

Where the Regional Vice President of Operations is located at the Corporate Offices, the auditor could set up a joint meeting with the Vice President of Finance or he could set up separate meetings, depending on the preferences of the executives. Even where the Regional Vice President of Operations is located in a different city, he could be included in the meeting with the Vice President of Finance via speaker phone. The auditor should send an advance copy of the draft to each participant in the meeting so they can review it and have their questions ready when the auditor meets with them.

The meeting with senior subsidiary management is a good forum for the auditor to measure the clarity and effectiveness of how he presented each finding in the report. If the executives have trouble understanding the issue, it generally means that the auditor was unclear in how he presented the finding. When he is back at his desk, the auditor should review those findings that management had trouble understanding, and reword them to make them clearer to the reader.

If management disagrees with an issue, the auditor should listen to the reasons for the disagreement. Upon conclusion of the meeting, the auditor should discuss the reasons for disagreement with the Internal Audit Director to determine whether the issue should remain in the report. The auditor may have misinterpreted the data and after careful consideration the Director and auditor may decide that the issue should not be included in the report.

While the auditor and Internal Audit Director should listen to the reasons for disagreement, they are the ones who should make the final decision whether an issue should be removed from the report. The argument that an issue, if disclosed, will embarrass subsidiary management is not a valid one. Likewise, the argument that remedial action was implemented while the auditor was in the field is not sufficient to remove it from the report. If it is a hot topic and it makes everyone feel better, the auditor can note in the report that management took corrective action before conclusion of the field work.

The Internal Audit Director should not allow Company politics to influence his decision whether an issue remains in the report. Only if subsidiary management is able to make the case that the facts were misinterpreted or the issue is insignificant should the Director agree to remove an audit finding from the report.

While the auditor does not need to send a draft of the report to the General Manager prior to issuance, he should telephone the General Manager and go over any additional findings resulting from follow up work at Corporate. He should also discuss with the General Manager any changes to recommendations that came out of meetings with senior management.

Report Writing Tips

In writing the audit report, the auditor should keep his audience in mind. Who is going to read your report and what do they want to know? The auditor writes his report to explain his findings and recommendations to the reader, not to document the work he has done. That was done in the workpapers. Thus, the auditor should keep the report as brief as possible.

While the auditor should explain each finding thoroughly so the reader has an understanding of the situation, he does not want to burden him with a lot of detail that the reader does not care about. Operations people are generally not interested in how the auditor obtained his samples. Going into a lot of detail on this subject guarantees that the reader will skim over it and may actually miss important information you are trying to convey. If management wants to know how you selected your sample, they will ask you.

The audit report is not the place to present the field location's financial statements, or detailed analyses of the variances from Plan and Last Year. As we discussed earlier, a summary of revenues and net income in the Background section is appropriate to give the reader a feel for the size of the operation and its financial success. However, including a detailed Income Statement, Balance Sheet, Statement of Cash Flows, etc. provides too much information. The reader probably will not even look at these statements and they only become fillers that lengthen the report unnecessarily. If management is interested in the detailed financial reports of the field location, they can look at the financial reports issued each month by Accounting.

Write in the active voice. It is much more effective than writing in the passive voice because it puts the emphasis on the person who should perform the task. Too often, the writer will say something like the following: "Disciplinary action should be taken against anyone who violates Company policies." This statement says what should be done but does not assign responsibility to anyone. Instead, the recommendation should be restated as follows: "The Executive Chef and Dining Room Manager should take disciplinary action against anyone who violates Company policies." This statement assigns the responsibility for corrective action to the Executive Chef and Dining Room Manager.

Another example of writing in the passive voice is the following: "Plastic bins should be obtained for bussers to place the dishes when clearing tables." This recommendation tells the reader what needs to be done, but does not assign responsibility to anyone to implement the recommendation. It should be reworded into the active voice as follows: "The Dining Room Manager should obtain plastic bins for the bussers to place the dishes when clearing the tables." This recommendation assigns the responsibility for obtaining plastic bins to the Dining Room Manager.

Keep sentences short. In reviewing his draft of the report, the auditor should be aware of sentences that are too long and should break them up. Sentences that ramble on with several clauses are difficult to read. The writer should get one thought across per sentence. Writing experts recommend that sentences should be no longer than 20 words.

The following is an example of a sentence that rambles on and strains the reader's thought processes in trying to decipher what the writer is trying to say:

For example, on Saturday, July 15, 2006, the three Valet Parking attendants turned in $1,275 in cash that agreed exactly to the cash register readings, but when we looked through the ticket stubs turned in, we noted that 553 ticket stubs were used, valued at $1,659, representing a $384 shortage for that day or 30%, although on the other 6 days we audited, the Valet Parking Supervisor did not account for approximately 30% of tickets issued.

The auditor can convey his findings to the reader much more effectively, by breaking up the sentence into several shorter ones, as follows:

For example, on Saturday, July 15, 2006, the three Valet Parking attendants turned in $1,275 in cash. This amount agreed exactly to the cash register readings. However, when we looked through the ticket stubs turned in, we noted that 553 ticket stubs were used, valued at $1,659. Thus, Valet Parking was actually $384 short on that day, or 30%. We found that on the other 6 days we audited that the Valet Parking Supervisor did not account for approximately 30% of tickets issued.

When writing the report, the auditor should use simple words whenever possible. People know you are smart, or you wouldn't be in a position where you are reviewing their work and commenting on it. You don't need to impress people by using big words that they need to look up in a dictionary to determine the message you are trying to deliver to them. Reading your report should not be a vocabulary lesson for the reader.

Explain terms that are unique to the industry or to the company. Don't assume your reader knows everything that you know. You are an expert in the field because you deal with the industry every day. The parent company may own subsidiaries in many unrelated fields, or some senior management people may come from different industries. Senior management is often hired because of their experience in problem solving, not necessarily because their background is in the food and beverage industry. Often an outside perspective sheds new light on worn out ideas. Thus, senior management may not be familiar with terms you take for granted.

When using a term that is unique to the industry or the Company, explain it to the reader. For example, the following statement contains a term unique to Jenny's Café: "We observed occasions where the bartender poured more than the standard shot in a drink glass." While the auditor knows that the standard shot for Jenny's Café is one ounce, senior management probably does not know whether a standard shot of liquor is one ounce, one and a quarter ounces, or one and a half ounces. Thus, the sentence should be written as follows: "We observed occasions where the bartender poured more than the standard one ounce shot into a drink glass."

The following is an example of a term that is familiar to the food and beverage industry but is not necessarily familiar to someone outside the industry: "Tipped employees are not completing and signing Tip Declarations each payroll period." While it seems self explanatory to the auditor, senior management may not be aware of the Tip Declaration rules. Thus, the auditor adds the following explanation:

> Tipped employees are not completing and signing Tip Declarations each payroll period. Federal regulations require all tipped employees to complete and sign a Tip Declaration form with all cash tips received during the payroll period, even if the employees declare zero tips received.

By reading the explanation of Tip Declaration, the reader now knows the federal requirements and what the field location needs to do to be in compliance with these regulations.

When using names of agencies, rules, forms, etc. that are lengthy, the writer can write the name and put the initials in parentheses. When using that name later in the report, the auditor can then use the initials only. Don't assume that the reader knows the meaning of the initials, even if they are commonly used.

Look at the following sentences:

> We tested 24 I9's and noted 11 exceptions to INS requirements. Each exception to a properly completed I9 carries a potential $10,000 fine in the event of an INS audit.

Even though the auditor may think INS is self-explanatory, it may not be to the reader. Thus, the auditor should spell out Immigration and Naturalization Service the first time it appears in the report section and then can use the initials going forward. If INS also appears in the Executive Summary, the auditor should write out the name in both places so the reader does not have to page back to the Executive Summary when he encounters the initials in the Findings and Recommendations section. Thus, the sentences should be written as follows:

> We tested 24 I9's and noted 11 exceptions to Immigration and Naturalization Service (INS) requirements. Each exception to a properly completed I9 carries a potential $10,000 fine in the event of an INS audit.

Some writers have a tendency to write long paragraphs. They are difficult to read and are a strain on the eyes. For example, look at the following:

Jenny's Café—Denver Restaurant opened on January 6, 1986 on Main Street in downtown Denver, Colorado. When it opened, the building was newly completed to Jenny's Café's specifications by Ready to Occupy Real Estate Developers, Inc., the landlord who still owns the building. The 25 year lease runs through January 4, 2011. There is a 10 year renewal option on the part of Jenny's Café. Rent is currently $20.2k per month, with an annual rent increase calculated by taking the increase in the Consumer Price Index plus 0.5%. Through June 30, 2006, Revenues were $7,706,351 a 4.3% increase in Planned Revenues of $7,386,700, and a 10.2% increase over Last Year's Revenues of $6,995,827. Net Income Before Taxes was $469,798 (6.1% of Revenues), a 64.9% decrease from Planned Net Income Before Taxes of $1,336,716 (18.1% of Revenues) and a 63.2% decrease from Last Year's Net Income Before Taxes of $1,277,985 (18.3% of Revenues). For the full 2006 year, Planned Revenues are $16.2M and Planned Profit Before Taxes are $2.8M. Mr. Robertson was promoted to the position of General Manager on January 16, 2006. The prior General Manager was Jim Rogers, who was the General Manager when Denver Restaurant was last audited in March 2002.

The information is easier to read when it is divided among several paragraphs, as follows:

Jenny's Café—Denver Restaurant opened on January 6, 1986 on Main Street in downtown Denver, Colorado. When it opened, the building was newly completed to Jenny's Café's specifications by Ready to Occupy Real Estate Developers, Inc., the landlord who still owns the building. The 25 year lease runs through January 4, 2011. There is a 10 year renewal option on the part of Jenny's Café. Rent is currently $20.2k per month, with an annual rent increase calculated by taking the increase in the Consumer Price Index plus 0.5%.

Through June 30, 2006, Revenues were $7,706,351 a 4.3% increase in Planned Revenues of $7,386,700, and a 10.2% increase over Last Year's Revenues of $6,995,827. Net Income Before Taxes was $469,798 (6.1% of Revenues), a 64.9% decrease from Planned Net Income Before Taxes of $1,336,716 (18.1% of Revenues) and a 63.2% decrease from Last Year's Net Income Before Taxes of $1,277,985 (18.3% of Revenues). For the full 2006 year, Planned Revenues are $16.2M and Planned Profit Before Taxes are $2.8M.

Mr. Robertson was promoted to the position of General Manager on January 16, 2006. The prior General Manager was Jim Rogers, who was the General Manager when Denver Restaurant was last audited in March 2002.

When listing a group of occurrences, it is easier to read when the writer uses bullets to separate the occurrences. For example, look at the following paragraph:

We noted several deviations from company policy. The bartender consistently filled wine to the rim of the wine glass, while the Company Standard calls for wine to be filled to one half inch from the rim of the glass. We noted carelessness in pouring draft beer where the bartender allowed beer to run down the drain in turning on the tap before putting a glass under the tap and while changing glasses. We also observed the bartender pour additional beer down the drain in attempting to remove all foam from the glass even though the Company Standard calls for a 10% head. We observed occasions where the bartender poured more than the standard one ounce shot into a drink glass. We observed the bartender refill a beer glass and record "No Sale" on the cash register. We observed the bartender fill beverage orders from the wait staff based on verbal requests rather than the orders printed on the order entry system's printer. We observed the bartender commingling tips with Company funds in the cash register. We observed the bartender remove a key from the cash register, leave the bar and return with a bottle of Seven Crown Whiskey, a bottle of Bacardi Rum, and a bottle of Grey Goose Vodka.

By using bullet points, the reader is able to digest the information much more easily. Consider the following revisions:

Specific deviations from company policy that we noted were as follows:

- We observed the bartender consistently fill wine to the rim of the wine glass, while the Company Standard calls for wine to be filled to one half inch from the rim of the glass,
- We noted carelessness in pouring draft beer where the bartender allowed beer to run down the drain in turning on the tap before putting a glass under the tap and while changing glasses. We also observed the bartender pour additional beer down the drain in attempting to remove all foam from the glass even though the Company Standard calls for a 10% head,
- We observed occasions where the bartender poured more than the standard one ounce shot into a drink glass,
- We observed the bartender refill a beer glass and record "No Sale" on the cash register,
- We observed the bartender fill beverage orders from the wait staff based on verbal requests rather than the orders printed on the order entry system's printer,
- We observed the bartender commingling tips with Company funds in the cash register,
- We observed the bartender remove a key from the cash register, leave the bar and return with a bottle of Seven Crown Whiskey, a bottle of Bacardi Rum, and a bottle of Grey Goose Vodka.

Auditors, particularly new ones, often have trouble expressing themselves on paper. In trying to write the perfect sentence or paragraph, they never really get started and sit there in front of a blank computer screen. The prospect of writing a 10-20 page report may seem intimidating!

Write down what comes to mind, even if it is not perfect. Once the thoughts have been written on paper or keyed into the computer, the auditor can go back and structure better sentences. You already have written the findings on the Discussion Points Worksheet. This makes an excellent starting point. When you have copied the discussion points onto your report, you can go back and make revisions to make them sound better.

Reread your draft several times. Remove unnecessary words. Clarify the points you are trying to make. Consider the following paragraph.

We noted that the last time someone from an outside service cleaned the grill hoods was 18 months ago. We also noted that the last time someone from an outside service tested the fire suppression system was 18 months ago. Finally, we noted that the last time someone from an outside service inspected the fire extinguishers was also 18 months ago. The Company standard requires that a professional cleaning company comes to the restaurant and cleans the grill hoods every 6 months. Company standards also require the fire suppression system to be tested on a six month basis. Finally, Company standards require that a certified safety contractor must test the fire extinguishers every 6 months.

The above paragraph is very wordy. It is a good start in that the writer has written down all of his ideas on the subject. However, it needs to be revised to make it sound better. Similar thoughts can be combined into one sentence. Thus, in rereading the draft of the report, the auditor made the following revisions:

We noted that it has been 18 months since the grill hoods were cleaned, the fire suppression system was tested, and the fire extinguishers were inspected. Company standards require that a professional cleaning company clean the grill hoods every 6 months. Also, a certified safety contractor must test the fire suppression system every 6 months and the fire extinguishers annually.

Sometimes it takes several rewrites to get the sentence structure correct. As the auditor gains more experience, he will naturally use better sentence structure and major revisions will not be needed as frequently. However, even experienced writers sometimes find better ways to express their thoughts or add additional ideas to the report, resulting in major revisions.

It is easy to make spelling errors or write sentences that are grammatically deficient. Fortunately, for the writer, today's word processing software usually has spell check and grammar check. These are two features that writers did not have before PC's and the accompanying software was developed. The auditor had to look at each word carefully to ensure that it was spelled correctly. And it seemed that no matter how often the auditor reviewed the report, he always found one or two words that were misspelled after he issued the report. In addition to checking for spelling errors, the writer had to look at each sentence carefully to ensure it was properly constructed, i.e. the verb agreeing with the subject in number and in person. With the PC, the software does it for you.

The writer should use caution when using the grammar check feature of the software (underlined in green in Word). When writing sentences with various clauses, the software sometimes flags the sentences for verbs not agreeing to the subject in number and in person when in fact they are correct. The software does not look at the word or phrase in context with the rest of the sentence. Thus, the writer must look at each flagged phrase carefully before making the suggested change.

In determining whether a verb agrees with its subject in number, the writer should look at the verb and ask who is performing the action. For example, consider the following sentence: "Our Accounts Payable testing revealed that 1 of 4 invoices that should have been accrued were missed in the accrual process." On the surface, the sentence appears to be correct, and will not be flagged by the software. However, when you ask the question "What was missed in the accrual process?" the answer is not invoices, but one. One was missed in the accrual process. Thus the subject is singular and the verb must also be singular. The correct sentence structure is thus, "Our Accounts Payable testing revealed that 1 of 4 invoices that should have been accrued was missed in the accrual process." Although the software will flag this sentence for not agreeing with the subject in number because it is comparing "was" to "invoices," we have proven that the sentence structure is correct and the writer should ignore the warning.

There are other types of errors that may also be flagged by the software but are actually grammatically sound. Thus, the writer should consider grammatical errors that the software flags but should use his own judgment in determining whether to correct the sentence structure.

While the software is good in flagging spelling errors (underlined in red in word), it does not recognize words that are unique to the industry. In the Food and Beverage industry, a busser is someone who clears tables. But spell check does not recognize the term and thus flags the word "busser" as a misspelled word. Again, the writer has to use his judgment in determining whether the word is actually misspelled or is a term unique to the industry.

Whenever the writer finishes a draft of the report, he should go to the beginning of the draft on the computer and click on Tools, Spelling and Grammar when using Word. The software will go through the entire report and stop at each word flagged as a misspelling and each phrase flagged as a grammatical error. The writer should consider each flagged word or phrase carefully and decide whether to correct it or leave it alone. This final check is invaluable in finding misspelled words and grammatical errors. When finished, the final document is usually a better one.

Summary

The auditor reviews the workpapers the night before the Exit Conference to ensure he has noted all exceptions in the Discussion Points Worksheet. He also goes through his To Do List to ensure that all To Do's that need to be done in the field have been completed.

During the Exit Conference, the auditor reviews the audit findings with location management. He explains how the report will be written and the response that the General Manager or Controller is required to make. The auditor should jot down any points of disagreement and revisit these issues to ensure his findings are correct. He should keep an open mind in points of disagreement but must use his own judgment in determining what goes into the audit report.

The scope statement explains what the auditor audited and how the audit was conducted, i.e. using the standard audit programs for that type of operation. It should be brief.

The Executive Summary should be a brief description of the principal findings in bullets, using 1-3 sentences to summarize each one. By reading the Executive Summary, management should get an idea of the issues to determine whether it wants to learn more by reading the Findings and Recommendations. The Titles used should be the same ones used in the Findings and Recommendations section and should be arranged in the same order with the most important topics listed first.

The Background provides a brief description of the field location's operation. It should provide the length of the lease or contract. Generally, Currently Year revenues and net income are compared to Plan and Last Year.

The Findings and Recommendations section uses titles to describe the topics, arranged in sequence of the most significant issues first and the least significant issues last. The auditor describes the issue and provides a recommendation that addresses it. When describing exceptions, the auditor should indicate the number of exceptions out of the number of items tested. Whenever possible, the auditor should quantify the dollar effect of the finding at cost over a one-year period. He should consider the cost-benefit relationship of each proposed recommendation.

The Required Response is where the auditor states what is expected from the General Manager and Controller regarding a reply to the audit report. The General Manager and Controller should put together an Action Plan addressing each issue in the Findings and Recommendations section and how the issues will be resolved. After consulting with senior management, the

General Manager and Controller may decide that the cost to correct the problem is more than the risk of loss, and decide not to take corrective action.

Distribution of the audit report should be kept to a minimum. If possible, the distribution list should only include the following: General Manager, Controller, Subsidiary President, Vice President of Finance, and Regional Vice President of Operations (in charge of the location), Corporate Executives, Audit Committee, and External Auditors.

In reviewing the draft of the report with senior management, the auditor should send them a draft of the report in advance of the meeting so they have an opportunity to review it and jot down questions. If the reader is unclear about what he read, it is an indication that the auditor needs to clarify the issue in the report. If there is disagreement about an issue, the auditor should listen to the reasons for disagreement and discuss them with the Internal Audit Director. The Internal Audit Director makes the final decision whether an issue remains in the report or is removed. The auditor should issue the report as quickly as possible, i.e. 2-3 weeks after the Exit Conference.

When writing the report, the auditor should keep it as brief as possible by not overburdening the reader with a lot of detail he does not care about. Detailed financial statements do not belong in the audit report. Write in the active voice—it is more effective. Keep sentences short. Use simple words whenever possible. Explain terms that are unique to the industry. If having trouble expressing your thoughts on paper, write down the thoughts as best as you can and go back later to make changes. Go through your Discussion Points and write the points in the same sequence. Rearrange the topics in order of importance when finished. Reread your draft several times, remove unnecessary words, and clarify your points.

Discussion Questions

1. When does the auditor perform the Auditor's Workpaper Review? What is the purpose of performing this review?
2. What is the purpose of the Exit Conference?
3. What is the purpose of the Scope Statement in the audit report?
4. What type of information should the auditor put in the Background section?
5. What is the purpose of the Executive Summary? How is the Executive Summary organized?
6. What type of information does the auditor put in the Findings and Recommendations section? How are the findings arranged? How does the

auditor make this section effective?

7. What is the purpose of the Required Response section? What type of response is normally required from the field location?

8. Why is the report distribution limited? Who should be included on the distribution list?

9. When reviewing the report draft with subsidiary management, why should the auditor provide management with a draft of the report prior to the meeting?

10. Why is it important to keep the report brief? What can the auditor do to keep the report brief?

11. Should the field location's financial statements (Balance Sheet, Income Statement, Cash Flows Statement) be included in the report? Explain your answer.

12. What tips can you provide that make the audit report more effective?

APPENDIX 1

Discussion Points Worksheet

Discussion Point	Disposition
1. Per B ICQ 1/2, the cash room door does not have any automatic door closer. Thus, it is possible for the door to be ajar while cash is counted in the cash room. The General Manager should make arrangements to have a door closer installed on the cash room door.	Discussed with field location management. Included in Internal Audit Report.
2. Per **B ICQ 1/2**, any supervisor is allowed access into the cash room while cash is counted. Supervisors have no reason to go into the cash room while cash is counted. Additional personnel in the cash room increase the risk of cash misappropriation. The General Manager should direct supervisors who need to talk to the cash room personnel to address them from the drop off window like any other employee.	Discussed with field location management. Included in Internal Audit Report.
3. Per **B ICQ 1/2**, the General Manager has not audited the $25,000 operating fund in 3 months. Company policy is for the General Manager to count the operating fund at the end of the month, to sign it, and submit it to the Bank Reconciliation Department	Discussed with field location management. Included in Internal Audit Report.

Jenny's Café, Inc.   A1 2/27
Denver Restaurant   *AS*
Points for Discussion   *8/25/06*
Audit Date: July 31, 2006

Discussion Point   **Disposition**

within 10 days after month end. The General Manager should begin auditing the safe monthly, documenting his count on the Monthly Safe Audit Sheet, signing the sheet, and faxing it to the Corporate Bank Reconciliation Department within 10 days of month end.

4. Per **B1**, a count of the $25,000 operating fund revealed that the safe was short $525. The General Manager said that he took $525 from the safe a few days earlier and forgot to put a petty cash voucher in the safe. He said he had not had a chance to buy the lighting fixtures he was planning to buy. GM should make purchase with credit card and get reimbursed through an expense report.

Discussed with field location management.

Included in Internal Audit Report.

5. Per **B1.2**, 2 of 26 petty cash vouchers included in the petty cash fund were not signed by the recipient. Each time an employee is reimbursed from the petty cash fund, the employee must sign a completed petty cash voucher.

Discussed with General Manager. He will address these issues with the individuals who forgot to sign.

Jenny's Café, Inc.   A1 3/27
Denver Restaurant   *AS*
Points for Discussion   *8/25/06*
Audit Date: July 31, 2006

Discussion Point   **Disposition**

6. Per **B1.1**, petty cash expenditure in the amount of $1,525 was not approved by the Vice President of Operations—Western Region. Petty cash expenditures in excess of $500 need written approval from the VP—Operations. In addition, expenditure should have gone through the capital approval process.

Discussed with field location management.

Included in Internal Audit Report.

7. Per **B1**, the General Manager has a personal check in the operating fund in the amount of $1,000, dated 5/31/06 that represents an unauthorized loan. Company policy forbids anyone to take a loan from the operating fund, without the written approval of senior management.

Discussed with field location management.

Included in Internal Audit Report.

8. Per **B2**, the Cash Room Cashier did not initial the Returned column of the Bank Sign Out Log. GARC policy requires that the Cash Room Cashier initial the Returned column of the Bank Sign Out log, documenting the return of the bank.

See Point #13 below.

Jenny's Café, Inc.   A1 4/27
Denver Restaurant   *AS*
Points for Discussion   *8/25/06*
Audit Date: July 31, 2006

Discussion Point	Disposition
9. Per **B ICQ 1/2**, cash handlers do not document their counts of their cash receipts on Cash Slips. Each cash handler should count his cash receipts and list the count by denomination on a Cash Slip and sign it. The cash slip should be inserted in the cash bag with the cash receipts.	Discussed with field location management. Included in Internal Audit Report.
10. Per **B ICQ 1/2**, a second person does not count the deposit before it is sealed in the deposit bag and there are no initials on the deposit slip documenting the person who prepared the deposit and the person who checked it. Company policy requires that a second person verify the cash deposit and both the deposit preparer and the person who checked the count initial the deposit slip.	Discussed with field location management. Included in Internal Audit Report.
11. Per **B3**, the restaurant cashier leaves rolled coin in an unlocked cabinet beneath her cash register because it does not fit inside the cash register. Since the cashier leaves her station periodically, the cash that can be as much as $62.50 is exposed to theft. A lock should be purchased for the cabinet so the cashier can lock it.	Discussed with General Manager. He said that he will tell the maintenance man to install a lock on the cabinet. The key will go on the ring with the cash register keys.

Jenny's Café, Inc.   A1 5/27
Denver Restaurant   *AS*
Points for Discussion   *8/25/06*
Audit Date: July 31, 2006

Discussion Point   **Disposition**

12. Per **A6**, 15 of 60 bank deposits were not transferred to GARC's main operating bank account within the required 2 business days of deposit. **REPEAT ISSUE**

Discussed with field location management.

Included in Internal Audit Report.

13. Per **B4**, exceptions noted in the Bank Sign Out Sheet and Armored Car Log testing are as follows: 2 of 7 days, 1 or more cashiers did not sign Bank Sign Out Sheet; 2 of 7 days, Cash Room Attendant did not initial the Bank Sign Out Sheet for 1 or more banks returned; 1 of 7 days, Main Cashier did not obtain signature of armed guard picking up the deposit.

Discussed with field location management.

Included in Internal Audit Report.

14. Per **I1**, we noted that one of the bussers, hurrying to get a table cleaned, dropped a tray full of dirty dishes on the floor and all dishes and glasses broke. Just before I left, another busser, hurrying to clear a table, dropped a tray of dishes just as he was entering the kitchen. In my review of the income statement, I noted that China, Glassware, and Silverware expense was double last year. Obtaining bins for the bussers to put the dishes in as they clear the tables could help to reduce breakage.

Discussed with field location management.

Included in Internal Audit Report.

Jenny's Café, Inc.　　　　A1 6/27
Denver Restaurant　　　　*AS*
Points for Discussion　　　*8/25/06*
Audit Date: July 31, 2006

Discussion Point　　　　　**Disposition**

15. Per **I1**, when reviewing the check, I noted that I was only charged for one glass of wine and I was not charged for the coffee. The check number was 34679. By not recording sales for products delivered to patrons, the waitress (Cathy) not only violated Company policy but this practice contributes to high product cost.

Discussed with field location management.

Included in Internal Audit Report.

16. Per **C ICQ**, the Sales/Accounts Receivable Clerk records Accounts Receivable sales, opens the mail and receives the checks, performs the collection process, reports on collection efforts, and writes the journal entry to record bad debt write-offs that have been approved by Corporate. This situation presents a segregation of duties concern. Mail should be opened by the receptionist who should make a copy of the check for the A/R-Sales Reporting Clerk and bring the original to the cash room to be deposited. Before writing off an account, the Controller should review the customer file with the documentation of the A/R Clerk's collection efforts. The journal entry to record bad debt should be written by the Accounts Payable Clerk.

Discussed with field location management.

Included in Internal Audit Report.

Jenny's Café, Inc.   A1 7/27
Denver Restaurant   *AS*
Points for Discussion   *8/25/06*
Audit Date: July 31, 2006

Discussion Point   **Disposition**

17. Per **C3**, 2 of 5 days selected had checks included in the deposit that were not listed on the Checks Received Log and not posted to the A/R Sub-Ledger. The receptionist needs to use more care to ensure all checks are listed and check copies are given to the A/R Clerk for posting to the A/R Sub-Ledger. In addition, the Controller needs to compare the checks received to the deposit slips at month end to ensure all checks were deposited.

Discussed with field location management.

Included in Internal Audit Report.

18. Per **C4**, 3 of 10 advance deposits on future events were recorded incorrectly. 2 of the deposits were not recorded as advance deposits when received but held in the safe until the date of the event. One deposit was recorded when the A/R Clerk was out sick. The A/P Clerk backed out the 5% sales tax from the deposit and incorrectly recorded Food Sales of $4,761.91 and Sales Tax Payable of $238.09 on the day she received the deposit instead of recording the full amount as an advance deposit. The Controller should be particularly careful in reviewing work performed by someone who does not normally do the work.

Discussed with field location management.

Included in Internal Audit Report.

Jenny's Café, Inc.   A1 8/27
Denver Restaurant   *AS*
Points for Discussion   *8/25/06*
Audit Date: July 31, 2006

Discussion Point   **Disposition**

19. Per **D1**, 2 of 5 fixed asset acquisitions did not have documentation for three bids as required by company policy. One of the five acquisitions was not from the lowest bidder. The Liquor Control System was purchased from Bartronics for $25,357. American Bar Supply bid $24,675 for the same Liquor Control System. There was no notation in the bidding documentation explaining why the higher bidder was selected.

Discussed with field location management.

Included in Internal Audit Report.

20. Per **D1**, Denver restaurant does not attach the fixed asset tags that are received from the GARC Property Accounting Department to fixed asset acquisitions, as required by GARC policy.

Discussed with field location management.

Included in Internal Audit Report.

21. Per **D3**, Denver restaurant sold a fully depreciated Fosters Convection Oven for $500, but did not complete a Retirement, Sale, or Transfer of Capital Asset form. As a result, the $500 was incorrectly recorded as Other Income, instead of a Gain on Sale of Capital Assets. In addition, the asset has not been removed from the Capital Asset Listing or the General Ledger.

Discussed with field location management.

Included in Internal Audit Report.

<table>
<tr><td>**Jenny's Café, Inc.**</td><td>A1 9/27</td></tr>
<tr><td>**Denver Restaurant**</td><td>*AS*</td></tr>
<tr><td>**Points for Discussion**</td><td>*8/25/06*</td></tr>
<tr><td>**Audit Date: July 31, 2006**</td><td></td></tr>
</table>

Discussion Point	Disposition
22. Per **D3**, Denver restaurant transferred a Really Kool Standup Cooler to San Diego Restaurant but did not complete a Retirement, Sale, or Transfer of Fixed Assets form. Thus, the cooler is still on the books of Denver instead of San Diego.	Discussed with field location management. Included in Internal Audit Report.
23. Per **E ICQ**, the Executive Chef does not retain the Bid Sheet where he or the Sous Chef documents the weekly bids from the produce, dairy, and bread suppliers or the price lists that he obtains from the meat and seafood suppliers. To provide an audit trail, the Executive Chef should retain bidding documentation and price lists for six months.	Discussed with field location management. Included in Internal Audit Report.
24. Per **E ICQ**, the Executive Chef does not maintain a PO Log as required by Company policy.	Discussed with field location management. Included in Internal Audit Report.

Jenny's Café, Inc.   A1 10/27
Denver Restaurant   *AS*
Points for Discussion   *8/25/06*
Audit Date: July 31, 2006

Discussion Point	**Disposition**
25. Per **E ICQ**, Receiving counts the bread and baked goods when the bread supplier delivers the bread and baked goods. However, when they deliver these products to the kitchen, no one in the kitchen checks the goods against the invoice to ensure they are receiving all products. To ensure all products charged to the kitchen are actually delivered, the Executive Chef should assign one of the kitchen staff to receive all product delivered and sign the invoice or transfer document.	Discussed with field location management. Included in Internal Audit Report.
26. Per **E1**, Denver Restaurant could have saved $232 by purchasing products covered by national supplier agreements from the national suppliers, instead of local ones. 13 of 13 items selected covered by national supplier agreements were purchased from local ones.	Discussed with field location management. Included in Internal Audit Report.
27. Per **F ICQ**, the Controller does not document her review of the invoices by initialing them.	Discussed with field location management. Included in Internal Audit Report.

Jenny's Café, Inc.	**A1 11/27**
Denver Restaurant	*AS*
Points for Discussion	*8/25/06*
Audit Date: July 31, 2006	

Discussion Point

Disposition

28. Per **F1**, testing of invoices for proper supporting documentation and approvals revealed the following:

Discussed all issues with field location management.

• 1 of 24 invoices was coded to an incorrect account—coded to Supplies, should have been Equipment Repairs,

1 of 24 invoices coded to wrong account is a minor discrepancy.

• 1 of 4 invoices tested that should have been accrued was not included on the Accrual List,

Invoice not accrued under $1k, as per company policy

• 1 of 4 invoices offering a cash discount for early payment was not paid within the discount period,

All other items are included in the Report.

• 2 of 8 invoices where sales tax was due was not taxed by the out of state supplier but use tax was not recorded to be remitted to the State,

• 3 of 21 invoices did not have a properly completed purchase order—2 did not have the individual items listed on the PO and 1 did not have prices listed on the PO,

• 14 of 21 purchases did not have the signature of the department manager on the PO, documenting the manager's approval,

• 3 of 21 invoices did not have proof of receipt—1 did not have a signed packing slip attached and 2 did not have the receiver's signature on the invoice.

Jenny's Café, Inc.	A1 12/27
Denver Restaurant	*AS*
Points for Discussion	*8/25/06*
Audit Date: July 31, 2006	

Discussion Point   **Disposition**

29. Per **F2**, Company policies were not consistently followed when completing expense reports. We reviewed 13 expense reports and noted the following:
• 2 had receipts randomly taped on 8.5 by 11 inch pieces of paper, making them difficult for the Accounts Payable Clerk to audit,
• 1 did not have a receipt for $395 airfare or a $50 taxi expense,
• 1 expense report was used for relocation expenses—Relocation Expense Report must be used so Human Resources can treat the expenses as required under federal law (some are required to be added to W2 earnings),
• 5 had all hotel expenses lumped into one day on the Lodging line even though they included other expenses, i.e. meals, telephone calls, etc.,
• 4 expense reports included expenses that were not legitimate business expenses: $295 dinner charge for GM and Bar Manager that the Bar Mgr picked up—GM was senior and should have picked up—appears to be excessive; $75

Discussed with field location management.

Included in Internal Audit Report.

Jenny's Café, Inc.   A1 13/27
Denver Restaurant   *AS*
Points for Discussion   *8/25/06*
Audit Date: July 31, 2006

Discussion Point	Disposition
laundry charge had no explanation—appears to be excessive, $65 laundry charge with no explanation—appears excessive; $195 dinner charge appears excessive and in-house movie not reimbursable, • 2 of 10 expense reports for travel did not have the purpose of the trip explained, • 2 of 6 expense reports with Entertainment Expenses had no explanation of who was entertained, where it took place, or the business purpose.	
30. Per **F3**, test of 28 manual checks showed the following exceptions: • 2 checks paid for unauthorized purposes (Marty's Repair Service and Handy Hardware Store)—only to be used for alcoholic beverages and entertainers, • 6 were signed by the Head Waitress, an unauthorized signer, • 3 checks were missing—no indication in check book who they were made out to—voids should be clearly marked as such,	Discussed with field location management. Included in Internal Audit Report.

Jenny's Café, Inc.　　　　　A1 14/27
Denver Restaurant　　　　　*AS*
Points for Discussion　　　　*8/25/06*
Audit Date: July 31, 2006

Discussion Point　　　　　　**Disposition**

• 2 checks were not supported by
an invoice (Seattle Sue's Country
Band and Handy Hardware Store),
and not recorded in G/L,
• 4 payments to entertainers were
not reported to Corp A/P as 1099
vendors even though they received
over $600 in payments (Country
Rag Time Band—$650, Robert
Rymes Country Band—
$1,300, Sheila McCray's Country
Band—$650, Singing Suzy
Silverman—$975).

31. Per **H1**, we observed Bar　　Discussed with field location
Operations on Sunday, July 23, 2006　management.
and noted the following exceptions:
　• Bartender filled wine to the rim　Included in Internal Audit Report.
　instead of standard half inch from
　rim,
　• Bartender opened beer tap, let
　beer run down drain as he
　attempted to remove all foam and
　let beer go down the drain as he
　obtained a second glass to put
　under the tap,
　• Bartender poured more than the
　standard 1 ounce shot of liquor in
　drink glass,

Jenny's Café, Inc.	A1 15/27
Denver Restaurant	*AS*
Points for Discussion	*8/25/06*
Audit Date: July 31, 2006	

Discussion Point   **Disposition**

• Bartender has access to the Liquor Room—Manager on Duty should issue additional liquor,

• Bartender filled drink orders based on verbal requests, not from the orders printed on the order entry system's printer.

• Observed bartender refill a beer glass and record "No Sale" on the cash register and put the dollar the customer gave him for a $2.25 beer in the cash register, commingling tip money with cash receipts,

• Confirmed with General Manager that there was no Manager on Duty Sunday night, the Bartender had the key to the Liquor Room and the Head Waitress had the key to close the restaurant.

The Bar Manager should take Disciplinary action against anyone who violates the Company's policies.

Jenny's Café, Inc.   A1 16/27
Denver Restaurant   *AS*
Points for Discussion   *8/25/06*
Audit Date: July 31, 2006

Discussion Point	Disposition
32. Per **I3**, observed Valet Parking operations on Tuesday, July 25, 2006, and noted the following:	Discussed with field location management.
• Every 3rd or 4th transaction the attendant did not record the transaction on the cash register and did not put the cash in the cash drawer—our calculations show that $110k per year may not be recorded,	Included in Internal Audit Report.
• There was no daily reconciliation of cash to tickets and thus there was no accountability of the cars parked.	
33. Per **J2**, 3 of 23 test counts in the food inventory differed from counter's counts:	Discussed with field location management.
• Milk—Gal. Counter counted 27—Auditor counted 25,	Included in Internal Audit Report.
• Cantaloupes—Counter counted 27—Auditor counted 51,	**REPEAT ISSUE**
• Extra Virgin Olive Oil— Counter counted 25—Auditor counted 37.	

Jenny's Café, Inc.   A1 17/27
Denver Restaurant   *AS*
Points for Discussion   *8/25/06*
Audit Date: July 31, 2006

Discussion Point   **Disposition**

2 differences were due to cases missed
on the other side of room because
counters counted from the count sheet
to product instead of counting
systematically from one spot, counting
left to right, top to bottom and adding
on additional counts found later. The
General Manager should take
disciplinary action against anyone who
violates company Policies regarding
cash handling and completing the
proper paperwork.

34. Per **J2.1**, we noted 57 of 142 bar   Discussed with field location
inventory items in the Liquor   management.
Commissary had differences because
the Bar Manager did not actually   Included in Internal Audit Report.
count the inventory in the Liquor
Room each month but relied on the
perpetual inventory balances to
record the ending inventory. Actual
inventory cost values were different
from the perpetual inventory balances
as follows: Liquor—$3,186
understated, Beer—$2,245
overstated, and Wine—$1,986
overstated. The Bar Manager must
actually count the inventory in the
Liquor Commissary each inventory
period.

Jenny's Café, Inc.	A1 18/27
Denver Restaurant	*AS*
Points for Discussion	*8/25/06*
Audit Date: July 31, 2006	

Discussion Point   **Disposition**

35. Per **J3**, we tested 36 Food and Bar inventory cost prices and noted that 20 had incorrect cost prices for a net understatement of $488. Management needs to do a better job of keeping its cost prices on the inventory current.

Discussed with field location management.

Included in Internal Audit Report.

36. Per **A7**, Denver Restaurant has large unfavorable variances between This Year versus Plan and This Year versus Last Year as follows (Year to Date through 6/30/06):

Discussed with field location management.

Included in Internal Audit Report.

Descrip This Yr Plan Last Yr.
Food Cost 38.6% 32.0% 31.7%
Beer Cost 28.6% 22.0% 21.8%
Liq Cost 29.4% 24.0% 24.5%
Wine Cost 32.9% 26.0% 26.4%
Sal & Wage 39.6% 34.7% 34.3%
Ch,Glass, Sil $116k $55k $55k
There is no evidence that any investigations have been performed as to the causes for these variances. Every month, the Controller and General Manager should investigate significant variances and document the results of those investigations.

Jenny's Café, Inc.   A1 19/27
Denver Restaurant   *AS*
Points for Discussion *8/25/06*
Audit Date: July 31, 2006

Discussion Point

Disposition

37. Per **L1**, we observed a cook prepare a hamburger based on the waitress's request rather than off a chit taken from the station printer. Thus, the order was never entered in the order entry system and the customer was not charged for it. This is a violation of company policy that requires all products prepared in the kitchen to be the result of receiving an order on the station printer.

Discussed with field location management.

Included in Internal Audit Report.

38. Per **L1**, we observed a waitress go behind the dessert station when the attendant had left for a few minutes to get a shrimp cocktail. We also observed the waitress add two shrimp to the shrimp cocktail, making it 50% larger than standard. There was no chit in the station printer; thus the order was never entered in the order entry system and the customer was not charged for it.

Discussed with field location management.

Included in Internal Audit Report.

253

Jenny's Café, Inc.   A1 20/27
Denver Restaurant   *AS*
Points for Discussion   *8/25/06*
Audit Date: July 31, 2006

Discussion Point   **Disposition**

39. Per **L1**, we observed the dessert station attendant prepare a pie ala mode based on a waitress's verbal request, rather than from an order printed on a chit obtained from the station printer. This is in violation of company policy that requires every order prepared in the kitchen to be the result of a chit printed on the station printer. Management should take disciplinary action against anyone who violates Company policies.

Discussed with field location management.

Included in Internal Audit Report.

40. Per **M ICQ**, tipped employees are not signing Tip Declarations for cash tips received each payroll period. Federal regulations require all tipped employees to complete and sign a Tip Declaration with all cash tips received even if they are declaring zero tips received.

Discussed with field location management.

Included in Internal Audit Report.

Jenny's Café, Inc.   A1 21/27
Denver Restaurant   *AS*
Points for Discussion   *8/25/06*
Audit Date: July 31, 2006

Discussion Point	Disposition
41. Per **M1**, our review of payroll records showed the following exceptions: • on 4 of 24 Employee Maintenance Forms tested, the rate on the Payroll Register did not agree to the Employee Maintenance Form, • 8 of 24 Time Cards tested were not initialed by the supervisor, • 5 of 7 manual entries on the Time Cards were not initialed by the supervisor.	Discussed with field location management. Included in Internal Audit Report.
42. Per **M2**, we noted an instance where an employee signed in one half hour before starting time but was not paid for that half hour. Federal labor laws require employers to pay employees from the time they clock in until the time they clock out. The employee should not be allowed to come in to work earlier than 7 minutes before the 4:00 p.m. starting time. Jenny's Cafe must pay this employee one half hour back pay.	Discussed with field location management. Included in Internal Audit Report.

255

Jenny's Café, Inc.   **A1 22/27**
Denver Restaurant   *AS*
Points for Discussion   *8/25/06*
Audit Date: July 31, 2006

Discussion Point	Disposition
43. Per **M2**, we noted an instance where an employee did not sign out for lunch and back in after lunch. The Dining Room Manager, after discussions with the employee, determined that she did take a lunch but forgot to sign out. The half hour lunch was deducted from the time paid. In this situation, the Dining Room Manager should ask the employee to go to the Sign In/Sign Out Sheet and enter the time she left for lunch and the time she returned from lunch. If no lunch was taken, the employee must be paid the extra half hour.	Discussed with field location management. Included in Internal Audit Report.
44. Per **M3**, 8 of 11 tipped employees tested did not declare enough in tips to achieve minimum wage of $5.15 per hour, but Denver Restaurant did not pay these employees wage adjustments that would bring them up to minimum wage. Payroll Clerk should go back to the beginning of the year and pay the amounts due to each tipped employee to bring them up to minimum wage.	Discussed with field location management. Included in Internal Audit Report.

Jenny's Café, Inc.   A1 23/27
Denver Restaurant   *AS*
Points for Discussion *8/25/06*
Audit Date: July 31, 2006

Discussion Point	**Disposition**
45. Per **M4**, productivity in the Dining Room and Valet Parking are consistently under the Company Standard of $600 in Sales per Employee in the Dining Room and $300 in Revenues per Employee in Valet Parking. For the month of June, average sales per employee was $488 for the Dining Room and $249 for Valet Parking. This situation points to overstaffing as also noted in our review of Salaries and Wages compared to Plan (39.6% vs. 34.7%) and Last Year (39.6% vs. 34.3%). There is no documented investigation in Denver's files and there does not appear to have been any effort made to address the overstaffing issues.	Discussed with field location management. Included in Internal Audit Report.
46. Per **N1**, our testing of the Human Resources files showed the following exceptions: • 4 of 24 EMF's were not signed by the employee, 4 of 24 were not signed by either manager, and an additional 2 were not signed by a second manager,	Discussed with field location management. Included in Internal Audit Report.

Jenny's Café, Inc.   A1 24/27
Denver Restaurant   *AS*
Points for Discussion   *8/25/06*
Audit Date: July 31, 2006

Discussion Point   **Disposition**

• 2 of 21 employees did not sign a
Consent and Release form prior to
being drug tested and 3 of 3 minors
did not have their parent's signature
on the Consent and Release form,
• 11 of 24 I9's were not properly
completed—
Attest section not completed—1
SS Card said "Not Eligible for
Work"-1
Driver's License & SS Card
attached but not listed on I9—1
Employer Certification not
complete-3
Did not note Work Permit
Expiration Date—1 SS # on I9 did
not match no. on card—1
Hire Date & Certification Date
more than 3 days apart—1
I9 was over-documented—2
• 1 of 11 aliens did not have the
Alien Registration number noted
on the I9 in the Attest Section,
• 2 of 7 alcohol serving associates
who were trained last year did not
have a current Alcohol Training
Awareness certification in their
files.

Jenny's Café, Inc.   **A1 25/27**
Denver Restaurant   *AS*
Points for Discussion   *8/25/06*
Audit Date: July 31, 2006

Discussion Point	Disposition
47. Per **O1**, it has been 18 months since the grill hoods were cleaned and the fire suppression system and fire extinguishers were inspected. Company standards require the grill hoods to be cleaned every 6 months, the fire suppression system to be inspected every 6 months, and the fire extinguishers to be inspected annually.	Discussed with field location management. Included in Internal Audit Report.
48. Per **O2**, CO_2 tanks and propane tanks throughout the building were not properly secured to the wall with a chain. In the warehouse, CO_2 tanks were standing unsecured in a corner. To prevent CO_2 and propane tanks from tipping over and injuring someone, all CO_2 and propane tanks, whether full or empty, should be chained to the wall or otherwise secured.	Discussed with field location management. Included in Internal Audit Report.

259

Jenny's Café, Inc.	**A1 26/27**
Denver Restaurant	*AS*
Points for Discussion	*8/25/06*
Audit Date: July 31, 2006	

Discussion Point	**Disposition**
49. Per **G1**, inventory levels of $150k are 22% higher than last year's $123k, resulting in capital invested in inventory that the Company could better invest elsewhere. Our observations of Stores confirmed that food inventory appeared to be excessive for a restaurant of this size and was poorly organized. The dry goods room and walk in coolers had cases of product lying on the floor and in multiple locations.	Discussed with field location management. Included in Internal Audit Report.
50. Per **G1**, stocks are not properly rotated so that the oldest product is used first. We noted rotting produce in the walk in produce cooler (2.75 cases of lettuce, 2.5 cases of tomatoes, 1 case celery, 2 cases egg plants, 1 bag of carrots—$128). No spoilage sheet was used to document spoilage thrown in the dumpster. Also, cans and packaged product were not dated to ensure that the oldest product was used first.	Discussed with field location management. Included in Internal Audit Report.
51. Per **G2**, the temperature of the walk in freezer was 25 degrees. Company standards require that freezers be kept at zero degrees.	Discussed with field location management. Included in Internal Audit Report.

Jenny's Café, Inc.   A1 27/27
Denver Restaurant   *AS*
Points for Discussion   *8/25/06*
Audit Date: July 31, 2006

Discussion Point	Disposition
52. Per **G3**, the receiving door was left open even though there was no truck in the receiving bay waiting to be unloaded. Company policy requires the receiving door to be unlocked whenever there is no truck waiting to be unloaded.	Discussed with field location management. Included in Internal Audit Report.
53. Per **G3**, the security cameras in the receiving area were not operational. The General Manager should have the security cameras serviced so the Warehouse Manager can observe the receiving area from his office.	Discussed with field location management. Included in Internal Audit Report.
54. Per **G4**, the porters issuing product to the kitchen did not complete issuance slips to document the product issued. All product issued from Stores must be listed on an issuance slip that is signed by the person issuing the product and the person receiving it.	Discussed with field location management. Included in Internal Audit Report.
55. Per **J4**, there is a segregation of duties concern in that the bartender counts the inventory in the Main Bar. Since the bartender sells liquor, beer, and wine at the Main Bar, he may not count the ending bar inventory.	Discussed with field location management. Included in Internal Audit Report.

APPENDIX 2

Jenny's Café—Denver

Internal Audit Report

GARC
GREAT AMERICAN RESTAURANT COMPANY
INTERNAL AUDIT REPORT
JENNY'S CAFÉ, INC.
DENVER RESTAURANT

General Manager: Joey Robertson
Controller: Heather Smith

Field Work: July 24–August 4, 2006

Date Issued: August 18, 2006

DISTRIBUTION

Field:
J. Robertson
H. Smith

Subsidiary Management:
E. Hernandez
C. Sims
S. Thompson

Corporate Management:
M. Chang
S. Grimm
K. Johnson
R. Kazmarek
R. Sartori
M. Swanson
C. Villanueva

Audit Committee:
J. Ellison
E. Merriweather
S. Takimoto

Deloitte and Touche

Reply Due on: September 18, 2006

TABLE OF CONTENTS

Scope 3
Required Response 3
Executive Summary 3
Background 8
Findings and Recommendations 8
Valet Parking Revenues 8
Monitoring Operations 10
Bar Operations 11
Kitchen Operations 13
Sales 14
Stores 15
Payroll 17
Human Resources 20
Cash 22
Inventory 26
Accounts Payable 27
Accounts Receivable 32
Fixed Assets 33
Purchasing and Receiving 35
Risk Management 36

SCOPE

We have completed our operational audit of Jenny's Café, Inc.—Denver Restaurant Food and Beverage and Valet Parking operations. Denver Restaurant is managed by Joey Robertson, General Manager. Denver Restaurant's Controller is Heather Smith.

Our audit was conducted utilizing our standard audit programs that were specifically designed for Jenny's Café restaurants. We conducted tests of transactions, management inquiries, and observations that we consider adequate to evaluate the key areas of internal control that management requires in this type of operation.

The key findings are summarized in the Executive Summary with additional detail in the Findings and Recommendations section of this report. We discussed all findings and recommendations with Jenny's Café local management: J. Robertson, General Manager, H. Smith, Controller, and Jenny's Café senior management: S. Thompson, Vice President of Operations—Western Region, C. Sims, Vice President of Finance.

REQUIRED RESPONSE

Jenny's Café—Denver Restaurant field management must respond to each recommendation in writing within 30 days of the report date. Management's response should include an Action Plan that specifies the action management will take to correct each deficiency and a timetable for implementing corrective action.

EXECUTIVE SUMMARY

The following summary highlights areas of particular concern for management's attention, resulting from our audit.

Valet Parking Revenues

- We observed valet parking attendants consistently failing to record cash transactions on the cash register and not putting the cash received in the cash drawer. Our calculations indicated that Denver restaurant revenues of $110k per year were misappropriated. The Valet Parking Supervisor's failure to reconcile tickets used to cash receipts resulted in the misappropriations going undetected.

Monitoring Operations

- In reviewing Denver Restaurant's Profit and Loss Statements through June 30, 2006, we noted that revenues were 4.3% over Plan and 10.2% over Last Year, profits were 64.9% below Plan and 63.2% below Last Year. However, despite the unsatisfactory results, there was no documented evidence that investigations were conducted by Denver management to determine the reasons for these variances.

Bar Observations

- During our observations of bar operations, we noted a bartender dispensing more than the standard serving in beer, liquor, and wine orders. In addition, we observed careless dispensing of draft beer resulting in significant spillage. We also observed a bartender filling beverage orders based on verbal requests rather than on chits printed on the station printer and a bartender refilling a patron's beer glass without collecting payment for the beer. These activities contributed significantly to the unfavorable Beer Cost variance to Plan (6.6%) and Last Year (6.8%), unfavorable Liquor Cost to Plan (5.4%) and Last Year (4.9%), and unfavorable Wine Cost to Plan (6.9%) and Last Year (6.5%) through June 30, 2006.

- The bartender had the keys to the Liquor Room and obtained additional liquor from this room when needed. Company policy requires that the Manager on Duty issues liquor from the Liquor Room as documented on a Liquor Requisition Slip.

Kitchen Operations

- We observed kitchen personnel preparing orders based on verbal requests instead of from a chit taken from the station printers. We also observed a waitress taking a shrimp cocktail from a cooler, instead of waiting for the salad station attendant to issue it, and adding additional shrimp to make it more costly than standard. This type of activity contributes to the unfavorable Food Cost variances to Plan (6.6%) and Last Year (6.9%).

Sales

- We noted that a waitress did not charge us for a second glass of wine or for coffee. By not recording sales for products delivered to patrons, the waitress contributes to the high product cost noted on the operating results through June 30, 2006.

- During our observations, we noted bussers drop trays of dishes twice within an hour. China and glassware breakage contributed significantly to the unfavorable China, Glassware, and Silverware replacement expense variances of $61k compared to Plan and $61k compared to Last Year.

Stores

- Inventory balances at June 30, 2006 totaled $150k, 22% higher than the $123k on hand at June 30, 2005. Our observations in Stores revealed that inventory was poorly organized, contributing to the high inventory balance.

- Inventory was not properly rotated in Stores resulting in several cases of produce in the walk in produce cooler that were spoiled at a cost of $128.

- While Company policy requires that the temperature of all freezers be maintained at 0 degrees Fahrenheit, we noted the temperature of the walk in freezer in Stores to be at 25 degrees Fahrenheit.

- We noted security issues in the receiving area that increased the likelihood of inventory misappropriation.

Payroll

- Productivity Analysis for the month of June revealed that productivity in the Dining Room and Valet Parking was consistently below the Company Standard of $600 in Sales per Employee in the dining room and $300 in revenues per employee in Valet Parking. Overall, productivity was $112 below the Company Standard for a Jenny's Café operation. Below standard productivity was a significant contributor toward unfavorable Salaries and Wages through June 30, 2006 of 4.9% compared to Plan and 5.3% compared to Last Year.

- Many tipped employees did not report enough in cash tips to bring them up to the $5.15 per hour minimum wage, but Denver did not pay the difference between effective hourly wages and minimum as gross adjustments, as required by the Fair Labor Standards Act.

Human Resources

- Our review of I9's showed that 11 of 24 I9's had exceptions to Immigration and Naturalization requirements. Each exception carries a potential fine of $10k in the event of an INS audit.

Cash

- When we audited the $25k operating fund, we noted the General Manager had his own personal check in the amount of $1,000 in the safe, dated May 31, 2006, representing an unauthorized personal loan.

- There was a petty cash voucher in the safe in the amount of $1,525 for a portable bar that was purchased. This expenditure was not approved by the Vice President of Operations—Western Region as required for expenditures over $500. In addition, this expenditure did not go through the capital expenditure approval process as required for capital asset purchases over $1k.

- The operating fund was $525 short due to the General Manager removing $525 to purchase lighting fixtures without putting a signed petty cash voucher in the safe.

Inventory

- The Bar Manager was not counting the ending inventory in the Liquor Room, Main Beer Cooler, or Wine Cellar but was recording inventory based on the perpetual inventory balances. When counted, actual inventory differed from the perpetual inventories as follows: Liquor Inventory was understated by $3,186, Beer Inventory was overstated by $2,245, and Wine Inventory was overstated by $1,986.

- There was a segregation of duties concern in that the bartender who is responsible for sales was counting the ending inventory at the Main Bar.

Accounts Payable

- Expense reports reviewed contained various discrepancies, including expenditures over $25 without receipts, relocation expenses reported on an expense report instead of a Relocation Expense Report, excessive travel expenses without explanations, and business entertainment expenses without IRS required documentation.

- The onsite disbursements account was used for unauthorized expenditures on two occasions between May 15 and June 30, 2006. In addition, 4 entertainers were paid more than $600 from the onsite checking account, but 1099 information was not relayed to Corporate so Form 1099's could be issued in compliance with government regulations.

Accounts Receivable

- There is a segregation of duties concern in that the Sales/Accounts Receivable Clerk performs every step in recording Accounts Receivable sales, receiving payments, collecting on open accounts, reporting on collection efforts, and writing off bad debts.

BACKGROUND

Jenny's Café—Denver Restaurant opened on January 6, 1986 on Main Street in downtown Denver, Colorado. When it opened, the building was newly completed to Jenny's Café's specifications by Ready to Occupy Real Estate Developers, Inc., the landlord who still owns the building. The 25 year lease runs through January 4, 2011. There is a 10 year renewal option on the part of Jenny's Café. Rent is currently $20.2k per month, with an annual rent increase calculated by taking the increase in the Consumer Price Index plus 0.5%.

Through June 30, 2006, Revenues were $7,706,351 a 4.3% increase in Planned Revenues of $7,386,700, and a 10.2% increase over Last Year's Revenues of $6,995,827. Net Income Before Taxes was $469,798 (6.1% of Revenues), a 64.9% decrease from Planned Net Income Before Taxes of $1,336,716 (18.1% of Revenues) and a 63.2% decrease from Last Year's Net Income Before Taxes of $1,277,985 (18.3% of Revenues). For the full 2006 year, Planned Revenues are $16.2M and Planned Profit Before Taxes are $2.8M.

Mr. Robertson was promoted to the position of General Manager on January 16, 2006. The prior General Manager was Jim Rogers, who was the General Manager when Denver Restaurant was last audited in March 2002.

FINDINGS AND RECOMMENDATIONS

Valet Parking Revenues

We observed Valet Parking transactions for about an hour on Tuesday, July 25, 2006. We noted that the three Valet Parking Attendants failed to record every third or fourth transaction on the cash register and did not put the cash received for those unrecorded transactions in the cash register.

Our calculations revealed that $110k in annual Parking Valet Revenues was misappropriated, as follows:

Average reported revenues on weekdays	$ 900
Number of weekdays	x 5
Reported revenues on weekdays	$ 4,500
Average reported revenues on weekends	1,260
Number of weekend days	x 2
Reported revenues on weekends	2,520
Reported revenues per week	7,020
Estimated percentage unreported	x 30%
Estimated amount misappropriated per week	2,106
Number of weeks in year	x 52
Total estimated misappropriated per year	$109,512

In reviewing the Daily Valet Parking Reports for one week, we noted that this report was not properly completed. While the Valet Parking Supervisor reconciled cash recorded on the cash register per the cash register readings to cash in the cash drawer, he did not reconcile tickets used to cash in the cash drawer.

For example, on Saturday, July 15, 2006, the three Valet Parking attendants turned in $1,275 in cash. This amount agreed exactly to the cash register readings. However, when we looked through the ticket stubs turned in, we noted that 553 ticket stubs were used, valued at $1,659. Thus, Valet Parking was actually $384 short on that day, or 30%. We found that on the other 6 days we audited that the Valet Parking Supervisor did not account for approximately 30% of tickets issued.

To provide proper accountability over Valet Parking Revenues, we recommend:

1. The Valet Parking Supervisor must reconcile the value of tickets used to cash receipts turned in to the cash room every day on the Daily Valet Parking Report. He must list the beginning ticket number and ending ticket number and account for every ticket issued, either as a ticket stub turned in or a complete ticket returned. Cash turned in must agree to the value of the tickets used.

2. At least once a week, on random days, the Sales/Accounts Receivable Clerk should audit the Daily Valet Parking Report, accounting for all tickets issued as either used and $3 turned in per ticket used, or returned as unused tickets.

3. The General Manager should take disciplinary action against employees who violate Company policies regarding cash handling and the failure to complete required paperwork.

Monitoring Operations

In reviewing the Profit and Loss Statements through June 30, 2006, we noted that while revenues of $7,706k were $320k (4.3%) over Plan and $711k (10.2%) over Last Year, profits of $470k were $867k (64.9%) below Plan and $808k (63.2%) below Last Year. The significant unfavorable variance in Net Income Before Taxes was due primarily to the following factors:

Description	This Year	Plan	Last Year	Var to Plan Fav (UnFav)	Var to Last Yr Fav (UnFav)
Food Cost	38.6%	32.0%	31.7%	(6.6%)	(6.9%)
Beer Cost	28.6%	22.0%	21.8%	(6.6%)	(6.8%)
Liquor Cost	29.4%	24.0%	24.5%	(5.4%)	(4.9%)
Wine Cost	32.9%	26.0%	26.4%	(6.9%)	(6.5%)
Salaries & Wages	39.6%	34.7%	34.3%	(4.9%)	(5.3%)
China, Glass, Silverware	$116k	$55k	$55k	($61k)	($61k)

Despite the significant unfavorable variances in Product Cost, Salaries and Wages, and China, Glassware, and Silverware, there is no evidence that investigations were conducted by Denver management to identify the causes for these variances. To ensure that Denver Restaurant achieves maximum profitability, we recommend:

1. The General Manager and Controller should review the results of operations for the month with the Executive Chef, Bar Manager, and Dining Room Manager. They should identify areas that are failing to

achieve Plan. The General Manager should assign the manager responsible for that area to investigate the cause of the unfavorable variance and to prepare a written report of the investigation with an Action Plan for correcting the deficiency.

Bar Operations

We observed Bar Operations on Sunday, July 23, 2006. During our observations, we noted procedural deviations that we believe contributed toward the high product cost noted for the first six months of 2006 compared to Plan and Last Year, as follows:

Product Cost	This Year	Plan	Last Year
Beer Cost	28.6%	22.0%	21.8%
Liquor Cost	29.4%	24.0%	24.5%
Wine Cost	32.9%	26.0%	26.4%

Specific deviations from company policy that we noted were as follows:
- We observed the bartender consistently fill wine to the rim of the wine glass, while the Company Standard calls for wine to be filled to one half inch from the rim of the glass,
- We noted carelessness in pouring draft beer where the bartender allowed beer to run down the drain in turning on the tap before putting a glass under the tap and while changing glasses. We also observed the bartender pour additional beer down the drain in attempting to remove all foam from the glass even though the Company Standard calls for a 10% head,
- We observed occasions where the bartender poured more than the standard one ounce shot into a drink glass,
- We observed the bartender refill a beer glass and record "No Sale" on the cash register,
- We observed the bartender fill beverage orders from the wait staff based on verbal requests rather than the orders printed on the order entry system's printer,
- We observed the bartender commingling tips with Company funds in the cash register,

- We observed the bartender remove a key from the cash register, leave the bar and return with a bottle of Seven Crown Whiskey, a bottle of Bacardi Rum, and a bottle of Grey Goose Vodka.

The following day, the General Manager confirmed that there was no Manager on Duty on Sunday night. The Bartender had the key to obtain additional liquor from the Liquor Room when he needed it and the Head Waitress had the key to lock the restaurant when she left. To bring actual Product Cost at the Bar in line with the 2006 Plan, we recommend:

1. The General Manager should schedule his management staff so that there is always a management person (Manager on Duty) at the restaurant when it is open for business. Only management may have keys to the restaurant.

2. The Manager on Duty is the only one who may have the keys to the Liquor Room. The Bartender should request additional Beer, Liquor, and Wine on a Requisition Slip and present it to the Manager on Duty. The Manager on Duty should fill the request, based on the Requisition Slip, sign it, and bring the order to the bar, where the Bartender counts the delivery, compares it to the Requisition Slip, and signs the Requisition Slip, acknowledging receipt of the delivery.

3. When pouring wine into a glass, the Bartender must follow the Company Standard in filling the glass to one half inch from the rim.

4. When pouring draft beer, all beer must go into the beer glass. The Bartender must follow the Company Standard of pouring beer with a 10% head. He should immediately report any problems with the beer dispensing equipment to the Manager on Duty so they can be rectified.

5. When dispensing liquor, the Bartender must use a shot glass to measure the Company Standard one ounce shot. Bartenders may not overfill the shot glass.

6. Product may not be given away without specific permission of the Manager on Duty. Any complimentary beverages must be documented on the guest check or cash register receipt by the Manager on Duty by writing the reason for the complimentary beverage on the guest check or cash register receipt. The documentation must be put inside the cash register drawer and submitted with the paperwork for the shift to the Accounting Department.

7. The bartender may only fill beverage orders based on orders documented on the order entry system's printer that is located in the bar. This process ensures that the customer is charged for the order.

8. Employees may not commingle tips with company funds. The bartender must have a tip jar located under the bar where he puts his tips.

9. The Bar Manager should take disciplinary action against anyone who violates Company policies.

Kitchen Operations

On August 2, 2006, we observed kitchen operations while the dining room was serving dinner. We observed a cook prepare a hamburger based on the waitress's verbal request rather than off the chit taken from the station printer. Thus, the order was never entered in the order entry system and the customer was not charged for the hamburger. This practice is a violation of Company policy that requires all food prepared in the kitchen to be the result of receiving an order on the station printer.

We observed a waitress go behind the dessert station when the attendant had left for a few minutes to get a shrimp cocktail. We also observed the waitress add two shrimp to the shrimp cocktail , making the menu item 50% more costly than standard. There was no chit in the station printer; thus the order was not entered in the order entry system and the customer was not charged for it.

When observing the dessert station, we noted the dessert station attendant prepare a pie ala mode order based on the waitress's verbal request rather than from an order printed on a chit obtained from the station printer. These examples of Company violations are direct contributors to year to date Food Cost of 38.6% being 6.6% unfavorable to Plan and 6.9% unfavorable to Last Year. To minimize Food Cost and maximize profits, we recommend:

1. The Executive Chef should reemphasize to the kitchen staff that food orders may only be prepared based on orders documented on chits taken from the station printers.

2. The Dining Room Manager should reemphasize to her staff that waiters and waitresses may not take food directly from the kitchen unless it was given to them by a kitchen staff person.

3. The Executive Chef and Dining Room Manager should take disciplinary action against anyone who violates Company policies.

Sales

While having dinner in the dining room prior to announcing the commencement of the audit, we noted that the auditor was not charged for a second glass of wine or for the coffee. By not recording sales for products delivered to patrons, wait staff not only violate Company policy but also contribute to high product cost. For the six months ended June 30, 2006, Wine Cost was 32.9%, substantially over the Planned Wine Cost of 26.0% and Last Year's Wine Cost of 26.4%. Food Cost was 38.6%, substantially over the Planned Food Cost of 32.0% and Last Year's Food Cost of 31.7%. To help bring Wine Cost and Food Cost in line with Plan, we recommend:

1. The Dining Room Manager should take disciplinary action against any employee who serves beverages to patrons without recording the sale in the order entry system.

During our observations of restaurant sales operations, we noted two occasions within an hour of each other where a busser, hurrying to clean a table, dropped a tray of dirty dishes and glasses. In reviewing June's profit and loss statement, we noted a significant increase in China, Glassware, and Silverware replacements ($116k) of 111.3% over last year ($55k). To reduce breakage of china and glassware in the dining room, we recommend:

2. The Dining Room Manager should obtain plastic bins for the bussers to place the dishes when clearing the tables. We believe that plastic bins are less likely to be dropped than trays.

Stores

When comparing the Balance Sheet at June 30, 2006 to June 30, 2005, we noted that Inventory increased by 22% from $123k in 2005 to $150k in 2006. Our observations confirmed that inventory levels appeared to be very high for a restaurant of this size. In addition, inventory was poorly organized in the dry goods room and walk in coolers in that the same product had been placed in multiple locations. There were many cases of products lying on the floor, some opened, others unopened. Badly organized inventory makes it difficult to determine what product is available and results in purchasing product already in stock. To reduce the amount of inventory on hand, thereby freeing up funds for Corporate to use for more profitable purposes, we recommend:

1. The Warehouse Manager should organize Stores so that product is easier to find. In the dry goods room, all cases should be opened when received and product placed on the shelves in the places reserved for the product. In the walk in coolers, porters should remove all cases from the floor and set them on the shelving units. Produce can remain in cases, but they should be arranged so that all inventory of a particular type, i.e. tomatoes, bell peppers, carrots, etc. are stored in the same location.

2. The Controller should review inventory levels regularly and advise the General Manager and Warehouse Manager when levels are rising significantly so purchasing practices can be reviewed and adjusted.

We noted that inventory in Stores was not properly rotated resulting in several cases of spoiled produce (2.75 cases of lettuce, 2.5 cases of tomatoes, 1 case of celery, 2 cases of egg plants, and 1 bag of carrots) in the walk in cooler valued at $128 at cost. In discussing stock rotation with the Warehouse Manager, we noted that there was no method used to ensure that the oldest dry goods were used first.

The Warehouse Manager did not document spoilage on a Spoilage Report. Company policy requires that all spoilage be documented on a Spoilage Report to help the location explain high Food Cost. To minimize spoilage, thereby improving Food Cost, and to maintain documentation to explain high Food Cost, we recommend:

3. The Warehouse Manager should institute a method of ensuring that goods are rotated so the oldest is used first. Receivers should mark cases and cans with the receiving date so Stores personnel know which product to issue first.

4. The Warehouse Manager should document all spoilage on a Spoilage Report and send the completed Spoilage Report to the Controller to help her explain High Food Cost.

In reviewing the temperature maintained in the walk in freezer in Stores, we noted that the temperature was 25 degrees Fahrenheit. Company policy is for all freezers to be kept at zero degrees Fahrenheit or colder. To ensure that all frozen foods are maintained in a completely frozen state, we recommend:

5. The Warehouse Manager should maintain the temperature in the walk in freezer at zero degrees Fahrenheit. If he is not able to maintain the walk in freezer at the proper temperature, the Warehouse Manager should make arrangements to have the compressor repaired.

The receiving door was left open even though there was no truck waiting in the receiving bay to be unloaded. Company policy is to lock the receiving door whenever the receiving docks are not in use. To ensure that theft is minimized by making it difficult to remove product from Stores without authorization, we recommend:

6. The Warehouse Manager should instruct Receiving personnel to lock the receiving door whenever they have completed unloading a truck and brought the products into storage.

The security cameras in the receiving area were not operational. Thus, the Warehouse Manager cannot observe activity in the receiving area from his office. To permit the Warehouse Manager to observe activity in the receiving area, thereby discouraging employees or other personnel from removing unauthorized goods through the receiving doors, we recommend:

7. The General Manager should contact a repair service to come to the restaurant and repair the security cameras.

Porters issued product from Stores without the product being listed on an issuance slip. Company policy requires the Warehouse Manager to write each requested item on a requisition slip. The porters should pull the requested items from Stores and load them on a cart. The Warehouse Manager should check the order against the issuance slip, sign, and date it. When the porter delivers the products to the kitchen, a kitchen staff person should receive the order against the issuance slip and sign it. To ensure all goods are properly transferred as requisitioned, we recommend:

8. The Warehouse Manager should implement the Company's issuance policies.

Payroll

In reviewing Productivity Analyses completed for June 2006, we noted that productivity in the Dining Room and Valet Parking was consistently under the Company Standard of $600 in Sales per Employee in the dining room and $300 in revenues per Employee in Valet Parking. For the month of June, Average Sales per Employee was $488 for the Dining Room and $249 in Valet Parking.

We have already discussed the problem of cash misappropriation in the Revenues section of this report. The $112 per Employee under standard for the entire operation appears to be primarily due to overstaffing. Overall salaries and wages were 39.6% compared to 34.7% Plan and 34.4% Last Year. However, there is no documented investigation in Denver's files and there does not appear to have been any effort made to address the overstaffing issues. To bring Salaries and Wages in line with Plan, we recommend:

1. The General Manager and Controller should review the summary of the Productivity Analysis each month and meet with the department managers to resolve the issues brought up by this analysis. The results of the meeting should be documented in a memo issued to the meeting participants.

In reviewing tipped employees to determine whether they received enough in tips to bring them up to the $5.15 per hour minimum wage, we discovered that 8 of 11 tipped employees tested did not achieve minimum wage. While the employer is required to pay the employee the difference between what the employee received in total compensation (wages, tips, and the cost value of employee meals) and minimum wage, Denver Restaurant did not do this. To comply with Federal and State minimum wage requirements, we recommend:

2. The General Manager should direct the Payroll Clerk to compare wages and declared tips to the minimum wage for each employee and pay the difference as a wage adjustment on the payroll.

3. The Payroll Clerk should go back to the beginning of the year and determine how much in back wages is due to each employee and pay those amounts as adjustments to wages.

Tipped employees are not completing and signing Tip Declarations each payroll period. Federal regulations require all tipped employees to complete and sign a Tip Declaration form with all cash tips received during the payroll period, even if the employees declare zero tips received. To comply with government regulations regarding tip reporting, we recommend:

4. The Dining Room Manager and Bar Manager should advise each tipped employee that he must complete a tip declaration each week. They should monitor the tip declarations received each week and follow up with those tipped employees who did not complete the required form.

In reviewing Sign In Sign Out sheets for week ending July 15, 2006, we noted an instance where an employee signed in one half hour before starting time but was not paid for that half hour. Federal labor laws require employers to pay employees from the time they clock in until the time they clock out. To comply with Federal labor laws, we recommend:

5. Department managers should advise their employees that they may not come in to work earlier than 7 minutes before the scheduled starting time.

6. Management must pay the noted employee one half hour back pay for the time he had signed in but was not paid.

During our review of Sign In Sign Out Sheets, we noted an instance where an employee did not sign out for lunch and back in after lunch. The Dining Room Manager, after discussions with the employee, determined she did take a lunch but forgot to sign out. The half hour lunch was deducted from the time paid. To ensure documented time worked agrees to time paid, we recommend:

7. Where an employee forgot to sign out and in for a lunch period that was taken, the department manager should ask the employee to go to the Sign In Sign Out Sheet and enter the time she left for lunch. If no lunch was taken, the employee must be paid for the extra half hour.

Our review of the payroll records for week ending July 15, 2006, revealed the following exceptions:
- On 4 of 24 Employee Maintenance Forms tested, the rate on the Payroll Register did not agree to the most recent Employee Maintenance Form in the employee's Human Resources folder,
- 8 of 24 time cards tested were not initialed by the supervisor or department manager,
- 5 of 7 manual entries on the time cards were not initialed by the supervisor.

To ensure all payroll activity is properly authorized, we recommend:

8. When an employee's pay rate changes, the Human Resources Manager should ensure that the rate change is documented with a new Employee Maintenance Form signed by the employee and two managers.

9. Each supervisor or department manager must review and initial each time card for each employee he supervises.

10. Whenever there is a manual entry or manual adjustment to a time card, the supervisor or department manager must initial the manual entry.

Human Resources

We tested 24 I9's and noted 11 exceptions to Immigration and Naturalization Service (INS) requirements as follows:
- 1 did not have the Attest section completed,
- 1 was supported with a Social Security Card with the caption "Not Eligible for Work" printed across the face of the card,
- 1 had a driver's license and Social Security Card attached but not listed on the I9 as List B and List C items,
- 3 did not have the Employer certification completed,
- 1 did not note the Work Permit expiration date,
- 1 Social Security number on the I9 did not match the card,
- 1 had the Hire Date and Certification Date more than 3 days apart,
- 2 I9's were over-documented, i.e. a List A, List B, and List C document were listed on the I9.

Each exception to a properly completed I9 carries a $10k potential fine in the event of an INS audit. To ensure that every I9 is properly completed according to INS regulations, we recommend:

1. When the Human Resources Clerk has completed an I9, she should give it to the Human Resources Manager for review prior to filing it in the I9 binder.

In reviewing I9's for proper documentation of Alien Registration numbers, we noted that 1 of 11 aliens did not have the Alien Registration Number noted on the I9. To ensure proper documentation of all aliens as required by the INS, we recommend:

2. As part of the Human Resources Manager's review of I9's, she should make sure that each alien has his alien registration number noted on the proper line of the I9.

Our testing of the Human Resources files showed the following exceptions:
- 4 of 24 Employee Maintenance Forms were not signed by the employee, 4 of 24 were not signed by either manager, and an additional 2 were not signed by a second manager,
- 2 of 21 employees did not sign a Consent and Release form prior to being drug tested,
- 3 of 3 minors did not have their parents' signature on the Consent and Release form,
- 2 of 7 alcohol serving associates who were trained last year did not have a current Alcohol Training Awareness certification in their files.

To ensure all employees added to the payroll are legitimate employees, applicants agree to be drug tested, parents (in the case of minors) consent to their children being drug tested, and only employees properly trained are serving alcohol, we recommend:

3. Prior to giving the Employee Maintenance Form to the Human Resources Clerk for inputting into the Human Resources/Payroll system, the Human Resources Manager should review all Employee Maintenance Forms to ensure the employee, the hiring manager, and a second manager signed the form.

4. Prior to sending an applicant for drug testing, the Human Resources Manager should ensure that the employee signed a Consent and Release form.

5. Where the applicant is a minor, the Human Resources Manager should ensure that the applicant's parent signed the Drug Test Consent and Release form prior to sending the minor applicant for drug testing.

6. Each year, the Human Resources Manager should draft a schedule for training existing alcohol serving employees in alcohol awareness training. She should schedule the employee for a training session 30 days before the one year anniversary of the last training session so the certification does not expire. Alcohol serving employees should not be allowed to work in an alcohol serving position if the date of the employee's training certification is more than one year old.

Cash

When we counted the operating fund, we noted that the General Manager had his own personal check in the amount of $1,000 in the safe dated May 31, 2006. As the check was two months old, it represented a personal loan from the operating fund, a violation of Company policy. To ensure unauthorized loans are not made from the operating fund, we recommend:

1. Employees may not cash checks from the operating fund without written approval from the Vice President of Operations—Western Region.

In reviewing petty cash expenditures reimbursed through the operating fund, we noted that an expenditure from the operating fund in the amount of $1,525 was not approved by the Vice President of Operations—Western Region. GARC policy requires that all petty cash expenditures in excess of $500 be approved by the regional Vice President of Operations. In addition, funds were used to buy a portable bar, a capital expenditure that should have gone through the capital expenditure approval process. To document the approval of expenditures over $500, we recommend:

2. When a petty cash expenditure is made in excess of $500, the General Manager must request written approval from the Vice President of Operations—Western Region. The General Manager may request approval through email, and approval will be given through return email.

In this situation, the General Manager should print the email and staple it to the applicable petty cash voucher.

3. Where the General Manager desires to purchase a capital item, he should complete a Capital Expenditure Request and go through the normal capital expenditure approval process.

When we audited the $25k operating fund, we noted that the fund was $525 short. When we asked the General Manager about the shortage, he stated that he had taken $525 from the safe to purchase lighting fixtures, but had forgotten to put a petty cash voucher for $525 in the safe. At the time of our audit, he had not had the opportunity to purchase the lighting fixtures. To keep the operating fund primarily for making change during restaurant operations, we recommend:

4. The General Manager and other management staff should make reimbursable purchases with their credit cards and submit the receipts on an expense report. Petty cash expenditures should be limited to small petty cash purchases made by hourly employees.

REPEAT ISSUE

GARC policy requires that deposits of cash receipts be transferred to GARC's main operating fund within two business days. As noted in our prior audit report, the Controller is not consistently meeting this mandate. We noted that 15 of 60 bank deposits had not been transferred to GARC's main operating bank account within the required two business days. To make funds available for GARC's use as soon as possible, we recommend:

5. The Controller should make it a priority to initiate the required funds transfer when she arrives for work in the morning.

The cash room door did not have an automatic door closer. Thus, it was possible for the door to be ajar while cash was counted in the cash room. To enhance cash room security by ensuring that the door closes and locks whenever someone enters the cash room, we recommend:

6. The General Manager should make arrangements to have a door closer installed on the cash room door.

We noted that supervisors entered the cash room while staff was counting cash. There is no reason why supervisors need access to the cash room while cash is counted. Additional personnel in the cash room increase the risk of cash misappropriation. To maximize security in the cash room, we recommend:

7. The General Manager should limit access to the cash room to the Manager on Duty, Controller, and General Manager while cash is counted. He should direct other personnel who need to talk to cash room staff to address them from the cash room window.

At the time of our audit, the General Manager had not counted the $25,000 operating fund in 3 months. Company policy is for the General Manager to count the operating fund at the end of each month, reconcile the count to the General Ledger balance, sign it, and send it to the Bank Reconciliation Department within 10 days. To comply with Company policy, we recommend:

8. The General Manager should count the operating fund at the end of each month, documenting his count on the Monthly Safe Audit Sheet. He should sign the Monthly Safe Audit Sheet, and fax it to the GARC Bank Reconciliation Department within 10 days of month end.

Cash handlers do not document the count of their cash receipts on a Cash Slip. Company policy requires every cash handler to document his count on a Cash Slip and sign it. To provide the cash room with a record of the original count, we recommend:

9. Each cash handler must complete a Cash Slip by listing his count by denomination and signing the form. He should insert the completed Cash Slip in the cash bag with the cash receipts. When verifying the count, the cash room attendant should check off each count by denomination on the Cash Slip with a red pen, and initial the Cash Slip.

When observing cash room operations, we noted that a second person does not count the deposit before it is sealed in the deposit bag. GARC policy requires that one cash room attendant prepares the deposit and a second person verifies the deposit. Both people should initial the deposit slip. To ensure the deposit slip is properly completed, we recommend:

10. After the cash room attendant completes the deposit slip, a second person should verify the deposit. Both personnel should document their counts by initialing the deposit slip.

We reviewed the Bank Sign Out Log and Armored Car Log for compliance to company policies. As a result of our review, we noted the following:
• During 2 of 7 days tested, one or more cashiers did not sign the Bank Sign Out Sheet,
• During 2 of 7 days tested, the cash room attendant did not initial the Bank Sign Out Sheet for one or more banks returned,
• For 1 of 7 days tested, the Main Cashier did not obtain the signature of the armed guard who picked up the deposit.

To provide management with documentation that banks were issued and returned, and to document the pick up of the cash deposit in the event of loss by the armored car company, we recommend:

11. The cash room attendant should insist that each cashier signs for the bank issued from the cash room.

12. The cash room attendant must initial the Bank Sign Out Sheet when the bank is returned.

13. The Main Cashier should ensure that the armed guard does not leave the cash room with the cash deposit until he signs the Armored Car Log for the deposit(s).

Inventory

The Bar Manager was not actually counting the Liquor Room but was relying on the perpetual inventory system to record the cost value of the ending inventory in the General Ledger. When we counted the inventory in the Liquor Room, Main Beer Cooler, and Wine Cellar with the Bar Manager, we noted 57 of 142 items where the perpetual inventory balance was different from the actual inventory counts. When totaled, the miscounts resulted in misstatements of the Liquor Commissary inventory as follows: Liquor Inventory was understated by $3,186, Beer Inventory was overstated by $2,245, and Wine Inventory was overstated by $1,986. To ensure the Liquor Commissary Inventory that is recorded in the General Ledger is correct, we recommend:

1. At the end of each inventory period, the Bar Manager must count the inventory in the Liquor Room, Main Beer Cooler, and Wine Cellar and enter the counts in the perpetual inventory system.

When observing the count of the inventory at the Main Bar, we noted that the bartender counted the inventory while the Bar Manager wrote down the counts while sitting at a table at the other end of the lounge. This represents a segregation of duties concern in that the bartender sells the product and could manipulate Liquor, Beer, and Wine Costs by misstating the ending inventory counts. To ensure that inventory at the Bar is counted correctly, we recommend:

2. The Bar Manager should ask someone who does not work at the bar to count the inventory at the Main Bar. The Bar Manager should write the counts while standing at the bar so he can observe the person counting the inventory.

REPEAT ISSUE

We observed the physical inventory on Monday, July 31, 2006 in the Food Warehouse. Our tests of inventory counts showed that 3 of 23 test counts in the Food Warehouse had differences as follows:

Item	Food Whse Count	Auditor's Count	Difference
Cantaloupes	27	51	(24)
Extra Virgin Olive Oil	25	37	(12)
Milk—Gallon	27	25	2

The two larger differences were due to cases that the counters missed on the other side of the cooler or storage room because the counters counted from the count sheet, and looked for the product in the room. To ensure all products in a count area are included in the count, we recommend:

3. The counter should start in one spot in the room and systematically count left to right, top to bottom, working his way around the room. The person writing the counts should find the inventory items on the count sheet and enter the count. When the counter comes to an item that was previously counted in the room, the count writer should add on to the previous count with a plus sign and the additional count.

When we tested Food and Bar inventory items for correct cost prices, we noted that 20 of 36 items had incorrect cost prices for a net understatement of $488. To ensure that the inventory is valued properly, we recommend:

4. The Food Warehouse Manager and Bar Manager should check cost prices at least once per month so that inventory reports are updated when cost prices change.

Accounts Payable

Company policies were not consistently followed in the 13 expense reports we reviewed. Specifically we noted the following discrepancies:
- 2 expense reports had receipts randomly taped on 8.5 by 11 inch pieces of paper, making it difficult to match receipts against specific expenses entered on the expense report when audited by Accounts Payable,
- 1 expense report did not have a receipt for a $395 airfare or a $50 taxi expense,

- 1 expense report was used for relocation expenses,
- 5 expense reports had all hotel expenses lumped into one day on the Lodging line even though they included other expenses, i.e. meals, telephone calls, etc.
- 4 expense reports included expenses that were not legitimate business expenses:
  - $295 dinner for the General Manager and Bar Manager that the Bar Manager included on his expense report had no explanation for the unusually high cost;
  - $75 laundry charge from the Executive Chef had no explanation for the unusually high cost,
  - $65 laundry charge from the Executive Chef had no explanation for the unusually high cost,
  - $195 dinner charge for the Bar Manager had no explanation for the unusually high cost; in house movies included in the expense report is not a reimbursable expense,
- 2 of 10 expense reports for business travel did not have the purpose of the trip explained,
- 2 of 6 reports with business entertainment expenses had no explanation of who was entertained, where it took place, or the business purpose, as required by IRS regulations.

To comply with GARC policies regarding reimbursement for travel and other business expenses and to ensure management employees are not hiding questionable travel and entertainment expenses from their supervisors, we recommend:

1. When two employees have a business meal, the senior employee should pay for the meal and document it on his expense report.

2. When taping supporting receipts on 8.5 by 11 inch pieces of paper, the person completing the expense report should attach receipts in the order they appear on the expense report, separated by day.

3. The person completing the expense report should obtain and attach receipts for all expenses over $25.

4. A relocating employee must submit a Relocation Expense Report for all relocation expenses so Human Resources can treat these expenses as required under federal law (some expenses are required to be added to W2 earnings).

5. Employees traveling on business must separate hotel expenses by day and by type of expense, such as Lodging, Meals, Telephone, etc.

6. Employees may only be reimbursed for reasonable travel expenses. If there are unusual circumstances why expenses are higher than normal, the employee should document the reason for the unusually high business expense on the expense report.

7. Employees traveling on business must document the purpose of the trip on the expense report.

8. Employees incurring Entertainment Expenses must document who was entertained, where the entertainment took place, and the business purpose of the entertainment.

9. During her review of expense reports, the Accounts Payable Clerk should bring any non-reimbursable expenses, i.e. in-house movies, and other violations of company policies in expense report preparation to the attention of the Controller. The Controller should deduct non-reimbursable expenses from the expense reports. If an expense report is not completed according to Company policy, the Controller should return it to the preparer to remedy the deficiency.

Denver Restaurant has an onsite disbursements account that is only to be used to pay for alcoholic beverages at the time of delivery and entertainers performing in the lounge. In reviewing 28 manual checks written from the onsite disbursements account between May 15 and June 30, 2006, we noted the following exceptions:

- 2 checks were written for unauthorized purposes: one to Marty's Repair Service and the other to Handy Hardware Store,
- 6 checks were signed by the Head Waitress, an unauthorized signer,

- 3 checks were missing—no indication in the checkbook who the payee was on the checks,
- 2 checks were not supported by an invoice: Seattle Sue's Country Band and Handy Hardware Store, and were not recorded in the General Ledger as Entertainment Expense,
- 4 payments to entertainers were not reported to Corporate Accounts Payable as 1099 vendors even though they received over $600 in payments (Country Rag Time Band—$650, Robert Rymes Country Band—$1,300, Sheila McCray's Country Band—$650, Singing Suzy Silverman—$975),

To be in compliance with Company policies regarding the use of manual checks and government regulations, we recommend:

10. Checks should be written only for authorized purposes. Denver management should establish credit with other vendors it desires to utilize and pay those invoices through the Accounts Payable system.

11. Only authorized signers may sign checks on the onsite disbursements account. There should be a Manager on Duty scheduled to work whenever the restaurant is open who should sign the checks from the onsite disbursements account.

12. The Manager on Duty should clearly write "VOID" on the check stub in the checkbook when a check is voided to account for all checks used in numerical sequence.

13. The Manager on Duty should obtain an invoice from the payee before writing a check from the onsite disbursements account. He should make a copy of the check, attach it to the invoice and put the documents in the Accounts Payable Clerk's In Box so she can record the transaction in the Accounts Payable system as a purchase and manual disbursement.

14. The Accounts Payable Clerk should obtain 1099 information from each entertainer who is paid through a manual check. She should set up a spreadsheet where she tracks each entertainer paid through the disbursements

account. At year end, the Accounts Payable Clerk should send the spreadsheet to Corporate Accounts Payable so a Form 1099 can be issued to each entertainer who was paid $600 or more during the year.

While the Controller said that she reviews all invoices to ensure that they are for legitimate purchases, she did not document her review by initialing them. To ensure that the Controller does not miss any invoices in her review, we recommend:

15. The Controller should document her review by initialing each invoice as she reviews it.

We tested 24 invoices for proper supporting documentation and approval. Our testing revealed the following:
- 3 of 21 invoices (2 food and 1 beer) did not have a properly completed purchase order,
- 14 of 21 purchases did not have the signature of the department manager on the purchase order, evidencing the department manager's approval,
- 1 of 4 invoices offering a cash discount for early payment was not paid within the discount period,
- 2 of 8 taxable invoices were not taxed by the out of state supplier and not picked up for use tax payments by the Accounting Department,
- 3 of 31 invoices did not have proof of receipt (1 did not have a signed packing slip attached and 2 did not have the receiver's signature on the invoice.

To ensure that all purchases are approved prior to placing the order, cash discounts are received where offered, use taxes are paid when due, and payment is made only for goods actually received, we recommend:

16. Personnel placing orders may not order product until a purchase order is completed and approved by a superior who evidences approval by signing the purchase order.

17. Receiving should send invoices to Accounting promptly and Accounting should immediately process invoices from vendors offering cash discounts for early payment so payment is made within the discount period.

18. The Controller should set up a process where invoices for taxable purchases from out of state suppliers who do not charge sales tax are flagged and self assessed for use tax by recording the use tax due in the Use Tax Payable account. When completing the Sales and Use Tax return, the Controller should enter the Use Tax Payable balance in the Use Tax section of the return. Use Tax Due should be added to Sales Tax Due in processing the payment to the State.

19. Receiving personnel should sign invoices when receiving product to document that all goods on the invoice were received. Signed packing slips should be sent to Accounting. When the Accounts Payable Clerk subsequently receives the invoice, she should match the items on the packing slip to the invoice and attach the packing slip to the invoice as proof of delivery.

Accounts Receivable

There is a segregation of duties concern in that the Sales/Accounts Receivable Clerk records Accounts Receivable sales, opens the mail and receives the checks in payment of Accounts Receivable sales, performs the collection process, reports on collection efforts, and writes the journal entry to record bad debt write-offs that have been approved by Corporate. To strengthen internal control by segregating duties, thus providing a system of checks and balances over the Accounts Receivable process, we recommend:

1. The receptionist should open all mail. She should make a copy of the check for the Sales/Accounts Receivable Clerk to use in recording the payment received. The receptionist should bring the actual checks to the cash room to be included in the next deposit. Before recommending to Corporate that an account be written off, the Controller should review the customer file with the documentation of the Sales/Accounts Receivable Clerk's collection efforts. The journal entry to record the bad debt should be written by the Accounts Payable Clerk and approved by the Controller.

We selected the sales deposit slip for 5 days to determine whether all checks received in the mail were listed on the cash log. Our review determined that on 2 days, there were checks included in the deposit that had not been listed on the Checks Received Log. To ensure all checks received in the mail are properly tracked so the Controller can be sure they were deposited, we recommend:

2. The receptionist should take more care to ensure she lists every check received in the mail on the Checks Received Log.

3. At the end of each week, the Controller should compare the checks listed on the deposit slip to the Checks Received Log to ensure all checks received were deposited.

In reviewing advance deposits for proper treatment, we noted that 3 of 10 advance deposits for future events were recorded incorrectly. Two of these advance deposits were held in the safe until the event date. A third advance deposit was deposited but the Sales/ Accounts Receivable Clerk was out sick and the Accounts Payable Clerk recorded the transaction. Instead of recording the transaction as an Advance Deposit Payable, she incorrectly backed out the 5% sales tax and recorded Food Sales of $4,761.91 and Sales Tax Payable of $238.09. To ensure that payments for future events are recorded correctly, we recommend:

4. The Controller should issue a memo to pertinent staff reminding them that checks may not be held in the safe but must be deposited with the next sales deposit.

5. When an accounting staff member is out and the work is done by someone else, the Controller should pay particular attention to the work performed by the substitute to ensure it is done correctly.

Fixed Assets

We reviewed fixed asset acquisitions for compliance with GARC capital expenditure procurement policies. Our review revealed that 2 of 5 fixed asset acquisitions did not have documentation from three bidders. In addition, of the remaining three acquisitions that did have documentation of three bids, the purchase of one was not made from the lowest bidder. There was no explanation in the project file why the Liquor Control System was purchased from Bartronics for $25,357, while American Bar Supply bid $24,675 for the same Liquor Control System. To ensure that Denver Restaurant obtains the best price for given specifications, we recommend:

1. The General Manager should purchase capital expenditures only after receiving three bids on a particular project. The bid documentation should be retained for 3 years after the capital expenditure project has been closed.

2. If there are legitimate reasons why three bids cannot be obtained or why the lowest bidder is not selected, the General Manager must document those reasons and keep the documentation in the project folder.

When performing our tests of fixed assets by identifying fixed assets from the Fixed Asset Listings, we noted that Denver Restaurant does not affix the fixed asset tags it receives from the GARC Property Accounting Department to the corresponding assets. Thus, in some cases, it is impossible to determine what specific asset relates to the notation on the Fixed Asset Listing. To facilitate fixed asset identification, we recommend:

3. When the Controller receives fixed asset tags from GARC Property Accounting, she should ask the maintenance man to attach the tags to the appropriate assets.

4. Since the Controller has many fixed asset tags in her office, she should go through the Fixed Asset Listing, determine which tag belongs on which asset, and ask the maintenance man to affix them to the appropriate assets.

In our discussions with the Controller, we learned that Denver restaurant sold a fully depreciated Fosters Convection Oven for $500, but did not complete a Retirement, Sale, or Transfer of Capital Asset form. As a result, the $500 was incorrectly recorded as Other Income, instead of a Gain on Sales of Capital Assets. In addition, the asset has not been removed from the Capital Asset Listing or the General Ledger.

Our discussions with the Controller also revealed that Denver Restaurant transferred a Really Kool Standup Cooler to San Diego Restaurant but did not complete a Retirement, Sale, or Transfer of Fixed Assets form. Thus, the cooler is still on the books of Denver, instead of San Diego. To ensure the Fixed Asset Listing reflects only assets that are in service at Denver Restaurant, we recommend:

5. The Controller should complete Retirement, Sale, or Transfer of Capital Asset forms for the Fosters Convection Oven and the Really Kool Standup Cooler and submit them to GARC Property Accounting so they can remove the assets from Denver's books.

6. When assets are retired, sold, or transferred in the future, the Controller should complete the Retirement, Sale, or Transfer form and send it to GARC Property Accounting so they can make the proper journal entry and remove the asset from the Fixed Asset Listing.

Purchasing and Receiving

We tested recent purchases that were covered under national supplier agreements to determine whether they were purchased from national suppliers. Our testing revealed that 13 of 13 items selected that were covered under GARC national supplier agreements were purchased from alternative suppliers at higher cost. Denver restaurant could have saved $232 by purchasing these items from suppliers covered under the national supplier agreements. To ensure that Denver Restaurant pays the lowest possible prices for all food and beverage purchases, we recommend:

1. The Executive Chef should purchase goods from the national suppliers whenever they are covered by a national supplier agreement.

When we reviewed purchasing procedures with the Executive Chef, we learned that he does not maintain documentation of the weekly bids he or the Sous Chef receives from the produce, dairy, or bread suppliers. He also does not maintain the price lists that he receives from the meat or seafood suppliers. To provide an audit trail of bid prices that allows sound purchasing practices to be verified, we recommend:

2. The Executive Chef should retain bidding documentation and price lists in files labeled with the week they were obtained for six months.

In our discussions with the Executive Chef, we learned that the Executive Chef does not maintain a Purchase Order Log as required by Company policy. The purpose of the Purchase Order Log is to track all purchase orders used and to track product received without invoices so the Controller knows what accruals need to be recorded at month end. Our Accounts Payable testing revealed that 1 of 4 invoices that should have been accrued was missed in the accrual process. To ensure all purchase orders are tracked and purchases are accrued where appropriate, we recommend:

3. The Executive Chef should institute a Purchase Order Log where all purchase orders are tracked.

4. At month end, the Executive Chef should forward a copy of the month's Purchase Order Log to the Controller so she can determine what invoices are still outstanding for goods received and can accrue the costs of these deliveries into the current month.

When observing receiving procedures in the warehouse, we noted that Receiving receives baked goods from the bread supplier at the receiving dock by comparing the counts against the invoice. However, when the porter delivers the baked goods to the kitchen, no one in the kitchen counts the product and compares the count against the invoice to ensure that the kitchen is actually receiving all goods charged to it. To ensure that no goods are diverted between the receiving dock and the kitchen, we recommend:

5. The Executive Chef should appoint one of the kitchen staff to count all products delivered to the kitchen and sign the invoice or transfer document.

Risk Management

We noted that it has been 18 months since the grill hoods were cleaned, the fire suppression system was tested, and the fire extinguishers were inspected. Company standards require that a professional cleaning company clean the grill hoods every 6 months. Also, a certified safety contractor must test the fire suppression system every 6 months and the fire extinguishers annually. To ensure that a fire does not start in the grill hoods and that fire suppression system and fire extinguishers are operational when needed, we recommend:

1. Rather than relying on memory to make an appointment to have the grill hoods cleaned, the fire suppression system tested, or the fire extinguishers inspected, the Executive Chef should set up an appointment when these services are performed to have the cleaning and inspections done at the next required time of service.

During our review of Denver Restaurant, we noted that CO_2 tanks and propane tanks throughout the restaurant were not properly secured to the wall with a chain. In the warehouse, CO_2 tanks were standing unsecured in a corner. If a tank containing pressurized gas were to tip over and the head break off, the tip would be propelled like a missile and cause serious injury were it to hit someone. Even empty tanks are still heavy and can cause injury if one fell on someone's foot. To prevent CO_2 and propane tanks from tipping over and injuring someone, we recommend:

2. The General Manager should direct the maintenance man to chain all CO_2 and propane tanks, whether full or empty, to the wall or otherwise secure them.

Throughout our field work, the staff at Jenny's Café—Denver was very cooperative, making our job easier. We would like to thank Joey Roberson, Jenny's Café General Manager, and his staff at Jenny's Café—Denver for the excellent cooperation they gave us during the audit.

Aimee M. Stone
_____

Aimee M. Stone
Senior Auditor

Approved:
David G. Hasselback
_____

David G. Hasselback
Director, Internal Audit

APPENDIX 3

Sample Audit Program

Jenny's Café, Inc.
Denver Restaurant
Audit Program—General Matters
Audit Date: July 31, 2006

Audit Objectives

1 To ensure all relevant aspects have been considered in determining scope and budget requirements.
2 To ensure all pertinent information has been obtained prior to leaving for the field location.
3 To determine the specific areas of concentration for the upcoming audit.
4 To determine whether Corporate management has specific concerns regarding the upcoming audit.

Audit Steps	Initials	Ref.	Comments

1. Obtain audit assignment from the Director of Internal Audit.
a. Discuss upcoming audit with the Director of Internal Audit.
b. Book airline, hotel, and car rental (if needed) reservations through the Internal Audit Administrative Assistant.
c. Obtain time budget and divide it among the different audit sections.

2. Write the Engagement Letter:
a. Take the original to the Director of Internal Audit for his signature.
b. Make a copy for the workpapers.
c. Put original in envelope with a business card from each member of the audit team to present to the General Manager upon arrival at the field location.

Jenny's Café, Inc.
Denver Restaurant
Audit Program—General Matters
Audit Date: July 31, 2006

Audit Steps	Initials	Ref.	Comments

d. Provide an electronic version to the Administrative Assistant to issue to subsidiary management on the day the field work begins.

3. Obtain the permanent file for the audit location, or if this is a new location, set up the permanent file binder.

a. Set up a Table of Contents and index documents obtained for the permanent file.

b. Review documents in the permanent file and make yourself familiar with their contents. Obtain new documents that have been issued since the last audit, and insert in the permanent file, i.e. last audit report, updated organization charts, new contracts, leases, amendments, etc.

c. Add additional procedures to applicable audit programs resulting from unique provisions in contracts, leases, etc.

d. Review last audit's workpapers for documentation that should go into the permanent file, i.e. procedural narratives, flowcharts, etc.

Jenny's Café, Inc.
Denver Restaurant
Audit Program—General Matters
Audit Date: July 31, 2006

Audit Steps	Initials	Ref.	Comments

e. Obtain a copy of the current union contract from the Labor Relations Department, make yourself familiar with its provisions, and modify the Payroll section as necessary to adequately test the labor contract's provisions.

4. Obtain the standard audit programs designed for the subsidiary to be audited.
a. Review the scope of the audit and determine whether additional steps need to be added to the audit programs.
b. Put the audit programs in the workpaper binder.

5. Obtain a copy of the most recent Balance Sheet and Income Statement and put a copy in the workpapers:
a. Perform an analytical review of the Balance Sheet and Income Statement.
b. Make notes on large variances to be followed up at the field location.
c. Add additional audit procedures to individual sections as needed as a result of large variances noted.

Jenny's Café, Inc.
Denver Restaurant
Audit Program—General Matters
Audit Date: July 31, 2006

Audit Steps	Initials	Ref.	Comments

d. When at the field location, follow up with the General Manager on the large variances noted and put explanations in the workpapers.

6. Obtain any information about the field location from Corporate Headquarters, i.e. newspaper articles, magazine articles, company newsletter, etc. and put them in the permanent file.

7. Audit the rent payments to ensure the field location is in compliance with the provisions of the lease regarding rent payments.

8. As you are preparing for the audit, make a list of items needed from the field location's Controller.
   a. If the visit is announced, email the list of items needed to the General Manager and Controller.
   b. If the visit is unannounced, print a copy of the list and insert it in the envelope with the Engagement Letter.

Jenny's Café, Inc.
Denver Restaurant
Audit Program—General Matters
Audit Date: July 31, 2006

Audit Steps	Initials	Ref.	Comments

9. Go through the audit programs of each section to prepare for the upcoming audit.
   a. Set up standard workpapers as needed and organize audit binder into sections, using subject dividers.
   b. Where possible, select samples for testing at the field location.

10. Review the prior audit report.
    a. While at the field location, determine whether each audit finding has been resolved.
    b. For repeat audit findings, indicate in the audit report that this is a repeat finding.

11. Schedule meetings with Home Office personnel.
    a. Meet with subsidiary senior management to discuss any specific concerns they have with the field location and document the results of the meeting in the workpapers.
    b. Contact Home Office department heads about any problems they have noted with documentation sent to the Home Office, and document any problems noted in the workpapers.

Jenny's Café, Inc.
Denver Restaurant
Audit Program—General Matters
Audit Date: July 31, 2006

Audit Steps	Initials	Ref.	Comments

12. If possible, perform unannounced observations of field location operations upon arrival.
a. Document results of observations in the workpapers.
b. Discuss any deviations from company policy with field location management.

13. Write a Planning Memo that summarizes the information learned during the planning process.
a. Review the planning memo with the Director of Internal Audit.
b. Insert the completed Planning Memo in the workpapers.

14. Upon arrival at the field location, introduce yourself to the General Manager and present him with the Engagement Letter.
a. Note whether the General Manager asked to see identification.
b. During the Introduction Meeting, explain the purpose of the audit.

Jenny's Café, Inc.
Denver Restaurant
Audit Program—General Matters
Audit Date: July 31, 2006

Audit Steps	Initials	Ref.	Comments

c. Set up a tour of the facility. During the tour, be alert to any unusual situations and note them in the workpapers.

d. Set up the date and tentative time for the Exit Conference.

15. Upon conclusion of the audit, write the audit report.

a. Discuss the audit report with senior subsidiary management.

b. Upon final review of the report with the Director of Internal Audit, issue the report.

16. Follow up on the field location's response.

a. Determine whether the field location's response adequately addresses each issue raised in the report.

b. If not, follow up with the field location by email or telephone call until every issue in the report is adequately addressed.

Jenny's Café, Inc.
Denver Restaurant
Audit Program—Cash
Audit Date: July 31, 2006

Audit Objectives

1. The operating fund is counted and the count is agreed to the General Ledger balance.
2. The operating fund is secured at all times.
3. Petty cash expenditures are made only for purchases of small items that cannot be processed through Accounts Payable.
4. Bank accounts are reconciled and reconciling items are promptly cleared.

Audit Steps	Initials	Ref.	Comments
1. Upon identifying yourself to the General Manager, begin counting the operating fund.			
a. Using the automated count sheet, count the operating fund and reconcile it to the General Ledger balance.			
b. Tie each bank issued to a document where the cash handler signed for the amount of the bank.			
c. Review petty cash vouchers for unauthorized advances and expenditures that should have been incurred through a vendor paid through the accounts payable system.			
d. When the count is completed, print the final report and ask the General Manager to sign it, acknowledging all funds were returned.			

Jenny's Café, Inc.
Denver Restaurant
Audit Program—Cash
Audit Date: July 31, 2006

Audit Steps	Initials	Ref.	Comments

e. Follow up on any reconciling items, i.e. funds in transfer to the bank, amounts in the coin account, etc.

f. Tie the Cash Count Sheet to the balance in the General Ledger.

2. While reviewing the cash function, verify the following security issues through discussions with unit management and physical observations:

a. Money room/vault area is physically secure and alarmed (if required by Corporate Security) with the use of separate alarm codes for each individual, and security devices are in working order.

b. Door automatically closes and lock is not capable of being bypassed with a button or knob.

c. Money room possesses an approved safe. Money room has a safe/vault that is kept locked when room is unattended.

d. Non-money room employees are prohibited access to the vault area of the money room while cash is in the room, with the exception of the General Manager and Office Manager.

Jenny's Café, Inc.
Denver Restaurant
Audit Program—Cash
Audit Date: July 31, 2006

Audit Steps	Initials	Ref.	Comments

3. Complete the Internal Control Questionnaire for Cash.

4. Observe cash room operations, including the following:
   a. Bank issuance process, including signing for the banks.
   b. Observing the cash pick up process where a Cash Room attendant goes around to each cash handler and picks up excess cash.
   c. Banks returned at the end of the shift, including the Cash Room Attendant initialing the Bank Sign Out Sheet, acknowledging return of the bank.
   d. Cash verification process where the Cash Room attendant compares her count to that on the Cash Slip.
   e. Making up the deposit and getting it ready for pick up by the armored carrier.
   f. Returning the banks to the safe at the end of the cash counting process.
   g. Armored carrier arrives to pick up the cash deposit.

Jenny's Café, Inc.
Denver Restaurant
Audit Program—Cash
Audit Date: July 31, 2006

Audit Steps	Initials	Ref.	Comments

5. Select one week's Bank Sign Out Sheets and determine whether each cashier has signed for the bank and the Main Cashier initialed its return.

6. Select one week's deposits from the General Ledger Cash Depository account, trace the amounts to the deposit slips, and trace the deposit slips to the Armored Car Log.

7. Test change orders by performing the following:
a. Observe a change order received and determine whether the Cash Room Manager counts the change order delivery and agrees the count to the delivery documents and the Change Order Slip.
b. Review the Change Order Log from the most recently completed month and determine whether all cash movement between the field location and the bank are recorded on the log.
c. Select several change orders and deposits and trace them to the Coin Account bank statements.

Jenny's Café, Inc.
Denver Restaurant
Audit Program—Cash
Audit Date: July 31, 2006

Audit Steps	Initials	Ref.	Comments

8. Where the location has an onsite checking account, perform the following:
a. Review the signature cards to ensure they are current.
b. Obtain a recent month's bank statement and determine whether only authorized signers sign the checks and all checks comply with multiple signer requirements.

9. Select the most recent Petty Cash Reimbursement Request and determine whether all petty cash expenditures were for expenditures that comply with Company policies.

10. Where checks are accepted, perform the following:
a. Review the location's Check Acceptance Policy to ensure it is adequate and meets Company standards.
b. Select some checks from a recent deposit and review them for compliance with the established Check Acceptance Policy.

Jenny's Café, Inc.
Denver Restaurant
Audit Program—Cash
Audit Date: July 31, 2006

Audit Steps	Initials	Ref.	Comments

11. Where credit cards are accepted for payment, perform the following:
a. Select 3-4 days and examine the Credit Card Settlement report for each shift.
b. For each day selected, add the credit card totals for each type of credit card from the Credit Card Settlement reports and agree them to the totals on the cash register sales reports for the day.

12. Select the most recent bank reconciliation for the depository account, on-site checking account, and the coin account, and perform the following:
a. Foot the bank reconciliation.
b. Tie the Bank Balance to the Bank Statement.
c. Tie the Balance per the General Ledger on the Bank Reconciliation to the General Ledger.
d. Trace any Deposits in Transit to the following month's Bank Statement.
e. Trace any Outstanding Checks to the following month's Bank Statement.
f. Follow up on any old reconciling items.

Jenny's Café, Inc.
Denver Restaurant
Audit Program—Cash
Audit Date: July 31, 2006

Audit Steps	Initials	Ref.	Comments

13. Summarize any exceptions on the Discussion Points Worksheet, discuss them with the General Manager, and include them in the Audit Report, where appropriate.

Jenny's Café, Inc.
Denver Restaurant
Audit Program—Accounts Receivable
Audit Date: July 31, 2006

Audit Objectives

1. The Aged Accounts Receivable Trial Balance reflects all Accounts Receivables outstanding.
2. There is an effective collection process in place that collects most delinquent accounts.
3. Bad debts are written off according to Company policy.
4. Deposits on future events are recorded as Advance Deposits and applied to the event when it occurs.

Audit Steps	Initials	Ref.	Comments
1. Complete the Internal Control Questionnaire for Accounts Receivable.			
2. Select 3-7 days Accounts Receivable activity and determine whether all Accounts Receivable charges were billed to the customer the following business day.			
3. Ask the Banquet Manager for a list of banquets held during the test period selected in No. 2. a. Tie the detailed invoices from the banquet system to the invoices generated from the Accounts Receivable system. b. Tie the invoices to the posting to the Sales Journal and to the Accounts Receivable Aged Trial Balance.			

Jenny's Café, Inc.
Denver Restaurant
Audit Program—Cash
Audit Date: July 31, 2006

Audit Steps	Initials	Ref.	Comments

c. Determine whether each invoice was billed properly for the correct amount.

4. Select several days' check deposit slips, list the checks on a workpaper, and tie each check to the Checks Received Log.

5. Select several days' Accounts Receivable payments and determine whether they were properly posted to the Accounts Receivable Sub-Ledger.

6. Obtain the Accounts Receivable Aged Trial Balance for the prior month and perform the following:
a. Tie the total from the A/R Aged Trial Balance to the Balance Sheet or Trial Balance.
b. Obtain the A/R Aged Trial Balance from two additional months and see if the Controller signed and dated all three months' reports.

Jenny's Café, Inc.
Denver Restaurant
Audit Program—Cash
Audit Date: July 31, 2006

Audit Steps	Initials	Ref.	Comments

7. Obtain the most recent Collection Status of Past Due Accounts report and perform the following:
a. Select some 5-10 past due invoices from the Accounts Receivable Trial Balance and trace them to the Collection Status of Past Due Accounts report.
b. In reviewing the Collection Status of Past Due Accounts report, determine whether the collections person is vigorously pursuing the accounts.
c. Where an account is more than 120 days old and has not been turned over to a collection agency, ask the Controller or General Manager why the account has not been turned over for collection.

8. Obtain the Controller's most recent Analysis of Collectibility of Past Due Accounts to determine whether the Allowance for Bad Debts is adequate.

Jenny's Café, Inc.
Denver Restaurant
Audit Program—Cash
Audit Date: July 31, 2006

Audit Steps	Initials	Ref.	Comments

9. Select some recent bad debt write offs and review the supporting Bad Debt Write Off forms and attached documentation to determine whether Company procedures were followed.

10. Select several recent functions and determine whether the deposits for these functions were handled correctly.

11. Obtain a copy of the Advance Deposit detail from the Controller, foot the schedule, and tie the total to the General Ledger.

12. Summarize any exceptions on the Discussion Points Worksheet, discuss them with the General Manager, and include them in the Audit Report, where appropriate.

Jenny's Café, Inc.
Denver Restaurant
Audit Program—Capital Expenditures
Audit Date: July 31, 2006

Audit Objectives

1. The Fixed Asset accounts reflect all capital expenditure activity.
2. Company policies are followed in purchasing capital equipment and contracting for capital improvements.
3. Proper accounting treatment is utilized when recording China, Glassware, and Silverware purchases.
4. Repairs and Maintenance account reflects only those items that were properly expensed.

Audit Steps	Initials	Ref.	Comments
1. Complete the Internal Control Questionnaire for Capital Expenditures.			
2. Prior to going to the location, obtain a list of capital projects and capital equipment purchases completed in the last 6 months.			
3. Select all capital projects completed in the last 6 months and capital equipment purchases made in the last 6 months (5-10 in a new operation) and request the Controller to provide the capital project folders for the capital projects with all supporting documentation.			

Jenny's Café, Inc.
Denver Restaurant
Audit Program—Capital Expenditures
Audit Date: July 31, 2006

Audit Steps	**Initials**	**Ref.**	**Comments**

4. For each capital project or capital equipment purchase selected, obtain the project file and perform the following:

a. Determine whether the field location has completed a Capital Expenditure Request Form and obtained the required approvals according to the approval hierarchy based on the total project dollar amount.

b. Determine whether the field location obtained at least 3 bids for the capital project and retained all bid documentation.

c. Determine whether the field location selected the lowest bidder or documented the reason for not selecting the lowest bidder.

d. Determine whether a Capital Expenditure Purchase Order was completed.

e. If there was a cost overrun greater than 10%, determine whether a supplementary CER was completed and appropriate approvals were obtained.

Jenny's Café, Inc.
Denver Restaurant
Audit Program—Capital Expenditures
Audit Date: July 31, 2006

Audit Steps	Initials	Ref.	Comments

f. Determine whether the appropriate location personnel documented the receipt of the asset or completion of the capital improvement project, and approval was documented with a signature and date.

g. Determine whether a capital asset tag was affixed to the capital asset.

h. Determine whether the invoice for the capital project or asset was recorded in the proper General Ledger account.

i. When the Capital asset or improvement was put in service, determine whether the appropriate form was completed and sent to Corporate Property Accounting so monthly Depreciation Expense journal entries were made.

j. Tie each capital asset selected to the General Ledger journal entry putting the asset in service.

Jenny's Café, Inc.
Denver Restaurant
Audit Program—Capital Expenditures
Audit Date: July 31, 2006

Audit Steps	Initials	Ref.	Comments

5. Select a few recent capital asset retirements, sales, and transfers from the General Ledger and determine whether a Retirement, Sale or Transfer of a Capital Asset form was properly completed and sent to Corporate Property Accounting.

6. Review the Repairs and Maintenance General Ledger account for the last 3 months and select the larger items (> $1,000) for testing.
a. Obtain the invoices of the items tested and determine whether they were legitimate expenses or should have been capitalized.
b. Determine whether the invoice was properly approved.

7. Review the capital expenditure accounts for the past 6-12 months to ensure there were no replacement purchases of China, Glassware, and Silverware that should have been expensed.

Jenny's Café, Inc.
Denver Restaurant
Audit Program—Capital Expenditures
Audit Date: July 31, 2006

Audit Steps	Initials	Ref.	Comments

8. Obtain a copy of the Fixed Asset Listing from Corporate Property Accounting and perform the following:

a. Select 10-20 items from the Property Management System: a few smaller dollar items and the rest high dollar items, and list them on your workpaper, including asset tag number.

b. When at the location, ask the Controller or General Manager to locate the assets on your list.

c. Identify the asset by tag number, if possible, or examine the asset to ensure it matches the description in the Property Management System.

9. Summarize any exceptions on the Discussion Points Worksheet, discuss them with the General Manager, and include them in the Audit Report, where appropriate.

Jenny's Café, Inc.
Denver Restaurant
Audit Program—Purchasing
Audit Date: July 31, 2006

Audit Objectives

1. Purchases are made from the national supplier whenever possible.
2. Purchases are made from the lowest bidder for a specified quality of product.
3. Goods received were actually ordered and agree to the invoice.
4. Credit is received for all rejected goods, shortages, and damaged goods.

Audit Steps	Initials	Ref.	Comments
1. Complete the Internal Control Questionnaire for Purchasing.			
2. Obtain the list of products covered by national purchasing agreements from the Corporate Purchasing Department. a. Go through local supplier invoices and determine whether any of those purchases are covered by a national supplier agreement. b. Where products were purchased locally that should have been purchased from national suppliers, list them on a workpaper and review them with local management.			

Jenny's Café, Inc.
Denver Restaurant
Audit Program—Purchasing
Audit Date: July 31, 2006

Audit Steps	Initials	Ref.	Comments

3. Select a recent week and obtain the bidding documentation.

a. Select several items purchased during that week and determine whether the product was purchased from the lowest bidder.

b. On any products purchased from a vendor who was not the lowest bidder, follow up with management to determine why the bidder was selected.

4. Select several invoices and determine whether a purchase order was completed and approved for each invoice of tangible goods prior to placing the order.

5. Review the details of the purchasing accrual for the last closed month and determine whether all purchases received without an invoice were accrued into the proper month.

**Jenny's Café, Inc.
Denver Restaurant
Audit Program—Purchasing
Audit Date: July 31, 2006**

Audit Steps	Initials	Ref.	Comments

6. Observe 2-3 deliveries and perform the following:

a. Determine whether all goods received were actually counted or weighed and compared to the invoice or packing slip and the purchase order.

b. Determine whether all paperwork is properly handled by the receiving personnel according to company policy.

c. Determine whether any goods not ordered or that do not meet company specifications were rejected.

d. Determine whether credits are properly tracked on a Credit Log and that the Warehouse Manager or Chef follows up monthly on credits due but not received.

e. Observe how the product received is stored and determine whether Company policy is followed in storing goods received.

7. Summarize any exceptions on the Discussion Points Worksheet, discuss them with the General Manager, and include them in the Audit Report, where appropriate.

Jenny's Café, Inc.
Denver Restaurant
Audit Program—Accounts Payable & Manual Checks
Audit Date: July 31, 2006

Audit Objectives

1. All expenditures are for properly approved purchases or legitimate services provided, and are properly recorded in the General Ledger.
2. Manual checks are cut to authorized vendors for approved purposes.
3. All Expense Report reimbursements are for reimbursable expenses incurred in pursuing the Company's objectives.
4. Sales and Use tax on taxable items are paid to the appropriate government authorities.

Audit Steps	Initials	Ref.	Comments
1. Complete the Internal Control Questionnaire for Accounts Payable and Manual Checks.			
2. Check with the Corporate Sales Tax Department what types of items used in the restaurant are taxable, i.e. ice, napkins, condiments, bags, toothpicks, etc., and take list to field location.			
3. Obtain recent cancelled checks from the onsite checking account, list 20-30 checks and perform the following: a. Obtain copies of the signature cards from the Treasury Department and determine whether each signer was authorized to sign the checks.			

Jenny's Café, Inc.
Denver Restaurant
Audit Program—Accounts Payable & Manual Checks
Audit Date: July 31, 2006

Audit Steps	Initials	Ref.	Comments

b. Determine whether each signer on the on-site checking account, per the signature cards, still works at the field location.

c. Tie the checks to invoices to ensure the payments were made to an authorized vendor.

d. Determine whether each disbursement was made for the purpose for which the account was established.

e. Determine whether each check was used in numerical sequence.

f. Determine whether each payment was supported by a legitimate invoice.

g. If the vendor was a 1099 vendor, determine whether the payment was reported to Corporate A/P for 1099 reporting purposes.

h. While at the field location, determine whether there are any presigned checks in the check book.

i. Determine whether the on-site check book is properly secured, i.e. in the safe or in a locked file cabinet in a locked office.

Jenny's Café, Inc.
Denver Restaurant
Audit Program—Accounts Payable & Manual Checks
Audit Date: July 31, 2006

Audit Steps	Initials	Ref.	Comments

4. Select 30-40 invoices and perform the following:

a. Where applicable, determine whether the invoice was processed in time to take advantage of the early payment discount.

b. Determine whether the invoice was coded to the correct General Ledger account.

c. If the purchase was taxable, determine whether Sales Tax was paid or self assessed.

d. Where the products were carried by a national supplier, determine whether the product was purchased from the national supplier.

e. Determine whether a purchase order was properly prepared.

f. Where applicable, determine whether the invoice was properly accrued.

g. Determine whether the purchase was approved by the department manager by signing the purchase order.

h. Determine whether the receiver signed the invoice.

Jenny's Café, Inc.
Denver Restaurant
Audit Program—Accounts Payable & Manual Checks
Audit Date: July 31, 2006

Audit Steps	Initials	Ref.	Comments

5. Select several Expense Reports for review, including the General Manager's (filed at Corporate) and determine whether company procedures and reimbursement policies were followed in completing the Expense Reports.

6. If an employee at the location incurred relocation expenses during the last year, determine whether the Relocation Expense Report was used.

7. Summarize any exceptions on the Discussion Points Worksheet, discuss them with the General Manager, and include them in the Audit Report, where appropriate.

Jenny's Café, Inc.
Denver Restaurant
Audit Program—Food Warehouse (Stores)
Audit Date: July 31, 2006

Audit Objectives

1. All products are organized in the Food Warehouse in a manner that ensures product is fresh and spoilage is minimized.
2. Product movement into and out of the Food Warehouse is documented.
3. Product stored in the Food Warehouse is secure.

Audit Steps	Initials	Ref.	Comments
1. Complete the Internal Control Questionnaire for the Food Warehouse (Stores).			
2. During your tour of the Food Warehouse, look at the product in Stores to determine whether the receiving date has been marked on the cans, boxes, and cases, and whether goods are properly rotated.			
3. Review warehouse operations and describe the procedures used in storing product, issuing product, organizing product in the warehouse, and the temperatures maintained in the coolers and freezers. Comment on any deviations from Company policy.			

Jenny's Café, Inc.
Denver Restaurant
Audit Program—Food Warehouse (Stores)
Audit Date: July 31, 2006

Audit Steps	Initials	Ref.	Comments

4. Observe a delivery of product issued by Stores and determine whether the person receiving the product counts it and compares the counts to the Requisition Slip or Issuance Slip.

5. Select a sample of Requisition Slips or Issuance Slips and perform the following:
a. Determine whether the issuance documentation is complete, i.e. every item is listed on the slip and checked off by the person picking the product, checking the product, and receiving the product.
b. Determine whether the appropriate personnel signed the Requisition or Issuance slips.

6. During your audit work, note the security devices and practices in the Food Warehouse and note any deviations from Company policy.

Jenny's Café, Inc.
Denver Restaurant
Audit Program—Food Warehouse (Stores)
Audit Date: July 31, 2006

Audit Steps	Initials	Ref.	Comments

7. Where the location has an inventory control system with a perpetual inventory, select 10-20 inventory items, count them, and compare your counts to the perpetual inventory balances, making adjustments for inventory currently in process.

8. Summarize any exceptions on the Discussion Points Worksheet, discuss them with the General Manager, and include them in the Audit Report, where appropriate.

Jenny's Café, Inc.
Denver Restaurant
Audit Program—Bars
Audit Date: July 31, 2006

Audit Objectives

1. All alcoholic and non-alcoholic beverages produced at the bar are recorded on the Point of Sale system or cash register.
2. All liquor, beer, and wine issued to the bar are documented and traceable to the bar.
3. Beer, Liquor, and Wine Costs are tracked by Bar and significant variances from Plan are investigated.
4. Beer, liquor, and wine are dispensed according to established portion specifications.

Audit Steps	Initials	Ref.	Comments
1. Complete the Internal Control Questionnaire for Bars.			
2. Perform observations of the bar (unannounced, if possible) and note the following: a. Determine whether bartenders follow Company policies in dispensing alcoholic beverages and recording them on the cash register. b. Determine whether bartenders follow portion control policies in dispensing alcoholic beverages. c. Determine whether bartenders fill orders placed by the wait staff only from orders printed on the chit printer. d. Determine whether the bartender sticks chits from filled orders on a spindle.			

Jenny's Café, Inc.
Denver Restaurant
Audit Program—Bars
Audit Date: July 31, 2006

Audit Steps	Initials	Ref.	Comments

3. Tour the Liquor Room, Main Beer Cooler, and Wine Cellar, and determine whether the liquor room is properly organized with all liquor removed from cases and put in the shelves, where possible.

4. Review the effectiveness of the Liquor Sticker control system by performing the following:
a. Examine a number of bottles randomly selected in the Liquor Room to see whether they have liquor stickers affixed to them.
b. Go to the bar, randomly select a number of liquor bottles, and determine whether they have liquor stickers affixed to them.

5. Test the effectiveness of the Liquor Control Log by performing the following:
a. Select some liquor sticker numbers from the shelf in the Liquor Room and trace them to entries in the Liquor Control Log.
b. Select some entries from the Liquor Control Log and trace them to bottles on the shelf.

Jenny's Café, Inc.
Denver Restaurant
Audit Program—Bars
Audit Date: July 31, 2006

Audit Steps	Initials	Ref.	Comments

c. Select some sticker numbers from bottles in the Bar and trace them to the Liquor Log.

d. Select some entries from the Liquor Control Log of bottles issued to the Bar and trace them to bottles at the bar.

6. Obtain the Liquor, Beer, and Wine issuance slips for a recent week and perform the following:

a. Determine whether the issuance slips contain all required signatures.

b. Take one of two slips and trace each item to the inventory system to ensure the issuance was properly posted.

7. Select a week of Liquor Control System reports approximately one month prior to the audit and perform the following:

a. Determine whether the daily reconciliation was done properly.

b. Take the most recent Liquor Control System Report and compare the meter readings to those on the report.

Jenny's Café, Inc.
Denver Restaurant
Audit Program—Bars
Audit Date: July 31, 2006

Audit Steps	Initials	Ref.	Comments

8. Select a week of Beer Usage Reports and supporting Draft Beer Control System Usage Reports approximately one month prior to the audit and perform the following:

   a. Determine whether the daily reconciliation was done accurately.

   b. Take the most recent Draft Beer Control System Report and agree to the draft beer meter readings. Count the beer bottles left in the bar and agree to the Beer Usage Report.

9. Select a week of Wine Usage Reports approximately one month prior to the audit and perform the following:

   a. Determine whether the daily reconciliation was done accurately.

   b. Take the most recent Wine Usage Report, count the wine left in the bar, and agree it to the ending counts on the report.

10. Select a week of Bar Usage Reports and determine whether the reconciliation was done correctly.

Jenny's Café, Inc.
Denver Restaurant
Audit Program—Bars
Audit Date: July 31, 2006

Audit Steps	Initials	Ref.	Comments

11. Determine whether the location follows through on disciplinary action on bartenders that have product usage variances greater than the acceptable limit by noting any product usage shortages over the limit and reviewing the employee's personnel file to see whether there is a record of disciplinary action taken in the file.

12. Select recent Bar Control Reports for a recent month, and perform the following:
a. Trace the beginning counts to the ending counts of the previous period's Bar Control Report.
b. Agree quantities received to issuance slips.
c. Tie ending counts to the count sheets.
d. Agree unit costs to recent invoices.
e. Verify the accuracy of the Selling Price used in the Bar Control Report.
f. Tie the credits to the Liquor metering system.

Jenny's Café, Inc.
Denver Restaurant
Audit Program—Bars
Audit Date: July 31, 2006

Audit Steps	Initials	Ref.	Comments

g. Tie the total Liquor, Beer, and Wine Costs to the P & L.

h. If there are significant variances from the P&L, determine whether the Bar Manager or Controller investigated the reasons for the variance and documented the results of the investigation.

i. If there are significant variances from Plan at specific bars, determine whether management investigated the reasons for the variances and documented the results of the investigation.

13. Summarize any exceptions on the Discussion Points Worksheet, discuss them with the General Manager, and include them in the Audit Report, where appropriate.

Jenny's Café, Inc.
Denver Restaurant
Audit Program—Sales
Audit Date: July 31, 2006

Audit Objectives

1. Sales recorded in the General Ledger represent products and services provided to customers.
2. All sales are recorded on a POS device, cash register, or other means of tracking sales.
3. All revenues are balanced to recorded sales.

Audit Steps

1. Complete the Internal Control Questionnaire for Sales.

2. Perform unannounced observations of the dining room, if possible, and continue to observe dining room operations throughout the audit to determine whether Company policies are followed by location employees.

3. Observe the POS system or the cash register in operation and determine whether proper procedures are followed in recording sales.

4. Select several days' Daily Sales Journals and tie the reconciliations used to record sales on the Daily Sales Journal to the supporting documentation.

Jenny's Café, Inc.
Denver Restaurant
Audit Program—Sales
Audit Date: July 31, 2006

Audit Steps	Initials	Ref.	Comments

5. Obtain copies of the menu and a report from the POS system that lists every menu item with the selling price.

   a. Select 10-20 items from each menu and tie the selling prices to the POS menu report.

   b. Advise the Dining Room Manager or General Manager of any differences noted so they can immediately correct the errors.

6. Select one recent day's guest checks and perform the following:

   a. Compare the used guest checks against the serial numbers on the Guest Check Control Log and determine whether every guest check issued was returned.

   b. Trace any unused guest checks to a subsequent Guest Check Control Log to determine whether they were reissued later.

   c. Where missing guest checks were noted, check the employee's personnel file to determine whether disciplinary action was taken.

Jenny's Café, Inc.
Denver Restaurant
Audit Program—Sales
Audit Date: July 31, 2006

Audit Steps	**Initials**	**Ref.**	**Comments**

7. Select one week's cash register readings and perform the following:
   a. Agree each cash register tape to the readings on the Internal Cash Register Reconciliation or to the Reconciliation of POS Grand Totals.
   b. Where cashiers have variances greater than the allowable amount, obtain the employee's personnel file and determine whether there is a record of disciplinary action taken.

8. Test the accuracy of sales tax paid to the State by performing the following:
   a. Select one day and calculate the sales taxes to determine whether the cash registers or POS system is calculating sales tax correctly.
   b. Review the most recent Sales and Use Tax return by tying amounts to subsidiary schedules.
   c. Tie a few of the amounts on the subsidiary schedules to the Sales Journals and supporting reports used to post to the Sales Journals.

Jenny's Café, Inc.
Denver Restaurant
Audit Program—Sales
Audit Date: July 31, 2006

Audit Steps	Initials	Ref.	Comments

9. Select 1-3 Daily Sales Journals and perform the following:
   a. Foot the Tips Received column on the Charge Tips Received Form.
   b. Agree the Total Tips Paid on the Charge Tips Received Form to the Profit Center Sales Report.
   c. Tie the payments listed on the Charge Tips Received form to the applicable guest checks.

10. Select 3 days of the Daily Sales Journal for testing and perform the following:
    a. Tie each number on the Daily Sales Journal to the appropriate source documents.
    b. Tie each number on the Daily Sales Journal to the General Ledger posting.
    c. Trace the cash and credit card deposits to the postings on the bank statement.

Jenny's Café, Inc.
Denver Restaurant
Audit Program—Sales
Audit Date: July 31, 2006

Audit Steps	**Initials**	**Ref.**	**Comments**

11. Obtain a printed copy of the Void, Overring, Refund, and No Sale Log for a recent month, and perform the following:

a. Select some entries and tie them to the source documents.

b. Review the notes about unusual trends and note the action taken.

c. Determine whether appropriate action was taken on unusual trends noted.

12. Where the location utilized a secret shopper service or detective agency during the past year, obtain a copy of the report and perform the following:

a. Insert the report copy in the workpapers.

b. Review the report and highlight any manipulative practices documented in the report.

c. Determine what corrective action was taken, and review documentation of the corrective action.

d. During observations, determine whether problems noted in the report still exist.

Jenny's Café, Inc.
Denver Restaurant
Audit Program—Sales
Audit Date: July 31, 2006

Audit Steps	Initials	Ref.	Comments

13. Select 2-3 days from the most recent Monthly Per Capita Report and perform the following:
a. Insert the copy of the Monthly Per Capita Report in the workpapers.
b. Check the mathematical calculations on the Monthly Per Capita Report.
c. Tie the Sales to the Daily Sales Journals.
d. Tie the Number of Guests to the Profit Center Sales Reports (POS system) or to the guest checks (cash register system).

14. Select 10-12 transactions that were closed out to House Charge on the Profit Center Sales Report, and perform the following:
a. Obtain the supporting guest checks and note the guest check numbers on a workpaper and the audit work performed.
b. Review the supporting guest checks and determine whether there are authorized signatures on the guest checks approving the comps.
c. Determine whether the comps were handled correctly, according to Company policy.

Jenny's Café, Inc.
Denver Restaurant
Audit Program—Sales
Audit Date: July 31, 2006

Audit Steps	Initials	Ref.	Comments

15. Obtain a copy of the Gift Certificate Log from the prior month and perform the following:
a. Insert the copy of the Gift Certificate Log into the workpapers.
b. Tie the Total Amount Outstanding at the end of the month to the General Ledger balance.
c. Select 5-10 gift certificates that have recently been redeemed and tie them to the Gift Certificate Log, and determine whether they were properly logged when issued and when redeemed.
d. Determine whether the gift certificates selected were cancelled with a paid stamp or some other method that prevents reuse.

16. Obtain the last 2-3 vending machine settlement statements (at least one audited) and perform the following:
a. Copy the vending machine statements and insert them in the workpapers.

Jenny's Café, Inc.
Denver Restaurant
Audit Program—Sales
Audit Date: July 31, 2006

Audit Steps	Initials	Ref.	Comments

b. Determine whether there is a signed contract with the vending machine company on file, and that both parties are in compliance with its provisions.

c. Determine whether there are unexpired certificates of insurance naming the Company coinsured on file.

d. Determine whether commissions were properly calculated.

e. If an error was made, determine whether the Controller caught the error and resolved it with the vending machine company.

f. Determine whether there is documented evidence of a quarterly audit of the commission statement.

17. Review sublet operations by performing the following:

a. Observe the sublet operation to determine whether all sales are recorded on the cash register, and document your observations.

b. If any instances of sales not recorded are noted, advise the General Manager immediately so he can address it with the sublet's manager.

351

Jenny's Café, Inc.
Denver Restaurant
Audit Program—Sales
Audit Date: July 31, 2006

Audit Steps	Initials	Ref.	Comments

c. Determine whether there is a signed contract with the sublet company on file, and that both parties are in compliance with its provisions.

d. Determine whether there are unexpired certificates of insurance naming the Company coinsured on file.

e. Select a recent month's rental statement, copy it, and insert it in the workpapers.

f. Ask the Controller to request the source documents supporting the rental statement tested from the sublet manager.

g. Check the math and tie the components of the rental statement to the source documents.

18. Select 3-5 Daily Valet Parking Ticket Reconciliations and perform the following:

a. Make copies of the reconciliations and insert them in the workpapers.

b. Review the reconciliations and determine whether they were properly prepared, including required signatures.

Jenny's Café, Inc.
Denver Restaurant
Audit Program—Sales
Audit Date: July 31, 2006

Audit Steps	Initials	Ref.	Comments

c. Go through the ticket stubs supporting the reconciliations and tie them to the appropriate reconciliations.

d. Check the next day's reconciliation to determine whether unused tickets were reissued the next day.

e. Tie total cash per the reconciliation to the Main Cashier's Report, completed by the Cash Room.

f. Agree Ending Cash Register Readings per the reconciliation to the cash register reading tapes and the Beginning Reading to the prior day's reconciliation.

g. Where there are attendants with variances greater than the established limits, review the employee's personnel file to determine whether disciplinary action was taken.

19. Summarize any exceptions on the Discussion Points Worksheet, discuss them with the General Manager, and include them in the Audit Report, where appropriate.

Jenny's Café, Inc.
Denver Restaurant
Audit Program—Inventory
Audit Date: July 31, 2006

Audit Objectives

1. The inventory value on the balance sheet reflects inventory on hand at month end.
2. Proper receiving, warehouse issuance, and sales cut-offs ensure the accuracy of the inventory.
3. Cost prices on the inventory listing reflect current invoice prices.

Audit Steps	Initials	Ref.	Comments
1. Complete the Internal Control Questionnaire for Inventory.			
2. Review the product costs from the most recent Profit and Loss statements. a. Note significant variances from Plan and Last Year and obtain explanations from the Controller for these variances. b. Where there are large variances from Plan, review the Controller's documentation on investigations made and determine whether the investigations were adequate.			
3. If present at the field location during the month-end physical inventory, perform the following:			

Jenny's Café, Inc.
Denver Restaurant
Audit Program—Inventory
Audit Date: July 31, 2006

Audit Steps	Initials	Ref.	Comments

a. Meet with the General Manager a day or two before the inventory to determine who is responsible for counting each area.

b. Plan your observations so that you can observe each team of counters count part of their assigned locations.

c. When observing counting teams count, determine whether each team counts in a systematic manner, beginning in one place, counting left to right, top to bottom, until all inventory in an assigned location has been counted.

d. Determine whether one person in the team is counting inventory while the second person on the team is writing the counts on the preprinted count sheets in ink.

e. Perform test counts of items selected and list them on a worksheet for subsequent follow up.

f. Compare your test counts to those of the counters and resolve any differences.

g. Make copies of all count sheets and insert them in the workpapers.

Jenny's Café, Inc.
Denver Restaurant
Audit Program—Inventory
Audit Date: July 31, 2006

Audit Steps	Initials	Ref.	Comments

4. Obtain a copy of the final inventory listings and perform the following:

a. Insert a copy of the final inventory listing in the workpapers.

b. Tie the test counts to the final inventory listings and follow up with the Department Manager on any differences.

c. Tie the remaining counts from the count sheets that you did not test to the final inventory listing.

d. Where the final inventory listings are manual, test the calculations and foot the inventory listing, paying particular attention to large and small extensions.

e. Count the number of beer kegs on the premises (full, partials, and empties) and agree the count to the Keg Deposit Log.

f. Cross reference the Final Inventory Listing pages into the Inventory Summary for Food and Bar.

g. When the month is closed, tie the Inventory Summary for the Food and Bar inventories to the General Ledger balances.

Jenny's Café, Inc.
Denver Restaurant
Audit Program—Inventory
Audit Date: July 31, 2006

Audit Steps	Initials	Ref.	Comments

5. If not present to observe the month-end physical inventory, obtain the count sheets and inventory listing from the last month end physical inventory and perform the following:

a. Copy the inventory listing and count sheets and insert them in the workpapers

b. Tie the counts from the count sheets to the inventory listings.

c. Clearly note any differences on the count sheet or final inventory listings in red ink.

d. Cross reference the Final Inventory Listing pages into the Inventory Summary for Food and Bar.

e. Tie the Inventory Summary for the Food and Bar inventories to the General Ledger balances.

6. Select 10-20 food items and 10-20 bar items and tie the cost prices on the inventory listings to recent invoices.

Jenny's Café, Inc.
Denver Restaurant
Audit Program—Inventory
Audit Date: July 31, 2006

Audit Steps	Initials	Ref.	Comments

7. Select one week's employee meal calculations and perform the following:

a. Determine whether the employee meals were calculated according to company policy.

b. Check the calculation and determine whether the credit taken was accurate.

c. Ask the Controller to explain the rationale for the amount of the credit taken and determine whether it is reasonable.

8. Summarize any exceptions on the Discussion Points Worksheet, discuss them with the General Manager, and include them in the Audit Report, where appropriate.

Jenny's Café, Inc.
Denver Restaurant
Audit Program—Menu Costing
Audit Date: July 31, 2006

Audit Objectives

1. Cost Specification Sheets are used to cost each menu item and unit costs are updated quarterly.
2. Menu items are costed and put into a Menu Mix with sales prices and the anticipated mix of items sold to determine whether the prices will achieve the desired Standard Cost Percentage.
3. The Menu Mix is adjusted for food served but no payment was received.
4. Buffets are costed by inventorying items going into the buffet and subtracting items returned from the buffet.

Audit Steps	Initials	Ref.	Comments
1. Complete the Internal Control Questionnaire for Menu Costing.			
2. Obtain the Cost Specification Sheets for the various menus and perform the following: a. Compare the menu items from the menus to the Cost Specification Sheets on a test basis to determine whether each menu item has a cost specification sheet. b. Select several menu items and determine whether the selling prices on the Cost Specification Sheets are correct. c. Look at the date at the top of the Cost Specification Sheets and determine whether the costs were updated within the last 3 months.			

Jenny's Café, Inc.
Denver Restaurant
Audit Program—Menu Costing
Audit Date: July 31, 2006

Audit Steps	Initials	Ref.	Comments

d. Check the mathematical accuracy of the items selected.

e. Review the Cost Specification Sheets selected and determine whether the assumptions that went into the Cost Specification Sheets are reasonable.

f. Observe the cooks prepare the menu items selected and determine whether they are preparing the item according to specifications.

g. Obtain invoices of the ingredients from the items selected, and determine whether the items have current ingredient costs (make allowances for items whose costs fluctuate frequently, i.e. produce, dairy, bread, etc.).

h. On ingredients whose costs fluctuate frequently, ask the chef about the reasonableness of prices used that seem to be significantly different from current prices, and determine whether the prices used are reasonable.

Jenny's Café, Inc.
Denver Restaurant
Audit Program—Menu Costing
Audit Date: July 31, 2006

Audit Steps	Initials	Ref.	Comments

3. To test the Menu Mix, perform one of the following, depending on the type of system used to record dining room sales:

a. Take the most recent Menu Mix and tie the number of month to date items sold from the Order Entry System's last day of sales into the number of items sold in the sales mix.

b. Where a cash register is used, take a few days cash register reading tapes and tie the number of menu items sold per the cash register readings into the spreadsheet tallying the items sold, and tie the totals from this spreadsheet into the Menu Mix.

4. Tie some of the selling prices in the Menu Mix into the actual menus and tie some of the costs in the Menu Mix into the Cost Specification Sheets.

Jenny's Café, Inc.
Denver Restaurant
Audit Program—Menu Costing
Audit Date: July 31, 2006

Audit Steps	Initials	Ref.	Comments

5. To test the Employee Meal Credit on the Menu Mix, perform the following:

a. Obtain the Controller's Employee Meal Credit Calculation spreadsheet and select a few days to test the calculation.

b. Count the number of meals on the test days and tie the number of meals into the spreadsheet.

c. Verify with the Chef the amount of credit per meal that should be given is the amount the Chef determined is the average cost of the employee meal.

d. Tie the total Employee Meal Credit for the month to the Menu Mix Standard Cost calculation.

6. To test the Coupon Credit Report, perform the following:

a. Select a few days and obtain the actual coupons supporting the numbers entered on the Coupon Credits Report for those days.

b. Count the number of coupons in each denomination and agree the count to the count on the Coupon Credit Report.

Jenny's Café, Inc.
Denver Restaurant
Audit Program—Menu Costing
Audit Date: July 31, 2006

Audit Steps	Initials	Ref.	Comments

c. Check the accuracy of the multiplication.

d. Add the values of the Buy One Entrée, Get One Free coupons and tie the total to the amount posted to the Coupon Credit Report.

7. To test the Comp Report, perform the following:

a. Select a few days from the Comp Report and obtain the supporting guest checks.

b. Tie the sales per the guest checks to the appropriate sales columns on the Comp Report.

c. Check each guest check to ensure it was signed by a management person and that the business purpose or the notation "management meal" is written on the back.

Jenny's Café, Inc.
Denver Restaurant
Audit Program—Menu Costing
Audit Date: July 31, 2006

Audit Steps	**Initials**	**Ref.**	**Comments**

8. Compare Actual Food Cost percentage to Standard Food Cost percentage for several months and perform the following:
a. If there was a variance greater than the Company Standard (2-3 percentage points), determine whether an investigation was conducted, documented and signed by the Executive Chef and General Manager.
b. Review the results of the investigation and determine whether an adequate effort was made to determine why the variance was so high.

9. Review the accuracy of one buffet costing by performing the following:
a.Review the Cost Specification Sheets used to cost the trays of product and the buffet cost spreadsheet.
b. Select some ingredients from the menu costings and tie the unit costs used to current invoices.

Jenny's Café, Inc.
Denver Restaurant
Audit Program—Menu Costing
Audit Date: July 31, 2006

Audit Steps	Initials	Ref.	Comments
c. Ask the Executive Chef how the menu was costed and determine whether the method used was reasonable.			
d. Review the spreadsheet used in the Menu Mix to inventory the items going into the buffet and those returned from the buffet and determine whether the method used was reasonable.			
10. Summarize any exceptions on the Discussion Points Worksheet, discuss them with the General Manager, and include them in the Audit Report, where appropriate.			

Jenny's Café, Inc.
Denver Restaurant
Audit Program—Kitchen Operations
Audit Date: July 31, 2006

Audit Objectives

1. Product is only removed from the kitchen after it is recorded on a guest check.
2. Spoilage and waste are minimized.
3. There are sufficient internal controls over the linen room that ensure all linens issued are promptly returned.
4. There is sufficient security over the kitchen and dining room that prevents theft of inventory and minimizes breakage of china and glassware.

Audit Steps	Initials	Ref.	Comments
1. Complete the Internal Control Questionnaire for Kitchen Operations.			
2. As part of the planning process, review the Linen and China, Glassware, and Silverware accounts and note whether there are large variances between This Year and Last Year and This Year and Plan. When at the location, follow up on any large variances.			
3. Observe kitchen operations and write your observations in the workpapers while considering the following: a. Determine whether Company policies are followed in filling orders only off chits and tearing chits part-way when completing the order.			

Jenny's Café, Inc.
Denver Restaurant
Audit Program—Kitchen Operations
Audit Date: July 31, 2006

Audit Steps	Initials	Ref.	Comments

b. Determine whether kitchen personnel use portion control scales, ladles, soufflé cups, and standard bowls to ensure portion control.

c. Where manual dups are used, determine whether the checking function is sufficient to catch any product removed from the kitchen that was not documented on the guest check and recorded on the cash register.

d. Discuss any variances from company policy with the Executive Chef.

4. Select a recent day where dups have been matched to the guest checks and select 20-50 guest checks with substantial activity, and perform the following:

a. List the guest checks on a schedule and tie the orders from the dups to the main guest check.

b. Determine whether all orders were properly recorded and validated by the cash register on the main guest check.

Jenny's Café, Inc.
Denver Restaurant
Audit Program—Kitchen Operations
Audit Date: July 31, 2006

Audit Steps	Initials	Ref.	Comments

c. Where items on the dups were not recorded on the cash register, examine the personnel files of the responsible employee and determine whether appropriate disciplinary action was taken.

5. Through observations (eating meals in the dining room and observing kitchen operations), determine whether the wait staff is recording non-alcoholic beverage purchases on the guest checks.

6. Review the Spoilage Sheets for the inventory period you are testing and determine whether proper procedures were followed in documenting the spoilage, reviewing the Spoilage Sheets, and approving them.

Jenny's Café, Inc.
Denver Restaurant
Audit Program—Kitchen Operations
Audit Date: July 31, 2006

Audit Steps	Initials	Ref.	Comments

7. Determine whether the Linen Room has proper internal controls by performing the following:

a. If the initial comparison of Linen Expenses to Plan and Last Year shows significant variances, ask the Dining Room Manager for an explanation and determine whether the explanation is reasonable.

b. Observe Linen Room procedures and determine whether Company procedures are followed in issuing and returning linens, chef's gowns, and towels.

c. Look through large invoices from the linen company to determine if there are unusually large invoices (indication that the restaurant is being charged for lost linens).

d. Review several days of Linen Room Sign Out Sheets to determine whether linens and other issues were properly documented.

e. If possible, observe a linen delivery and determine whether the Linen Room Supervisor is properly counting out returned linens with the Linen Service representative and counting linens received.

Jenny's Café, Inc.
Denver Restaurant
Audit Program—Kitchen Operations
Audit Date: July 31, 2006

Audit Steps	Initials	Ref.	Comments

8. Review the China, Glassware, and Silverware replacements costs and perform the following:

a. Where there is a high China, Glassware, and Silverware replacement cost on the P&L, discuss the reasons with management and determine whether the explanations are reasonable.

b. While observing kitchen and dining room operations, determine whether sufficient care is exercised in handling China, Glassware, and Silverware to minimize breakage.

9. Review the restaurant's policy of what employees do with their personal belongings, observe the security of the restaurant, and determine whether Company policies are followed and good internal controls are in place.

10. Summarize any exceptions on the Discussion Points Worksheet, discuss them with the General Manager, and include them in the Audit Report, where appropriate.

Jenny's Café, Inc.
Denver Restaurant
Audit Program—Payroll
Audit Date: July 31, 2006

Audit Objectives

1. All hourly employees are paid for time worked based on documented time in and time out.
2. All employees are paid in accordance with Federal and State wage and hour laws.
3. Payments to employees for hours worked are documented.
4. Manual checks are processed only when required and in accordance with Company policies.

Audit Steps	Initials	Ref.	Comments
1. Complete the Internal Control Questionnaire for Payroll.			
2. Obtain the Sign In Sign Out Sheets, Time Cards, or Time Keeping Reports for one week, select 20-30 employees and perform the following: a. Determine whether the hourly rate on the Payroll Register agrees to the current Employee Maintenance Form signed by the General Manager. b. Where there is a labor union, determine whether the hourly rates on the Payroll Register agree to the rates on the union contract.			

Jenny's Café, Inc.
Denver Restaurant
Audit Program—Payroll
Audit Date: July 31, 2006

Audit Steps	Initials	Ref.	Comments

c. Calculate the time worked from the time keeping documents (time clocked in to time clocked out) and compare your results for the week to the Payroll Register.

d. Where there are manual entries on time cards, determine whether the department manager initialed each manual entry.

e. Where there are 5 or fewer cards with manual entries, go through the remaining time cards and select time cards with manual entries so there are 5 examples. Determine whether the manual entries were initialed by the supervisor.

f. Discuss any differences with the department manager and determine whether the explanation is reasonable.

g. Determine whether employees are clocking out for lunch and back in after lunch. If not, the employee must be paid continuously from the time he clocks in to the time he clocks out.

h. Determine whether the department manager or supervisor initialed each time card, documenting approval of the number of hours worked.

Jenny's Café, Inc.
Denver Restaurant
Audit Program—Payroll
Audit Date: July 31, 2006

Audit Steps	Initials	Ref.	Comments

i. Determine whether each employee signed the time card or Payroll Check Log, documenting the employee's agreement to the accuracy of time worked.

j. Determine whether overtime hours are paid premium pay, i.e. time and a half, according to Federal and State labor laws.

3. Observe employees clock in at the beginning of a shift and clock out at the end of a shift and note any unusual behavior, i.e. one employee punching in/out or swiping ID cards for several employees. Advise General Manager immediately of someone punching in or out or swiping ID cards for more than one employee.

4. Where a Time Keeping system is used, perform the following:
a. Review one week's Daily Time Worked Reports to determine whether adjustments were handled properly.
b. Determine whether the department managers signed the Daily Time Worked Reports.

Jenny's Café, Inc.
Denver Restaurant
Audit Program—Payroll
Audit Date: July 31, 2006

Audit Steps	Initials	Ref.	Comments

c. Obtain the Weekly Time Summary for the week selected and tie any corrections noted on the Daily Time Summaries to the Weekly Time Summary.

d. Determine whether the department managers and supervisors signed the Weekly Time Summaries for their departments.

5. Obtain the Wage and Hour Report for the week previously selected and perform the following:

a. Tie the total hours worked on the Wage and Hour Report to the Payroll Clerk's adding machine tape of the hours worked per the source documents.

b. Tie the adjustments to wages to the appropriate source documents, signed by management.

c. Tie charge tips per the Wage and Hour Report to the Dining Room Manager's signed and dated List of Charge Tips Paid.

d. Tie the charge tips total on the Wage and Hours Report to the sum of each day's charge tips reported on the Daily Sales Journal.

Jenny's Café, Inc.
Denver Restaurant
Audit Program—Payroll
Audit Date: July 31, 2006

Audit Steps	Initials	Ref.	Comments

e. Tie some of the entries on the List of Charge Tips Paid to the individual credit card slips.

f. Tie 5-10 cash tips declared entries on the Wage and Hour Report to the Cash Tips Declaration Slips.

g. Compare the signed individual employee Cash Tip Declaration slips to the entries on the Dining Room Manager's Cash Tips Declared spreadsheet.

h. For the time cards previously selected, tie the hours worked to the Wage and Hour Report.

6. Select 10-15 tipped employees whose wage rates are less than minimum wage and perform the following:

a. Prepare a spreadsheet that takes the hours worked multiplied by the minimum wage (overtime hours must be paid at time and a half) and compare it to Wages plus Tips plus Employee Meals.

b. Where total compensation did not at least equal minimum wage, determine whether the restaurant paid the difference to the employee in an adjustment to wages.

Jenny's Café, Inc.
Denver Restaurant
Audit Program—Payroll
Audit Date: July 31, 2006

Audit Steps	Initials	Ref.	Comments

7. To determine the accuracy of sales entered into the Payroll system for tip allocation purposes, compare the sales from the Daily Sales Journal for one week to the sales entered into the Payroll System.

8. Select 4-5 sets of payroll reports and perform the following:
   a. Determine whether the Controller or General Manager signed and dated the Employee Maintenance Reports, Payroll Registers, and High Dollar Reports.
   b. Determine whether there is evidence that the Controller tied the hours and dollars to the Wage and Hour Report, i.e. check marks.

9. Select 5-10 minor employees and determine whether the hours worked comply with the Federal and State child labor laws.

Jenny's Café, Inc.
Denver Restaurant
Audit Program—Payroll
Audit Date: July 31, 2006

Audit Steps	Initials	Ref.	Comments

10. Using the employees selected earlier for testing, perform the following:

a. Trace each employee to the Payroll Check Log and determine whether each employee signed the Payroll Check Log.

b. Look through the Payroll Check Log for employees who did not sign it and ask the Pay Master to see those checks.

c. If checks are missing, ask the Pay Master for an explanation and determine whether the explanation is reasonable.

11. Select 5-10 manual checks that were cut in the last few months and determine whether Company procedures were followed in processing the manual checks.

Jenny's Café, Inc.
Denver Restaurant
Audit Program—Payroll
Audit Date: July 31, 2006

Audit Steps	Initials	Ref.	Comments

12. Obtain the Productivity Analysis for a few days and perform the following:

    a. Tie the sales in the Productivity Analysis to the Daily Sales Journal.

    b. Tie the number of employees worked by position to the payroll records.

    c. Determine whether the staffing in the restaurant is in line with the revenues of the restaurant and discuss your findings with the General Manager.

13. Summarize any exceptions on the Discussion Points Worksheet, discuss them with the General Manager, and include them in the Audit Report, where appropriate.

Jenny's Café, Inc.
Denver Restaurant
Audit Program—Human Resources
Audit Date: July 31, 2006

Audit Objectives

1. Each new hire is properly documented on an Employee Maintenance Form (EMF) signed by the employee and two managers.
2. The restaurant is in compliance with all Federal and State regulations regarding the employment of minors.
3. All alcohol serving employees are trained annually in alcohol serving practices.
4. Progressive discipline is administered where notable shortages occur and other violations of company policy are noted.

Audit Steps	Initials	Ref.	Comments
1. Complete the Internal Control Questionnaire for Human Resources.			
2. Prior to leaving for the field, obtain a summary of the Child Labor laws and required posters applicable to the State where the field location is located.			
3. Through observations and questioning of Human Resources personnel, determine whether security of HR files is adequate.			

Jenny's Café, Inc.
Denver Restaurant
Audit Program—Human Resources
Audit Date: July 31, 2006

Audit Steps	Initials	Ref.	Comments

4. Select 20-30 employee files and perform the following:

a. Determine whether each EMF is properly completed and was signed by the employee and two managers.

b. Tie the wage rates on the EMF's to the union contract rates.

c. Check each employee's HR file to determine whether he has a current EMF signed by the employee and two managers, or a memo from the General Manager listing the old and new rates for blanket pay increases, based on the union contract.

d. Look up each employee on the Drug Test Log and determine whether the drug test results were received before the applicant was hired.

e. Determine whether each employee had a negative drug test result.

f. Determine whether all INS regulations were followed in completing each I9.

Jenny's Café, Inc.
Denver Restaurant
Audit Program—Human Resources
Audit Date: July 31, 2006

Audit Steps	Initials	Ref.	Comments

5. Determine the field location's compliance to Child Labor laws by selecting 5-10 minors and performing the following:

a. Where state laws require work permits, examine each minor's work permit that the location has on file.

b. Where required, determine whether the location posts the current week's minor employees' work schedule on the employee bulletin board.

c. Determine whether the location has some type of system in place to flag minors and make department supervisors and managers aware of the minors working in the department.

6. To measure the location's compliance with the Company mandated Alcohol Service Training program, perform the following:

a. Determine whether the field location has a written Alcohol Service Training program that has been approved by the Corporate Human Resources Department.

Jenny's Café, Inc.
Denver Restaurant
Audit Program—Human Resources
Audit Date: July 31, 2006

Audit Steps	Initials	Ref.	Comments

b. Select 5-10 alcohol service employees and determine whether their employee files contain a signed certification that they have attended an Alcohol Awareness training program within the last year.

7. Determine whether there is a relative reporting to another relative or significant other by performing the following:

a. Ask the restaurant's Human Resources Manager and other management personnel if there is anyone reporting directly or indirectly to a relative or significant other.

b. Where such a relationship exists, review the affected employee's personnel file and determine whether there is documented permission from the subsidiary President or Corporate Vice President of Human Resources allowing the relationship to continue.

Jenny's Café, Inc.
Denver Restaurant
Audit Program—Human Resources
Audit Date: July 31, 2006

Audit Steps	Initials	Ref.	Comments

c. When reviewing employee files during Human Resources testing, be aware of the possibility of nepotism in people with the same last names. Check the street addresses of people with the same last names where one reports to the other.

8. Through inspection, determine whether all Federal, State, and Company posters and job postings are posted in conspicuous locations.

9. Determine whether the Human Resources Manager is maintaining an OSHA 300 Log, whether workplace injuries are properly reported on the log, when applicable, and whether the OSHA 300A Summary is posted from February through April.

Jenny's Café, Inc.
Denver Restaurant
Audit Program—Human Resources
Audit Date: July 31, 2006

Audit Steps	Initials	Ref.	Comments

10. Determine whether progressive discipline is taken for notable variances by performing the following:

a. Obtain a copy of the restaurant's cash variance policy and note the definition of a notable variance.

b. Select at least one week in the prior month and list each notable variance on a workpaper.

c. Review the applicable employee files and note if there is a Record of Employee Counseling form on file for each notable variance listed.

11. While testing employee files, note whether there is one or more Records of Employee Counseling in the file, and determine whether discipline was handled according to Company policy.

12. Summarize any exceptions on the Discussion Points Worksheet, discuss them with the General Manager, and include them in the Audit Report, where appropriate.

Jenny's Café, Inc.
Denver Restaurant
Audit Program—IT, Risk Management, Other
Audit Date: July 31, 2006

Audit Objectives

1. Computer hardware and software are protected against unauthorized access.
2. Equipment is properly maintained and tested.
3. The restaurant is in compliance with all lease provisions and municipal requirements.

Audit Steps	Initials	Ref.	Comments
1. Select several PC and mainframe users and ask each user whether the password is unique and consists of letter, numbers, and special characters.			
2. Ask several employees who utilize the POS system what types of transactions they can initiate on the POS system and determine whether that access is appropriate for the position.			
3. Review computer hardware security through observations during the period of the audit to ensure all hardware is properly secured.			

Jenny's Café, Inc.
Denver Restaurant
Audit Program—IT, Risk Management, Other
Audit Date: July 31, 2006

Audit Steps	Initials	Ref.	Comments

4. Determine whether all PC's in the restaurant are protected by Company standard anti-virus software.

a. Discuss anti-virus software with the Controller and General Manager to determine whether the location has the Company standard software on every PC.

b. Select several PC's and look at the bottom right corner of the screen to determine whether the symbol of the anti-virus software is present.

5. Determine whether the grill hoods have been cleaned and the fire suppression systems have been tested in the past 6 months, and the fire extinguishers have been tested in the last year by performing the following:

a. Look at recent invoices from the service provider to determine whether the grill hoods were cleaned in the last six months.

b. Look at recent invoices from the service provider to determine whether the fire suppression system was inspected in the last six months.

Jenny's Café, Inc.
Denver Restaurant
Audit Program—IT, Risk Management, Other
Audit Date: July 31, 2006

Audit Steps	Initials	Ref.	Comments

c. Determine whether all fire extinguishers have been inspected during the last year by examining the inspection tag on each fire extinguisher.

6. Go to each location that has CO_2 or propane tanks and determine whether the tanks (including empties) are properly secured with a chain or other device that prevents them from tipping over.

7. Read the restaurant's lease and perform the following:
a. Verify the rent calculation for the past two months.
b. Review the check date for the last two payments and determine whether the payment was made on time.
c. Review other provisions of the lease and determine whether the restaurant is in compliance with those provisions.

8. Determine whether the location is in compliance with all municipal requirements by performing the following:

Jenny's Café, Inc.
Denver Restaurant
Audit Program—IT, Risk Management, Other
Audit Date: July 31, 2006

Audit Steps	Initials	Ref.	Comments

a. Check with the Corporate Legal Department whether they are aware of any unique municipal requirements of the restaurant.

b. During the initial meetings, ask local management whether the restaurant is subject to any unique municipal requirements.

c. Through observations, determine whether all municipal requirements are followed by all employees.

9. Discuss the restaurant's record retention policies with the General Manager and Controller and perform the following:

a. Determine whether records are well organized and readily retrievable.

b. Review the organization of file boxes in the record retention room to determine whether file boxes are properly labeled and organized in a manner that records are readily retrievable.

c. Determine whether the record retention room contains file boxes with records that are older than 6 years that should be destroyed.

Jenny's Café, Inc.
Denver Restaurant
Audit Program—IT, Risk Management, Other
Audit Date: July 31, 2006

Audit Steps	Initials	Ref.	Comments

10. Examine the general business and liquor license to determine whether they are current and are hanging in a place viewable by patrons.

11. Ask the General Manager for a copy of the most recent health inspection report and determine whether any deficiencies noted have been corrected.

12. Determine whether the General Manager, Controller, or other management person you met when arriving at the restaurant asked to see Company photo identification before showing you around the facilities and providing you with records.

13. Summarize any exceptions on the Discussion Points Worksheet, discuss them with the General Manager, and include them in the Audit Report, where appropriate.

389

APPENDIX 4

Sample Internal Control Questionnaire

Jenny's Café, Inc.
Denver Restaurant
Internal Control Questionnaire—Cash
Audit Date: July 31, 2006

Internal Control Question	Yes/No	Comments

1. Segregation of Duties:

   a. Who issues banks to the cashiers?

   b. Who is responsible for recording sales on the POS terminals?

   c. Who counts the cash and makes up the cash slip?

   d. Who verifies the cash in the cash room?

   e. Who makes up the deposit?

   f. Who puts the banks and other funds making up the operating fund in the safe after the deposit has been made up?

   g. Who performs the monthly safe audit?

   Are the duties properly segregated?

2. Cash Room Security:

   a. Is the Money Room / vault area physically secure and alarmed (if required by Corporate Security) with the use of separate alarm codes for each individual?

   b. Who has a security code to turn off the alarm?

   c. Does each person with an alarm code need access to the Cash Room?

Jenny's Café, Inc.
Denver Restaurant
Internal Control Questionnaire—Cash
Audit Date: July 31, 2006

Internal Control Question	Yes/No	Comments
d. Does each person authorized to arm and disarm the alarm have individual passwords?		
e. Are security devices in working order?		
f. Are security cameras pointed at all areas so there are no blind spots where cash could be counted without surveillance?		
g. Is the surveillance recorder locked up and surveillance tapes or disks kept for at least two weeks?		
h. Are all doors and windows that provide access to the Cash Room alarmed?		
i. Are there one or more motion detectors in the Cash Room?		
j. Does the Cash Room door close and lock automatically when released?		
k. Is the lock incapable of being bypassed with a button or knob?		
l. Does the Cash Room possess an approved safe?		
m. Is the Money Room safe/vault kept locked when the room is unattended?		

Jenny's Café, Inc.
Denver Restaurant
Internal Control Questionnaire—Cash
Audit Date: July 31, 2006

Internal Control Question	Yes/No	Comments

n. Are non-money room employees prohibited access to the vault area of the money room while cash is in the room, with the exception of the Manager on Duty, General Manager and Controller?

o. Is all cash stored inside the safe when the Cash Room closes for the day?

3. Safe Combination:

a. Who currently has the safe combination?

b. Do each of these people need the safe combination to perform their duties?

c. Is there adequate backup to the safe combination in case the custodian is not able to report for work?

d. Is the safe combination changed each time someone with the safe combination leaves the Company or is transferred to another location?

e. Is the current list of employees with access to the safe on file with the Corporate Security Department?

Jenny's Café, Inc.
Denver Restaurant
Internal Control Questionnaire—Cash
Audit Date: July 31, 2006

Internal Control Question	Yes/No	Comments

f. Are the current safe combinations (not necessary if electronic safe is used) on file with the Corporate Security Departments?

4. Cash Pick Ups:

a. Does the cash handler have the cash pick up ready at the designated time?

b. Does the cash handler complete a Cash Pick Up Slip, listing the count by denomination?

c. Does the cash handler seal the original Cash Pick Up Slip inside the bag so it can be seen through the bag, and retain a copy?

d. Does the Cash Room attendant have a Cash Pick Up Log where she lists each cash bag picked up from the cash handlers?

e. Upon return to the Cash Room, does a second Cash Room attendant compare the bags to the Cash Pick Up Log and sign the log?

Jenny's Café, Inc.
Denver Restaurant
Internal Control Questionnaire—Cash
Audit Date: July 31, 2006

Internal Control Question	Yes/No	Comments

5. Cash Room Cashiering Process:

a. Do cash handlers sign for their banks when they pick them up from the Cash Room?

b. At the end of the shift, does the cash handler complete a cash slip listing the count by denomination and signs the Cash Slip?

c. Does the Cash Room Attendant receiving the cash receipts and banks at the end of the day initial the Bank Sign Out sheet, acknowledging return of the bank?

d. Does the Cash Room Attendant use a red pen in verifying cash returned, checking off the counts by denomination and initialing the Cash Slip?

e. If banks are returned as one lump sum, does the Manager on Duty verify the total issued, including the working fund issued to the Cash Room, before returning the amount to the safe?

Jenny's Café, Inc.
Denver Restaurant
Internal Control Questionnaire—Cash
Audit Date: July 31, 2006

Internal Control Question	Yes/No	Comments

6. Credit cards and coupons:
   a. Does the Cash Room attendant verify the credit cards by taking an adding machine tape of the credit card slips and comparing the total to the Credit Card Batch Settlement Slip?
   b. Does the Cash Room Attendant verify the coupons turned in by each cashier?
   c. Does the Cash Room Attendant follow up on any exceptions and initial the tape?

7. Main Cashier's Report:
   a. Does the Main Cashier enter all cash and cash items in the Main Cashier's Report?
   b. When all cash receipts have been counted, does the Main Cashier count all cash, credit cards, and coupons at his counting station and balance them to the Main Cashier's report?

8. Sales Deposit:
   a. Do two people count the final deposit?
   b. Do these people initial the deposit slip?

Jenny's Café, Inc.
Denver Restaurant
Internal Control Questionnaire—Cash
Audit Date: July 31, 2006

Internal Control Question	Yes/No	Comments

c. Does the cash attendant tear off the tear strip with the serial number and attach it to the location's copy of the deposit slip?

d. Does the Main Cashier enter each deposit bag on the Armored Car Pick Up Log?

9. Armored Carrier Pick Up:

a. Are armored car pick ups scheduled at least 6 days per week (if Sunday pick up is not feasible)?

b. Does the Main Cashier consult the photo identification list or check the guard's photo ID before giving him the deposit bags?

c. Is the photo identification list hanging on the wall of the Cash Room near the door?

d. Does the armed guard sign the Armored Car Log when picking up the cash bags from the location?

10. Change Orders:

a. Does the Cash Room Manager complete a Change Order Slip where the change ordered is listed by denomination?

Jenny's Café, Inc.
Denver Restaurant
Internal Control Questionnaire—Cash
Audit Date: July 31, 2006

Internal Control Question	**Yes/No**	**Comments**

b. Is the Change Order Slip signed by the person placing the order and the person receiving the change and the date received noted?

c. Does the person receiving the change count it and agree the count to the Change Order Slip?

d. Is the movement of cash to and from the bank for change ordered tracked in a Change Order Log?

11. Petty Cash Expenditures:

a. Are all Petty Cash Received Vouchers properly completed with the Date, Amount, Name, Description, and signature of the person receiving reimbursement and the person authorizing the petty cash expenditure?

b. Are all petty cash expenditures only made for authorized purposes?

c. Is all movement of cash for petty cash purposes supported by a properly signed and authorized Petty Cash Received Voucher?

Jenny's Café, Inc.
Denver Restaurant
Internal Control Questionnaire—Cash
Audit Date: July 31, 2006

Internal Control Question	Yes/No	Comments

d. At least monthly, does the Cash Room Manager summarize the petty cash expenditures on an Excel spreadsheet by General Ledger account, obtain the General Manager's signature, and submit the reimbursement request to the Accounts Payable Clerk for reimbursement, supported by the Petty Cash Received Vouchers?

e. Is one copy of the Reimbursement Request kept in the safe as documentation for the Petty Cash Received Vouchers submitted to Accounts Payable for reimbursement?

12. Where checks are accepted, does the location have written check acceptance procedures distributed to all personnel who deal with checks?

13. Are reconciling items on bank reconciliations researched and cleared promptly?

Jenny's Café, Inc.
Denver Restaurant
Internal Control Questionnaire—Cash
Audit Date: July 31, 2006

Internal Control Question	**Yes/No**	**Comments**

14. Are tips kept separate from company funds in a separate tip jar, away from the customers' view?

15. Do waiters and waitresses provide their own change?

16. Do waiters and waitresses settle with the restaurant cashier before they leave for the day?

17. Are all cash room shortages greater than $100 promptly reported to Corporate Security?

Jenny's Café, Inc.
Denver Restaurant
Internal Control Questionnaire—Accounts Receivable
Audit Date: July 31, 2006

Internal Control Question	Yes/No	Comments

1. Segregation of Duties:
   a. Who opens the mail?
   b. Who deposits the checks?
   c. Who posts Accounts Receivable payments?
   d. Who posts daily sales to the General Ledger?
   e. Who processes Accounts Payable credits?
   f. Who collects outstanding receivables?
   Are the duties properly segregated?

2. Does the Accounts Payable Clerk post payments from check copies made by someone not involved in the payment collection or posting process?

3. Granting credit:
   a. Does the General Manager require companies to complete a credit application that requests Corporation Name, Telephone Number, Address, E-Mail Address, and Credit Amount Requested?
   b. Does the Controller obtain a credit report, i.e. Dun & Bradstreet, before granting credit?

Jenny's Café, Inc.
Denver Restaurant
Internal Control Questionnaire—Accounts Receivable
Audit Date: July 31, 2006

Internal Control Question	Yes/No	Comments

4. Invoicing:

    a. Do the invoice forms have the Company logo and remittance address on them?

    b. Is banquet software used where the Banquet Manager mails the contract for the event to the customer for his signature, documenting the understanding of the banquet requirements?

    c. Where banquet software is not used, does the Banquet Manager list the details on a manual invoice that is used to produce the invoice billing the customer?

5. Where the Accounts Receivable sub-ledger does not interface to the General Ledger, does the Controller compare each invoice to the invoice posting report to ensure the journal entry is correct?

6. Checks Received Log:

    a. Does the person opening the mail list each check on the Checks Received Log?

    b. At month end, does the Controller compare each day's total on the Checks Received Log to the day's deposit slip?

Jenny's Café, Inc.
Denver Restaurant
Internal Control Questionnaire—Accounts Receivable
Audit Date: July 31, 2006

Internal Control Question	**Yes/No**	**Comments**

7. Posting payments:

    a. Does the person opening the mail make copies of the checks, gives the check copies to the A/R Clerk for posting, and takes the checks to the Cash Room to be deposited?

    b. Does the Controller review the total postings to the Sub-Ledger for the day per the posting report and agree them to the General Ledger journal entry?

    c. Where the Company uses a lock box for Accounts Payable remittances, does the location send any checks received at the location to the lock box?

8. Where the A/R system does not allow the user to go back and age the receivables at any point in time, does the Controller ensure that the aging is run on the first day of the new month?

9. Collecting Past Due Accounts:

    a. Has the Controller assigned someone the task of collecting on past due accounts?

    b. Has the Controller established written collection procedures?

Jenny's Café, Inc.
Denver Restaurant
Internal Control Questionnaire—Accounts Receivable
Audit Date: July 31, 2006

Internal Control Question	Yes/No	Comments

c. Does the Controller regularly monitor the collection process?

d. Does the person pursuing collection maintain a telephone log where she documents the result of each collection call?

e. Does the person pursing collections maintain a Collection Log sheet for each delinquent customer where notes on each action taken are noted?

10. Each quarter, does the Controller go through the past due accounts and perform a collectibility analysis to determine whether the Allowance for Doubtful Accounts is adequate?

11. Bad Debts:

a. When the Controller determines that an account will not be collected, does he complete a Bad Debt Write Off form and obtain proper approvals before writing off the account?

b. Is the bad debt written off against Allowance for Doubtful accounts?

12. Are deposits on future events promptly deposited and recorded as Advance Deposits?

406

Jenny's Café, Inc.
Denver Restaurant
Internal Control Questionnaire—Capital Expenditures
Audit Date: July 31, 2006

Internal Control Question	Yes/No	Comments

1. Segregation of Duties:
   a. Who completes the Capital Expenditure Request (CER) form?
   b. Who approves the CER?
   c. Who handles the procurement of the capital assets?
   d. Who solicits bids on the capital asset or project?
   e. Who makes the final decision from whom to purchase the capital asset or have the capital improvements made?
   f. Who ensures the capital assets are working properly, progress targets have been met, or that the capital improvements have been satisfactorily completed?
   g. Who approves the capital invoices for payment?
   h. Who processes the capital invoices for payment?
   Are the duties properly segregated?

2. Emergency Capital Expenditures
   a. In an emergency, does the General Manager obtain verbal approval from the Regional Vice President of Operations to make the capital expenditure purchase?

Jenny's Café, Inc.
Denver Restaurant
Internal Control Questionnaire—Capital Expenditures
Audit Date: July 31, 2006

Internal Control Question	Yes/No	Comments

b. Is the verbal approval followed up with an email from the Regional Vice President of Operations to the General Manager?

c. Does the General Manager print the email and save it in the folder set up as a Capital Asset file?

d. Once the emergency asset has been installed, does the General Manager complete a CER form and go through the proper approval channels?

3. As part of the budgeting process, does the General Manager put together a Capital Project Budget with written justification for each capital project on the list, and submit it to Corporate for approval?

4. Capital Expenditure Request (CER) form:

a. When it is time to begin the capital project approved as part of the Capital Project Budget, does the General Manager complete the CER and attach the bid documentation?

b. Does the General Manager complete a Request for Bid form and send it to at least three contractors or equipment suppliers?

Jenny's Café, Inc.
Denver Restaurant
Internal Control Questionnaire—Capital Expenditures
Audit Date: July 31, 2006

Internal Control Question	Yes/No	Comments

c. Does the General Manager submit the CER to the appropriate levels of management for approval prior to awarding the capital improvement projects and capital asset purchases to the winning bidders?

d. Once the CER has been approved, does the General Manager complete a Capital Expenditure Purchase Order and contact the winning bidder to begin work?

e. When the General Manager selects the winning bid from a supplier or contractor who did not submit the lowest bid, does he document his rationale for his selection in the Capital Project folder?

5. Cost Overruns:

a. Where capital project costs exceed the approved CER by more than 10%, does the General Manager complete a new CER for the cost overrun and put it through the approval process?

b. If the original CER amount plus the cost overrun goes over the threshold for the next level of approvers, is the CER approved by the next level of approvers?

Jenny's Café, Inc.
Denver Restaurant
Internal Control Questionnaire—Capital Expenditures
Audit Date: July 31, 2006

Internal Control Question	Yes/No	Comments

6. Receiving Capital Equipment:
   a. Does the receiving department have a copy of the Capital Expenditure Purchase Order when the capital assets arrive from the supplier?
   b. Do receiving personnel count the number of crates or cartons and compare the count to the number of boxes listed on the packing slip?
   c. Where there is a difference in the container count, does the receiver note the difference on the packing slip or bill of lading and ask the driver to sign the notation?
   d. Does the General Manager or department manager who ordered the equipment promptly follow up on any differences with equipment supplier?
   e. Does the General Manager or department manager who ordered the equipment promptly inspect the installed equipment to ensure it meets the original capital asset specifications?

7. In the case of capital improvements, do the General Manager and the maintenance person inspect the completed work for flaws that need remediation before approving the invoice for payment?

Jenny's Café, Inc.
Denver Restaurant
Internal Control Questionnaire—Capital Expenditures
Audit Date: July 31, 2006

Internal Control Question	Yes/No	Comments

8. Are capital asset tags promptly affixed to new capital assets after installation?

9. Capital Expenditure Payments:
a. Where contracts are signed for capital improvements, does the General Manager submit the contract to the Corporate Law Department for review before signing it?
b. When receiving a progress billing, do the General Manager and the maintenance person review the work with the contractor to ensure the milestone has been satisfactorily reached before approving the billing for payment?
c. When processing progress billings for payment, does the Accounts Payable Clerk record the payments in the Construction in Progress account?
d. When the capital project is complete, does the General Manager complete a Capital Project Completion form listing the details of the completed capital project and related costs with copies of the invoices and sends the package to the Corporate Property Accounting Department?

411

Jenny's Café, Inc.
Denver Restaurant
Internal Control Questionnaire—Capital Expenditures
Audit Date: July 31, 2006

Internal Control Question	**Yes/No**	**Comments**

10. For equipment purchases that are not part of a capital project, does the Accounts Payable Clerk record approved invoices into the Equipment Additions account?

11. When a capital asset is placed in service, does the Controller complete a Capital Equipment Purchase form and send it to the Corporate Property Accounting Department so it begins recording Depreciation Expense?

12. When an asset is retired, sold, or transferred to another location, does the Controller complete a Retirement, Sale or Transfer form, obtain the proper signatures, and send it to the Property Accounting Department?

13. Repairs and Maintenance:
a. Are routine equipment repairs and maintenance recorded in an expense account when paid?
b. Are service agreements sent to the Corporate Law Department for review before the General Manager signs them?
c. When a repair significantly extends the life of a capital asset, is the cost of the repair capitalized?

Jenny's Café, Inc.
Denver Restaurant
Internal Control Questionnaire—Capital Expenditures
Audit Date: July 31, 2006

Internal Control Question	Yes/No	Comments
14. China, Glassware, Silverware: a. Is the initial purchase of China, Glassware, and Silverware (new restaurant or entire replacement) capitalized? b. Are replacement purchases of China, Glassware, and Silverware expensed?		

Jenny's Café, Inc.
Denver Restaurant
Internal Control Questionnaire—Purchasing
Audit Date: July 31, 2006

Internal Control Question	Yes/No	Comments

1. Segregation of Duties:
   a. Who solicits bids?
   b. Who completes the Purchase Order?
   c. Who approves the Purchase Order?
   d. Who places the orders?
   e. Who receives the products when delivered?
   f. Who approves the invoice for payment?
   Are the duties properly segregated?

2. Does the location utilize national suppliers whenever a national supplier carries an item the location needs to purchase?

3. Bid Solicitation:
   a. Does the Executive Chef solicit bids weekly for products whose prices fluctuate frequently, i.e. produce, dairy, meats, and seafood?
   b. Does the Executive Chef solicit bids monthly from several suppliers for dry and frozen goods?
   c. Does the Executive Chef specify the grades of products for which he is soliciting bids?
   d. Are bids documented on Bid Sheets that are filed by week and retained for 6 months?

Jenny's Café, Inc.
Denver Restaurant
Internal Control Questionnaire—Purchasing
Audit Date: July 31, 2006

Internal Control Question	Yes/No	Comments

4. Purchase Orders:
    a. Is a purchase order completed for all tangible items purchased?
    b. Does the supervisor of the person completing the purchase order sign it, documenting his approval?
    c. Does the receiver write the quantities received of each item on the purchase order?

5. Purchase Order Log:
    a. Are purchase orders listed from a central location and each purchase order logged on the log, including voids?
    b. Is a new purchase order log sheet started each month?
    c. Does the Controller use the Purchase Order Log to determine which invoices need to be accrued at month end?
    d. If the Controller does not use the Purchase Order Log for the month end accrual, does he use another method of determining which goods received without an invoice should be accrued?

Jenny's Café, Inc.
Denver Restaurant
Internal Control Questionnaire—Purchasing
Audit Date: July 31, 2006

Internal Control Question	Yes/No	Comments

6. Receiving:

a. Are deliveries scheduled when receiving personnel are present?

b. Does the receiver have the purchase order with him and compares the goods received to the items listed on the purchase order to ensure all goods were actually ordered?

c. Are goods on the truck that do not appear on the purchase order rejected?

d. Does the receiver count all product received and compare the counts to the invoice or packing slip?

e. Does the receiver weigh all goods billed by weight and compare the weights to the invoice?

f. Are produce cases weighed on a test basis under the supervision of the Warehouse Manager to ensure they meet minimum weights specified in the bid solicitation?

g. Is the scale calibrated annually to ensure it provides accurate weight?

h. After agreeing the counts to the invoice or packing slip, does the receiver sign and date the invoice or packing slip?

Jenny's Café, Inc.
Denver Restaurant
Internal Control Questionnaire—Purchasing
Audit Date: July 31, 2006

Internal Control Question	Yes/No	Comments

i. Does the receiver note any differences in counts on the invoice and have the differences been initialed by the truck driver?

j. Does the Warehouse Manager inspect the perishable goods to ensure they meet the restaurant's specifications?

k. Are goods that do not meet specifications returned to the vendor and a credit obtained?

l. When there are shortages or rejected goods, does the Warehouse Manager or chef contact the supplier and obtain a credit?

m. Is a Credit Log used to track credits that are due from the supplier?

n. When an after hours delivery is needed, does the Chef or General Manager make someone available to wait for the emergency delivery so it is received using normal receiving procedures?

o. Once received, is the invoice number and date received noted in the Purchase Order Log?

p. Has someone been assigned the responsibility for taking all paperwork to accounting at the end of the day?

Jenny's Café, Inc.
Denver Restaurant
Internal Control Questionnaire—Purchasing
Audit Date: July 31, 2006

Internal Control Question	Yes/No	Comments

7. Storage:
  a. Once goods have been received, do the receivers immediately store the goods?
  b. Are dry goods removed from their cases and stored in shelving units in the Dry Goods Room?
  c. Are perishable goods immediately stored in the produce cooler, dairy cooler, or freezer?
  d. Are products removed from cases and stored in shelves?
  e. Are cases kept off the floor in the walk in cooler, walk in freezer, and dry goods room?
  f. Is new product stored behind old product so the old product is used first?
  g. Is the date received clearly marked on cartons or cans to identify the oldest product?
  h. Is liquor and wine immediately delivered to the Bar Manager so he can add them to the perpetual inventory records?
  i. Is the Bar Manager alerted to beer deliveries so he can verify the count and add the beer to the perpetual inventory records?

Jenny's Café, Inc.
Denver Restaurant
Internal Control Questionnaire—Purchasing
Audit Date: July 31, 2006

Internal Control Question	Yes/No	Comments
j. Are all liquor, wine, and beer immediately locked in the Liquor Room, Wine Cellar, or Beer Cooler?		
k. Are baked goods and other products that Receiving delivers to the Kitchen counted by a kitchen person and compared to the invoice?		

Jenny's Café, Inc.
Denver Restaurant
Internal Control Questionnaire—Accounts Payable & Manual Checks
Audit Date: July 31, 2006

Internal Control Question	Yes/No	Comments

1. Segregation of Duties:
   a. Who sets up vendors in the master file?
   b. Who enters invoices in the A/P system?
   c. Who are the check signers on the on-site checking account?
   d. Where are A/P checks cut?
   e. Who purchases products?
   f. Who receives products?
   g. Who reviews invoices that were keyed into the A/P system?
   h. Who posts the invoices to the General Ledger?
   Are the duties properly segregated?

2. Reviewing Purchase Orders:
   a. When reviewing Purchase Orders, does the approver ensure that each item is actually needed before approving it?
   b. Does the reviewer document his review and approval by signing the Purchase Order?

Jenny's Café, Inc.
Denver Restaurant
Internal Control Questionnaire—Accounts Payable & Manual Checks
Audit Date: July 31, 2006

Internal Control Question	Yes/No	Comments

3. Processing invoices for payment:

a. Does the Accounts Payable Clerk match the quantities and unit prices on the invoice to the purchase order and packing slip, where applicable?

b. Where there are price differences between the purchase order and invoice, does the Accounts Payable Clerk advise the person who placed the order of the differences so he can follow up with the vendor for a credit?

c. Does the Accounts Payable Clerk staple the purchase order, packing slip, bill of lading, etc. to the invoice?

d. Where there is a discount offered for early payment, does the Accounts Payable Clerk make the invoice a priority so it is processed in time to take advantage of the discount?

e. Does the location have a program where it assesses itself for sales tax on taxable items purchased from out of state suppliers who do not charge sales tax on the invoice?

Jenny's Café, Inc.
Denver Restaurant
Internal Control Questionnaire—Accounts Payable & Manual Checks
Audit Date: July 31, 2006

Internal Control Question	Yes/No	Comments

4. Does the department manager or General Manager sign the invoice for services, repairs, equipment maintenance, and utilities, documenting his approval?

5. Expense Reports:
   a. Is the purpose of the trip documented on the Expense Report?
   b. Are hotel expenses broken out by date and type of expense?
   c. Are travel expenses over $25 supported by receipts, attached to 8.5 x 11 inch sheets of paper in logical sequence?
   d. Are all expenses listed on the expense reports reimbursable under company policy?
   e. When several employees dine out, does the highest level employee pay for the meal?
   f. Are Business Meals and Entertainment documented on the expense report with the names of the persons entertained, the place, the business association, and the business purpose of the meal or entertainment?

Jenny's Café, Inc.
Denver Restaurant
Internal Control Questionnaire—Accounts Payable & Manual Checks
Audit Date: July 31, 2006

Internal Control Question	**Yes/No**	**Comments**

6. Are Relocation Expenses processed on a separate Relocation Expense Report and sent to the Corporate Human Resources Department for processing?

7. When keying Accounts Payable invoices, does the Accounts Payable Clerk run an adding machine tape and compare the total to the Accounts Payable Invoice Listing to ensure the amounts keyed were correct?

8. Accounts Payable Review:
   a. When reviewing Accounts Payable invoices, does the Controller compare the invoices keyed to the Accounts Payable Invoice Listing to ensure all pertinent information was keyed correctly?
   b. Does the Controller check that all required signatures are present on the invoice and supporting documentation?
   c. Does the Controller review the General Ledger account distribution to ensure the correct General Ledger account is charged?

Jenny's Café, Inc.
Denver Restaurant
Internal Control Questionnaire—Accounts Payable & Manual Checks
Audit Date: July 31, 2006

Internal Control Question	**Yes/No**	**Comments**

d. When errors are corrected, does the Controller review the corrections to ensure that all corrections were actually made?

e. Does the Controller document his review by initialing the invoice?

f. In locations that do not have a Controller, does the General Manager or some other independent person perform the invoice review function?

9. Once the invoices are posted to the General Ledger, does the Accounts Payable Clerk stamp them "Posted" to they are not accidentally rekeyed into the General Ledger system?

10. Manual Checks:

a. Are manual checks only written for the purpose intended for the on-site checking account?

b. Are manual checks only written for the purpose intended for the on-site checking account?

Jenny's Café, Inc.
Denver Restaurant
Internal Control Questionnaire—Accounts Payable & Manual Checks
Audit Date: July 31, 2006

Internal Control Question	Yes/No	Comments
c. If subsidiary management allows the on-site checking account to be used for other purposes than to pay for delivery of alcoholic beverages as required by State law, have these purposes been authorized by a senior executive in writing?		
d. Are manual checks used in numerical sequence?		
e. Are manual checks only written and signed when the check signer has an invoice to a valid vendor?		
f. Is the manual check book properly secured, i.e. kept in the safe or in a locked file cabinet in a locked office?		
g. Is a copy of the manual check attached to the invoice?		
h. Does the Accounts Payable Clerk promptly key the invoice information for the manual check, including the check number, into the Accounts Payable system?		
i. Where manual checks are cut to unincorporated vendors, does the location obtain 1099 information and send this information to Corporate so it can issue Form 1099's at year end?		

Jenny's Café, Inc.
Denver Restaurant
Internal Control Questionnaire—Accounts Payable & Manual Checks
Audit Date: July 31, 2006

Internal Control Question	Yes/No	Comments
j. For 1099 vendors, does the Controller keep track of payments and notify Corporate Accounts Payable at year end of all vendors receiving $600 or more in payments so Form 1099's can be issued?		
k. Is the person responsible for processing invoices for payment prohibited from being a signer on the on-site checking account?		

Jenny's Café, Inc.
Denver Restaurant
Internal Control Questionnaire—Food Warehouse (Stores)
Audit Date: July 31, 2006

Internal Control Question	Yes/No	Comments

1. Segregation of Duties:
   a. Who oversees warehouse operations?
   b. Who completes the issuance or requisition slip?
   c. Who signs the issuance slip documenting product issued from the Food Warehouse?
   d. Who picks the product from the storage locations?
   e. Who reviews the issuance slips?
   f. Who verifies the product received at the receiving location and signs the issuance slip as received?
   Are the duties properly segregated?

2. Warehouse Organization:
   a. Are cases of product promptly emptied and their contents stored in shelving units?
   b. Are products labeled with the receiving date and rotated so oldest product is used first?
   c. Are cases kept off the floor of the dry goods room, walk in coolers, and walk in freezers?

Jenny's Café, Inc.
Denver Restaurant
Internal Control Questionnaire—Food Warehouse (Stores)
Audit Date: July 31, 2006

Internal Control Question	Yes/No	Comments

3. Storage:
   a. When product is delivered, is it stored immediately upon receipt?
   b. Is product stored in a manner that facilitates inventory counting, i.e. stored in the same order as it appears on the inventory count sheets?
   c. Is all inventory of a particular product stored in the same location so it is easy to find?

4. Dry Goods Room:
   a. If shelves are high, is there a step ladder, kept in the corner of the room, so personnel can easily retrieve goods from the top shelf?
   b. Are bulk goods, such as flour, sugar, rice, etc. that are purchased in 50 lb. bags, kept on a bottom shelf so they are easy to remove?
   c. Is product purchased in bulk, delivered to the kitchen in unopened bags?

5. Coolers:
   a. Does each walk-in cooler have shelving units lining the walls of the cooler?
   b. Are there separate coolers for produce, dairy, and meat/seafood?

Jenny's Café, Inc.
Denver Restaurant
Internal Control Questionnaire—Food Warehouse (Stores)
Audit Date: July 31, 2006

Internal Control Question	**Yes/No**	**Comments**

c. Is produce stored in clearly labeled cases or in plastic bins?

d. Is meat and seafood removed from cases, placed on trays or in bins, and stored in the shelving units?

e. Do the walk-in coolers have working thermometers on the outside to facilitate reading the temperature inside the coolers?

f. Is the produce cooler kept at 39 degrees Fahrenheit and the meat and dairy coolers kept at 36-38 degrees Fahrenheit?

g. Does the Warehouse Manager check the temperature at least three times a day and record it on a Cooler/Freezer Temperature Log to ensure they are in the safe range?

6. Freezers:

a. Does the walk-in freezer have shelving units lining the walls of the freezer?

b. Are the labels on cases facing the front so they are easily read?

c. Is there a working thermometer outside the walk-in freezer so the temperature inside can be monitored?

429

Jenny's Café, Inc.
Denver Restaurant
Internal Control Questionnaire—Food Warehouse (Stores)
Audit Date: July 31, 2006

Internal Control Question	Yes/No	Comments

d. Is the temperature of the walk in freezer kept at 0 degrees Fahrenheit or colder?

e. Is the compressor kept on while issuing product from the walk-in freezer and only turned off when a longer period of time is needed, i.e. counting inventory?

7. Issues from Stores:

a. Are all issuances documented on multi-part issuance slips so both the issuer and the receiver have a copy?

b. Are products picked based on the items listed on the issuance slips?

c. Does the porter check off each item on the Requisition or Issuance Slip as he picks it?

d. Does the Warehouse Manager or a checker compare each item on the cart against the issuance slip, check it off before it leaves Stores, and sign the issuance slip as the issuer?

e. At the Kitchen, does a kitchen person count the product delivered, compare it against the issuance slip or requisition slip, check it off, and sign the document as the receiver?

Jenny's Café, Inc.
Denver Restaurant
Internal Control Questionnaire—Food Warehouse (Stores)
Audit Date: July 31, 2006

Internal Control Question	**Yes/No**	**Comments**

f. Does the porter take the signed issuance or requisition slip to the Warehouse Manager who files it with the inventory documentation for the current inventory period?
g. Where changes are made to the issuance slip due to shortages, does the porter initial the change?

8. Warehouse Security:
a. Is the receiving door kept locked until a delivery truck arrives and closed and locked once the delivery has been received?
b. Are coolers and freezers locked once deliveries for the day have ceased?
c. Prior to leaving for the day, does the Warehouse Manager check to ensure each cooler and freezer in Stores is locked?
d. Is the Manager on Duty the only person other than the Warehouse Manager with keys to the Stores area and its coolers and freezers?
e. Are security cameras in place in the receiving area and throughout the Food Warehouse, and are they in working order and monitored?

Jenny's Café, Inc.
Denver Restaurant
Internal Control Questionnaire—Food Warehouse (Stores)
Audit Date: July 31, 2006

Internal Control Question	Yes/No	Comments

9. Does every walk-in cooler or freezer have a door handle on the inside that permits the door to be opened from the inside?

10. Where emergency product is needed from Stores after hours, does the Manager on Duty follow the normal procedures, including documentation and signatures, when obtaining product from Stores?

Jenny's Café, Inc.
Denver Restaurant
Internal Control Questionnaire—Bars
Audit Date: July 31, 2006

Internal Control Question	Yes/No	Comments

1. Segregation of Duties:
   a. Who issues beer, liquor, and wine from the Liquor, Room, Main Beer Cooler, and Wine Cellar?
   b. Who receives beer, liquor, and wine at the bar issued from the Liquor Room, Main Beer Cooler, and Wine Cellar?
   c. Who dispenses alcoholic beverages?
   d. Who dispenses non-alcoholic beverages from the bar?
   e. Who completes the daily reconciliation of Liquor, Beer, and Wine usage to the cash register?
   f. Who counts inventory at the bar at the end of the inventory period? Are the duties properly segregated?

2. Liquor Room Organization:
   a. Are there sufficient shelving units so all liquor can be stored neatly on a shelf?
   b. Is liquor organized by type of liquor and then by brand?
   c. Is liquor organized in the same order as it appears on the count sheets?
   d. Is liquor that cannot be put on a shelf due to insufficient shelf space left in sealed cases?

Jenny's Café, Inc.
Denver Restaurant
Internal Control Questionnaire—Bars
Audit Date: July 31, 2006

Internal Control Question	**Yes/No**	**Comments**

e. Are all empty boxes removed from the liquor room?

3. Are the Liquor Room, Main Beer Cooler, and Wine Cellar locked whenever there is no one in these areas?

4. Liquor Stickers:
   a. Does the Company have sequentially numbered liquor stickers with the Company Logo?
   b. Once affixed to the bottle, is the adhesive strong enough so the sticker cannot be removed without damaging the sticker?
   c. Does the Bar Manager affix a liquor sticker to every bottle removed from a case when received in the liquor room and put on a shelf?
   d. Are all liquor stickers secured in the Liquor Room?

5. Liquor Control Log:
   a. Does the Bar Manager maintain a Liquor Control Log where he tracks every liquor bottle that enters the premises from the day the case is opened?

Jenny's Café, Inc.
Denver Restaurant
Internal Control Questionnaire—Bars
Audit Date: July 31, 2006

Internal Control Question	Yes/No	Comments

b. Is every liquor sticker entered in the Liquor Control Log by sticker number, liquor type, bottle size, date issued, issuer, bar issued, date returned, and person receiving the empty bottle.

c. Does the Bar Manager only issue liquor upon receipt of an empty bottle?

d. Does the Bar Manager log the bottle in the Liquor Control Log as returned with the date returned?

e. Does the Bar Manager draw a line through the liquor sticker with a magic marker so it cannot be reused?

f. Is the bar kept at a par inventory so there are always a set number of bottles at the bar?

6. Liquor Issuances:

a. Are issuance slips prenumbered?

b. Is every bottle or keg issued from the Liquor Room, Main Beer Cooler, or Wine Cellar listed on an issuance slip?

c. Does every issuance slip indicate the bar to which the product was issued?

Jenny's Café, Inc.
Denver Restaurant
Internal Control Questionnaire—Bars
Audit Date: July 31, 2006

Internal Control Question	**Yes/No**	**Comments**

d. Does the person issuing the product sign the issuance slip?

e. Does the person receiving the product count the product, compare it to the issuance slip, and sign the issuance slip?

f. Does the Bar Manager retain issuance slips in folders set up for each week?

7. Liquor Meter Dispensing System:

a. Does the bar utilize a liquor meter dispensing system?

b. Other than sticky liqueurs, is every liquor bottle used at the bar metered?

c. Are system heads sealed to the bottle with a prenumbered seal?

d. Is the seal number logged in the Liquor Log?

e. Does the Bar Manager perform a daily reconciliation of the retail value of liquor dispensed, per the liquor metering system, to liquor sales recorded on the POS system, accounting for the usage of any liqueurs not metered?

Jenny's Café, Inc.
Denver Restaurant
Internal Control Questionnaire—Bars
Audit Date: July 31, 2006

Internal Control Question	Yes/No	Comments

8. Draft Beer Metering/Dispensing Systems (where used):

   a. Does the Bar Manager reconcile the retail value per the metering system to beer sales per the cash register?

   b. Does the Bar Manager take a daily count of all bottled beer each day, subtract it from the prior day's count plus issues, calculate the retail value of usage and add it to draft meter sales for comparison to beer sales on the cash register?

9. Wine Controls:

   a. Are expensive wines locked in a wine cellar or liquor room until sold?

   b. When an expensive wine is sold, does the Bar Manager or Manager on Duty complete an issuance slip and issue it to the bar?

   c. Does the Bar Manager take a daily inventory of the wine at the bar, calculate the retail value of wine usage, and compare it to sales per the cash register?

Jenny's Café, Inc.
Denver Restaurant
Internal Control Questionnaire—Bars
Audit Date: July 31, 2006

Internal Control Question	**Yes/No**	**Comments**

10. Where the product usage variance for the bar is greater than the allowable variance, does the Bar Manager take disciplinary action against the bartender responsible?

11. Do the bartenders follow the Company's portion control policies in dispensing alcoholic beverages?

12. Do the bartenders fill orders placed by waitresses only from the orders printed on the chit printer?

13. Bar Reports:
a. Does the Controller compare the Liquor, Beer, and Wine Costs per the Bar Reports to the applicable P&L accounts each month?
b. Does the Bar Manager or Controller investigate large variances between the Bar Reports and the General Ledger and document the results of the investigation?
c. Does management review the Bar Reports for the individual bars, investigate significant variances from Plan, and document the results of the investigation?

Jenny's Café, Inc.
Denver Restaurant
Internal Control Questionnaire—Sales
Audit Date: July 31, 2006

Internal Control Question	Yes/No	Comments

1. Segregation of Duties:
   a. Who obtains the cash register readings or POS cash balancing reports?
   b. Who counts the cash in the cash register?
   c. Who verifies the cash turned in to the cash room?
   d. Who reconciles the cash to the POS or cash register sales?
   e. Who prepares the Daily Sales Journal that records the sales in the Accounts Receivable Sub-Ledger?
   f. Who keys the Daily Sales Journal into the Accounts Receivable Sub-Ledger?
   g. Who approves the Daily Sales Journal?
   h. Who posts the Daily Sales Journal to the Accounts Receivable Sub-Ledger and to the General Ledger?
   i. Who approves voids and overrings?
   Are the duties properly segregated?

Jenny's Café, Inc.
Denver Restaurant
Internal Control Questionnaire—Sales
Audit Date: July 31, 2006

Internal Control Question	**Yes/No**	**Comments**

2. When payment is made on a guest check, does the Dining Room Cashier close the check on the POS system?

3. Guest Check Controls:
   a. Are unused guest checks kept in a locked room with key access limited to the General Manager, Dining Room Manager, Bar Manager, and Controller?
   b. Do the guest checks have the Company logo on them?
   c. Does the Controller log the beginning and ending guest check numbers when the guest checks are received from the printer?
   d. Does the Dining Room Cashier sign a log for guest checks issued to her?
   e. Does the Dining Room Cashier utilize a Guest Check Control Log where each waiter or waitress signs for guest checks received?
   f. At the end of the shift, does the Dining Room Cashier reconcile the guest checks issued to guest checks returned?

Jenny's Café, Inc.
Denver Restaurant
Internal Control Questionnaire—Sales
Audit Date: July 31, 2006

Internal Control Question	Yes/No	Comments

4. Overrings or Voids:
   a. When an overring occurs, does the cashier complete an overring slip with the details of the overring?
   b. Does the Manager on Duty review the reason for the overring and sign the overring slip?
   c. On a POS system, is security access to initiate voids only given to the cashier's supervisor?

5. Internal Cash Register Readings:
   a. Does the Sales Reporting Clerk reconcile the internal cash register readings from each cash register to the previous day's readings and balance to the current day's activity?
   b. On a Point of Sales system, does the Sales Reporting Clerk reconcile the current day's activity to the change in the Grand Total for each cashier?

Jenny's Café, Inc.
Denver Restaurant
Internal Control Questionnaire—Sales
Audit Date: July 31, 2006

Internal Control Question	**Yes/No**	**Comments**

6. Tip Reporting:

    a. Are charge tips paid through the payroll system?

    b. Where charge tips are paid through cash receipts the day they were earned by the employees, does each tipped employee sign a Charge Tips Received Form next to the amount of the cash payment received?

    c. Does the Sales Reporting Clerk make a copy of the Charge Tips Received Form for the Payroll Clerk to use in reporting these payments in the payroll system?

7. Sales Reporting:

    a. Does the Sales Reporting Clerk use the cash counted in the cash room as the Cash amount on the Daily Sales Journal?

    b. Are the credit card amounts on the Daily Sales Journal the amounts from the Credit Card Settlement slips?

    c. Are Gift Certificates and Coupons Received amounts on the Daily Sales Journal supported by adding machine tapes of the Gift Certificates and coupons counted?

Jenny's Café, Inc.
Denver Restaurant
Internal Control Questionnaire—Sales
Audit Date: July 31, 2006

Internal Control Question	Yes/No	Comments

d. Are the revenue amounts on the Daily Sales Journal taken from the POS Profit Center Sales Reports or from the cash register readings?

e. Does the Sales Tax Payable amount agree to the underlying sales accounts multiplied by the applicable sales tax rates?

f. Does Gift Certificate Sales agree to the supporting sales documentation?

g. Does Charge Tips agree to the Revenue Center Sales Report or other means of collecting charge tip data?

8. Voids, Overrings, Refund, and No Sale Tracking:

a. Does the Sales Reporting Clerk maintain a log of voids, overrings, refunds, and "No Sale" Transactions by cashier?

b. Does the Dining Room Manager or General Manager review the log weekly to determine whether there are any disturbing trends?

443

Jenny's Café, Inc.
Denver Restaurant
Internal Control Questionnaire—Sales
Audit Date: July 31, 2006

Internal Control Question	Yes/No	Comments

9. Counterfeit Currency Detection:
   a. Have cashiers been trained to detect counterfeit currency?
   b. Does each cashier station have a counterfeit detection device?

10. Does each employee wear a Company issued photo ID that is clearly visible to customers with the employee's name clearly printed in large letters?

11. Does the Company periodically utilize a secret shopper service or detective agency to obtain an assessment of how the employees are performing?

12. Per Capita Spending:
   a. Does the Daily Sales Reporting Clerk obtain the number of guests for per capita reporting purposes?
   b. Each day, does the Controller calculate the Per Capita Spending and send an email to the General Manager and other management personnel with the statistical figures?
   c. Does the Controller prepare a Per Capita Spending spreadsheet that she issues to management at month end?

Jenny's Café, Inc.
Denver Restaurant
Internal Control Questionnaire—Sales
Audit Date: July 31, 2006

Internal Control Question	**Yes/No**	**Comments**

13. Comped Transactions:
    a. For comped transactions, does the guest sign the guest check?
    b. Does the Manager on Duty sign the comped guest check thereby authorizing the comp?

14. Gift Certificates:
    a. Do gift certificates have the Company logo, the restaurant's name, address, serial numbers, and a place to type the customer's name?
    b. Are gift certificate amounts printed on the certificate only upon sale of the gift certificate?
    c. Is gift certificate stock stored in a locked file cabinet or locked desk drawer, controlled by the Manager on Duty?
    d. When a customer buys a gift certificate, does the Manager on Duty log the sale in a Gift Certificate Log?
    e. Is a check imprinter used to imprint the value of the gift certificate?

Jenny's Café, Inc.
Denver Restaurant
Internal Control Questionnaire—Sales
Audit Date: July 31, 2006

Internal Control Question	Yes/No	Comments
f. When the gift certificate is sold, does the Manager on Duty type the customer name on the gift certificate and sign it?		
g. Does a cashier record the gift certificate sale on the cash register?		
h. Is the gift certificate sale recorded as a liability?		
i. When the gift certificate is redeemed, does the Cash Room Attendant cancel it with a "PAID" stamp?		
j. Does the Sales Reporting Clerk enter the date redeemed and amount in the Gift Certificate Log?		
k. At month end, does the Controller print the Gift Certificate Log, agree the total to the Gift Certificate Payable account in the General Ledger, and resolve any differences?		

Jenny's Café, Inc.
Denver Restaurant
Internal Control Questionnaire—Sales
Audit Date: July 31, 2006

Internal Control Question	Yes/No	Comments
15. Vending and Amusement Machine Revenues: a. Does the General Manager send vending machine contracts to the Corporate Legal Department for review prior to signing the contract? b. Does the vending machine contract stipulate that the vending machine company have a General Liability policy in effect of at least $1 million coverage? c. Each year, does the General Manager obtain a certificate of insurance from the vending company that names the Company as coinsured? d. When the vending company empties the vending machines, does it provide the General Manager with a reconciliation of cash collected to the machine meter readings and a calculation of commissions due? e. Where there are no meters in the machine, does the vending company reconcile the value of merchandise usage to cash?		

Jenny's Café, Inc.
Denver Restaurant
Internal Control Questionnaire—Sales
Audit Date: July 31, 2006

Internal Control Question	Yes/No	Comments

f. Does the Controller assign someone to verify machine meter readings and cash collected from the machines at least once per quarter?

g. Does the Company representative document the meter readings and cash collected for subsequent comparison to the commission statement?

h. When meter readings and cash are not verified, does the Controller compare the reconciliation with verified reconciliations to determine whether commissions paid are similar?

16. Sublet Revenues:

a. Does the General Manager send sublet contracts to the Corporate Legal Department for review prior to signing the contract?

b. Does the vending machine contract stipulate that the vending machine company have a General Liability policy in effect of at least $1 million coverage?

Jenny's Café, Inc.
Denver Restaurant
Internal Control Questionnaire—Sales
Audit Date: July 31, 2006

Internal Control Question	Yes/No	Comments
c. Each year, does the General Manager obtain a certificate of insurance that names the Company as coinsured?		
d. Does the Controller audit sublet sales at least once a year by comparing cash register reading tapes to the Sales Reconciliation and Rent Statement provided by the sublet each month?		
e. When auditing the sublet, does the Controller document the work performed?		
17. Valet Parking:		
a. Does the Valet Parking operation utilize a pre-numbered, three-part ticket: customer, windshield wiper, key?		
b. Does the attendant record the fee collected on the cash register and insert the cash in the cash drawer?		
c. Does the attendant keep tips separate from company funds?		
d. Are unused tickets secured in a locked cabinet with limited access?		

Jenny's Café, Inc.
Denver Restaurant
Internal Control Questionnaire—Sales
Audit Date: July 31, 2006

Internal Control Question	Yes/No	Comments
e. Does the Controller or other management person control the reserve supply of valet parking tickets in a locked storeroom?		
f. Does the Valet Parking Supervisor sign for all tickets received?		
g. Does the Valet Parking Supervisor track tickets issued to the Valet Parking Attendants by having them sign for them on the Daily Valet Parking Ticket Reconciliation?		
h. Does the Valet Parking Supervisor reconcile tickets used to cash turned in on the Daily Valet Parking Ticket Reconciliation?		
i. Does the Sales/Accounts Receivable Clerk check the Daily Valet Parking Ticket Reconciliation against the ticket stubs turned in to determine whether all tickets accounted as used were actually used?		

Jenny's Café, Inc.
Denver Restaurant
Internal Control Questionnaire—Inventory
Audit Date: July 31, 2006

Internal Control Question	Yes/No	Comments

1. Segregation of Duties:
   a. Who counts the Inventory in Stores?
   b. Who counts the inventory in the Liquor Room, Main Beer Cooler, and Wine Cellar?
   c. Who counts the inventory in the kitchen?
   d. Who counts the inventory in the bars?
   e. Who enters the counts into the inventory software?
   f. Who is responsible for Bar Cost?
   g. Who is responsible for Food Cost?
   Are the duties properly segregated?

2. Does someone periodically count the inventory who is independent of the Sales process, i.e. Accounting?

3. Inventory Counting and Recording:
   a. Is a complete physical inventory performed at least monthly?
   b. Are two people assigned to each inventory location, one to count and one to write the counts?

Jenny's Café, Inc.
Denver Restaurant
Internal Control Questionnaire—Inventory
Audit Date: July 31, 2006

Internal Control Question	Yes/No	Comments

c. Is there a proper cut off of goods received when counters begin counting inventory?

d. Are all inventory locations well organized to facilitate the count?

e. Is the Kitchen counted after it closes for the day?

f. Are emergency issues from product counted subtracted from the counts?

g. Is inventory counted systematically in a location, starting in one place, counting left to right, top to bottom, until all inventory in the location has been counted?

h. Are inventory counts written on preprinted count sheets with several columns for additional counts?

i. Are counts written in ink on the count sheets?

j. Is all product purchased by weight (meat, poultry, seafood, cheese, etc.) weighed on a scale during the inventory count process?

k. Is the weight of the container subtracted from the gross weight when entering the weight on the inventory?

Jenny's Café, Inc.
Denver Restaurant
Internal Control Questionnaire—Inventory
Audit Date: July 31, 2006

Internal Control Question	Yes/No	Comments

l. Are additional counts of the same product added to the original count with a plus sign?

m. Do both people on the count team sign each page of the count sheets?

n. Are new items that are not preprinted on the count sheets hand-written on the bottom of the page on the count sheets?

o. Are changes due to recounts documented on the count sheets by crossing out the original count and writing the revised count next to it?

p. Are hand-written items added to the inventory system through system maintenance?

4. Liquor, Beer, and Wine Inventory:
   a. Does the Bar Manager actually count the entire Liquor Room, Main Beer Cooler, and Wine Cellar instead of using the perpetual inventory balances as the ending counts?
   b. Are the bars counted after they close for the day?
   c. Are partial liquor bottles counted to the nearest tenth of a bottle?

Jenny's Café, Inc.
Denver Restaurant
Internal Control Questionnaire—Inventory
Audit Date: July 31, 2006

Internal Control Question	Yes/No	Comments

d. Are beer kegs estimated to the nearest quarter keg by shaking the keg?

e. Are the deposits on beer kegs, including partial kegs and empty kegs, counted on the Keg Deposit Log and included in the Beer Inventory value?

5. Keying Inventory Counts:

a. Are new inventory items added to the master file?

b. Are prices updated on the master file each inventory period?

c. When the inventory is printed, does someone compare the count sheets to the final inventory listing to ensure all counts were keyed correctly?

d. Are final inventory listings printed and distributed to the department heads for review by the end of the day after the counts were made?

e. Does the Controller calculate the Product Cost based on purchases, accruals, transfers, ending inventory, etc. and advise Department Managers of significant differences from Plan?

Jenny's Café, Inc.
Denver Restaurant
Internal Control Questionnaire—Inventory
Audit Date: July 31, 2006

Internal Control Question	Yes/No	Comments

f. Do Department Managers investigate significant product cost differences from Plan, including recounts of inventory items that appear too high or too low?

g. Once the inventory is finalized, does the Department Manager sign and date the final inventory listing?

h. Do the Controller and General Manager sign the final inventory listing, documenting their review and approval?

6. Inventory Costing:

a. Has someone in the Food Warehouse (Stores) been assigned the responsibility of keeping the inventory cost prices current on the Inventory?

b. Does the Bar Manager update the cost prices on the Bar inventory regularly?

c. Does the person keying maintenance in the inventory reports update the cost prices upon receipt of the changes?

Jenny's Café, Inc.
Denver Restaurant
Internal Control Questionnaire—Inventory
Audit Date: July 31, 2006

Internal Control Question	**Yes/No**	**Comments**

7. Product Cost Calculation:
   a. Does the Controller calculate Product Cost by category from information available?
   b. Does the Controller investigate significant variances in product cost percentages from Plan, including asking department managers to perform recounts of items that appear to be too high or too low?
   c. Where the cause of the significant variance from Plan cannot be determined, does the Controller document the investigation performed?

8. Spoilage:
   a. Is spoilage minimized by rotating product?
   b. Is spoilage listed on a spoilage sheet, given to the Controller to calculate the cost of spoilage, and retained as back up for product cost variances from Plan?
   c. Is spoiled product discarded after it has been documented?

Jenny's Café, Inc.
Denver Restaurant
Internal Control Questionnaire—Inventory
Audit Date: July 31, 2006

Internal Control Question	Yes/No	Comments
9. Employee Meals: a. Does the chef have a method of tracking employee meals served and report this information to the Controller daily? b. Does the Controller calculate the cost of employee meals, deduct it from Food Cost, and charge Employee Benefits through a journal entry?		

Jenny's Café, Inc.
Denver Restaurant
Internal Control Questionnaire—Menu Costing
Audit Date: July 31, 2006

Internal Control Question	Yes/No	Comments

1. Cost Specification Sheets:
   a. Does the chef break down each menu item into its ingredients on Cost Specification sheets and determine the costs of each ingredient on these sheets?
   b. Does the chef add the costs of the ingredients together to determine the total cost of the menu item?
   c. Does the chef divide the total cost of each menu item by its selling price to calculate the standard food cost percentage?
   d. Is a base consisting of items common to several menu items calculated and added to the other ingredients of each menu item?
   e. In costing menu items that have ingredients where part of the raw ingredients contain parts that are not usable, i.e. bell peppers, does the chef include the unusable portion in the cost calculation?
   f. Where the chef is costing meat that is purchased in bulk and sliced after cooking, i.e. prime rib, does the chef use the total raw weight in the calculation and divide it by the number of servings obtained?

Jenny's Café, Inc.
Denver Restaurant
Internal Control Questionnaire—Menu Costing
Audit Date: July 31, 2006

Internal Control Question	Yes/No	Comments
g. Where the chef is costing soups, gravies, etc. when he makes a batch and divides it among several servings, does he determine the cost of the batch, divide it among the number of servings, and then cost individual servings by adding the ingredients to finish the serving?		
h. Where the customer has a choice of several ingredients, i.e. salad dressing for a salad, does the chef use the average cost of the salad dressings available on the Cost Specification sheets?		
i. Where the customer can obtain additional products at no additional charge, i.e. additional rolls, or additional cups of coffee, does the chef use an average number consumed in the Cost Specification sheets?		
j. Does each menu item contain the date the unit cost of the ingredients was last updated?		

Jenny's Café, Inc.
Denver Restaurant
Internal Control Questionnaire—Menu Costing
Audit Date: July 31, 2006

Internal Control Question	Yes/No	Comments

2. Developing Menus:
a. In developing menus, does the chef calculate the standard cost of each menu item and then meet with the General Manager to set prices based on the standard cost percentage they wish to achieve?
b. Are the menu items put into a sales mix to determine whether the different menu items set at different food cost percentages will achieve the desired food cost percentage for the restaurant?

3. Menu Mix:
a. Does a clerk drop actual numbers of menu items sold into the menu mix each inventory period to calculate the Standard Cost percentage that should have been achieved based on the mix of items sold?
b. Where specials are added to the menu, does the chef cost the special and add it to the menu mix?

Jenny's Café, Inc.
Denver Restaurant
Internal Control Questionnaire—Menu Costing
Audit Date: July 31, 2006

Internal Control Question	Yes/No	Comments

c. Does the Executive Chef or Controller compare Actual Food Cost to Standard Food Cost based on the menu mix and investigate Actual Food Cost that is outside + - 2 percentage points from standard?

d. Are the results of the investigation documented?

e. Do the Executive Chef and General Manager review the documentation of the investigation and sign it?

4. Menu Mix Credits:

a. Does the location make adjustments to the Menu Mix for items such as employee meals (when absorbed into food cost), comped meals, coupons, etc.?

b. When accepting a "buy one, get one free" coupon, does the cashier write the value of the free meal (lower priced meal) on the back of the coupon?

c. Does the Controller or designee summarize coupons redeemed on a Coupon Credits Report?

Jenny's Café, Inc.
Denver Restaurant
Internal Control Questionnaire—Menu Costing
Audit Date: July 31, 2006

Internal Control Question	**Yes/No**	**Comments**
d. Are coupons collected by denomination, rubber banded, and put into a separate envelope each day as support for the Daily Sales Journal?		
e. When eating in the dining room, does management sign the guest check, write comp on its face, and write the reason for the comp on the back of the guest check and the names of the other members of the party?		
f. When recording sales the following day, does the sales clerk add the comped guest checks and tie the total to the comp key on the order entry system's sales report?		
g. Does the sales clerk check to see that each comp was properly authorized?		
h. Does the sales clerk summarize the Comps on a Comp Report by Food , Liquor, Beer, Wine, and Sales Tax and give it to the Controller for review?		

Jenny's Café, Inc.
Denver Restaurant
Internal Control Questionnaire—Menu Costing
Audit Date: July 31, 2006

Internal Control Question	Yes/No	Comments

5. Does the Executive Chef review the menu items at least annually, and add and delete items based on sales?

6. Buffet Costing:
   a. Does the Executive Chef cost the buffet on several days and average the cost of those buffets?
   b. Does the Executive Chef cost the different menu items going into the buffet by tray, pan, pot, etc.?
   c. Does the Executive Chef inventory all items going into the buffet and all items returning from the buffet (except food going into the trash), including trash and beverages included in the selling price?
   d. As additional trays are added to the buffet table during the evening, are they added to the Beginning Inventory of items going into the buffet?

**Jenny's Café, Inc.
Denver Restaurant
Internal Control Questionnaire—Kitchen Operations
Audit Date: July 31, 2006**

Internal Control Question	**Yes/No**	**Comments**

1. Segregation of Duties:
   a. Who schedules the kitchen employees?
   b. Who works the broiler, deep fryer, grill, and stove?
   c. Who prepares salads and appetizers?
   d. Who prepares desserts?
   e. Who enters orders in the order entry system?
   f. Who issues linens?
   Are the duties properly segregated?

2. Order Entry System:
   a. Do the wait staff enter all orders into the Order Entry System?
   b. Do kitchen personnel fill orders based only on what is printed on the station printer?
   c. When filling an order, do the cooks tear the chit off the printer and clip it on an overhead clip until the order is ready?
   d. When completing an order, do kitchen personnel tear the chit halfway and set it next to the order?

Jenny's Café, Inc.
Denver Restaurant
Internal Control Questionnaire—Kitchen Operations
Audit Date: July 31, 2006

Internal Control Question	Yes/No	Comments

e. Are all beverage orders for the bar entered into the order entry system and a chit listing the items ordered prints in the bar?

f. During employee training sessions, does management emphasize that no product may leave the kitchen without appearing on a chit (except non-alcoholic beverages, i.e. coffee, tea, etc.)?

3. Manual Dup Controls:

a. Do waiters and waitresses write entrée orders on two part guest checks where the top copy is presented to the cooks on the production line?

b. Do cooks on the production line only fill orders based on what is written on the dup?

c. Do waiters and waitresses use dup pads to order other items such as salads, appetizers, desserts, etc.?

d. Do personnel at the salad station and dessert station only fill orders based on what was written on the dup?

e. Does the cashier validate the orders written on the guest check by recording each item on the cash register?

Jenny's Café, Inc.
Denver Restaurant
Internal Control Questionnaire—Kitchen Operations
Audit Date: July 31, 2006

Internal Control Question	Yes/No	Comments
f. Does the bartender fill beverage orders only from what was written on the dup presented to him?		
g. Are all filled dups driven through spindles when the orders are picked up?		
h. At the end of the day, does someone pick up the dups, put them in separate bags labeled Bar, Salad Station, Dessert Station, and Production Line and take them to the Dining Room Manager's office or General Manager's office?		
i. Does a clerk compare dups to guest checks and cash register validations at least weekly to ensure that each item written on a dup was recorded on the cash register?		
j. Are all exceptions noted during the comparison of dups to guest checks brought to the Dining Room Manager for resolution with the waiter or waitress?		
k. Is disciplinary action taken where items recorded on dups were not recorded on the cash register?		

Jenny's Café, Inc.
Denver Restaurant
Internal Control Questionnaire—Kitchen Operations
Audit Date: July 31, 2006

Internal Control Question	Yes/No	Comments
4. Portion Control: a. Are kitchen staff made aware of the standard portion sizes of each item going into an entrée, appetizer, dessert, etc.? b. Are standard measuring devices used to ensure portion sizes are according to standard, i.e. portion control scale, ladle, standard bowl, soufflé cup, etc.? c. Does the chef periodically observe the kitchen staff to ensure that the portion sizes are correct?		
5. Where manual dup systems are used, does the expediter or cashier check the items the waiters and waitresses remove from the kitchen against what was recorded on the cash register per the guest check validations?		
6. Does the location have procedures in place that ensure non-alcoholic beverages are recorded on guest checks?		

Jenny's Café, Inc.
Denver Restaurant
Internal Control Questionnaire—Kitchen Operations
Audit Date: July 31, 2006

Internal Control Question	Yes/No	Comments

7. Spoilage and Waste:

a. Does the Executive Chef periodically observe his kitchen help to ensure they are cutting up produce and meat in a manner than minimizes waste?

b. Are fruits and vegetables rotated properly so the oldest is used first?

c. Does the Executive Chef use leftovers in soups, employee meals, etc. to minimize the amount that is thrown in the trash?

d. Where there is spoilage, is spoilage documented on Spoilage Sheets before throwing it in the trash and cost prices determined?

e. Is the Spoilage Sheet signed by the person completing it and the person reviewing and approving it?

f. Is the Spoilage Sheet sent to the Controller as support in explaining high Food Cost?

Jenny's Café, Inc.
Denver Restaurant
Internal Control Questionnaire—Kitchen Operations
Audit Date: July 31, 2006

Internal Control Question	Yes/No	Comments

8. Linen Room Controls:

a. Has a par been established consisting of the number of linens that are issued to the dining room?

b. Is there a Linen Room Sign Out Sheet where the Head Waitress or Head Waiter signs for linens received and returned?

c. Does the Linen Room Supervisor count out the number of linens issued with the Head Waiter or Head Waitress ?

d. Once the par stock is issued for the day, are additional linens issued only on a one for one exchange of dirty linens for clean linens?

e. At the end of the day, does the Linen Room Supervisor count back the number of linens returned and agree them to the number issued?

f. Do kitchen personnel sign the Linen Room Sign Out Sheet for the number of chef's gowns and towels received?

Jenny's Café, Inc.
Denver Restaurant
Internal Control Questionnaire—Kitchen Operations
Audit Date: July 31, 2006

Internal Control Question	Yes/No	Comments
g. Does the Linen Room Supervisor investigate differences between the number of linens issued and returned?		
h. When using a linen service, does the Linen Room Supervisor count the number of linens returned with the Linen Service representative and compare the count to the receipt issued by the Linen Service rep?		
i. When receiving linens from the Linen Service, does the Linen Room Supervisor count the linens received, compare the count to the invoice or packing slip, and follow up any differences with the Linen Service to ensure she receives credit?		
9. China, Glassware, Silverware:		
a. Do bussers use plastic bins in collecting dirty dishes from the tables?		
b. Does management have procedures in place that deter employees from throwing usable china, glassware, and silverware in the trash?		

Jenny's Café, Inc.
Denver Restaurant
Internal Control Questionnaire—Kitchen Operations
Audit Date: July 31, 2006

Internal Control Question	Yes/No	Comments

10. Kitchen Security:

a. Is there supervision of kitchen personnel and dining room staff at all times?

b. Is bringing personal possessions into the kitchen or dining room forbidden?

c. Are there locker rooms where employees can change into uniforms?

d. Are employees assigned lockers where they can keep their personal possessions?

e. Are all coolers and freezers locked when the Kitchen closes?

f. Are the Executive Chef, Sous Chef, and General Manager the only employees with keys to the kitchen coolers and freezers?

g. Is the room where china, glassware, and silverware are stored kept locked and keys limited to the Dining Room Manager, Executive Chef, and General Manager?

Jenny's Café, Inc.
Denver Restaurant
Internal Control Questionnaire—Kitchen Operations
Audit Date: July 31, 2006

Internal Control Question	**Yes/No**	**Comments**
h. Is the Linen Room locked when the Linen Room closes for the day?		
i. Are keys to the Linen Room limited to the Linen Room Supervisor, Dining Room Manager, and General Manager?		
j. Is the restaurant locked and the alarm set when the last management person leaves for the day?		

Jenny's Café, Inc.
Denver Restaurant
Internal Control Questionnaire—Payroll
Audit Date: July 31, 2006

Internal Control Question	Yes/No	Comments
1. Segregation of Duties:		
a. Who calculates the number of hours each employee worked per the time cards?		
b. Who approves time cards or Time Keeping Reports?		
c. Who performs payroll master file maintenance?		
d. Who performs Human Resources functions?		
e. Who inputs time worked into the payroll system?		
f. Who approves the payroll prior to transmitting it?		
g. Who receives the payroll checks?		
h. Who cuts manual payroll checks?		
i. Who signs manual payroll checks?		
j. Who runs the payroll reports?		
k. Who reviews the payroll reports?		
Are the duties properly segregated?		

HANS L. STEINIGER

Jenny's Café, Inc.
Denver Restaurant
Internal Control Questionnaire—Payroll
Audit Date: July 31, 2006

Internal Control Question	Yes/No	Comments

2. Time Keeping:

   a. Is the time worked for each hourly employee recorded in some fashion: Time Cards, Sign In Sign Out Sheets, or Time Keeping System?

   b. When using Sign In Sign Out Sheets, does the Department Manager calculate time worked each day and initial each entry?

   c. When using time cards, does the Department Manager initial all manual entries on the time cards?

   d. Does the Department Manager approve time worked by initialing the completed time card or signing the Time Keeping report each day?

   e. Are employees paid from the time they clock in to the time they clock out?

   f. Does the employee sign the time card indicating agreement to the hours worked or does the employee document this agreement in some other method?

474

Jenny's Café, Inc.
Denver Restaurant
Internal Control Questionnaire—Payroll
Audit Date: July 31, 2006

Internal Control Question	Yes/No	Comments

3. Adjustment Reports:

a. Where Time Keeping systems are used, do the department managers review the Daily Time Worked Reports, make corrections to hours worked, sign the reports, and return them promptly to the payroll clerk?

b. Does the payroll clerk make daily adjustments to the Time Keeping system's hours worked based on the signed reports returned by the department managers?

c. At the end of the week, does the Payroll Clerk print the Weekly Time Summaries, distribute them to the department managers who review them to ensure all changes were made correctly, sign them, and return them to the Payroll Clerk?

Jenny's Café, Inc.
Denver Restaurant
Internal Control Questionnaire—Payroll
Audit Date: July 31, 2006

Internal Control Question	Yes/No	Comments

4. Payroll Input:

a. On Monday morning, are the signed time records from each department on the Payroll Clerk's desk?

b. Does the Payroll Clerk key changes to employee master file records based on authorized (signed) Employee Maintenance Forms?

c. Do the department managers calculate total hours worked for each employee and write the total on the time records?

d. Does the Payroll Clerk enter hours worked into the Payroll system based on approved time records?

e. Does the Payroll Clerk enter miscellaneous adjustments into the Payroll system based on properly approved source documents?

f. If the restaurant is located in New York, Texas, California, or Oregon, does the payroll system add the value of employee meals to gross wages for purposes of calculating state unemployment taxes?

Jenny's Café, Inc.
Denver Restaurant
Internal Control Questionnaire—Payroll
Audit Date: July 31, 2006

Internal Control Question	Yes/No	Comments
g. Does the Payroll Clerk key charge tips into the Payroll system from a charge tips received spreadsheet that the Dining Room Manager completes each week and signs?		
h. Does the Dining Room Manager require each tipped employee to sign a Cash Tips Declaration Slip each week, even if the employee reports zero tips received?		
i. Does the Dining Room Manager summarize the Cash Declaration Slips signed by each tipped employee on a Cash Tips Declared spreadsheet that he signs and dates?		
j. Does the Payroll Clerk key cash tips from the Cash Tips declared spreadsheet?		
k. Are the Cash Declaration Slips, signed by tipped employees, filed with the Cash Tips Declared spreadsheet as support for the current payroll?		
l. Are deductions entered into the Payroll system supported by properly completed and approved source documents, signed by the employee, authorizing the employer to make the deduction?		

Jenny's Café, Inc.
Denver Restaurant
Internal Control Questionnaire—Payroll
Audit Date: July 31, 2006

Internal Control Question	Yes/No	Comments

m. After entering the payroll and printing the Wage and Hour Report, does the Controller review, sign, and date the Wage and Hour Report?

n. Is the field location paying overtime in accordance with the Federal and State labor laws?

5. Tip Reporting and Minimum Wage:

a. Where tipped employees receive wages below minimum wage, does the Payroll Clerk prepare a spreadsheet where she calculates whether each employee's wages, plus tips, plus cost of employee meals at least equals the minimum wage (higher of Federal or State)?

b. Where the tipped employees' wages plus declared tips plus cost value of employee meals do not equal minimum wage, does the restaurant pay the employees the difference as an adjustment to Gross Wages?

Jenny's Café, Inc.
Denver Restaurant
Internal Control Questionnaire—Payroll
Audit Date: July 31, 2006

Internal Control Question	Yes/No	Comments

6. Payroll Reports:

a. Does the payroll package come directly to the Controller or General Manager?

b. Is the Payroll Clerk forbidden to have access to the payroll checks?

c. Does the Controller compare the Wage and Hour Report to the Payroll Register to check that Total Hours by Department, Regular Wages, Overtime Wages, Adjustments, Charge Tips, and Cash Tips agree?

d. Does the Payroll Clerk research differences between the Wage and Hour Report and Payroll Register and resolve them to the Controller's satisfaction?

e. Does the Controller compare the entries on the Employee Maintenance Report to the supporting Employee Maintenance Form?

f. Does the Controller check the hours of employees appearing on the High Dollar Report to ensure they were entered correctly?

Jenny's Café, Inc.
Denver Restaurant
Internal Control Questionnaire—Payroll
Audit Date: July 31, 2006

Internal Control Question	Yes/No	Comments
g. Does the Controller send the Payroll Registers to the department heads for them to review, sign, and date?		
h. Are any errors in payroll checks noted on a Payroll Adjustment form with the details of the error and department head's signature for entry into the following week's payroll?		
i. Does the Controller or General Manager document his review by signing the Employee Maintenance Report, Payroll Register, and High Dollar Report?		
j. Do employees working with payroll reports take care not to leave payroll reports lying around on their desks when leaving so unauthorized people walking by cannot look at them?		
k. Are payroll reports locked in a locked file cabinet at night?		

Jenny's Café, Inc.
Denver Restaurant
Internal Control Questionnaire—Payroll
Audit Date: July 31, 2006

Internal Control Question	Yes/No	Comments

7. Signing for Payroll Checks:

a. Does the employee sign an acknowledgment that the hours worked are correct, i.e. time card, Payroll Check Log (with acknowledgment statement), etc.?

b. Does the employee sign the Payroll Check Log acknowledging receipt of the payroll check?

c. Are undistributed payroll checks returned to the Pay Master to be locked in a locking file cabinet?

d. Is the Payroll Check Log returned to the Payroll Clerk to be filed with the payroll documentation for the Payroll?

e. Where the Pay Master mails a payroll check to an employee, does he note on the Payroll Check Log that the payroll check was mailed and the date it was mailed?

Jenny's Café, Inc.
Denver Restaurant
Internal Control Questionnaire—Payroll
Audit Date: July 31, 2006

Internal Control Question	**Yes/No**	**Comments**

8. Manual Payroll Checks:
    a. Are small payroll errors added to the following week's payroll?
    b. Where a manual payroll check is required, are there detailed procedures on requesting or processing a manual payroll check?
    c. Does the Payroll Clerk complete a Manual Payroll Check Request form?
    d. Does the Controller review and sign the Manual Payroll Check Request form?
    e. Does the employee sign the Payroll Check Log or separate acknowledgment that documents receipt of the manual check?

9. Is all casual labor hired as employees and paid through the payroll system?

Jenny's Café, Inc.
Denver Restaurant
Internal Control Questionnaire—Payroll
Audit Date: July 31, 2006

Internal Control Question	Yes/No	Comments

10. Overtime Pay:
   a. Are all hourly employees paid overtime pay in accordance with Federal or State overtime requirements (more favorable to employee applies)?
   b. Do salaried employees qualify as exempt employees under the duties test and salary test?

11. Productivity Report:
   a. Does the Payroll Clerk complete the Productivity Analysis each day?
   b. Does the Controller review, sign, and date the Productivity Analysis each day?
   c. Does the Controller distribute the Productivity Analysis to department heads and to Corporate as required?

Jenny's Café, Inc.
Denver Restaurant
Internal Control Questionnaire—Human Resources
Audit Date: July 31, 2006

Internal Control Question	Yes/No	Comments

1. Segregation of Duties:
   a. To whom does the Payroll Clerk report?
   b. To whom does the Human Resources person report?
   c. Who screens and hires prospective employees?
   d. Who processes payroll?
   e. Who performs file maintenance to the Human Resources database?
   f. Who completes the paperwork for new hires?
   g. Who approves the Employee Maintenance Form?
   h. Who is the second approver on the Employee Maintenance Form? Are the duties properly segregated?

2. Does the Human Resources database link to the payroll system so that the Payroll Clerk does not perform file maintenance?

3. Human Resources Files:
   a. Is there a separate Human Resources file maintained for each employee?
   b. Does each folder contain a completed employment application and resume, if salaried or office employee?

Jenny's Café, Inc.
Denver Restaurant
Internal Control Questionnaire—Human Resources
Audit Date: July 31, 2006

Internal Control Question	Yes/No	Comments
c. Does the Human Resources Department contact each former employer to determine whether the employee had a satisfactory relationship?		
d. Does the HR person document each conversation with an outside source regarding a potential employee on an Applicant Inquiry form?		
e. Does the HR file contain the completed Employee Maintenance Form with required signatures to hire the employee and subsequent properly approved EMF's for status changes?		
f. Where the Company requires new hires to be drug tested, does each HR file contain a properly completed and signed Drug Test Consent and Release form?		
g. Does each employee's folder contain a current W-4 form?		
h. Are all Company required certifications contained in the employee folders?		
i. Are completed Records of Employee Counseling maintained in the HR file?		

Jenny's Café, Inc.
Denver Restaurant
Internal Control Questionnaire—Human Resources
Audit Date: July 31, 2006

Internal Control Question	Yes/No	Comments

4. File Security:

    a. Do HR personnel put files in locked desk drawers while leaving temporarily to go on a break so unauthorized people walking by cannot look at them?

    b. Are HR files locked in a locked file cabinet at night?

5. Employee Maintenance Forms (EMF):

    a. Does the new hire sign the completed EMF?

    b. Does the hiring manager sign the EMF?

    c. Is the Human Resources Manager (may not be Human Resources Clerk) or General Manager the second management signer on the EMF?

6. Pay Rates:

    a. Does each employee's HR file contain a properly approved EMF with the employee's current pay rate?

    b. Where there is a union, does each union employee have a pay rate that agrees to the union contract for that position?

Jenny's Café, Inc.
Denver Restaurant
Internal Control Questionnaire—Human Resources
Audit Date: July 31, 2006

Internal Control Question	Yes/No	Comments

c. When making an offer of employment, does the Human Resources Manager make an offer that has been previously approved by the General Manager?

d. Where a blanket increase affects all employees, i.e. a rate increase stipulated in the union contract, does each HR folder contain a memo signed by the General Manager that lists the old rate and new rate for each affected position?

7. Drug Testing:

a. Where the Company has a drug testing policy, does the prospective employee complete and sign a Drug Test Consent and Release form?

b. When the prospective employee is a minor, is the minor required to obtain the parent's signature documenting the parent's consent to have his child drug tested?

c. Does the Human Resources Manager maintain a drug test log that is used to track each applicant sent to the drug test lab for drug testing?

Jenny's Café, Inc.
Denver Restaurant
Internal Control Questionnaire—Human Resources
Audit Date: July 31, 2006

Internal Control Question	Yes/No	Comments
d. Is the drug test log stored in a locked file cabinet?		
e. Where the drug test log is kept in an Excel spreadsheet, is a paper copy printed at least once a month?		
f. When the paper copy of the Drug Test Log is discarded, is it shredded?		
g. Does the field location wait with hiring the prospective employee until the drug test results are received?		
h. Where a prospective employee tests positive to the drug test, is he disqualified from being hired?		

8. I9 Documentation:

    a. Does every new employee complete an I9 on the first day of work?

    b. Does the employee complete Section 1 of the I9, including the attest section of Section 1, and his signature and date?

    c. Where a translator is used to assist the employee in completing Section 1, does the translator complete, sign, and date the Translator Certification?

Jenny's Café, Inc.
Denver Restaurant
Internal Control Questionnaire—Human Resources
Audit Date: July 31, 2006

Internal Control Question	Yes/No	Comments
d. Does a Human Resources person obtain one List A item or a List B and a List C item from the employee and complete Section 2 of the I9?		
e. Does the Human Resources person make copies of the I9 documentation and staple the copies to the completed I9?		
f. Does the person reviewing the documentation sign and date the Certification?		
g. Does the person reviewing the documentation date the I9 within three days of the date of hire (the date the employee signed the I9)?		
h. When reverifying (rehiring) or updating the I9, does the HR person complete Section 3 of the I9, sign and date it?		
i. Are I9's maintained separately from the HR files in a separate 3-ring binder?		
j. Are I9's kept for 3 years from the date of hire or one year after the employee terminates, whichever is later?		

Jenny's Café, Inc.
Denver Restaurant
Internal Control Questionnaire—Human Resources
Audit Date: July 31, 2006

Internal Control Question	Yes/No	Comments

k. When an employee terminates, is the I9 removed from the active I9 binder and filed in a separate terminated I9 binder?
l. Does a second person verify each completed I9 to ensure it is completed properly?

9. Employee Termination:
a. When an employee terminates, is a Termination Check List completed that lists all company assets that need to be returned and all steps that need to be followed in terminating the employee?
b. Is an EMF completed with the reason for termination documented on the EMF?
c. If termination is due to unsatisfactory performance or violation of work rules, is a brief description of the violation or a reference to an Employee Evaluation or Record of Employee Counseling noted in the Notes section of the EMF?

Jenny's Café, Inc.
Denver Restaurant
Internal Control Questionnaire—Human Resources
Audit Date: July 31, 2006

Internal Control Question	Yes/No	Comments

10. Child Labor Laws:

a. Do minors work only the hours permitted under the US Fair Labor Standards Act or the applicable State Child Labor Laws (whichever is stricter)?

b. Is there some type of system in place (e.g. different color time cards) to remind supervisors and managers that certain employees are minors?

c. Does Human Resources continually review the hours that minors are working to ensure they work only the hours that they are legally permitted to work?

d. Are department supervisors and managers disciplined for repeated violations of minors working beyond the legal maximum number of hours permitted by law?

e. Where required, does the HR Department obtain work permits from minors before allowing them to begin work?

f. Are the work permits returned to the minor employees upon termination of employment?

Jenny's Café, Inc.
Denver Restaurant
Internal Control Questionnaire—Human Resources
Audit Date: July 31, 2006

Internal Control Question	Yes/No	Comments
11. Alcohol Service Training:		
a. Is there an Alcohol Service Training program in place?		
b. Has the Alcohol Service Training program been documented and is it updated annually?		
c. Is the Alcohol Service Training program approved by the General Manager in writing and submitted to Corporate Human Resources for approval?		
d. Is the approval from the Corporate Vice President of Human Resources or the Director of Human Resources stapled to the Alcohol Service Training program?		
e. Does the Alcohol Service Training Program require each alcohol serving employee to attend training annually?		
f. Upon conclusion of the training program, does the employee sign a certification stating that he attended training, understood the content, was given the opportunity to ask questions and had those questions answered?		

Jenny's Café, Inc.
Denver Restaurant
Internal Control Questionnaire—Human Resources
Audit Date: July 31, 2006

Internal Control Question	Yes/No	Comments
g. Where the State has an alcohol service training program, does the location have a copy of each employee's completion of the State's Alcohol Service Training certificate in the employee's HR file?		
h. Where the State's alcohol service training program is held every two years, is the alcohol serving employee required to attend the location's alcohol service training program during the years he does not attend the State program?		
12. Nepotism:		
a. Are there any relatives reporting to other relatives directly or indirectly?		
b. Where there is a relative reporting to another relative or significant other, is the relationship disclosed to the subsidiary President and Corporate Vice President of Human Resources, with a carbon copy to the Regional Vice President of Operations?		

493

Jenny's Café, Inc.
Denver Restaurant
Internal Control Questionnaire—Human Resources
Audit Date: July 31, 2006

Internal Control Question	Yes/No	Comments

c. Is there a paper copy of an email in the employee's file from the subsidiary President or Corporate Vice President of Human Resources acknowledging the relationship and agreeing to let it continue?

13. Federal, State and Company Poster Requirements:
a. Are all required Federal, State, and Company posters posted in conspicuous locations that all employees frequent regularly?
b. Are all Company employment opportunities posted for a two-week period?

14. OSHA Reporting:
a. Is the restaurant maintaining an OSHA 300 Log of reportable injuries and illnesses at the workplace?
b. Is the OSHA 300A Summary posted in a conspicuous location for a three-month period in February through April?

Jenny's Café, Inc.
Denver Restaurant
Internal Control Questionnaire—Human Resources
Audit Date: July 31, 2006

Internal Control Question	Yes/No	Comments
15. Cash Variances: a. Has the General Manager established a cash variance policy in writing and made all cash handlers aware of this policy? b. Where a cash handler has a notable variance, is the employee subjected to progressive discipline? c. Is discipline documented on a Record of Employee Counseling form?		
16. Other Discipline: a. Are other disciplinary matters handled through employee counseling and documented on a Record of Employee Counseling form? b. When the employee demonstrates consistent improvement in performance, does the supervisor complete a Record of Employee Counseling form that officially removes the employee from counseling? c. Where major offenses are committed, is the employee suspended pending investigation?		

Jenny's Café, Inc.
Denver Restaurant
Internal Control Questionnaire—Human Resources
Audit Date: July 31, 2006

Internal Control Question	Yes/No	Comments
d. Does the Human Resources Manager document the results of the investigation, sign and date the report, and insert it in the employee's folder with copies of signed witness statements stapled to the report?		
e. Does the location's Human Resources Manager send copies of the report to the Corporate Human Resources representative and the Corporate Director of Labor Relations?		
f. If the investigation reveals that the employee did commit the major offense as charged, is the employee terminated?		

Jenny's Café, Inc.
Denver Restaurant
Internal Control Questionnaire—IT, Risk Management, Other
Audit Date: July 31, 2006

Internal Control Question	Yes/No	Comments

1. Segregation of Duties:
   a. Who has access to the POS systems?
   b. Who has security clearance in the POS system to grant access levels to employees who need access?
   c. Who performs void approval, file maintenance, and report printing on the POS systems?
   d. Who assists the locations with computer related issues?
   Are the duties properly segregated?

2. Computer Backup:
   a. Are all POS systems backed up every night?
   b. Are critical accounting systems backed up every night, i.e. Accounts Payable, Payroll, General Ledger, etc.?
   c. Are other critical systems backed up, i.e. inventory control software?
   d. Are important spreadsheets backed up onto a disk, flash drive, etc.?
   e. Are critical systems backed up on a tape or other storage device and taken to an offsite storage location once a week?

Jenny's Café, Inc.
Denver Restaurant
Internal Control Questionnaire—IT, Risk Management, Other
Audit Date: July 31, 2006

Internal Control Question	Yes/No	Comments

3. Passwords:

   a. Are all online systems, i.e. Accounts Payable, Payroll, Sales Reporting, etc, password protected?

   b. Is each PC password protected to prevent access to company files, word processing documents, and spreadsheets?

   c. Are passwords changed every 30 days?

   d. Are passwords unique words unrelated to the system the password is accessing, formed by using letters, numbers, and special characters?

   e. Does the Company's data security shut out any user who enters six incorrect passwords?

4. POS System Access:

   a. Is POS system access limited to those employees who need to use it, i.e. waiters, waitresses, bartenders, supervisors, etc.?

   b. Is each person with POS access issued a swipe card with a unique access code?

   c. Does the cashier close the cash drawer after every transaction?

Jenny's Café, Inc.
Denver Restaurant
Internal Control Questionnaire—IT, Risk Management, Other
Audit Date: July 31, 2006

Internal Control Question	Yes/No	Comments
5. Hardware Security: a. Is computer hardware (PC's, printers, scanners, etc.) properly secured? b. Are file servers located in a separate room that is kept locked 24 hours a day? c. Are laptops locked in a locked file cabinet or in an overhead cabinet? d. Does the Manager on Duty check that all doors are locked when leaving the premises at night? e. Do the outer doors to the premises have deadbolt locks?		
6. Anti-Virus Software: a. Does every PC on the premises have the Company standard anti-virus software on it? b. Is the anti-virus software updated as updates are issued by the software provider? c. Are users alerted not to open attachments from unfamiliar sources?		

Jenny's Café, Inc.
Denver Restaurant
Internal Control Questionnaire—IT, Risk Management, Other
Audit Date: July 31, 2006

Internal Control Question	Yes/No	Comments
7. Grill Hoods & Fire Suppression System Maintenance: a. Have the grill hoods over the stoves been cleaned in the past 6 months? b. Have the fire suppression systems been tested in the last six months? c. Has each fire extinguisher on the premises been inspected during the last year?		
8. CO_2 and Propane Tank Storage: a. Are all CO_2 and propane tanks chained to a wall to prevent them from tipping over? b. Are empty tanks secured to prevent them from tipping over?		
9. Lease Compliance: a. Does the Controller calculate the rent due each month and remit the payment by the due date? b. Is the restaurant in compliance with all provisions of the lease?		

Jenny's Café, Inc.
Denver Restaurant
Internal Control Questionnaire—IT, Risk Management, Other
Audit Date: July 31, 2006

Internal Control Question	Yes/No	Comments

10. Municipal Requirements:
a. Is the location in compliance with all municipal requirements?
b. Does management make employees aware of the municipal requirements during orientation and periodic training meetings?

11. Record Retention:
a. Are records clearly labeled and stored in file cabinets?
b. Are older records moved to retention boxes and clearly labeled as to their contents?
c. Are current year and prior year retention boxes stored in logical sequence in a place where they are easily retrievable?
d. Are retention boxes stacked in rows so people can easily move among the boxes and retrieve boxes that are needed?
e. Is the file retention room kept locked at all times and keys limited to management?
f. Are records destroyed after aging past the legally required retention period?

Jenny's Café, Inc.
Denver Restaurant
Internal Control Questionnaire—IT, Risk Management, Other
Audit Date: July 31, 2006

Internal Control Question	Yes/No	Comments
12. Does the restaurant have a general business license and liquor license hanging in the restaurant in a location that is visible to patrons?		
13. Do location personnel ask official visitors for photo identification from the agency they represent or Corporate before providing them with access to the restaurant's records or assets?		

CPSIA information can be obtained
at www.ICGtesting.com
Printed in the USA
BVOW03s1943081116
467220BV00001B/107/P